Healthy Carb Cookbook FOR DUMMIES®

by Jan McCracken

WILEY

John Wiley & Sons, Inc.

Healthy Carb Cookbook For Dummies®

Published by
John Wiley & Sons, Inc.
111 River St.
Hoboken, NJ 07030-5774
www.wiley.com

For general information on our other products and services, please contact our Customer Care Department within the U.S. at 877-762-2974, outside the U.S. at 317-572-3993, or fax 317-572-4002.

For technical support, please visit www.wiley.com/techsupport.

Wiley publishes in a variety of print and electronic formats and by print-on-demand. Some material included with standard print versions of this book may not be included in e-books or in print-on-demand. If this book refers to media such as a CD or DVD that is not included in the version you purchased, you may download this material at http://booksupport.wiley.com. For more information about Wiley products, visit www.wiley.com.

Library of Congress Control Number: 2005923783

ISBN 978-0-7645-8476-3 (pbk); ISBN 978-0-471-75659-0 (ebk); ISBN 978-1-118-07012-3 (ebk); ISBN 978-1-118-07167-0 (ebk)

10 9 8 7 6 5 4 3 2

1O/SQ/QW/QV/IN

WILEY

About the Author

Jan McCracken was born and raised in the Midwest, in a small, farming community in Illinois. Adopted by her grandparents, Jan grew up gardening with her grandfather and canning and cooking with her grandmother. She spent most of her early life in Illinois, Iowa, and Kansas.

In the early '80s, Jan and her faithful friend, Mr. Bear, a fluffy husky-chow mix, relocated to a cabin in the mountains above Santa Barbara, California. Given her love of country living, the mountains, and cooking, Jan later opened a country bed-and-breakfast in the Ozark Mountains of Branson, Missouri. It was during her inn-keeping years in Branson that Jan wrote her first self-published book, the *Ozark Mountain Christmas Recipe Collection,* First Edition. With the grand success of her first book, her extensive recipe collection, and her love of cooking, Jan continued to write "little books of recipes" that included the *Garden Recipe Collection* and the *Fruit Sampler Collection.* Her personal favorite is a gift book collection of eighteen *Little Books of Tea.*

Jan began living the low-carb lifestyle about ten years ago and is an advocate of preventive medicine through diet, exercise, and lifestyle. As a proponent of healthy lifestyles, her love of research keeps her tuned into the pulse of what's happening in the low-carb genre as well as in nutrition and wellness. Jan's works in these areas include *Low Carb Christmas Cookin'* and the *Carb Countin' Holiday Cookbook with Sassy Stepper.*

You can count on Jan's recipes to always be easy and delicious, and her motto is, "Fresh is always best."

Jan has two grown children, Katie and Ray. Katie has blessed Gammy Mac with twins, Sara Jane and John Edward, and Ray and Lori have blessed her with Kaylie Elise. Jan's ever-present smile is especially warm and proud when she talks about her grandchildren.

Jan's long-term goal for her books, speaking engagements, and teaching is to help people understand that food truly is great medicine; it can prevent and heal disease by making a positive impact on the health of people around the world. As a health advocate for all ages, Jan has set up an international group of Sassy Steppers to combat obesity and disease, stepping out with people all over the world on the road to wellness.

In addition to her other endeavors, Jan continues her freelance writing career and is currently at home in California. She feels very blessed to have been given the opportunity to write *Healthy Carb Cookbook For Dummies.*

When you see Jan's name in print you'll usually see her personal slogan, which comes from her heart:

Change Your Mind . . . Change Your Heart . . . Lose Weight for Life!

Dedication

To all of you with "low-carb" in your vocabulary who never want to diet again and who want to pursue a healthy, low-carb, active lifestyle for life — yes, the very life of you! I wrote this book for each of you!

Author's Acknowledgments

Sincere, heartfelt thanks to the entire team at Wiley Publishing. They have become like family to me. I have learned so much that I almost feel as if there should be some sort of graduation ceremony for all authors that write *For Dummies* books.

A very special thank you goes to my agent, Grace Freedson, for so graciously getting me off on the right foot and for her ongoing guidance and warm support.

My heartfelt thanks to Stacy Kennedy, my acquisitions editor, who has been a gem and a delight to work with since Day One. Big thanks to my project editor, Mike Baker, for his patience, his ability to keep me and the project on track, his willingness to go the extra mile, and his great sense of humor. Mike gets stellar points! Sincere appreciation and marvel for what they do goes to my copy editors, Trisha Strietelmeier and Tina Sims. Special thanks to Lesa Grant, my marketing manager and a talented lady whose enthusiasm is contagious. I got the luck of the draw with my recipe tester — very warm thanks to Emily Nolan. Thanks to technical reviewer and nutritional analyst Patty Santelli, who made sure all the net carb math was done precisely.

My dear friend Debra Hartman, who, long distance from Branson, has been so supportive throughout this entire project. A very special thanks to Deb for being such an ongoing source of encouragement and delight in my life! The praise and glory of this book goes to the Lord, with thanks for His blessing me with the authorship of this book. Without Him I could not have written a word.

Publisher's Acknowledgments

We're proud of this book; please send us your comments through our Dummies online registration form located at www.dummies.com/register/.

Some of the people who helped bring this book to market include the following:

Acquisitions, Editorial, and Media Development

Project Editor: Mike Baker

Acquisitions Editor: Stacy Kennedy

Senior Copy Editor: Tina Sims

Copy Editor: Trisha Strietelmeier

Editorial Program Assistant: Courtney Allen

Technical Reviewer and Nutrition Analyst: Patty Santelli

Recipe Tester: Emily Nolan

Senior Permissions Editor: Carmen Krikorian

Editorial Manager: Christine Meloy Beck

Editorial Assistants: Hanna Scott, Melissa Bennett

Cover Photos: © iStockphoto.com/Дарья Петренко

Cartoons: Rich Tennant, www.the5thwave.com

Composition Services

Project Coordinator: Nancee Reeves

Layout and Graphics: Kelly Emkow, Stephanie D. Jumper, Barry Offringa, Lynsey Osborn, Julie Trippetti

Special Art: Elizabeth Kurtzman

Photos: © T.J. Hine Photography

Food Stylist: Lisa Bishop

Proofreaders: Carl William Pierce, Jessica Kramer, TECHBOOKS Production Services

Indexer: TECHBOOKS Production Services

Special Help: Elizabeth Rea

Publishing and Editorial for Consumer Dummies

Kathleen Nebenhaus, Vice President and Executive Publisher

David Palmer, Associate Publisher

Kristin Ferguson-Wagstaffe, Product Development Director

Publishing for Technology Dummies

Andy Cummings, Vice President and Publisher

Composition Services

Debbie Stailey, Director of Composition Services

Contents at a Glance

Recipes at a Glance

Wraps

Fish and Seafood

Beef, Lamb, and Pork

Poultry

Meatless Main Dishes

Vegetables and Side Dishes

Appetizers, Snacks, and Dips

Less than 10 Net Grams of Carbs per Serving

Less than 20 Net Carbs per Serving

Table of Contents

Introduction

• •

*A*re you hankering for some new horizons for cooking low-carb? Well, you've come to the right place. This book is fun, and I've developed and de-carbed some pretty awesome recipes for you to incorporate into your daily low-carb lifestyle whether you're cooking for one, two, or an entire family. Low-carb never tasted so good!

Regardless of the meal or food you have in mind, I think you'll find a recipe that hits the spot here. From breakfast to soup, salads, sides, and main courses, I have you covered with these recipes, which are all about variety, great flavors, and healthy meals that don't take forever to prepare. But it only gets better from there: I also include recipes for desserts (including some sweet surprises), fresh wraps, and snacks. I give you slow cooker recipes so that your low-carb meal is ready for you when you walk through the door, and I provide ideas for dishes to cook in a hurry (on days when you haven't used your slow cooker!). And did I mention that there are veggies galore that are great for your health and will please your tummy, too? I hope you enjoy preparing these recipes as much as I have enjoyed putting together this book just for you. A majority of the recipes contain less than 10 grams of net carbs per serving.

About This Book

So what's this book all about? It's a mix of low-carb lessons that I've learned the hard way along my low-carb road, plus a ton of recipes that will satisfy your comfort-food cravings and your low-carb sweet tooth — a mix of comfort-food cooking sprinkled with my California-cuisine influences and a heavy serving of low-carb variety and healthy eating. The simple cook in me likes to get things on the table in a very timely manner and you'll see that influence in the recipes in this book.

I grew up in a small Midwestern farming community on good, old-fashioned comfort food, and that's what I learned to cook — three squares a day and plenty of desserts. Then, about 20 years ago, I moved to California, and my entire eating lifestyle changed. Even though I'd grown up eating veggies fresh from the garden and canning every year, the word *fresh* took on a whole new meaning for me when I was introduced to California cooking. Grilling became a year-round sport. Fruits and vegetables became even more prominent. And fish — even though I'd caught and cooked my fair share of freshwater fish in the Midwest, being able to walk down to the dock and buy seafood right off the boats was a treat beyond measure. (And let's not forget exercise: I became a runner and ran the beach almost every day. I was one healthy California girl.)

But I had a dream of opening a bed and breakfast, and Branson, Missouri, and the Ozark Mountains beckoned me on a journey that became yet another culinary experience. My breakfasts at the Inn at Fall Creek reflected an interesting mix of my Midwest comfort-food cooking and the California cuisine that I had learned to love. I looked at the interior design of my B&B as country — my guests called it California County — and saw that the mix was clear both in the décor and in the food. I tried for comfort food and folded in the healthy with a splash of laughter and grand presentation.

I gained some weight while at the B&B — not from a lack of running around 24/7 but from eating late at night and irregular meals. It was then that my best friend steered me to a low-carb diet. It wasn't all about weight even back then — it was about my health, which was deteriorating — and my friend was concerned. I literally shrieked when she introduced me to the low-carb diet, "What do you mean I can't have white bread and sugar?" We laugh about it to this day, and we both support each other on our continuing low-carb lifestyle paths.

I continued the low-carb diet and dropped some major pounds. And I moved back to California. I discovered that if I ate sugar I was out of whack for days. So I decided that it wasn't on my list of things to eat any more — not just for a few weeks but for a lifetime. I'm not telling you that I won't have a small slice of birthday cake at my grandchildren's birthday parties, but I am telling you that sugar is off my grocery list for good. And so low-carb became a lifestyle for me that worked and still does today.

It's not just about the recipes. I have a sincere desire to help you be successful with your low-carb healthy lifestyle. I'm a health advocate and a low-carber of ten-plus years who has fallen off the low-carb wagon many times; dusted myself off and sheepishly climbed back on; been through my share of stalls, confusion, and boredom; and finally discovered the truth about controlling my carb intake. For me, it means not only looking at my carbs but looking at my calories and taking calories seriously too — as seriously as I take my carbs. I've blended my carb and calorie intakes to find what works for my body. The other biggie is moving my body more; I use a pedometer to count my steps every day and try my best to meet my daily goals and keep increasing my daily steps.

I can think of no greater joy than sharing with you what I know works through this book. My goal is to help you become more aware of carb and calorie counts, find out more about nutrition, become motivated to move your body more, and cook up a storm with mouthwatering low-carb recipes. Applying the ideas in this book to your healthy low-carb lifestyle will help you lose weight and keep off those pounds for the rest of your life and encourage you on the road to health, longevity, and wellness.

Conventions Used in This Book

I present the recipes in this book in a conventional style, listing the ingredients, the preparation time, the time it takes to cook the recipe, the amount of time the dish needs to be refrigerated before serving, and the number of servings to divide the finished product into. Some of these recipes are so good that you're going to want to eat the whole thing. (But remember, although the phrase *low-carb* means that you can eat until you're satisfied, you still have to keep track of those carb counts.)

A nutritional analysis at the end of each recipe gives you the total carbohydrates, the amount of fiber, and the net carb counts per serving, along with other important nutrition information to apply to your low-carb healthy lifestyle.

I've tried to keep things simple in the ingredient lists for these recipes. So, unless otherwise stated, you can assume the following:

- **Butter** is unsalted.
- **Eggs** are large.
- **Salt** is regular ol' table salt.
- **Pepper** is freshly ground black pepper (believe me, the fabulous flavor more than makes up for the extra ten seconds it takes to grind it yourself).
- **Vegetables and fruits** are washed under running water.

And here are some other recipe-related issues to keep in mind as you dive into the fabulous low-carb foods in this book:

- If you're looking for vegetarian recipes, look for this tiny little tomato — ○ — in front of the recipe name in the Recipes at a Glance section toward the front of this book, in the list of Recipes in This Chapter on the first page of each chapter in Part II and Part III, and next to the recipe name on the little recipe-card tab that begins each recipe.

✔ Some of the sidebars I include (those little gray boxes) contain starter ideas and variations of other recipes found in the chapter. In those cases, I provide you with some basic ingredients and preparations and let you take it from there. I promise that none of them are rocket science, but they're pretty tasty, so have a look-see. What I think you'll find is the amazing dietary variety and opportunity for improvisation that healthy low-carb lifestyles can provide.

And now for a few non–recipe-related issues:

✔ *Italic* is used for emphasis and to highlight new words or terms that are defined in the text.

✔ **Boldfaced** text is used to indicate keywords in bulleted lists or the action parts of numbered steps.

✔ `Monofont` is used for Web addresses. When this book was printed, some Web addresses may have needed to break across two lines of text. If that occurs, just know that no extra hyphens have been added. So, when using one of these Web addresses, just type in exactly what you see in this book, pretending as though the line break doesn't exist.

✔ Sidebars are shaded gray boxes that contain text that's interesting to know but not necessarily critical to your understanding of the chapter or section topic.

In Chapter 4, I cover all the low-carb conventions I use in the recipes.

What You're Not to Read

I give you extra added attractions to the subject at hand in the sidebars in this book. It won't ruin my day (or yours) if you don't read them.

Foolish Assumptions

All authors have to make a few assumptions about their audiences, and this low-carb lady is no different. If any of these descriptions hit the mark, you have the right book in your hands:

✔ You're a low-carb fan with some basic knowledge of the low-carb world, and you're looking for a ton of fabulous recipes that fit your lifestyle.

✔ You're considering lowering the carbohydrates that you consume on a daily basis, you've heard a little about low-carb dietary plans, and you want to know a little more about how they work and get an idea of all the great foods you *can* eat and the easy recipes you can prepare.

✔ You're looking for quick snacks and munchies that make the adjective *easy* seem like an understatement.

✔ You have basic cooking skills — you know what "preheat the oven" means, you can measure ingredients, and you can keep your fingers out of the beaters on your mixer.

How This Book Is Organized

I start this book out by talking to you about diets in general, suggesting that you throw away your diet yo-yo, and basically explaining what's involved in adopting a healthy low-carb active lifestyle — everything from grocery shopping to table presentation. I cover topics ranging from fiber to phytochemicals to pedometer walking. But I focus on the food and the recipes — bunches of great low-carb recipes with variations.

This book is divided into five parts for basic organization, with chapters by subject in each part for easy access for you. Here's an overview of what you find in each part.

Part 1: Creating a Healthy Lifestyle Counting Carbs

A lot of smart people are confused about counting and controlling carbs — bad carbs, good carbs, and no carbs. In this part, I clear this matter up for you, setting you on the straight and narrow of your choice of a great healthy low-carb lifestyle. You'll decide to throw your diet yo-yo in the ocean forever and aim directly for a lifestyle of health, wellness, and longevity. Along the way in this part, I accompany you to the grocery store with a prepared list of basic low-carb staples. While cruising the aisles, you'll become an expert at label reading and looking for hidden sugars and carbs. I teach a couple of short classes — one on net carb math and another on low-carb nutrition and the glycemic index. But don't worry: You don't have to take any written tests. I also show you how to become an amazing grazer, grazing your way to weight loss along with moving more with the help a new friend, a pedometer, to count your steps for you everyday. In between all of this serious stuff, I expect you to at least grin a few times because I wrote this book so you can have fun leafing through its pages.

Part II: Low-Carb Cooking Made Easy

This part will whet your appetite, and I have a feeling that you just won't know which recipe to try first. I separate the recipes into chapters by categories, making it easy to choose an entree in one chapter, go to another chapter for a side of veggies, and then hop over to the desserts chapter for a perfect sweet ending to your low-carb meal.

Part III: Expanding Everyday Low-Carb Cooking

In this part, I give you some easy options for whipping up great low-carb snacks and dips, rolling up recipes for fun and tasty low-carb wraps, getting your low-carb meals on the table almost effortlessly with a slow cooker, and preparing quick recipes with 5 carbs or less.

Part IV: Eating Low-Carb on the Town and on the Run

I know that you won't cook all your own meals, so in this part I offer you ideas on how to dine out and still stick to your low-carb lifestyle. I also provide suggestions on packing a low-carb lunch and include a special recipe to tote with you. Finally, I give you ideas about cooking low-carb in hurry with recipes for quick, tasty meals.

Part V: The Part of Tens

This part starts with a chapter on strategies to simplify your carb-counting cooking. Next, I list 10 foods that you can eat more of and lose weight at the same time. Finally, I give you ten great Web sites to visit online for free low-carb information, e-zines, and great nutritional information.

Icons Used in This Book

I want to give you a heads up about the icons that I use throughout the book, or you may just miss something important. Here's a list of all the icons I use:

 You'll see a lot of these as you flip through the pages of this book. I give you tips galore on everything. The tips are little extras and embellishments to help you on your low-carb lifestyle path.

 Think of the remember icon as just a little help from your friends about some things that are important to your low-carb lifestyle. I wouldn't want you to forget them.

 The warning icon is meant to raise a red flag to you about something important in your low-carb lifestyle or the recipe you're about to prepare, so please take heed when you see it.

 Sometimes I lapse into the technical realm about nutrition and other techie elements of your low-carb lifestyle. I use this icon to alert you where this information is. If it's not your thing, skip it.

 When you see this icon, you'll know that I'm suggesting ways to take the information I provide and head off down your own culinary path. Try some of these lip-smacking good suggestions marked with this icon.

 Time in a bottle? Unfortunately not — you can't buy it in a bottle. So I use this icon throughout the book to flag some areas in your low-carb healthy cooking where you can save some time.

 This icon accompanies all recipes that have less than 5 grams of net carbs per serving — and there are a bunch of them.

 This icon helps you immediately find the recipes that have less than 10 grams of net carbs per serving — and there are a bunch of these too.

Where to Go from Here

The recipes and other info in this book are all so good that you may just want to close your eyes and start reading from wherever you happen to open the book. And if you want dessert, go immediately to the dessert chapter and get cookin'. *For Dummies* books usually tell you that you don't have to remember anything you read, and this book is no different — it's designed so you can easily find what you need if you forget something that you read earlier. I do have one favor to ask of you: Remember when you cook something great from this book, will you?

If you ask me (you didn't, I know), I suggest reading all of Part I first and then jumping to whatever recipe chapters interest you the most. Wherever you start, please have some fun browsing through these pages while preparing and eating some great low-carb food!

Part I
Creating a Healthy Lifestyle Counting Carbs

The 5th Wave   By Rich Tennant

"Oooo, what's in there? Low—carb eye of newt? I can barely tell the difference."

In this part . . .

In this part, I help you take control of your low-carb dietary choices as part of an overall healthy and active lifestyle. You'll be jumping off the diet merry-go-round forever, aiming directly for a lifestyle of health, wellness, and longevity. Knowledge is wonderful stuff, so I clear up confusion about counting carbs, bad carbs, good carbs, no carbs, and controlling carbs. I speak "low-carb nutrition," which may be somewhat of a foreign language to you, but you'll pick it up quickly and begin fitting all the pieces of the wellness puzzle together in your lifestyle. I show you how to do the calculations for net carb math. I explain the glycemic index and the glycemic load of foods, and I tell you how to become an amazing grazer so that you can keep your blood sugars on an even keel.

I help you make some changes in your low-carb kitchen and discuss good low-carb staples to keep on hand. I provide you with tons of tips on how to make the transition to the low-carb lifestyle and how to stay on track after you're up to speed, like planning your meals in advance by taking advantage of your carb awareness and cooking skills. Finally, I encourage you to get moving, preferably by walking. To help motivate you, I discuss the benefits of using a pedometer — a dandy little device to keep track of your daily steps.

Chapter 1

Taking Control of Carbs In and Out of the Kitchen

*L*iving an active low-carb lifestyle is a great way to lose those extra pounds, maintain a healthy weight, and ensure top-notch overall health. And there's no better way to implement and maintain a low-carb plan than to cook many of your meals at home. Doing so allows you to know exactly what's in the majority of the food you eat on a daily basis, which is a key piece of information to have when you're controlling or counting carbs.

In this chapter, I welcome you to the world of low-carb living. I introduce the basics behind low-carb dietary plans. I present some advice for taking a low-carb diet to the next level by incorporating it into a healthy, active low-carb *lifestyle,* in which the recipes in this book can play a tremendous role in offering fabulous flavors and variety, variety, variety. Did I mention variety? I help you take stock of your current eating habits to help identify areas for improvement, and I provide a bit of perspective on making weight management and healthy nutrition a life-long commitment.

Revealing the Low-Carb Revolution

The first two words in the title of this book are *low* and *carb.* So I guess it only makes sense to start at the beginning. If you're new to the world of low-carb cooking, don't worry. I take you on a quick tour of the low-carb basics before you delve into all things cooking. In short, a *carbohydrate* is a nutrient found in foods that your body can readily turn into energy (for a more complex definition of a carbohydrate, see Chapter 2). But carbs also have the ability to be stored as fat if they're not used for energy. Sounds pretty straightforward, right? However, if ever there was a controversial subject, it has to be low-carb dieting. But remember that things that aren't worth talking about are rarely controversial and certainly don't make headlines.

Low-carb diet programs were originally promoted as high-protein diets. The initial low-carb diets claimed that you could eat as much fat as you wanted to and still lose weight. Nutritional research showed that consuming all of that fat wasn't the healthiest approach in creating a long-term healthy lifestyle, even though some fats are necessary and healthy (cruise over to Chapter 2 and read about knowing your fats). As competitive diets surfaced and different low-carb plans emerged, the ratio of protein, carbs, and fats that low-carb diets called for changed, too. And that ratio is still at the root of the low-carb controversy today. But despite the differences in the approach of various low-carb dietary plans, all of them basically agree on the fundamental principle that too many carbs in your diet will cause weight gain and prevent weight loss.

The number of carbs that work for you on a daily basis is up to you, the individual. Some people can get away with simply controlling their carbs and eating over 100 grams of carbs a day, and some folks need to count closely because they gain weight if they even approach 50 for the day. The "acceptable" carb range that all the different dietary plans out there call for varies from the very restrictive, which limits the consumption of some food groups such as fruit and grains, to a more balanced, less restrictive approach that focuses on carb control. Here's a snapshot of the low-carb spectrum:

- **Most restrictive:** Some plans limit you to only 5 percent of your daily calorie intake from carbohydrates. This works out to be around 20 grams of carbs a day.

- **Moderate:** These more moderate low-carb plans allow 40 percent of your daily calorie intake to come from carbohydrates.

- **Least restrictive:** On a lesser restrictive low-carb plan, you're not required to count carbs, but instead you make choices about the type of carbs you eat.

The good news, at least in terms of how useful you'll find this book, is that regardless of the low-carb dietary approach you currently subscribe to or are considering, you can find tons of fabulous recipes here that will fit squarely into your plans. With all the recipes I include that are super skinny on carbs, you can inject even the most restrictive plans with a huge jolt of variety.

 A low-carb lifestyle shouldn't eliminate attention paid to calorie counts. Calorie intake versus calorie output is the real bottom line to weight loss and maintenance. Combine the work of tracking your daily carb intake with balancing calories, and you create a healthy low-carb lifestyle that you can live with for life — a healthy and rewarding life. (Check out Chapter 2 for more on calories.)

 Always check with your personal healthcare practitioner before beginning any major change in your dietary lifestyle or starting a new exercise program.

Keeping your eye on the carb

Most low-carb dietary plans ask you to walk away from carbs that have little nutritional value, make your blood-sugar levels spike, and pack on the pounds (see Chapter 2 for more information on your blood-sugar levels). Even though low-carb dietary plans definitely differ on the details, these are the basics. Learning what's really in foods and products is vital to make sure that you're not consuming a bunch of hidden sugars, hidden carbs, and excessive calories (find out more about reading labels in Chapter 3). So put yourself on carb patrol and avoid these foods for no one's sake but your own:

- Candy
- Cookies, cakes, pies, and other baked goods (I'm not talking sugar-free here — see more about artificial sweeteners in Chapter 2)
- Most pastas
- Processed snack foods such as chips, pretzels, and crackers
- Refined sugars
- Sodas and fruit juices that are loaded with sugar
- White flour and white breads
- White rice

Counting on friendly low-carb foods in the kitchen

Low-carb diets can get some unfavorable press, as can low-fat diets, low-calorie diets, fad diets, and practically any other diet in the universe. But if you make your decisions from the perspective of living an overall healthy lifestyle, the word *diet* can be stricken from your vocabulary.

A healthy low-carb lifestyle allows you to keep all of the nutritious carbs from all five of the food groups. Each food group is important because no one group can supply your body with all of the necessary nutrients. Variety is still the spice of life. Here's a bird's-eye view of some of the more low-carb friendly foods, along with some recipe suggestions if you're itchin' to get in the kitchen:

- **Vegetables:** The more colors the better. Leafy greens and lettuces — the darker green, the better — are a great place to start (see Chapter 8 for more information on greens and lettuces, plus great salad recipes), but it's only a start. Low-carb vegetable options are plentiful (see Chapter 12 for a bunch of great recipes and a handy vegetable buying guide).

- **Fish and seafood:** Many fish have close to 0 carbs, and the health benefits in eating fish are huge (for recipes, turn to Chapter 9).

- **Poultry:** Chicken and turkey are very healthy sources of protein (Chapter 10 has all kinds of great recipes).

- **Lean meats:** Read both words here — *lean* meats are the best when you're looking for protein sources (check out Chapter 11 for recipes).

- **Some fruits:** Yes, fruits that are relatively low in carbs do exist (check out the shopping list in Chapter 3).

- **Nuts:** They're full of good nutrients and are a great source of protein. Nuts are great to graze on to keep your metabolism fires burning (see Chapter 2), and they can help curb cravings (for more on nuts and other great snack suggestions and recipes, see Chapter 14).

- **Whole grains:** Even though whole grains are mainly carbohydrates, refined grains are the guys to watch out for. Whole grains, in moderation, are a great source of fiber, with as much as seven times more fiber than refined grains.

- **Legumes:** Soybeans are very high in protein, contain no cholesterol (like all legumes), and are low in saturated fats and sodium, plus they're packed with dietary fiber and are rich in iron, calcium, zinc, potassium, magnesium, and B vitamins. Pretty impressive for a little bean, eh? The best-kept secret in the low-carb lifestyle is black soybeans, and they taste great. (See Chapter 7 for information about black soybeans and a recipe using black soybeans.)

- **Yogurts that are low in sugar and carbs:** If you look, you can find some great ones, especially Greek yogurt.

- **Cheeses of many varieties:** Cheeses are a great source of protein, but watch for the saturated fats. Keyword — balance. (Among many others, there's a great recipe for No-Pasta Lasagna in Chapter 12 with great cheesy stuff in it.)

Leaning toward a Lifestyle Approach: The Latest in Low-Carb Living

Low-carb dietary guidelines are a good thing. But I sometimes compare them to a pattern for a dress. The basics of the dress pattern and the dietary guidelines are both just *guidelines*. After the basic dress is sewn or the basic guidelines are laid down, it's necessary to perform alterations and embellishments to fit each individual's particular taste, style, and needs. In other words, one dietary lifestyle does not fit all! Use these low-carb dietary plans as *guides* for you to draw your own blueprint!

Empowering yourself to make a commitment to a healthy lifestyle is the only answer to maintaining your weight with the awesome rewards of wellness and longevity. Did you wake up one morning overweight? Did you pack on those pounds overnight? I didn't think so. So what's your hurry now? It all has to come off in two weeks?

Jump off that diet merry-go-round. Make a decision to lose weight for life! Be willing to look at the big picture (soon to be a picture of less of you)! Make the steps you're taking to lose pounds take you along a road that you'll continue traveling as you maintain and lose weight for life. You'll never go on a "diet" again. The word "diet" derives from the Greek *diaita,* of which the literal meaning is "way of life." For you, this translates into a constant way of living or *lifestyle.* Think of yourself as following a healthy, active low-carb lifestyle — not a diet!

Considering the components

All low-carb lifestyles are not created equal, and only you know what really works for you. You may be a real carb counter, or you may be a carb controller. This book isn't intended to tell you which healthy low-carb lifestyle that you should choose — it's a cookbook! You more than likely had already chosen your low-carb lifestyle before you bought this book, and you can adapt the recipes in this book to whatever low-carb lifestyle you choose. Roll the dice so that you come up with the healthy and active low-carb lifestyle that fits what you so deserve, including not only good food but also health and longevity.

You may want to find a lifestyle combination of all the low-carb "diets" out there that fits your specific needs. Find not just another diet that's going to keep you on the diet roller coaster, but a low-carb dietary plan that you can adapt for life as a personal healthy low-carb lifestyle. This entails some trial and error. I can't tell you what will and won't work for your body. But I can tell you that a low-carb lifestyle will not only help you lose and maintain your weight but also provide other perks. You'll have more energy, you'll feel better, chronic aches and pains may disappear, your health will likely improve, your risk of chronic diseases can lessen, and you'll look better. You'll probably buy a new mirror because you'll like the way you look, and your self-esteem will be higher than ever!

By living a healthy low-carb lifestyle, you can lose and maintain your weight with a vast array of foods that line up with the caloric needs of your body while eliminating refined carbs, unhealthy fats, white flour, and white sugar. If you want to adopt a basic low-carb lifestyle, these general guidelines may prove helpful:

- ✔ Choose carbs that are nutritious and not full of empty calories.
- ✔ Eat more foods high in fiber content, such as vegetables, whole grains, and fruits.
- ✔ Eat more fish.
- ✔ Eat more nuts.
- ✔ Move more every day.
- ✔ Watch for added sugar in fruits and minimize caloric artificial sweeteners.
- ✔ Avoid processed foods and others containing partially hydrogenated oils and trans fats (see Chapter 2 for more information on all fats).
- ✔ Be selective about the fats you eat, because all fats are not bad.
- ✔ Select foods based on your individual calorie needs according to your body. Remember that calories do count and that balancing calories is important in losing and maintaining weight.

You're not supposed to cut carbs totally out of your healthy lifestyle. It's not about elimination; it's about carb control and the types of carbs consumed. Your body processes and breaks down foods differently than any other processor on the planet. You have to find your own sweet spot of balance. Every book tells you something a little different, and almost every person has a different answer. It's about the basic equipment — your body. So listen to it. Drop those initial pounds and then begin enjoying your new healthy lifestyle of choice — low-carb.

Valuing variety

You may hear people talk about all the foods that they can't have on a low-carb diet. But the list of foods you *can* have when you're controlling your daily carb intake is so long that it really dwarfs the list of foods you should shy away from. So try switching gears in your head. Don't think deprivation — think choices, choices, choices. (Check out Chapter 3 for all the great items you get to add to your low-carb shopping list.)

Some people say that eating the low-carb way is a juggling act. I say, "Great. Look at all I have to juggle!" The possibilities and combinations are endless. If you choose to be bored with this lifestyle, you have no one to blame but, well, yourself. One of my objectives in this book is to demystify the belief that low-carb is boring. I do this by bringing you choices, choices, choices with great low-carb recipes and suggestions for low-carb snack foods. I guarantee that if you prepare some of the low-carb recipes in this book for your guests, they won't have a clue that they're low-carb because they are so good! Stop thinking that something can't be good for you unless it hurts or tastes bad. A healthy lifestyle doesn't hurt, the food can be great, and you don't suffer from pangs of hunger and deprivation. You're in the driver's seat, and you can have a joyous and very healthy ride. So come on along!

Healthy nutritional eating doesn't have to be ho-hum. Eating what's good for you and available to you on your low-carb eating plan is easy when it tastes great (see the recipes later in this book, many with less than 5 grams of carbs). The problem with falling off the wagon of any healthy lifestyle usually comes down to boredom. But there's no reason to be bored with the food in your low-carb lifestyle. The boredom comes only when you prepare broccoli the same way for the 98th time!

After you discover the grand flexibility of all the whole fresh foods that are there for your enjoyment, you'll stop mourning the absence of the foods you can't have and start thinking, "Wow! Look at all the awesome foods that I can have — foods that will not only satisfy my appetite but also taste delicious and have the added benefit of enhancing my health every day."

Variety is truly the spice of the low-carb lifestyle. By adding new foods with low carb counts, you'll not only avoid boredom and stay with your low-carb lifestyle, but I'll bet you'll smile more because of how you look and feel. Try two new recipes a week to expand your low-carb cuisine horizon. You won't be sorry.

Becoming an active low-carb consumer: Get the nutrition facts

Become nutrition minded — not food minded. I think you'll be amazed at how good nutritional foods can taste! Taking charge of your health and your lifestyle is very empowering. These days, knowing what to eat and where to get reliable information can be challenging. Take a little time to learn just a little about nutrition. I'm not asking you to get a degree. Just commit to reading one short nutrition article a week, whether it's online, in a magazine, or in a newspaper.

Food satisfies hunger, but food is also about giving your body energy. The right kind of energy is about nutrition. When you begin to get a glimmer of the connection between nutrition and wellness, you'll be even more excited about the smart choice you're making in controlling your carbs with your healthy low-carb lifestyle. You're on the road to losing weight for life! (See more about low-carb nutrition in Chapter 2 and a discussion of reading those Nutrition Facts panels in Chapter 3.)

Reducing your reliance on diet products

The diet industry is a billion-dollar industry, but for many people, the only thing that gets skinnier are their wallets. Ante up for the pleasures of your healthy low-carb lifestyle, not for diet hype full of empty promises. Put your money where your mouth is (sorry, I just couldn't resist). Spend your money on foods that you really enjoy and learn how to cook different ways. For example, try some ethnic dishes and get familiar with fresh herbs and spices. Discover new and easy ways to prepare great food (see Chapter 20 for quick and easy recipes). Treat yourself to a low-carb cooking class, which you can find offered at lots of places these days!

Very simply, if manufacturers of diet products and packaged foods are selling extreme promises, beware. What they're really selling is *hope* — simple and empty hope along with hidden ingredients and preservatives. There is no magic bullet to weight control. Stop the extremes. Check out Chapter 3, where I provide all kinds of shopping lists with all kinds of foods that are naturally low in carbs, many of which are better alternatives to dietary products.

Assessing Your Situation: Developing a Carb-Patrol Report

Food journaling has been proven to work, so I want you to try this exercise. For one week, you're going to eat as you normally do, whether you usually pay little attention to what you put in your mouth or you're a pretty active carb counter already. During this week, write down everything you eat and drink — and I mean *everything*. Don't worry about writing down carb counts or calorie counts (unless you usually do) or getting fancy and trying to construct some sort of spreadsheet. Just get a little notebook and take it everywhere with you and scribble down everything you put in your mouth. After a couple days, you'll begin to think of it as a little game you're having with yourself. This is a very personal exercise, so you don't have to share it with anyone unless you want to.

At the end of the week, assess what you've eaten. A couple of things could happen here. You could give yourself a big pat on the back or yell "Yikes!" That's why food journaling works — you just don't realize what you really eat in a day. Writing down all the foods that you eat every day will help you begin to make small changes, setting you up for success in adopting a low-carb lifestyle.

Losing Weight for Life

You've heard many times that life isn't about the destination; it's about the journey. As you embark upon life's journey, you encounter change and challenge, just as you do in your low-carb lifestyle. And much like life, if you stick to the basics and throw out the extremes, things flow much more smoothly. You also know that some goals in life are more quickly realized than others. Some take more time and patience. So why does the world not apply these theories to quick-loss fad diets? Because there is always a better mousetrap, and most people are guilty of wanting a quick fix, especially when it comes to weight loss. You have the power — it's the power within you. You have the desire to lose and maintain your weight for life, or you wouldn't have this book in your hand right now.

Reality check: There is no quick fix to losing weight and keeping it off. Following a healthy, active low-carb lifestyle is your ticket to losing weight for life. Slow and steady wins the race forever. The rewards can be huge! You may be able to eliminate chronic disease and illness and enjoy wellness and longevity. What better pot of gold at the end of the rainbow could you possibly ask for? Health is wealth, and there isn't enough money in the world to buy health.

Focusing on today

Don't always be living in the future (looking forward to "when I do this" or "when this happens") and certainly don't dwell in the past, with all its *would haves, could haves,* and *should haves.* Today is all you have, so make the most of it. Appreciate today and live today. Expand your horizons today. Expand your low-carb lifestyle and stretch yourself. Get excited about a new recipe or treat yourself because you deserve it. You'll love yourself even more tomorrow because of what you do today.

And you'll find that low-carb is your yellow-brick road to losing weight for life and that it just gets easier to maintain your healthy low-carb lifestyle. Start liking yourself and accepting yourself today.

Ditching your bathroom scales

Begin moving in a different direction now. I'm not telling you to never weigh yourself, but I am suggesting that you not be a slave to your bathroom scale. Shift your focus from dieting to leading a healthy low-carb lifestyle. Notice that your clothes are suddenly looser? I recall a time not too long ago that I had fallen off the proverbial low-carb wagon and climbed sheepishly back on. I had an important meeting to attend and wanted so badly to get into a brand-new pair of great dress pants in my closet. I hesitated as I slid one leg into the chic, new pants and then began to zip them up. Wow — they were actually a little loose around the waistband. Did I feel good about myself or what? The scale, however, didn't reflect any great weight loss. Expectation is killer stuff, so don't ruin your progress and your glory by stepping on the scale, because with the low-carb lifestyle, you'll find that you sometimes lose inches before you lose pounds. It'll all eventually mesh, and the pounds will disappear with the inches as you continue your active, healthy low-carb lifestyle. Just take it one step at a time.

Chapter 2

Raising Your Total Carb Awareness

*N*o one diet or lifestyle works for everyone. You probably already selected the low-carb lifestyle that works best for you before you opened this book. You may count *every* carb that you put into your mouth; you may take a more relaxed, yet still focused approach by carefully monitoring the carbs that you choose to eat every day; or you may have found that eliminating refined sugar, white flour products, and processed foods is adequate to maintain your carb-conscious lifestyle. I say whatever works for you is great.

Or maybe you're just beginning to explore what this low-carb thing is all about. If that's the case, welcome to the low-carb world (and you may want to consider *Low-Carb Dieting For Dummies,* written by Katherine B. Chauncey and published by Wiley, as you try to find a dietary and lifestyle approach that works for you).

But no matter where you fall on the low-carb spectrum, information is key. And that's where this chapter comes in. In this chapter, I present some of the nuts and bolts of low-carb living. If you're new to the lifestyle, you'll find this information very useful as a primer of sorts. But like any good low-carb lifestyle, I'm flexible. So I've been sure to pack this chapter with enough tips and information to pique your interest even if you're an old pro at this stuff.

Research shows that rapid weight loss rarely lasts. Take heed — slow and steady wins the race in weight loss. Keep those pounds off as you shed them.

Introducing the Carbohydrate

Carbohydrates are molecules made of hydrogen, carbon, and oxygen. They are sometimes referred to as *carbs* or *carbos*. Carbs include:

- ✔ Starches
- ✔ Sugars
- ✔ Fiber

Carbohydrates are the body's main source of energy and the first energy that the body uses (though fiber is calorie free, and therefore doesn't provide energy). Carbohydrates are found mostly in plant foods such as vegetables, fruits, and whole grains. Low-carb dietary approaches attempt to minimize the consumption of foods containing starches and sugars, while encouraging the consumption of carbohydrate foods that are high in fiber.

Usually carbohydrates are classified as complex or simple:

- ✔ *Complex carbohydrates* require digestion before the energy released can be used by the body. Therefore, low-carb dietary plans usually stress that the carbs you do consume should be of the complex variety because they lead to steady energy levels as opposed to the peaks and valleys of energy and sluggishness that usually occur when you eat simple carbohydrates.

- ✔ *Simple carbohydrates,* such as sugars, white flour, white rice, and foods containing high amounts of starches, go directly into the bloodstream, causing a spike in blood sugar levels. This spike gives the body a boost of energy for a short period of time. The blood sugar levels then drop, and a sense of depletion results. Therefore, low-carb dietary plans stress the need to avoid simple carbohydrates as priority number 1.

Singing the sugar blues: Replacing sugar with other sweeteners

Most low-carb dietary plans place refined sugars high on the list of dietary components to avoid, the same area they occupy in any healthy lifestyle. Here are some reasons to replace refined sugars for your sweet fix:

✔ Sugar is full of empty calories. Sugar provides no nutrients to your body.

✔ Sugar breaks down quickly in your bloodstream, dumping high levels of insulin.

✔ Sugar is high on the list of the causes of weight gain, mood swings, and even depression (sugar blues).

✔ Sugar wreaks some real havoc with your overall health and longevity by suppressing your body's immune response.

✔ Sugar, like all simple carbs, can create cravings, leaving your body wanting more. The more sugar you eat, the more you want.

Plus, most of the sweet stuff (sugar) is high in calories and can also have a high fat count, especially baked goods. (See the "Meeting Your Metabolism: Becoming Carb and Calorie Conscious" and "Knowing Thy Fats" sections later in the chapter for more information on why healthy low-carb *lifestyle* approaches stress the need to be aware of both calories and fats as well as carbs.)

"The sweetening of America" has become a popular phrase, but one that isn't looked upon favorably. Sugar is one of the primary causes of a world of obese people, with the numbers climbing every day. Sugar has no nutritional value and is jam-packed with calories, calories, calories. Well, we do like it sweet, so what now? Simple — find something that sweetens in place of sugar. There are two types of sweeteners:

✔ **Non-nutritive sweetener:** These are referred to as *sugar substitutes* or *artificial sweeteners.* The two terms are used interchangeably, so don't let it confuse you. Non-nutritive sweeteners supply neither energy nor calories to the body. Most sugar substitutes simply pass through the body and are excreted in urine.

✔ **Nutritive sweeteners:** These sweeteners do supply the body with energy and calories. A couple examples of this category of sweeteners are corn syrup and honey. Also included in this group are sugar alcohols and polyols.

Sweet facts

The average sugar consumption in the United States and around the world has skyrocketed. In 1899, the average sugar consumption per person in the United States was about 10 pounds of sugar per year. One hundred years later, in 1999, the sugar consumption had increased to an average of 170 pounds per person per year. Interestingly enough, in 1899, the incidence of heart disease, stroke, and diabetes was minimal. By 1999, those same diseases were raging throughout the United States and are reaching epidemic numbers today.

In the following sections, I help you sort out the sweetener thing in your low-carb lifestyle.

Assessing artificial sweeteners

Sugar substitutes/artificial sweeteners are a very individual choice because one may have an aftertaste for you and taste heavenly to another. One or a combination of two may make drinks and foods taste sweeter to you, while someone else finds the combination almost repulsive. I'm sure that you have your very own favorite. The level of sweetness greatly varies with different brands. Sometimes combining two different sweeteners creates a synergistic effect, resulting in added sweetness from the combination. (See more about the sugar substitute that I've chosen to use in the recipes in this book in Chapter 4. And check out the "Sweet, sweeter, sweetest" sidebar in this chapter for the history of some common sweeteners on the market today.)

Sugar substitutes make food taste sweet without the calories, but watch the carb counts. By the teaspoon, they may have less than one gram of carbs, but if you have a whole cupful, that's a different story. A big marketing game is played with the carb count of artificial sweeteners. Keep in mind that if a teaspoon of an artificial sweetener only contains a half of a carb and you need a whole cup of that same sweetener in a recipe, those half carbs add up. Pay attention to the calories as well because some sweeteners are being advertised as *no calorie* but do indeed stack up calories in the same manner.

Be sure to always read labels to see what has been added to the foods that you're buying. You'll see lots of food products on the market that are indeed labeled sugar-free and low in net carbs. But when you read the labels, you find that they are off the charts in calories, making them not good choices for your low-carb healthy lifestyle (discover more about reading labels in Chapter 3).

Sugar alcohols (Polyols)

Polyols and *sugar alcohols* are one and the same. Polyols are sugar-free sweeteners that are derived from plant products such as berries and fruits, various corn syrups, from grain products like surplus corn. They're used extensively as sweeteners and bulking agents in a wide variety of foods including chewing gums, candies, ice cream, baked goods, and fruit spreads. They're also used in toothpastes, mouthwashes, breath mints, and medicinal products such as cough syrups and throat lozenges. The latest and greatest extensive use for them is in low-carb sweets and treats such as low-carb protein bars, cookies, candies, and ice cream — the list is a long one. Unlike sugar substitutes/artificial sweeteners, they don't come in little packets. They're found more readily in prepared low-carb sweet products than in your low-carb pantry.

Sweet, sweeter, sweetest

What you use to satisfy your sweet tooth is your choice, but here's a brief look at the history of sweetening the pot without refined table sugar (please note that this is not an all-inclusive list). All of these products are still available to you today:

1879: Saccharin was discovered. It's derived from a natural substance in grapes and is 300 times sweeter than table sugar.

1931: Stevia is a plant from which two French chemists produced a white crystalline substance that they named Stevioside. It's 300 times sweeter than table sugar. Stevia is currently sold as a dietary supplement.

1965: Aspartame was discovered. It's made of amino acids and is 180 times sweeter than table sugar. It was first approved by the U.S. Food and Drug Administration (FDA) in 1981.

1967: Acesulfame potassium was discovered. It's 200 times sweeter than table sugar. It was first approved by the FDA in 1988.

1978: Sucralose was discovered and then tested for over 20 years. The FDA first approved it in 1998. Sucralose is 600 times sweeter than table sugar.

The name "sugar alcohol" is misleading to many because polyols are neither sugar nor alcohol. It's about their molecular construction. Part of the structure of sugar alcohols is similar to that of sugar, and some is similar to alcohol. Sugar alcohols contain no nutrients and no dietary fiber and are a low digestible carbohydrate, which means that they have less of an impact on blood glucose levels. Moderation is again the key. Because of the confusion around the name "sugar alcohol," these ingredients are referred to more and more as polyols. The Food and Drug Administration will make the final decision whether sugar alcohols are actually renamed polyols.

Sugar alcohols are sometimes perceived as being calorie and carbohydrate free but that's not the case. Table sugar contains 4 calories per gram. The calorie content of different sugar alcohols varies from 0.2 to 3.0 calories per gram, so don't be fooled. Be a savvy label reader. (In Chapter 3, I provide some tips on reading nutrition labels, including sugar alcohol considerations.)

The sweetness varies among these sugar replacements. The most commonly used polyols are

- Erythritol
- HSH (hydrogenated starch hydrolysates)
- Isomalt
- Lacitol
- Maltitol and maltitol syrup

✔ Mannitol

✔ Sorbitol

✔ Xylitol

Broad controversy exists in the entire diet community of the universe, and the subject of polyols is no different. Researchers can't seem to agree whether polyols are absorbed by your body or if they simply pass right on through. Some folks in the "not absorbed" camp say that because they pass through your body without absorption, it's a good thing for your low-carb lifestyle and doesn't harm your body. Others jump up and down shouting that if polyols merely pass through your body, because there's no mechanism within your body to process polyols, then they can't possibly be good for you or your health. Manufacturers add to the fires of the controversy by touting that even if a portion of the polyol is absorbed into the bloodstream, it requires little or no insulin, thus causing no spike in blood sugars. Here are a few points to consider in making your dietary decisions:

✔ **Looking at the upside of polyols:** The sweet treats that can be made with polyols are pretty incredible. You'll find some tastier than others, and some will be based on your personal preference, like anything else. Polyols provide manufacturers with the bulk and texture of sugar for their food products, as well as making the products very sweet to please your low-carb sweet tooth. Some of the low-carb treats made with polyols that are on the market can be downright decadent, making you beg for more.

✔ **Looking at the downside of polyols:** Some polyols linger in your intestines, inducing uncomfortable bloating, gas, and sometimes diarrhea. You may be extra sensitive to all or some polyols and experience a sometimes-embarrassing laxative effect after eating them. Sometimes it hits you almost immediately, and other times the bloating comes a little later.

Factoring in fiber

Dietary fiber is essential in low-carb dietary plans. *Dietary fiber* is a complex carbohydrate that the body doesn't digest or absorb but moves through the body. Fiber occupies a special position in the low-carb world because you get to subtract it from your total carb counts when you track your carb intake (see the "Understanding Net Carb Math 101" section for more information). In fact, fiber is beneficial in weight management because it makes you feel full for longer periods of time, squelching some of those cravings. Fiber is also necessary stuff for regularity, especially with low-carb lifestyles.

High-fiber foods are beneficial for maintenance of your day-to-day health, but most folks don't get enough fiber in their diet. (The recommended daily intake of fiber is 21 to 38 grams, depending on your gender and age.) Most adults are lucky to get 10 to 15 grams. You find fiber in plant foods, such as vegetables, whole grains, nuts, seeds, beans, and fruits. There are two types of fiber, *soluble* and *insoluble,* and you can read about them in the easy to understand yet detailed chart in Figure 2-1, which outlines how fiber works in your body better than a page full of words could.

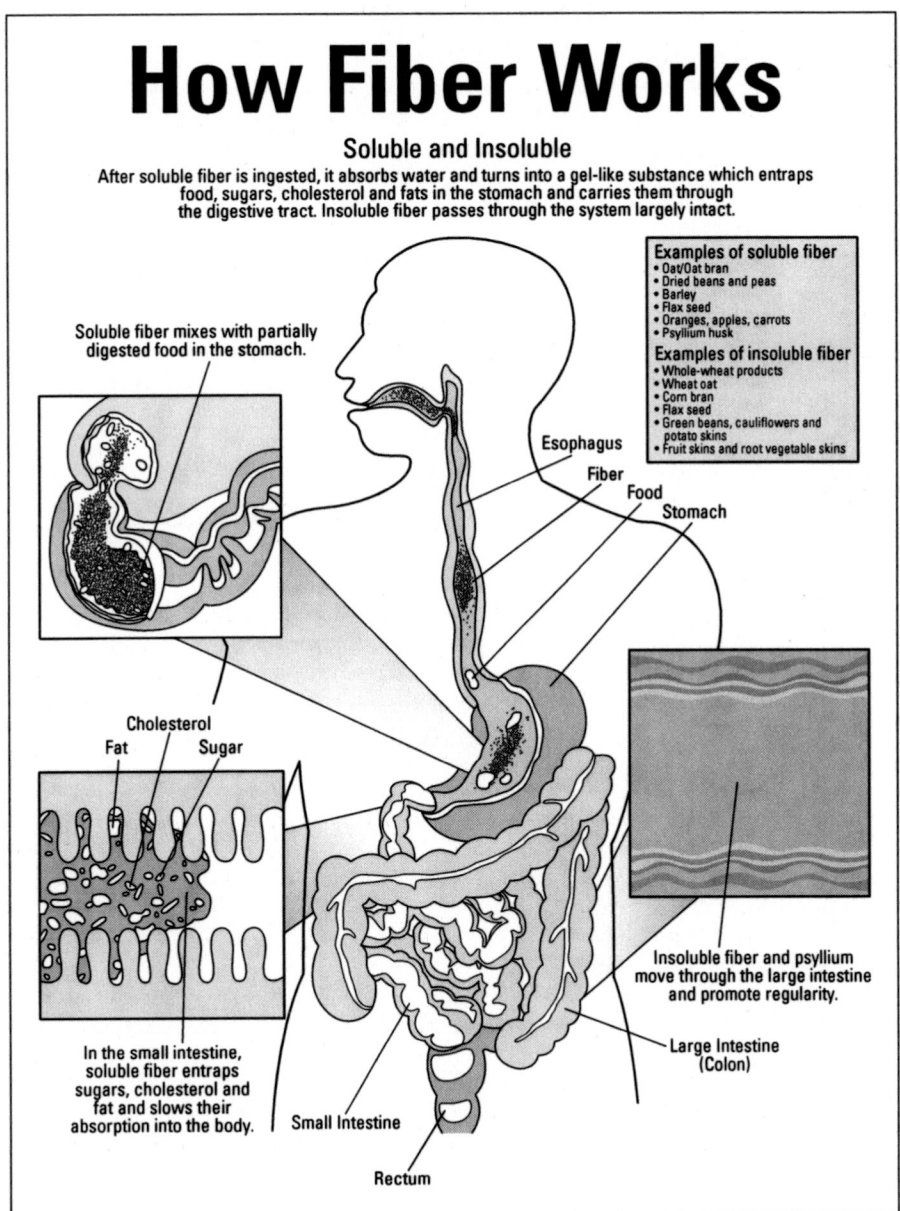

How Fiber Works
Soluble and Insoluble

After soluble fiber is ingested, it absorbs water and turns into a gel-like substance which entraps food, sugars, cholesterol and fats in the stomach and carries them through the digestive tract. Insoluble fiber passes through the system largely intact.

Examples of soluble fiber
• Oat/Oat bran
• Dried beans and peas
• Barley
• Flax seed
• Oranges, apples, carrots
• Psyllium husk

Examples of insoluble fiber
• Whole-wheat products
• Wheat oat
• Corn bran
• Flax seed
• Green beans, cauliflowers and potato skins
• Fruit skins and root vegetable skins

Soluble fiber mixes with partially digested food in the stomach.

Esophagus

Fiber
Food
Stomach

Cholesterol
Fat   Sugar

Insoluble fiber and psyllium move through the large intestine and promote regularity.

Large Intestine (Colon)

In the small intestine, soluble fiber entraps sugars, cholesterol and fat and slows their absorption into the body.

Small Intestine

Rectum

Figure 2-1: Take a look at the mechanics of fiber.

Courtesy of the National Fiber Council, www.nationalfibercouncil.org. Used by permission.

Understanding Net Carb Math 101

Though approaches may vary from plan to plan, a common thread runs throughout the game of counting carbs: Certain carbohydrates have more impact on the rise of blood glucose levels than others. For carb counters, you see carbs referred to as *high-impact* and *low-impact carbs. Low-impact carbs* simply mean that your body doesn't metabolize them. (Check out the section "Meeting Your Metabolism: Becoming Carb and Calorie Conscious," later in the chapter.) This is great news for the low-carb lifestyle! In a nutshell, when you're looking at a Nutrition Facts food label and you see the total carbohydrate count, you're not finished yet — this is where knowing net carb math 101 is invaluable to you. This simple net carb formula is a useful tool in planning meals and snacks in your everyday low-carb lifestyle.

Because your body doesn't digest dietary fiber and it's not absorbed in the body but rather "moves through" your body, you have the green light to subtract the total grams of fiber from the total grams of carbs in a particular serving of food, giving you your "net carbs" for that serving. If you're a smart low-carb cookie, you'll take this to heart — all those fresh veggies and fruits are full of fiber.

So the formula to determine net carbs in a given food is simply:

Total carbohydrates – Dietary fiber = Net carbs

A great example of net carb counts is a very healthy food — black soybeans. The total carb count for a serving of ½ cup of black soybeans is 8 grams of carbs. The dietary fiber count per ½ cup serving is 7 grams. When you subtract the fiber count from the carb count, you get a whopping total of 1 gram of net carbs for the entire ½ cup serving. This is healthy low-carb eating at its best! (See a great chili recipe in Chapter 16 with black soybeans.)

But the low-carb diet world is constantly changing. These days, another formula that some low-carbers use to mathematically eliminate additional carbs from their bottom-line carb counts is called Net Impact Carbs or the Effective Carb Count (ECC). The formula looks like this:

Total carbohydrates – Dietary fiber – Sugar alcohols (polyols) = Effective Carb Count (ECC)

As you can see, the difference between the effective carb count and the net carb count is a little thing called sugar alcohol. I'll warn you that controversy abounds over the use of this formula, and the heart of the controversy is whether sugar alcohols actually affect your blood sugar levels (see the section "Singing the sugar blues: Replacing sugar with other sweeteners," earlier in this

chapter). You may sometimes hear or see Effective Carb Counts referred to as "usable carb counts."

There's no legal definition of low carb, and carb counts vary greatly.

Weighing Your Carb Choices

All carbohydrates are not created equal. And carbs are not monsters. They are just a force to be reckoned with in your healthy lifestyle. I don't like the connotation of "good" and "bad" when referring to carbs, so I'll call them "healthy" and "not so healthy" in this section if that's okay with you. To make it easy, healthy carbs, in general, are unprocessed foods and contain a good amount of fiber. On the other side of the carb coin lie the not-so-healthy carbs, which are usually refined or processed foods. Take responsibility for being the judge and jury of the carbs in your food. Here are a few factors to consider in making your daily judgment calls:

- ✔ How the carbs you choose affect your blood sugar (check out the glycemic index and glycemic load info later in this chapter to see about carbs and blood sugars)
- ✔ Your metabolism (mosey on down in this section to bone up on mighty metabolism)
- ✔ The total calorie count (see the "Meeting Your Metabolism: Becoming Carb and Calorie Conscious" section later in the chapter).

Substitute a couple high-calorie foods, such as high-fat meats and fast foods, with natural foods like vegetables, fruits, whole grains, fish, and lean meat every day, and you can reduce your carbs as well as your calories while you increase your intake of nutrients that your body needs.

Healthy carbs

Healthy carbs are those that are as unprocessed as possible in their natural and whole form. Include more healthy carbs in your low-carb lifestyle. Some healthy carbs need to be consumed in moderation, and some choices in each group are considered more low-carb acceptable than others (see Chapter 3 for the details). Here are some examples of healthy carbs:

- ✔ Plant-based foods (veggies are key)
- ✔ Certain fresh fruits

- ✔ Certain dairy products
- ✔ Lean meats
- ✔ Fish and seafood
- ✔ Poultry
- ✔ Nuts and seeds
- ✔ Whole grains (in moderation)
- ✔ Legumes (in moderation)

Because healthy carbs are slow to metabolize in your body, they help you avoid spikes in your glycemic index (see more on the glycemic index in the section "Surveying Blood-Sugar Levels and Their Role in a Low-Carb Lifestyle," later in this chapter).

Sharpen your carb consciousness and discover that fresh is best. The more fresh foods that you can pack into your low-carb healthy lifestyle, the more of a winner you become. I provide you with a shopping list of healthy low-carb fresh foods in Chapter 3. (And you can also check out Chapter 23 for Web sites that provide both lists and searchable databases for determining exact carb counts in foods.)

Carbs that aren't so healthy

Simple carbs are absorbed by your body so quickly that they immediately hit your bloodstream with a rush, and an almost instantaneous gush of insulin follows. This gush floods the cells with the simple sugar of energy for your body. This process takes you on what you might know as a sugar high, whether you have ingested sugar or another simple carbohydrate. You experience a quick surge of energy and then a crash that usually comes with a craving. Not a healthy situation for you or your healthy low-carb lifestyle. (See the section "Surveying Blood-Sugar Levels and Their Role in a Low-Carb Lifestyle," later in this chapter.) Some of these "not-so-healthy carbs" include but are not limited to the following products:

- ✔ Refined sugars and products containing refined sugars, such as doughnuts, cookies, cakes, candies, and soda
- ✔ White flours and products containing white flours, such as breads, pizza, pastas, and noodles
- ✔ White rice
- ✔ Highly processed foods of all kinds, even foods like luncheon meats, some frozen meals, and meals in a box

Meeting Your Metabolism: Becoming Carb and Calorie Conscious

Despite what the headlines and ads say, low-carb dieting isn't a magic bullet that instantly sheds pounds and inches, never to have them return. I'm here to make the case that you should take your healthy low-carb active lifestyle very personally. Don't be afraid of blending low-carb lifestyle blueprints until you find the one that fits your body perfectly. And don't be afraid to become both carb and calorie conscious.

Reinserting calories into the metabolism discussion

Although many low-carb plans shy away from discussing the calories, calorie considerations are a reality. Where? In the focus on metabolism. *Metabolism* is very simply the rate at which your body burns calories. And although minding your metabolism is rightly a key plank in many low-carb approaches, somehow the *calorie* part drops out of the discussion. Well, I'm here to put it back in so that you can see it's okay to consider the calories.

A lot of low-carb diets pay little or no attention to calories — it's all about carbs. But if you can't figure out why you haven't lost many pounds, although you've been on a low-carb diet for six months and you're bored to tears with the food, it's high time you become carb and calorie enlightened. I know that a lot of the low-carb books won't even go here. But I will.

Be serious about controlling your carbs in your lifestyle, but don't fluff off the calories. You can see the importance of considering calories while trying to reach and maintain a healthy weight by simply considering what a calorie is. A *calorie* is simply a measure of *energy* that the food you eat produces when it's used by your body. Ah, but the key part in that definition of a calorie is the phrase *used by your body*. It's a fact that if you don't burn up those calories (use up that energy), you store them in your body as fat. There's no getting around it.

It's not rocket science, and it doesn't take a roomful of diet gurus to explain it. The math is actually very simple: If you take in 900 calories worth of energy in the foods you eat and you use only 600 of those calories, those other 300 calories have to go somewhere. So they pick a bunch of your body's cells to call home and set up camp. Camp calories have a more common name: fat.

Carbs and calories go hand in hand for long-term success with your healthy low-carb lifestyle, from the grocery store to the table to your tummy. Be aware that some processed foods out there that have low-carb stamped all over them have a calorie count that is sky high (see Chapter 3 for more on low-carb foods that can keep you fat).

Speaking of calories — eating just 100 more calories a day adds up to 10 extra pounds in one year. But the good news is that if you eat just 100 *less* calories every day, you would *lose* an extra 10 pounds in one year.

Working on metabolism mechanics

Being smart about your healthy lifestyle means you watch your carbs and your calories too and move your body more every day. You want to keep those metabolic fires a burnin' however you can and not give those fat cells squatter's rights to your body!

Everyone's *metabolic rate* (the rate at which your body uses calories) burns at a different level. No two bodies are alike. Metabolic rates can be affected by age, by gender, by how healthy your body is, by what you eat (different foods are metabolized at different rates), by how often you eat (or don't eat), by how much you move every day, and even sometimes by medications that you take. And not only does everyone's metabolic fire burn at a different level, but the fires change daily. This is why the formula of ingesting 2,000 calories and burning 2,000 calories has its merit, but it's not a watertight, absolute formula. We're all different, and it may take me a lot longer to burn 2,000 calories than it does you.

The metabolic key to losing and maintaining weight by using a healthy, low-carb lifestyle is kick-starting your metabolism in the morning, keeping it humming along at a constant pace by snacking on low-carb friendly foods throughout the day, and increasing that pace by moving your body more.

Stoking the fire with breakfast

Your metabolic rate also fluctuates throughout the day. When you go to bed at night, your metabolism slows. (So forget about that magical losing-weight-while-you-sleep stuff that you see on TV and in the magazines at the checkout counter in the grocery store. If it sounds too good to be true, it usually is.) Your metabolism is at its lowest point when you wake up in the morning. That's why breakfast is the most important meal — not only to feed your hungry body but also to fuel your metabolic furnace fires so they start burning calories (energy) early in the day. (See Chapter 6 for more on the importance of breakfast.)

When your brain says, "I'm hungry," what it's really telling you is that you need energy (calories). The minute you swallow some food, it ignites your metabolic fire and starts burning that energy. If you skip breakfast, your metabolic fires will keep on smoldering, as they do throughout the night.

Grazing on good carbs

After you have those metabolic fires kick-started, the key is to keep them going. It's just like throwing another log on the fire to keep it burning — that's what food does for your metabolic fire. *Grazing* is the art of not getting hungry by using smart snacks and goodies to keep your metabolic fires burning. This results in your being more satisfied, all the while burning calories and fat, which means that you are either losing weight or maintaining your ideal weight. Let me tell you what grazing is *not* in your low-carb healthy lifestyle: Grazing isn't a license to stuff yourself and overeat.

Eat several small meals a day — every two or three hours — and graze those cravings away before they pop up. Grazing has been a well-kept secret in the diet genre for years, but its merit is being more and more recognized as yo-yo diets fail and healthy lifestyles succeed. Chose smart low-carb snacks with plenty of fiber and protein, and your blood sugar levels will remain on an even keel. This prevents spikes in insulin levels, keeping your body more balanced and providing you with more energy and alertness and a better attitude. Be smarter than your hunger and get in front of it before that hunger screams, "I'm starving, feed me." When you become a grazer, you never feel deprived, and grazing just becomes routine — it's what you do when you're living low-carb for life. Feel full and lose weight!

I don't care what kind of excuse you have, never skip a meal. It doesn't have to be a full-on sit-down meal, and eating on the run sometimes is unavoidable. But just eat, okay?

Eating smaller and more frequent meals and snacking on healthy low-carb foods is a standard approach in many low-carb dietary plans. And it can work: It keeps the fires of your metabolism burning at a higher rate, thus preventing your body from storing the energy as fat.

The basic approach of many low-carb diets — eating as much as you want while losing weight — can be very attractive. However, buyer beware. The secret to eating more while losing weight is in *what you're eating*. The reality is that this is only true when you choose foods and snacks that are healthy carbs with low carb counts, high fiber counts, and low calories (see the section "Weighing Your Carb Choices," earlier in this chapter, for more on healthy and not-so-healthy carbs, and check out the low-carb shopping list I provide in Chapter 3).

Moving and metabolism

Try taking a short walk at break time or lunch during your busy day. The exercise of moving — yes, just moving your body does it — fuels your metabolic fire. Fueling your fires doesn't only burn calories; it gives you more energy. Want to know a secret about your metabolism and your weight? I don't care what diet you're on or what you eat (well, I really do, but . . .), if you don't combine your healthy low-carb lifestyle with moving more, the possibility of derailing your lifestyle increases greatly. Cutting through it all, if you burn energy (calories) equal to what you take in, you can maintain your weight. If you burn more energy (calories) than you take in, you lose weight, add tone to your muscles and your body, have more energy, and even eliminate stress.

Surveying Blood-Sugar Levels and Their Role in a Low-Carb Lifestyle

Once upon a time, you only heard about the *glycemic index* (GI) with reference to diabetes. But today, you can find entire diet plans that are structured purely around the glycemic index! Things do change. The GI was developed to provide a ranking of the potential of different types of carbohydrate-containing foods to raise the blood sugar levels in the body on a scale of 0 to 100. Carbohydrates that raise the blood sugar the fastest have the highest glycemic index.

Here's how the whole blood-sugar thing works. Eating foods high in carbohydrates, such as white potatoes, causes a rapid rise in blood sugar levels. Your body says, "Wait a minute. I need to regulate this — my blood sugar levels are going up!" Your pancreas is put on notice and begins to dump excessive amounts of insulin to level out your blood sugar. *Insulin* is a natural hormone that the body manufactures and is responsible for getting the sugar out of your blood by delivering it to most your body's cells at a rapid rate. Your cells absorb what's now simple sugar, or energy. Now here's the whammy: If your cells don't use this energy immediately, your body stores it as fat. How's that for the long way around to simply say weight gain and control is all about energy in equaling energy out? If you don't burn up the same amount of energy that you take in, you get fat or fatter!

To add insult to injury, because the insulin has done its job in leveling out your body's sugar levels by delivering the simple sugar in the form of energy to your cells, as your cells use the energy quickly, your blood sugar falls rapidly, creating low blood sugar and mood swings. This results in a sudden dip in energy and increased carbohydrate cravings. Your body is saying, "I want more sugar (technically referred to as *glucose*), please." These peaks and valleys of your blood sugar spiking and crashing become a vicious cycle that's not only uncomfortable for your body but also very unhealthy.

Many diet plans suggest eating foods that are low on the glycemic index with your low-carb lifestyle. These foods that are low in carbs and generally high in fiber keep you off the blood-sugar roller coaster. Because fiber is absorbed slowly, your blood sugar just merrily glides along fairly evenly without spiking. These foods satisfy your hunger for longer periods of time, and your cravings are better controlled. An added bonus to this whole schematic is that it aids in the prevention of diseases such as diabetes, coronary heart disease, and obesity.

Glycemic index scores

The GI was developed for research purposes and doesn't apply to portion sizes in your everyday meals, and that's where the confusion about the GI comes from. But here's a look at the standard glycemic index:

- ✔ **Low:** A rating of 0 to 54 turns to glucose more slowly.
- ✔ **Medium:** A rating of 55 to 69 turns to glucose at a moderate rate.
- ✔ **High:** A rating of 70 or higher turns to glucose very quickly.

Check out www.mendosa.com/gilists.htm for what I think to be the most comprehensive and complete list of glycemic index and glycemic load foods currently on the Web. This list can help you make good food choices for your healthy low-carb lifestyle. Basically, if a food is low on the GI/GL scale (see more about the GL in the next section, "Enter the glycemic load"), then it's generally low carb and doesn't cause what's known in the low-carb world as an *insulin spike*. Therefore, your blood sugars stay on an even keel. This is what the low-carb healthy lifestyle is really all about — keeping you off that blood-sugar roller coaster!

In addition to foods being low on the GI, it's important that they be low in sugar and salt, be high in fiber, and contain good fats. Another way to conceptualize this whole glycemic index thing is to check out the Glycemic Index Food Pyramid (in Figure 2-2). The base of the pyramid contains foods that are low on the glycemic index and are encouraged within low-carb lifestyles. The next level up from the base contains foods still at home in low-carb lifestyles. The top two levels contain high-glycemic foods. Foods at the top level of the pyramid are avoided in low-carb dietary plans, and foods in the second level from the top are eaten only in restricted moderation.

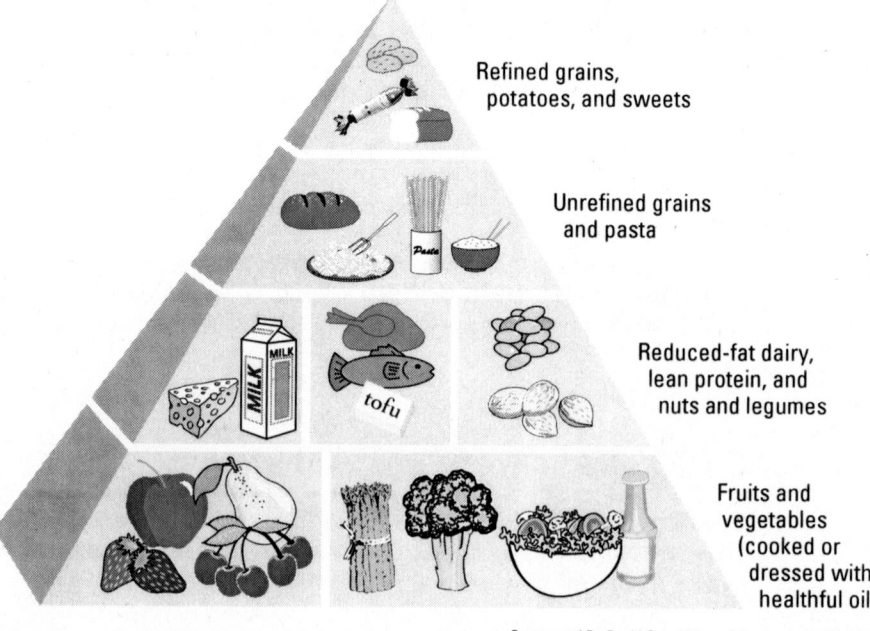

Refined grains,
potatoes, and sweets

Unrefined grains
and pasta

Reduced-fat dairy,
lean protein, and
nuts and legumes

Fruits and
vegetables
(cooked or
dressed with
healthful oil)

Figure 2-2:
The Low
Glycemic
Index
Pyramid.

Courtesy of Dr. David S. Ludwig and the Journal of Nutrition

Enter the glycemic load

The drawback of the glycemic index of foods is that it's not based on ordinary portion sizes. Instead, it's based on a *standard portion* containing 50 grams of usable carbs.

Take two and enter stage left — the glycemic load (GL). Now we're getting somewhere! The GL is much more user friendly because it takes into account the base of the glycemic index of carbohydrates in foods, and it's also based in standard portion measurements of foods. For glycemic load values for basic food types, go to www.mendosa.com/gilists.htm. (See Chapter 23 for more information about this Web site and more free low-carb information at your fingertips.)

The glycemic load ratings look like this:

- ✔ **Low:** A rating of 0 to 10
- ✔ **Medium:** A rating of 11 to 19
- ✔ **High:** A rating of 20 and higher

The following are foods high on the GL scale. Look familiar? Most of these foods are featured in the "Carbs that aren't so healthy" section, earlier in the chapter.

- ✔ Most processed foods
- ✔ White rice
- ✔ White flour and white flour products, such as white bread and dinner rolls
- ✔ Foods containing high amounts of refined sugar
- ✔ Soft drinks and fruit juices with high sugar content
- ✔ Cakes, candies, cookies, and brownies
- ✔ High sugar/white flour desserts

Choose foods with low GL ratings for your low-carb lifestyle, and it's a win-win situation. You're more likely to burn the calories from foods with a low GL as energy during the course of your day. Nonstarchy veggies have glycemic loads of almost zero because of their high fiber content, so they're great low-carb foods for you to nibble on.

Low GL carbs doesn't mean that they're free foods and you can just chow down. Be sure to look at the calorie counts on the charts, too, so you're not misled and end up gaining rather than losing weight. For instance, brown rice has a GI of 55 and a GL of 18, which puts brown rice in the medium range of the GL rating. Don't make this difficult, even though I've thrown some pretty technical stuff at you. Just remember that the GL rating of the food is important and get yourself a list of foods. As time passes, you'll just *know* as you settle into a low-carb lifestyle — you'll know what works for you.

When your body tells you that it's hungry, give it water first. If it still tells you that it's hungry, then feed it. Many times, people mistake being thirsty for being hungry. So initially try answering your body's request for replenishment with that nutritive carb- and calorie-free substance, water.

Knowing Thy Fats

Don't think you were going to get out of this chapter without a few words on fats. Your body requires fat to promote its energy reserves, which provide your body with more than double the energy of protein and carbs. Fats aid your body in the absorption of essential fat-soluble vitamins, including vitamins A, D, E, and K. Fats are regulators of nutrients in and out of your cells and supply insulation and protection of vital organs.

There are different types of fat that you should familiarize yourself with — some are good guys and some are bad guys. Sometimes, when people hear the words *low-carb dietary plan,* they instantly assume the plan must feature a high-fat diet. Don't get me wrong; some plans are clearly on the high-fat side. But many others take a more balanced view of all things nutrition and consider the amounts and types of fat involved. What's important is for you to know your fats and know which fats are good for you. Here's a brief overview of the good, the bad, and the very ugly:

- ✔ Saturated fats are the guys that give fats a bad rap. Some foods that are high in saturated fats include fatty fresh and processed meats, lard, high-fat dairy products, regular ice cream, the fat and skin of poultry, coconut oil, palm oil, and shortening. Excessive ingestion of saturated fats can raise your blood cholesterol, and that's not a good thing.

- ✔ Monounsaturated fats and polyunsaturated fats are considered healthy fats for you. Foods that are high in monounsaturated and polyunsaturated fats include olive oil, canola oil, flaxseeds, sesame seeds, most nuts, sardines, salmon, and avocados. Healthy fats regulate fat metabolism and aid in regulating insulin release. These fatty acids have little effect on the level of cholesterol in the blood (see more on healthy omega-3s in Chapter 9). Keep in mind to check the calorie count on healthy fats, with moderation as the keyword.

- ✔ Trans fats are partially hydrogenated oils that raise your LDL (bad cholesterol) and lower your HDL (good cholesterol). This double whammy should tell you to steer clear of trans fats. They're found in highly processed foods of all kinds, shapes, and sizes; the oil in margarines; french fries; beef; lamb; and dairy products — just to name a few. Please read your labels (see more about label reading in Chapter 3).

A diet high in saturated fat causes your body to make more cholesterol, which is linked with the risk of high blood pressure, diabetes, some cancers, and heart disease.

Chapter 3

Organizing and Shopping for the Low-Carb Kitchen

In This Chapter

▶ Making your kitchen low-carb friendly

▶ Putting together a stellar shopping list of low-carb staples

▶ Navigating the low-carb aisle at the grocery store

▶ Reading food labels

Managing your health begins in your pantry, fridge, and freezer and follows you up and down every aisle of the grocery store. And as you make your way home and prepare your low-carb, healthy meals and snacks, the details of managing your health are all around you! Making small changes in your kitchen is the first rung on the ladder of success of your healthy low-carb lifestyle, and the keyword is simplicity. With hectic lives abounding, the simpler you can approach your low-carb lifestyle, the more user friendly it becomes. And that spells positive results for you in weight loss, weight maintenance, and, most importantly, your present and future health.

In this chapter, I help you make sure that the key working environment of your lifestyle — your kitchen — passes the low-carb test, which comes in handy whether you've been a low-carber for a while or you're new to the low-carb lifestyle. I put you through sort of a carb cleansing process for your kitchen! Then I present a list of staples to fill your shelves, fridge, and freezer, and I take you to the grocery store for a little low-carb outing. While at the grocery store, there's a brief lesson on reading labels and scoping out the low-carb products that are on the shelves in the store. So stick with me; a lot of great foods are coming up.

Shaping Up Your Low-Carb Kitchen

Congratulations! You're going to clean out your kitchen and make a donation to your favorite shelter or soup kitchen. If this were a new reality television show, it might be called *Low-Carb Kitchen Makeover!*

Cutting carbs in the pantry

Face it — some items in your pantry have to go. They just don't belong in your healthy low-carb lifestyle. Pull out those high-carb and sugar-laden items lurking on your shelves. Box them up, and you're off to make your donation. Doesn't it feel great to help others while you make room for all the staples you need to whip up great low-carb meals? Here are the food items to look for to pack in your donation box or even boxes:

- Biscuit mixes
- Canned foods like baked beans, candied yams, and sugary pie fillings
- Cereals full of sugar and high in carbs
- Chocolate bars, chocolate syrups, and any other food covered in chocolate or accompanied by it
- Cookies, candies, packaged cakes, and sweet treats
- Crackers high in carbs, sodium, and fat, such as saltines
- Gelatins that aren't sugar-free
- Jams that aren't sugar-free, unless they're natural fruit spreads
- Mixes — cake, brownie, and muffin
- Oils high in saturated fats
- Packaged quick meals, such as macaroni and cheese
- Pasta
- Peanut butter, unless it's the natural kind
- Potato chips, corn chips, cheese puffs, pretzels, and any other high-carb snack items
- Puddings that aren't sugar-free
- Syrups and toppings, such as pancake syrup and ice cream toppings, laden with sugar
- Vegetable shortenings laden with trans fats
- White breads, including high-carb pita pockets, tortillas, dinner rolls, biscuits, croutons, and prepackaged breadcrumbs
- White flours
- White rice

Please note that I don't profess this to be an all-inclusive list but rather a guide, because every kitchen has different foods stuffed away that are labeled "temptation." Also, you may have already done some partial carb cleaning, and if you've already replaced some of the items I list here with carb-acceptable food, then of course you get to keep it! And if you're a parent of young kids or there are other folks in your house not quite willing to make the same changes, try isolating the remaining carb-laden foods in one cabinet.

Cleaning out the fridge and freezer

The next stop in your cleaning frenzy is the fridge and freezer. If you think you should just keep that frozen lasagna around for the day when a non-low-carb friend drops by, forget about it! It needs to go *now*. Otherwise, on a chilly, rainy night when you come home from work tired and hungry and don't know what's for dinner, guess what? That lasagna is history.

If you're going to donate your refrigerated and frozen stuff, you probably need to tackle this one on a Saturday morning so you can deliver it still cold or frozen. Here are the foods you should get rid of. They have high carb counts, and therefore, they no longer belong in your fridge or freezer:

- Frozen quick meals high in carbs, sodium, fats, and calories, like frozen lasagna and potpies
- Frozen cheesecakes and other sweet delights, such as pies
- Ice cream and other high-carb, high-sugar, frozen treats
- Jams that aren't sugar free, unless they're natural fruit spreads
- Juices high in sugar
- Marinades, sauces, and salad dressings high in sugar
- Milk (high in sugar and carb counts)
- Refrigerated biscuits, croissants, cinnamon rolls, Danishes, and other similar sweet rolls
- Soft drinks that aren't diet or made with Splenda

Creating a List of Low-Carb Staples, Aisle by Aisle

Your priority is to stock your kitchen with healthy, low-carb foods. Even though you have a good idea of what those foods are, you may not have a clue where to start in making a low-carb shopping list for staples. The whole idea is for you to have on hand what you need when you need it. Stocking up prevents unplanned trips to the grocery store, which in turn helps you avoid temptation and saves you time. Saving time is truly important in the rush of everyday life. And if you can whip up low-carb, delicious meals quickly because you've done just a smidgen of pre-planning and have shopped for necessary ingredients, you'll receive gold stars — in both preparing meals and saving time.

Keep in mind that some of the staples I list in this section may not apply to your household. And you don't have to buy them all; you have to make choices. This isn't a "must have" list by any means. To set yourself up for success in stocking your low-carb kitchen, be aware that you're realistically going to take two or three trips to the grocery store to be well stocked. You can't do it all in one fell swoop. Also, check out Chapter 20, where I provide additional tips and meal-planning advice to save you time and carbs.

Likewise, if you're following a particular low-carb dietary plan, not all of these staples may be on your personal list. The foods I cover in the following sections are generally low-carb friendly, and if they're a bit on the higher side of the ol' carb count, I let you know.

But if you're looking for exact carb counts, post a general carb gram counter on your fridge. If you prefer one of those little gram-counter booklets, get creative: Attach it to a magnet and stick it on your fridge! Put it right next to one of those magnetized shopping lists. You can pick these up at bookstores or in grocery stores by the magazines at the checkout counters. Check your gram counter while you make your list. For more information on nutritional analysis and carb counts, check out www.nutrtiondata.com for an extensive analysis and Chapter 23 for more on what this site has to offer you.

When you go to the grocery store, try not to go when you're hungry. If your stomach is growling, take along a zipper bag of your favorite nuts for a snack while you shop, and have a small bottle of water with you.

Produce department

Remember not to buy too many of one fresh fruit or vegetable. Consider how many days the item will store well — as you know, apples store much longer than lettuce, for example.

Some fruits and veggies that are high in carb counts are also high in fiber, which makes the net carb count fine for your lifestyle (see Chapter 2 on net carbs).

Veggies

The first stop is the veggie section (see Chapter 12 for more information on veggies). Veggies are both healthy and carb bargains whether they're on sale or regularly priced. They're brimming with nutrients and disease fighters.

The vegetables in the following list contain less starch than others, and they're all packed with fiber:

- Alfalfa sprouts
- Artichokes
- Asparagus
- Avocados
- Bean sprouts
- Bell peppers of all colors
- Bok choy
- Broccoli and broccoflower
- Brussels sprouts
- Cabbage
- Carrots
- Cauliflower
- Celery
- Fresh salad greens and lettuces
- Garlic
- Green beans
- Herbs of all kinds, like fresh basil, dill, rosemary, thyme, chives, cilantro, tarragon, and bay leaf
- Leeks
- Mushrooms of all kinds
- Okra
- Onions — red, yellow, and fresh green ones
- Parsley
- Pumpkin
- Radishes
- Rhubarb
- Scallions (green onions)
- Spinach
- String beans
- Squashes — zucchini, eggplant, and cucumbers

Other squashes are acceptable but have higher carb counts, so be sure to check the nutritional counts. Yellow and winter squash are good choices.

✔ Tomatoes of all varieties

✔ Turnips

✔ Wax beans

Even though some low-carbers look at carrots as having higher carb counts, the nutrient values are off the charts. Baby carrots are a great option for snacking and cooking too. You don't have to peel them or cut them up.

Remember that you can buy precut veggies for snacking and for cooking. They're a bit more expensive, but you have to be the judge on how valuable your time is in cutting all that stuff up!

Fruits

The next stop in the produce department is the fruit section. Unlike the advice I give concerning veggies in the preceding section, I advise you to skip the precut fruit. You'll find that some have added sugars and preservatives — two things that you want to steer clear of with your low-carb lifestyle. Fruits and low-carb living can be a controversial combination. It's about choices and balance, but fresh fruit should be a part of the rest of your life. Berries of all kinds are the least controversial in the fruit department because the fiber makes berries lower in carbs. Here are some other suggestions:

✔ Apples and pears (these are a little higher in natural sugar content and aren't for every day but are still on the list!)

✔ Apricots (another treat item)

✔ Blueberries, raspberries, strawberries, blackberries, and boysenberries

✔ Cranberries

✔ Grapes (in moderation)

✔ Kiwi fruit

✔ Mangoes (as a special treat — maybe a mango salsa)

✔ Melons — watermelon, honeydew, and cantaloupe (not for every day)

✔ Nectarines and peaches (also a little high on the natural sugar content)

✔ Pineapple (another moderation treat)

✔ Plums (the dark ones are the best)

✔ Sweet cherries

✔ Tangerines, oranges, grapefruit, and lemons

Nuts and seeds

In many grocery stores, you can also find nuts in the produce section. In specialty and health food stores, they're usually in the bulk goods area. I encourage you to buy nuts from the produce section or at a specialty or health food store — and avoid the nut offerings in the baking aisle. Why? You're looking for raw or minimally processed nuts. They're healthier, the carb counts are lower, and they don't contain preservatives.

Many nuts and seeds are acceptable in low-carb lifestyles. Ideas include almonds (raw, toasted, roasted, slivered), Brazil nuts, hazelnuts (you can make flour out of them too!), pecans (plain, toasted, sliced), pistachios, pumpkin seeds, sunflower seeds, and walnuts. Some are higher in fats and carb counts, such as cashews, macadamia nuts, peanuts, and pine nuts, but you can enjoy them in moderation. Check out Chapter 14, where I provide additional nutty tips, tricks, and recipes.

Canned and jarred goods

Let's move right along to the canned goods section. In this section, I include a few items that come in cans to embellish your fresh, low-carb cooking. I don't include canned veggies, because I encourage you to buy fresh or frozen ones. But you may want to keep particular canned veggies like water chestnuts on hand to include in some of your low-carb dishes if you really like them — it's one that I keep on hand to throw in my stir-fry dishes.

- Anchovies
- Applesauce with no added sugar
- Black soybeans
- Broth — chicken and beef

   Check the sodium counts, because they vary greatly.
- Capers
- Crab
- Dill pickles
- Fruit spreads with no added sugar
- Fruits with no added sugar or the low-carb brands
- Green chiles
- Horseradish
- Jellies and jams, sugar-free
- Low-carb ketchup

Regular ketchup has a very high sugar content, so it's best to pass it up.

✔ Maple syrup, sugar-free

✔ Mayonnaise, not salad dressing

✔ Mushrooms

✔ Mustard

Feel free to indulge in Dijon and specialty mustards; just check the sugar content.

✔ Olives — black and green

✔ Peanut butter, all natural

✔ Pumpkin

✔ Roasted red peppers

✔ Salad dressings

Watch the sugar and fat counts as similar prepared salad dressings held side by side may appear quite the same until you turn the bottle over and read the label.

✔ Sardines

✔ Shrimp

✔ Soy sauce

✔ Tomatoes — whole and some sauces

It's label-reading time because canned tomatoes vary dramatically in carb and sugar counts. Find one that you like that has low counts in both and then stick with that brand on your shopping list. (See Chapter 8 for more info on and recipes with tomatoes.)

✔ Tuna, white meat chicken, and salmon

All three of these come in vacuum-sealed pouches in spring water. I find that the quality is better in the pouch, but that's certainly a personal choice.

✔ Vinegars — balsamic, cider, and red wine

✔ Water chestnuts

✔ Worcestershire sauce

Many canned vegetables are high in sodium. To reduce the sodium and create a better tasting dish, drain and rinse the canned veggies.

Grains and breads

No entire food group should be totally eliminated from a healthy low-carb lifestyle. With grains and breads, you just have to tweak it to the low-carb side a little with moderation — not elimination — in mind. Whole grains provide your body with fiber and vitamins. When you're choosing a bread that you can enjoy, make sure that it's made from *whole grain* or choose a low-carb bread. I've been fortunate to find a whole-grain crunchy soy bread that has no flour added that's just delicious. The low-carb whole-wheat tortillas and pita pockets are also good. (Skip on over to Chapter 15 for some great wrap recipes.) The following is a list of grains and breads that can be a part of a healthy low-carb lifestyle in moderation:

- ✔ Bread — low-carb or one made with whole-grain wheat flour
- ✔ Crackers — whole-grain
- ✔ Oatmeal — steel cut or old-fashioned
- ✔ Pita pockets — low-carb whole-wheat
- ✔ Rice — brown or wild
- ✔ Tortillas — low-carb whole-wheat

Baking aisle

This is an aisle of temptation, so make your list, get your stuff, and get the heck out of there.

- ✔ Almond flour
- ✔ Bouillon cubes
- ✔ Cocoa powder
- ✔ Coconut, shredded and unsweetened
- ✔ Coconut milk, unsweetened
- ✔ Extracts — assorted flavors
- ✔ Gelatins, sugar-free
- ✔ Nonstick cooking spray
- ✔ Oils — canola, olive, and walnut (see Chapter 8 for a walnut oil salad dressing recipe)
- ✔ Puddings, sugar-free
- ✔ Sesame seeds
- ✔ Spices and dried herbs of all kinds

- ✔ Splenda or the sugar substitute of your choice
- ✔ Unsweetened baker's chocolate
- ✔ Whole-wheat flour (stone ground and white)
- ✔ Whole-wheat pastry flour

You have my permission to spend some time in the dried herbs and spices section. You can find wonderful items here that make all the difference in the world in your low-carb cooking. If you aren't familiar with cooking with herbs and spices, it's a tasty adventure to embark on. Because you're cooking lean meats, fish, poultry, and veggies in your low-carb lifestyle, and you're cutting down on fats and sweeteners, using spices can enhance the flavors dramatically.

Spices should always enhance the natural flavor of the food and never overwhelm it. A little often goes a long way, and it's always better to err on the light side, because you can always add more.

If spices seem expensive to you, watch for them on sale, because grocery stores run significant specials from time to time. My dollar store has a huge variety of spices, and they're just dandy.

Dairy case

Dairy products provide your body with calcium to build strong bones and nutrients that are necessary to help your body prevent osteoporosis. The key to the dairy case is label reading. Yogurt, for instance, isn't banned, but you need to compare the calories, the sugar, and the carbs and make a low-carb decision on which one to choose.

If you have a recipe that calls for milk, you can make your own version by using a light or heavy cream and mixing it with an equal amount of water. The carb counts are lower, there's little if any sugar content, and it makes dishes much creamier and tastier.

Here are some friendly dairy choices:

- ✔ Butter
- ✔ Cheeses of all kinds

    Don't forget shredded cheeses like mozzarella, cheddar, and Parmesan and the crumbly ones like blue and feta.
- ✔ Cottage cheese
- ✔ Cream cheese
- ✔ Mascarpone cheese

✔ Eggs, egg whites, and egg substitutes (see Chapter 13 for great meringue recipes)

✔ Half-and-half

✔ Heavy and light cream

✔ Hummus

✔ Milk

You may prefer soymilk, or you may use a low-carb milk product. Just be sure to check the carb and sugar counts.

✔ Sour cream

✔ Tofu

✔ Yogurt, plain

Some great Greek yogurts are available that are very low in carbs. There are also a lot of low-carb yogurts, but be sure to check the calorie counts on them.

Meat counter and fish market

The choices you make at the meat counter and fish market are very important to you and your low-carb lifestyle. Choosing lean meats and fresh fish gets you off to a great start. For more detailed information on fish, chicken, and meat, flip to Chapters 9, 10, and 11, respectively. Most fish have close to zero carb counts depending on the preparation and provide your body with some great nutrients. Lean meats provide you with lots of great protein. An outstanding benefit of both fish and meat is that they can be ready and on the table very quickly.

Deli counter

You know what you find at the deli counter — more temptation with all those carb- and sugar-laden salads and side dishes. But what you need to limit yourself to are fresh deli meats and maybe some cheeses sliced at the counter. Deli meats from the counter contain fewer preservatives than the prepackaged meats.

Frozen food section

I know you've shopped the produce section and the meat and fish counter for fresh. But you need back-up so you don't have to run to the store every day (see Chapter 20 on planning ahead). Also, you may prefer frozen veggies over fresh ones, which is fine, just as long as you eat those veggies! There are other good low-carb choices awaiting you in the frozen food section, including stir-fry veggie combinations, fruits, fish, shellfish, meats, low-carb acceptable frozen dinners, and some frozen low-carb dessert treats. I suggest you cruise the frozen-food section of several different stores. I don't know about where you live, but different grocery stores in my area don't always have the same products.

- ✔ **Edamame:** These frozen green soybeans are great in soups and stews. Sometimes I just boil some, add a little salt, and have them as a snack. They're filling and very good for you.

- ✔ **Frozen chicken fajitas and shrimp stir-fries:** Some of these are perfectly low-carb acceptable, so scope them out.

- ✔ **Frozen dinners:** Some of these entrees are especially prepared for the low-carb lifestyle. Still, the cardinal rule exists that you don't just read the front of the box. Turn it over and read all of the nutritional information.

- ✔ **Frozen desserts:** Sugar-free freezer pops are one of my favorite treats, and you'll find low-carb ice creams in lots of flavors, ice cream bars, and ice cream sandwiches. I send up a flag of caution to be sure and check the calorie counts, not just the net carbs on these products (collect more information on calories in Chapter 2). And watch those sugar alcohols too.

- ✔ **Frozen meats and fish:** Some folks prefer the convenience of having frozen meats and fish on hand. I mention this just so you know that you don't have to buy fresh to be successful at low-carb living.

- ✔ **Fruits:** Choose only the kinds with no added sugar. The quality of frozen fruits has come a long way. I buy frozen peaches for my smoothie treats all the time and just pop them in the blender. Frozen blueberries and red raspberries are other great choices.

- ✔ **Veggies:** They come in all kinds and are usually cut up and ready to be cooked. I suggest you try stir-fry vegetables. The combination of frozen stir-fried veggies has blossomed into a lot of choices. And many fit well in your low-carb lifestyle.

Be careful when choosing frozen stir-fry veggies, because some of them contain sauces that are loaded with sugars and preservatives. Choose the plain kind.

Putting the Low-Carb Aisle on the Map

You're cruising the grocery store with your fine list, and you have all your fresh foods in your low-carb grocery cart — way to go! And there it is — the low-carb aisle. You screech your cart to a halt, almost ramming into the little boy running after his mother, and take a quick right turn into the low-carb aisle. Have you ever seen so many products with "low-carb" tattooed on the front of them? May I offer a few words of advice? *Read the labels very carefully.*

Most grocery stores have put the low-carb aisle on their map of the store (did you know that most grocery stores actually have maps available?). All of the low-carb products may not be on the designated low-carb aisle. You may find some great low-carb cookies on the cookie aisle, and that would be a marketing issue. If you're craving cookies and following the low-carb lifestyle and you wander off track to the cookie aisle, the manufacturer has made it an easy choice for you! In some stores, you'll find duplicates depending on shelf space. For example, low-carb salad dressings are in the low-carb aisle and in the salad dressing section, too. All of this depends on the grocery store, so become familiar with the plans that the stores you shop most frequently have adopted.

Some of the new low-carb products you'll discover are nothing short of fabulous, and they make great additions to your low-carb lifestyle. They allow you to enjoy a variation of the tastes and textures of sugar-laden and carbohydrate-laden foods that are definitely off limits. What a blessing these fine products are. Unfortunately, there always have to be a few that jump on the bandwagon for reasons other than helping folks with their health goals.

Proceed through all the low-carb products with caution. Just because that sweet temptation says *low-carb* doesn't make it particularly user friendly to your body and your low-carb lifestyle. All low-carb products aren't created equal. Don't just look at the front of the packing that says, "Only 2 Net Carbs" — read the label and see what's inside that wrapper. Yep, the product may contain only 2 net grams of carbs with 375 calories — yikes! Combine all those calories with sugar alcohols, and you may be setting yourself up for a long-term sticking of your scales. Junk food in any form is still junk food even if it says low-carb. This is not user friendly to your low-carb lifestyle at all. And even if it's relatively healthy, just because it says "low-carb" doesn't mean that you can eat the whole thing.

Sometimes people are so diligent, or seemingly so, about their carb counts they just can't figure out why they aren't losing weight and/or why their energy levels are so low. When you find yourself in this situation, I urge you to look closely at what you're putting in your mouth that's labeled low-carb. If your weight loss is stalling, try writing down everything that you eat every day *plus the carb counts* (see more about patrolling your carbs with food journaling in Chapter 1). Food manufacturers can put "Less than 1 gram" of carbohydrate on the Nutrition Facts panel, if the food contains 0.5 to 0.9 grams. You may be amazed at how these *less than's* add up. Fresh and natural foods are the best for any healthy lifestyle, and low-carb is no exception.

Many of the low-carb products contain sugar alcohols, which some folks tolerate well and others don't tolerate at all (see Chapter 2 for information on sugar alcohols).

Some of the oldest and largest food companies are coming out with some awesome low-carb foods, and the prices are becoming much more reasonable (especially with the big name brands). But shop wisely for low-carb products because sometimes they're just not necessary and don't taste as good as the real thing does.

Reading the Nutrition Facts Panel

Food labels aren't optional reading. They're required reading within a healthy low-carb lifestyle. If you can't read the labels in the grocery store without your glasses, then don't leave home without them! The more you practice reading food labels, the more information you discover — some of which the food manufacturer may hope you don't notice or take the time to read. Basically, there are two label components you need to consider — the Nutrition Facts panel and the ingredient list.

Crunching the numbers

Look for the Nutrition Facts panel on the side or on the back of most food packaging (you can see an example of a Nutrition Facts panel in Figure 3-1). Required information on all Nutrition Facts panel includes: total calories, calories from fat, total fat, saturated fat, cholesterol, sodium, total carbohydrates, dietary fiber, sugars, protein, and essential vitamins. Trans fats are also set to make their required appearance soon.

Figure 3-1: Investigate these numbers closely.

Nutrition Facts	
Serving Size 1/2 cup (122 g)	
Servings Per Container about 3.5	
Amount Per Serving	
Calories 40	Fat Cal. 5
	% Daily Value*
Total Fat 0.5 g	1%
Sodium 5 mg	0%
Total Carb. 9 g	3%
Fiber 5 g	21%
Sugars 4 g	
Protein 2 g	
Vitamin A 300% (80% as beta-carotene)	
Calcium 2%	Iron 4%

Not a significant source of saturated fat, cholesterol, and vitamin C.
*Percent Daily Values are based on a 2,000 calorie diet.

Here are the basics on the Nutrition Facts panel jargon:

✔ **Serving size:** This is important because the serving size the manufacturer has defined may not reflect what you consider to be a standard serving. You may assume that a serving of your favorite food is about ¼ cup when it's really only 1 tablespoon. The information presented on the Nutrition Facts panel is for a single serving (check out the "Amount Per Serving" tagline in Figure 3-1). So, if this serving size doesn't fit with the amount of food you're about to eat, do the math.

For example, if you're going to eat 1 cup of a given food and the serving size is a ½ cup, you have to multiply the amount of carbs (and calories and fat and everything else) listed in the Nutrition Facts for that ½ cup serving by 2 to determine the number of carbs you're actually going to eat.

✔ **Servings per container:** Get into the habit of checking out this line when you check out the serving-size line. You may assume that tiny box or bag naturally contains one serving, but it may contain many more, meaning you once again have to do the math if you plan on eating the whole thing. Or better yet, don't eat the whole thing!

✔ **Calories:** Calories equal energy, so the calories listed on the Nutrition Facts panel indicate the amount of energy provided to the body for each serving of a given food. Don't forget: This calorie/energy thing is a two-way street. Energy coming in needs to be accounted for by energy going out. You have to burn the amount of calories you take in to maintain your desired weight.

✔ **Calories from fat:** This is the total amount of calories that are from fat.

✔ **Percentage of recommended daily value column:** The U.S. Department of Agriculture has determined the amounts (in grams) of the nutrients listed on the Nutrition Facts panel (fat, carbohydrate, fiber, and protein) that make up what it considers to be a well-balanced diet. The percentages listed here are the percent of each nutrient that a serving of the food contains, based on a 2,000-calories-a-day diet. A quick reference is a daily-value percentage of 5 percent is considered low, and 20 percent or more is considered high.

✔ **Total fat, saturated fat, and cholesterol:** These numbers are the amounts, in grams, and percentages of the total fat, saturated fat, and cholesterol per serving. (See Chapter 2 for more on distinguishing between healthy and unhealthy fats.)

✔ **Sodium:** Watch for high sodium counts. Small amounts of sodium are necessary for proper body function. Too much sodium can increase water retention and high blood pressure in some people. Especially watch the sodium content on processed foods.

✔ **Total carbohydrate:** This one is important to your low-carb lifestyle, because it shows the total grams of carbs in each serving. The total carbohydrates listed in grams equal the total grams of starches, fiber, and sugars that a serving of the product contains. You probably already know that this count isn't the final number you work with when calculating your carb counts. You can subtract the fiber count from the total carbohydrate count to determine the number of net carbs. (See Chapter 2 for more on carb calculations.)

✓ **Dietary fiber:** Fiber is a very important nutrient and one that most people don't get nearly enough of. Dietary fiber, itself, has no calories and is also listed as part of the total carbohydrate. See the preceding bullet for the formula that uses dietary fiber grams and total carbohydrate grams to determine the net carb count.

✓ **Sugars:** No daily value percentages are assigned to sugar, because there are no recommended daily amounts of sugar you should eat each day. The grams of sugar listed here include both naturally occurring sugars and added sugars.

There's a lot of controversy over the fact that current labeling rules don't require manufacturers to list added sugars separately, which makes deciphering how much added sugars are in a food or beverage sometimes not only challenging but very complicated. (Check out the "Searching for sugars" section, later in the chapter, for tips on finding these rascals in the ingredients list.)

✓ **Protein:** Some Nutrition Facts panels have a recommended daily value percentage for protein, and some don't. The percentage of daily value is only required if a claim is made for protein in the product.

✓ **Vitamins and minerals:** The percentage of the recommended daily amount of certain vitamins that you get from a serving of the food is also listed. A healthy goal is to reach the 100-percent mark for each vitamin and mineral every day. For example, if an orange juice label says that one serving has 80 percent of your vitamin C needs for the day, then you only need an additional 20 percent from other sources to fulfill your vitamin C quota.

Keep this in mind: The Nutrition Facts panel is undergoing a major overhaul and will be changing. Also, folks who are trying to lose weight or maintain weight don't normally consume 2,000 calories per day.

The Nutrition Facts panel includes the amount of sugar alcohols (polyols) per serving within its total carbohydrates calculations. As I write this book, it's optional to list the grams of sugar alcohols used on a separate line, unless a manufacturer uses the terms "no sugar added" or "sugar free" on the packaging. Then the manufacturer is required to list the grams of sugar alcohols used. If the product uses only one sugar alcohol, that sugar alcohol will be named in the Nutrition Facts panel; if more than one is used, the general term *sugar alcohols* is used. To clear up any confusion, you can always check the ingredient list, which always contains the names of each sugar alcohol that a product contains.

Searching for sugars

Nutrition labeling also includes ingredient lists. Here's where you put on your trench coat and become a hidden sugar detective when you're reading labels. I think you're going to be very surprised to discover how many sugars masked by different names are in so many food products. In the ingredient list, ingredients are listed by weight in a descending order from most to least. So the first ingredient listed is the most abundant in the food, and the last is the least abundant.

When manufacturers list *sugar* in the ingredient list, they're referring to sucrose only. The following are other names for "sugar" — hidden sugars — that manufacturers list so there doesn't appear to be much added sugar at all. Taken individually, there may not be. But add them up, and the amounts can be quite amazing. The real names for these sneaky little sugars include:

- Beet sugar
- Brown sugar
- Corn sweetener
- Corn syrup
- Dextrose
- Fruit juice concentrate
- Galactose
- Glucose
- High-fructose corn syrup
- Honey
- Invert sugar
- Lactose
- Malt
- Maltodextrin
- Maltose
- Malt syrup
- Maple syrup
- Molasses
- Polydextrose
- Raw sugar
- Sucrose
- Turbinado sugar

Chapter 4

Adopting a Healthy, Carb-Conscious Lifestyle with Ease

In This Chapter

▶ Looking at ways to lead a low-carb lifestyle

▶ Controlling carbs by cooking at home

▶ Getting back on track if you backslide

Many people seem to have an all-or-nothing attitude about losing weight. They think they either need to lose weight quickly, getting to that thin goal they have in their head, or it's all over. But if you want to live a healthy lifestyle, you need to be concerned about more than just reaching your ideal weight by going on a diet for a 30-day sprint. If you want to keep that weight off and be healthy for the rest of your life, you need to develop a lifestyle that incorporates nutritious cooking and eating plans you can easily follow for the rest of your life. You don't have to sacrifice culinary pleasures in order to adhere to sound nutritional principles in your healthy, low-carb lifestyle.

When you take a low-carb approach to dietary planning, you can still eat great food, you should never go hungry, and you can even have dessert. (See Chapter 13 for some great low-carb dessert recipes.) In this chapter, I help you see that to be successful adopting and maintaining a low-carb lifestyle requires an attitude adjustment. Your attitude toward food affects your body, your mind, and your spirit. I discuss how cooking at home can help you control your carbs. And I offer some advice on how to deal with those slips and misses that are a natural part of trying to change your entire lifestyle.

Making Your Low-Carb Lifestyle Work

Switching from your old habits and adopting a healthy and active low-carb lifestyle is a challenge. It involves making some changes in your life. But don't try to make all these changes overnight, or you'll set yourself up for failure. I want you to win this one because, although the stakes are high, so are the rewards.

The key to making your low-carb lifestyle work is flexibility. Establish which low-carb lifestyle road you're going down and set your goals. If you aren't reaching your goals in a reasonable amount of time, be prepared to change horses in midstream and evaluate what's going on with your body and make some tweaks in your approach. Living a healthy low-carb lifestyle is about *you,* and it begins with a choice of which low-carb lifestyle works for you. No one can make this decision for you — it's *your choice.* After making the choice, you must make a commitment — to yourself — to stick to that lifestyle.

Believing in your low-carb lifestyle

You're a believer in the benefits of a healthy lifestyle or you probably wouldn't be reading this book. If you don't believe in something, you sure can't implement it. If it's distasteful to you and not adaptable to your lifestyle, you're just setting yourself up for big-time failure. Don't be afraid to combine low-carb lifestyle plans, getting rid of what doesn't work for your body and adding what really works. All the while, keep balanced nutrition in the forefront to keep you going for the long haul. Life can be so fine — take charge of yours now!

Making a commitment

If achieving your weight goal and good health with your low-carb lifestyle is important to you, then it's worth working hard for. First and foremost, that means making a commitment. This doesn't mean that you won't ever slip and fall again — you're human, remember? (Check out the section "Fighting Back When You Backslide," later in this chapter, for help in maintaining a healthy perspective when you slip up.)

Commitment means that you set realistic long-term and short-term goals for your low-carb lifestyle and do everything in your power to work toward them everyday, one step at a time. Commitment means that when setbacks occur, you'll keep bouncing back because you're not quitting. The commitment that you make to yourself to lead a healthy lifestyle isn't about a temporary fix; it's about quality of life, health, elimination of chronic disease in your body, wellness, and longevity — it's about *your life.* Don't take your commitment lightly and you'll be thrilled with your results.

Doing it for yourself

Learning to love yourself is sometimes a difficult assignment. Step up to the challenge by looking yourself in the mirror and saying "I love you" and meaning it. Loving yourself is the best reason in the world to pursue a low-carb lifestyle, which for you may mean the desire to look and feel better. Pursuing a low-carb lifestyle works only when you're doing it for yourself.

Don't wait to enjoy the things that you want to do "until you lose weight" — begin now by making a list of all of your "wanna do's" and put yourself on a reward plan. Set your expectations at realistic levels so that when you exceed them you're pleasantly surprised and you feel good about yourself. Reward yourself with one of the things that's on your "wanna do" list — do it now!

Seeking out support

Find a friend or coworker who is a low-carb lifestyle advocate and team up. Two heads are often better than one when you have the same goal, and you can support each other in your quest for success in low-carb living for life. You can also celebrate improved health and wellness together by supporting each other through the process.

There are lots of great low-carb forums online that are very supportive. If you're a computer buff, jump online and give a couple a try. The online support groups are like anything else in life: You may have to try several before you find one that fits you. I know some moderators of several different groups, and you'll find the same people chatting about their low-carb lifestyle almost every day. Lots of these people have lost tons of weight and are very warm and willing to help newbies. (Surf some of the Web sites listed in Chapter 23 and find some forums online.)

You can sometimes be your own best support person. Leaving yourself little notes on your computer, the bathroom mirror, and the fridge can help encourage you to stick to your low-carb lifestyle. Post notes that affirm your lifestyle, act like a stop sign (for example, "stop and have a drink of water first"), and give you pats on the back for staying on track. You often need to give yourself the kudos that you so deserve because others may not realize your success. So go out and buy some cute new sticky notes and post them all around the house.

Fine-tuning your food-weakness radar

No one is shoving unhealthy foods into your mouth. Taking responsibility for what you eat is crucial to your success in living a low-carb lifestyle. Don't blame the restaurant, the hostess of the party, or your great-aunt Esther for your overeating or choosing foods that don't fit your low-carb lifestyle. Guess who's in charge here?

No one knows better than you the foods that you just can't resist. Fine-tuning your food radar and admitting your weaknesses to yourself catapults you ahead of the game. Awareness is about 95 percent of the battle. Admitting to yourself that certain foods are so tempting that they make your knees weak is the first step to conquering these little devils when you see them face to face. Being aware and making plans in advance to deal with these situations before they occur can give you more control when they arise.

Situations like these seem to rear their head a lot around the holidays, which can be a tough time of the year — if you let it be tough. Holidays are meant to be joyful and a time to get together with friends and family, and for eons, these celebrations have centered on food! Go to the parties and dinners. Just plan ahead with these tips that you can apply to any party or dinner:

- ✔ Take one of your favorite low-carb snack dishes, entrees, sides, or big salads — whatever is appropriate for the occasion.

- ✔ Eat a small meal before you go to the gala if you're really concerned about a test to your will power.

- ✔ Drink some water in the car on the way so you don't arrive on an empty stomach.

- ✔ Tuck some nuts in your pocket or purse in case there's just not enough variety on the table for you.

The upside of the holidays these days is that so many folks are watching their carbs, and new, exciting low-carb dishes are often being prepared for parties. I guarantee you won't be the only one with a low-carb lifestyle at the party.

If you really need a sobering moment to step away from that platter of cookies, step into the bathroom and take a look at the pretty dress or that great pair of pants and how well they fit you. Think about how hard you've worked to look that nice for the holidays or your big event. Want to slide down that big hill and have to climb it all over again? I didn't think so. (For related tips on planning ahead when you go out to eat, see Chapter 18.)

Learning to say, "No, thank you"

When you're offered certain foods at special gatherings, such as in a friend's home or at holiday parties, you may often hear a little voice that says, "Oh, I can't say no because I might hurt the hostess's feelings." When this happens to you, ask yourself very quickly, "Is this about *their* feelings or *my health*?" This isn't a trick question, and you know the answer. You don't need to offer a long-winded explanation about your low-carb lifestyle. You just need to simply and politely say, "No, thank you."

Taking Small Steps toward Success

Although the big picture has merit, you're probably better off to set small, attainable, specific goals. This approach won't be nearly as overwhelming for you, and you'll feel accomplishment along the way, spurring you on to your next goal. Don't forget to reward yourself each time you reach a goal. Oh, by the way, food rewards aren't an option.

If you have 90 pounds to lose, you may find that goal overwhelming. Or if you've lost and gained back that same 35 pounds for over 15 years because of yo-yo dieting, that can be disconcerting and downright depressing. Don't let your lifestyle or food decisions overwhelm you — remember that you're in charge! Making small changes is the key to finally hanging up your diet hat and trading it in for a successful low-carb, healthy lifestyle for life! When you begin stacking all of these small steps up, they become your stairway to a success story of wellness. How cool is that? Here are a few small steps to start you on the road to a low-carb lifestyle:

- ✔ **Eat.** Starving yourself isn't part of a low-carb lifestyle. Eating too little slows down your metabolism, which ends up working against your weight-loss goals. Unless those metabolic fires are burning, you aren't burning any calories. Become an amazing grazer (see Chapter 2 for more information on amazing grazing with your low-carb lifestyle).

- ✔ **Try one or two new foods a week.** There's just no excuse for boredom when you're following your low-carb lifestyle. There's so many great foods out there and the list of "can have's" is so much longer than the list of "can't have's." Your low-carb glass isn't half empty — or half full. It's brimming over with options!

- ✔ **Take your lunch to work.** If you've planned ahead and have your lunch, you won't be tempted to grab something unhealthy and full of carbs from the vending machine or snack bar. Toting your lunch gives you all kinds of flexibility and control in your healthy lifestyle. It's a good thing! See Chapter 19 for some ideas for lunches to go.

- ✔ **Never skip breakfast.** Always eat something before you leave home in the morning. See more on the importance of breakfast in Chapter 6.

- ✔ **Become food-label savvy.** Check portion sizes because they may not measure up to your appetite. See more on label reading in Chapter 3.

- ✔ **Be assertive.** Let others know what you want on your plate, whether you're in a restaurant or at your mother-in-law's house.

- ✔ **Take your measurements.** Body measurements are sometimes more accurate than the scale and much more motivating because you often drop inches before pounds. You're more likely to stay motivated this way.

✔ **Treat yourself.** Reward yourself for accomplishments with a movie, some new jeans (in a smaller size), a new shirt, or a new book on tape.

✔ **Eat fresh, raw vegetables for snacks at work and at home.** The texture and the crunchiness of raw veggies seem to satisfy cravings. I wonder how many pounds of baby carrots that I've eaten while sitting at the computer writing this book?

✔ **Plan your meals in advance.** Doing so will take you far down your road to success with your low-carb lifestyle (see more on meal planning in Chapter 20).

✔ **Drink more water.** Try to get in the habit of reaching for a bottle of water instead of a diet soda. You'll be amazed how much weight falls off if you do this. (See Chapter 5 for more about staying hydrated.)

✔ **Learn to cook with herbs and spices.** They add flavor when you cut back on fat and eat lean, plus the calorie and carb counts are low. An additional perk in herbs and spices is cutting out the boredom of the same old thing day in and day out.

Read at least one nutrition article a week! Fill up as much as you can on good nutritional data. You'll find it quite fascinating, and like feeding your body, you'll be feeding your nutritional soul. Most sound nutritional data that you digest will steer you not toward another fad diet but toward a life of good-tasting, satisfying, happy eating. When you go on a diet, it is assumed that you'll some day go off that diet. But if you know more about nutrition and how to prepare tasty, healthy, low-carb meals, you never have to go off that type of eating — that's your lifestyle for the rest of your life.

Cooking at Home to Control Carbs

The more satisfied you become with your low-carb lifestyle, the choosier you're going to get about what goes in your mouth — and rightly so. There's one surefire way to be absolutely certain what you're ingesting: Prepare it yourself at home (or have someone cook for you and you clean up). When you're at the helm in the kitchen, you don't have to guess whether ingredients are fresh and whether hidden sugars and carbs are lurking in your meals.

Healthy home-cooked meals don't have to take hours to prepare. Heck, sometimes they can be whipped up in less than 30 minutes. See Chapter 20 for some great recipes to prepare in a hurry.

Using the recipes in this book

Being the simple cook that I am, the level of difficulty of the recipes in this book is minimal. If you spot a recipe with a longer list of ingredients, don't let that intimidate you. It doesn't mean that the recipe is difficult, it just means there's more stuff in it. My goal in selecting recipes for this book was to bring you the tastiest and most nutritious dishes with the lowest number of carbs possible.

Some of the ingredients that I use in my everyday low-carb cooking may be "different" to you, so I want to run through them here with you. These ingredients are pretty basic — I don't use a lot of specialty products that are expensive or require a treasure hunt to locate. About the only "low-carb" products that I use in my everyday lifestyle are low-carb whole-wheat tortillas, and they're a staple in my kitchen. (And I confess that I have a stash of low-carb cookies that I treat myself to every so often with a cup of tea.) Most large grocery stores have all of the products that you need for the recipes in this book. I also do some of my shopping in a health-food store, and if you have one of those whole foods stores near you, you're one of the lucky ones. The following list highlights some of ingredients I use in this book that you may find a tad unfamiliar or wonder about:

- **Dairy products:** The recipes in this book make use of half-and-half and whipping cream. Just be aware that you can't use a ton of this stuff and lose weight! I also opt for regular cottage cheese and sour cream. Yes, I know that this is a major point of controversy in the low-carb world, so if you prefer reduced-fat and low-fat varieties, it's your grocery list! My favorite yogurt is Greek yogurt — it's really creamy and low in carbs, too. I don't care for the low-carb varieties myself, and I don't call for them in the recipes, but again it's a personal preference. I prefer plain yogurt both in my cooking and snacking. And please use real butter — margarine contains those fats that you don't want, like trans fats. Besides, butter lends such great flavor to any dish that you're preparing.

- **Flours:** The recipes in this book call for several different flours. I use the specific type of flour for each recipe that ensures success while balancing overall carb considerations. So, if you substitute a different type of flour, the results may vary. I keep whole-wheat pastry flour, white whole-wheat flour, and stone-ground flour in my pantry at all times. Whole-wheat pastry flour is like cooking with silk, but because it's so soft and fragile, you usually have to combine it with another of the flours I mentioned for some bulk.

- **Fresh ingredients:** More often than not, I choose fresh ingredients for these recipes. Fresh veggies galore, a variety of greens, fresh mushrooms, lots of baby carrots for snacking, and fresh fruits as well as fresh meats, poultry, fish, and eggs.

- **Sugar alcohols:** I don't cook with sugar alcohols, and I haven't included them as ingredients in this book, but if you're accustomed to doing so, please feel free to make substitutions in any of the recipes. After all, this book is all about what works for *you.*

- **Wines:** There are several recipes in this book that call for white and red wines, and I usually specify a dry wine. I use cheap (not just reasonably priced — cheap) wines for my cooking. But watch out for the fruity wines and flavored wines because they usually contain a ton of sugar. Merlot is both low in sugar counts and calorie counts, and if you want to sip just a tad while you're cooking, I'd suggest a nice Merlot!

My sugar substitute/artificial sweetener of choice is sucrolose, which goes by the brand name Splenda. I like it because of the taste, the texture, and the fact that it stands up to high heat. In the recipes in this book, there are two different types of Splenda:

- **Splenda:** Splenda comes in both packet and granular form. In recipe ingredient lists, I refer to this product as *Splenda sugar substitute.* Splenda in the packet is a concentrated sweetener, and one packet equals 2 teaspoons of sugar. Splenda in the granular form measures cup-for-cup like sugar because a bulking agent, maltodextrin, has been added. Although the granular form measures cup-for-cup with sugar, it's not the option I choose when baking — that's the job for Splenda Sugar Blend for Baking.

  Splenda doesn't contain any calories, but it's not carb-free. (There are calories, however, in the Splenda Sugar Blend for Baking because of the real sugar content.) The carb count on the Nutrition Facts panel states "Less than one gram" per teaspoon of the granular stuff and, of course, that's accurate. The granular Splenda contains about half a gram of carbs per teaspoon because of the bulking agent used. If you're using a cup of the stuff, you have to get your calculator out and add up all of those little *less than's!* A cup of granular Splenda contains about 24 grams of carbs. Splenda packets have less bulking agent, so you can save a few carbs if you use the packets. (For more details, check out www.splenda.com.)

- **Splenda Sugar Blend for Baking:** Splenda Sugar Blend for Baking is used in some of the dessert recipes in this book and others. This Blend for Baking does contain sugar, but a half-cup of it replaces a full cup of sugar. This product makes your low-carb baking just like old-fashioned baking. It doesn't get much low-carb better. See Chapter 13 for more on the carb and calorie counts of this product.

The vast majority of the recipes in this book contain less than 5 or 10 net grams of carbs per serving. Just flip through the chapters and look at all those Less-Than-5 and Less-Than-10 icons that accompany the recipes. (As I remind you in the Introduction, those icons refer to the net grams of carbohydrates per serving.) Overall, I've tried to offer you fabulous foods with minimal carbs. But I sometimes offer suggestions and even recipes that seem a little higher in carbs than others, so be sure to look at the big nutritional picture. The trade off for higher carb counts in some of my suggestions and recipes is an overall healthy, balanced lifestyle — except for some of the desserts that are just a plain ol' treat (treats lower in carbs than their carb-laden cousins, that is) because you deserve it once in a while. It is my sincere hope that you enjoy these low-carb recipes from this very old-fashioned cook. Bon appetite!

Planning easy low-carb meals

The secret to becoming a great low-carb cook is planning. Plan your meals and write them down. How far in advance you plan depends on what you're comfortable with. I suggest in Chapter 20 that you shop two times a week and have specific meals planned for a week at a time. This makes managing carbs easier and in the end saves you a lot of time. Planning meals a week in advance may take a little getting used to, but there are all kinds of advantages:

✔ You can look forward to your favorite foods.

✔ You can experiment with new recipes when you have time.

✔ You don't waste time after work trying to figure out what's for dinner, become frustrated, and wind up at the closest high-carb drive-thru.

✔ Planning easy, quick, and healthy low-carb meals gives you an overall sense of satisfaction and well-being. If it's your decision to actively pursue a low-carb lifestyle, you'll be delighted how planning meals with your carb intake in mind begins to show in your body weight, your overall health, and your attitude toward life.

✔ When you have leftovers, you can tote them for lunch the next day being confident that your lunch is low-carb. You can even get in the habit of cooking a little extra so you have lunch for a couple of days.

✔ Quick, easy, and planned meals give you more time for other things. When you can get in and out of the kitchen quickly because you're prepared and serve a great, healthy meal to boot, you have time to relax or work on a project that you've been trying to get to.

Planning means having ingredients on hand so that you make the most of your time spent in the kitchen. (See Chapter 3 for advice on stocking your low-carb kitchen.) Throughout this book, I provide you with tons of quick low-carb recipes. In fact, I devote a whole chapter to cooking low-carb quickly (see Chapter 20). But remember, some dishes are generally quicker than others to whip up:

✔ Fresh fish cooks very quickly, and it's full of nutrients and easy on the carb counts. Look at the timesaving recipes for fish in Chapter 9.

✔ Another way to literally have meals ready when you walk through the door is to invest in a slow cooker if you don't already have one (see Chapter 16 for low-carb slow cooker recipes).

✔ Wrap it up! You can throw whatever is in the fridge into a tad of olive oil and call it a stir-fry. Wrap it in a low-carb tortilla and you've got dinner. Or, scramble some eggs in the microwave, fold them in a low-carb tortilla, and you've got breakfast on the run. Wraps are quick and easy and offer so much versatility. (Take a walk over to Chapter 15 for some great wrap recipes.)

✔ Think salads. The greens are already combined, washed, and ready to go in a package in the produce department. Embellishments can make a salad a meal that's quick, easy, and low in carbs (see Chapter 8 for some great salad recipes).

Dishing up tasty low-carb portions

Something that some low-carb diet plans sometimes totally skim over is portion size (yes, I did use the "d" word). Size really does matter, especially in controlling your portions and your carb counts. Be mindful of your portions:

✔ You can't expect to eat platefuls of high-fat meats, foods dripping in fatty oils, tons of calories, or lots of highly processed foods and maintain your weight, your lifestyle, and your health.

✔ The amount of food you eat is closely related to blood sugar control. Don't let yourself get ravenously hungry. Always carry a snack of nuts or some other form of protein with you. And strive to become an "amazing grazer" to keep your blood sugar levels on an even keel.

According to the U.S. Department of Agriculture, Americans are eating about 150 to 200 calories more a day than they were 18 years ago, thanks to the super-sized portions that are available everywhere. Guess what that packs on in your body weight — 15 extra pounds a year.

Weight control goes hand in hand not only with carb control but also with portion control. See more about easily determining portion sizes in Chapter 21.

A good hostess always leaves her dining guests just a tad hungry and wanting more. Try to apply this guideline to your everyday eating habits. Research proves that it takes 20 minutes for your stomach to signal the brain that you're full. So make it a habit to stop eating before you feel stuffed. And if you're behind the stove, don't take it personally if your family or guests don't finish your fine meal.

Setting your low-carb table for success

The little things in life are often what make it worthwhile. The same is true in a healthy low-carb lifestyle. Everyone is going in 500 directions at once these days, and you're lucky to just get a not and healthy meal on the table after a day at work. But, as a former bed and breakfast innkeeper, I can tell you that presentation adds so much to your table. Treat yourself to a couple of no-iron tablecloths and some cloth napkins — you can even find easy-care terry-cloth ones. It'll take you only about five extra minutes (no more, I promise) to set the table.

I'm not trying to be your interior designer, but the color of your tablecloths matters. Bright colors like red, orange, and yellow actually stimulate your appetite. That's why you see so much red in restaurants! Darker color tablecloths in the gray, brown, and black family, on the other hand, won't make you any hungrier than you already are. If you're really out to impress, grab that big candle from the hallway or the coffee table, put it in the middle of the table, and fire it up. Ah — low-carb ambience at its best. If anyone says, "Hey, what are we celebrating?" you, as the star of the low-carb lifestyle, can answer, "We're celebrating life — yep, life and wellness."

Your china may be lovely, but if you put out fewer plates and bowls, you won't be tempted to fill them up and to overindulge. Keep it simple. The same advice goes for setting out a lot of entrée dishes and side dishes. Get in the habit of having your table as only a place to eat. Fill your plates in the kitchen and sit down at the table to eat. If people want seconds, they'll have to make a trip to the kitchen!

Fighting Back When You Backslide

Sometimes no matter what you do, the scale stays the same. Don't let that make you crazy. Lighten up on yourself. Give yourself time to adjust to new situations on a mental, emotional, and spiritual level. Your body needs time to adjust to your healthy lifestyle and weight loss. Be patient.

You may have days when you get up and weigh three more pounds than you did yesterday. Or maybe you crave sugar-free stuff, and before you know it, you've eaten six sugar-free chocolate chip cookies and you're still starving. Well, guess what — eating this food can send you into a plateau or a stall, and all of a sudden you think your scale is stuck. Well, it's more than likely not your scale — it's the foods you've been eating!

Climb back on that horse that just threw you with more conviction than ever. Go walk an extra 2,000 steps today with your pedometer, and you'll feel better, I guarantee it. (See Chapter 5 for more on pedometer walking.) The extra movement will get your metabolic furnace burning more, and you'll get beyond your stall more quickly and give your self-esteem a needed boost. Just don't give up. Remember, it's all about you. When you get this, you get it all.

You didn't gain all of this body fat and weight overnight, so don't get frustrated and agitated and give up. Hang in there because you are on the right road to wellness and longevity.

If and when you backslide a bit on the road to good health, take the direct and positive approach. Negative talk about what you could have or should have done will only make you feel badly about yourself and possibly make you just throw up your hands and eat foods that you'll really regret. Don't immediately recall only everything that you're doing wrong. Instead, look at everything that you've done right. You've done a lot of hard work and planning, and you don't want to ruin all you've accomplished. Remember that you can easily gain that 5 pounds back in just one weekend if you continue to beat yourself up and fail to get back on track.

Accept the fact that you're an oh-so-human being and you're just exactly where you are right now. Take back control of your healthy low-carb lifestyle and move forward. There ain't no going back now! Examine what you think happened to get you off track and what is going on in your life right now. Maybe some extra steps with your pedometer will help to rev up your metabolism and eliminate some of the stress you may be feeling. Sit down and plan your meals for the next few days to make sure they include your low-carb favorites. Most of all, be kind to yourself. Focus on your successes — not your failures!

Chapter 5

Completing the Wellness-for-Life Puzzle: Putting Your Body in Motion

In This Chapter

▶ Moving your body more
▶ Experiencing the wondrous ways of walking
▶ Trading in your diet yo-yo for a pedometer

You can diet and lose weight — it's a no-brainer. But do you want to go through all that deprivation and frustration just to put the weight back on? If you're like many folks who've tried to diet their way to a more slender self, you know the routine of yo-yo dieting and yo-yo weight gain. But losing and maintaining weight isn't just about dieting and eating healthy foods. You're reading this book, so I suspect you're either currently on one of the controlled-carb programs out there, or you're considering the switch to a low-carb lifestyle. Good for you.

A healthy low-carb lifestyle is made up of more than the dietary component. I also want you to complete the whole puzzle by adopting an *active* lifestyle by adding more movement to your day. True weight management is a balancing act of energy (calories) in versus energy (calories) out.

Don't throw your hands up in the air. I'm not talking about spending hours in the gym — just moving more. It isn't as difficult as it may sound, and the results can be life changing. Don't wait — start today by taking it one step at a time. Make the switch to a healthy, active, low-carb lifestyle. And make this lane change in your dietary lifestyle your last one.

In this chapter, I psyche you up and get you moving. Although I discuss different types of moving, I concentrate on one method in particular — walking, which I guess you could call my passion. It isn't earth shattering, but that's the point. Almost everyone can walk, and if you strap on a pedometer to count your steps (which I tell you all about in this chapter), you can easily

keep track of your progress. And though it may seem like one simple activity at first, I provide suggestions that put variety center stage.

Check in with your doctor before you start any diet or exercise program.

Moving More — Now

The ancient Chinese philosopher, Lao Tzu, said, "A journey of a thousand miles begins with a single step." Now is the time to take the first steps that'll help you reach your goal of moving more while keeping an eye on the big picture of health and wellness. Anytime you take the first step into something new, you're expanding your awareness about things around you and about yourself. The more you become aware of yourself and of what makes you tick, the more successful you'll be with a low-carb, healthy, active lifestyle.

Physical movement isn't punishment. For some reason, the thinking prevails that if you don't work up a sweat and exercise until your body hurts, you're not doing your body any good. Or that you have to immerse yourself in an unfriendly gym atmosphere that's filled with buff people that just seem to get more buff. This couldn't be further from the truth. Check out just a few of the fun possibilities that don't even seem like exercise:

- Line dancing or ballroom dancing
- Washing your car on a sunny day
- Tossing a ball with your kids in the back yard
- Raking leaves or sweeping the sidewalk
- Planting a garden, a flower bed, or even flower boxes on the patio
- Weeding your flower beds or vegetable garden

Unlike me, some of you don't cringe when the word *exercise* pops up. Check out some other sporty ideas that can be a fun way to get moving:

- Swimming or doing water aerobics
- Cross-country skiing
- Bowling
- Bicycling
- Playing softball, baseball, basketball, football, or soccer
- Playing table tennis
- Golfing
- Ice-skating

✔ Roller-skating

✔ Playing tennis, handball, or racquetball

You don't have to block off big chunks of time to move more. You can just start moving more one step at a time — no rushing allowed! The more you move, the more calories you're burning every hour.

If you have trouble making big changes, start with small ones. Think of your lifestyle change in terms of baby steps, and don't take the next step until you're comfortable with where you are in your daily exercise plan. Just ask any turtle, and he'll tell you that slow and steady wins the race. Your healthy lifestyle isn't just about dropping a few pounds or getting into that new suit and being able to button the jacket. The positive changes that you're making are about your life — a better, healthier, and more fulfilling life!

Walking Your Way to Wellness

Walking is a user-friendly movement. You can set your own pace, and it's almost injury-free at any age. You can just walk leisurely, or you can turn it into an aerobic movement. And you can easily increase your daily walking. Research has proven that the movement of walking at your normal pace is extremely vital to your overall health. In fact, studies are proving that the simple movement of walking may be better for your overall health than vigorous sports involvement or strenuous workouts. (For complete details about a walking program, check out *Fitness Walking For Dummies,* by Liz Neporent, published by Wiley.)

Walking is easy

Sure you have those minor details — like all the health benefits — that make walking so great, but there are many other reasons why walking fits nicely into your low-carb lifestyle:

✔ You already know how to do it.

✔ You can do it whenever you want — early in the morning, on your lunch hour, or late at night.

✔ You can do it anywhere — when you're traveling, camping in the woods, visiting a friend, and so on.

✔ You don't have to plan ahead to take a five-minute walk.

✔ You don't have to make an appointment or be on time to walk.

✔ There's no membership fee required for walking.

✔ You don't have to be focused to walk, which allows you to empty your brain and results in a feeling of refreshment.

✔ You don't have to go out and buy special clothes to walk; you can walk in your business suit or shorts.

✔ Your hair doesn't get hair messed up when you walk (unless it's windy).

Although you can walk in any shoes, if you're headed out for long or brisk walk, good, supportive walking shoes are necessary. Keep your walking shoes in your trunk — always. If you get to a doctor's appointment and the receptionist tells you that the doctor is running about 45 minutes behind, tell her you'll be back in a half-hour. Put those walking shoes on, and hit the pavement instead of sitting in the waiting room. Besides, everyone's sick at the doctor's office, so get out into the fresh air.

It benefits your body

Teaming up your low-carb, healthy lifestyle with simply moving more is a winner. You're doubling your health benefits. Here are a few health benefits of moving a little more and taking a few more steps every day:

✔ Curbs your appetite

✔ Burns almost as many calories as running or jogging

✔ Reduces stress

✔ Improves your circulation

✔ Improves your attitude and acts as a mood leveler

✔ Increases your self-motivation

✔ Increases your energy

✔ Improves your muscle tone

✔ Lowers your blood pressure

✔ Reduces your risk of heart attack and cardiovascular disease

✔ Can reduce bad cholesterol levels

✔ Can improve good cholesterol levels

✔ Causes you to sleep better and rest more peacefully

✔ Increases your alertness

✔ Helps you maintain and/or lose weight

Walking tall with good posture improves your walking form. Make sure you don't let your shoulders roll forward when you're walking.

Weighing in: Seeing is believing

If you want a real wake-up call about your weight and how many extra pounds you're carrying around, do this little exercise:

1. **Jump on the scale, and see what your weight is today. Write down your weight and your realistic ideal weight.**

   Make sure you're projecting a healthy weight for your height and body frame. (Check out the body-mass index information I include at the end of this chapter.) To illustrate my point, suppose that you weigh 166 pounds, and your ideal weight is 150 pounds.

2. **Subtract your desired weight from what you weigh today, and divide the answer by 8.**

   Subtract 150 from 166 to get 16. Divide that number by 8, and you end up with 2.

3. **Save enough gallon water bottles to equal the number you got when you divided your desired weight by 8 in Step 2.**

Sticking with the example, you need two 1-gallon bottles for this eye-opening experiment.

4. **Fill each gallon container with water. Each container should weigh about 8 pounds.**

5. **Set the containers in front of you on the countertop and declare a moment of silence.**

This visual experience enables you to actually see the extra weight you're carrying around. It can be a real inspiration to keep your low-carb lifestyle on track. Line the water bottles up on the back porch as a daily and sobering reminder. When you lose a couple pounds, be sure to pour out that much water. You'll feel so rewarded! And think how great you'll feel when they're both empty.

Stepping It Up: Pedometer Walking

Yo-yo dieting and lack of exercise (movement) are primary reasons for weight gain. You've already made the decision to change your life with a low-carb lifestyle, and now it's time to take the next step to wellness and longevity. Trade in your diet yo-yo for a pedometer. A *pedometer* is a littler device resembling a small pager that you clip on your waistband (see Figure 5-1). The pedometer's basic job is to count every step you take all day long. Inside this little guy is a lever, and your hip movements trip its trigger every time you take a step.

Add a pedometer to your belt first thing in the morning and follow a few simple ideas for stacking up steps. Before you know it, you'll be walking from 7,000 to 8,000 steps a day, and you may even reach the magic number of 10,000 steps a day. "Where did that magic number of 10,000 come from?" you ask. It all started in Japan with an interest in pedometers that began with a Japanese movement called 10,000 Steps a Day. The program claims that if you take 10,000 steps a day, your health will improve, and your waist will be slimmer as a result of this simple change.

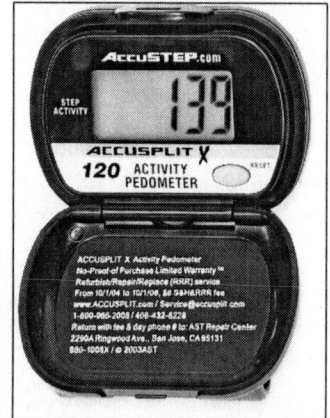

Figure 5-1:
Count those
steps with a
pedometer.

The pedometer and the 10,000 steps program have been widely accepted all over the world, and pedometer walking organizations and clubs are springing up everywhere. The 10,000 steps program is endorsed in the fight against obesity, because it encourages people to move more and to follow a healthy lifestyle. The program is both simple and inspiring. The most positive thing about the program is that it's doable for anyone and everyone no matter how busy they are. The 10,000 steps program is like a "move more toolkit" providing you with all the tools you need to plan and track your daily steps, all the while forming new healthy habits and making moving more of a permanent part of your healthy lifestyle. The President's Council on Physical Fitness and Sports recommends walking 30 minutes at least five days a week or 10,000 steps every day.

Don't try to accomplish 10,000 steps all in your first day of walking. Take the first step and then the next and don't beat yourself up if you don't do as well today as you did yesterday. After all, you're working toward a great goal — a major change in your lifestyle. You're a work in progress!

A short walk through the pedometer's history

As early as the 15th century, drawings indicate that Leonardo da Vinci was the conceptual originator of the pedometer when he designed a gear-driving device with a pendulum arm that moved back and forth with every swing of the leg during walking. Centuries later, on a visit to France, Thomas Jefferson purchased the hippest version of the pedometer available at the time. In 1965, pedometers hit the commercial market in Japan under the name *manpokei,* which means "10,000 steps meter" in Japanese. The Japanese are the leaders in pedometer use for counting steps, and it's said you can find two or three pedometers in each household in Japan.

In shopping for a good, reliable pedometer, you need to spend only about $30 or less. There are all kinds on the market that not only count steps but also count calories. Some even talk and play music. If you search on Google (www. google.com) for "pedometers," you'll have more than enough to choose from. I suggest the simpler the better — all you need is one that counts steps.

Taking your first step with a pedometer

Don't make pedometer walking difficult, because it's not. You simply clip it on at your waist every morning and hit the reset button. It counts your steps all day. You take it off at night and record the number of steps you took that day, and you start over the next day. Pretty easy, right?

For the first week you wear your new little friend on your waist, don't change anything in your daily activity. Be sure to log your steps every night when you take your pedometer off. You may be very surprised at how little you actually move during your waking hours. Divide your total number of steps for the week by seven, and you have what's called your *baseline steps* or your average daily steps. Don't be surprised if it comes in between 2,000 and 3,000 steps, or even less — well short of the ultimate 10,000 step counts. And, it's okay if the number is 500! Most people don't move much, I tell you. Figure 5-2 shows a simple log you can use to record your steps.

Day	Steps Taken
Monday	
Tuesday	
Wednesday	
Thursday	
Friday	
Saturday	
Sunday	
Total Steps Taken for the Week	
Divide Total Steps Taken for the Week by 7 to Get Your Average # of Steps per Day	

Figure 5-2: Record your steps for first seven days.

It takes 21 days to form a habit. So if you consistently move more and wear your pedometer 21 days in a row, you form a new habit that comes as a natural part of your lifestyle and daily routine. If you miss a day in wearing your pedometer during the 21-day period, you have to start all over. Some people start a new 21-day period after they've been successful with the first one just to keep focused on the new, healthy habit. At the end of the 21-day block, you have more energy, are less stressed, feel better, and look better. And if you play your cards right, you may even weigh less.

Drink up

If you take long walks, especially in warmer weather, you're likely to get thirsty. By the time your body tells you that you're thirsty, you're on your way to being dehydrated. So keep yourself hydrated. There's a reason for all the hype about drinking six to eight glasses of water per day. Water is a noncaloric and a basic essential nutrient for the maintenance of your life and the proper functionality of your body. About 60 to 75 percent of your body's weight is water — the most abundant nutrient in your body. Muscle tissue is about 70 percent water while in comparison fat contains only about 10 to 15 percent water. Every cell, organ, and tissue in your body requires water to function. Your body can go much longer without food than it can without water. Water helps carry valuable nutrients to the places your body needs them, it cleanses your body of toxins and fats, and it hydrates you. Ensure that you stay hydrated with your low-carb lifestyle — drink up! Visit www.water cure.com to find out all about the cures of good ol' water.

Stepping up to higher counts

Studies everywhere show that if you wear a pedometer and set daily goals, you become more active than people that don't wear one. Pedometers are quirky little critters, because they seem to have an almost magical power of motivation about them. When you wear one, it's like entering a contest with yourself. You clip your pedometer on every morning, and when you glance at it at noon, you think, "I gotta do something to get my steps in — I'm lagging today." After work, when you stop at the grocery store, you park your car in the back of the lot and make a couple extra trips around the perimeter of the grocery store with your cart just to get your steps in for the day. I'm telling you, this little device works like a charm!

After your first week, begin to set new goals for yourself based on your baseline number of steps. Don't set yourself up for failure. Set realistic and achievable goals, and then reward yourself for reaching them. The average person takes about a minute to walk 100 steps. So figure out your schedule, see if you can work in a couple five or ten minute walks several times a day, and begin scheming how you can increase your steps. At first, set your goal to increase your steps by 200 each day. When you get comfortable with that, challenge yourself and up the ante. Just one little step at a time can add up to giant steps in your active lifestyle, making you happier and healthier.

Here are some easy ways to sneak more steps into your day:

- Clean the house.
- March in place while you watch the news.

✔ Walk around the house while you chat on the phone.

✔ Walk the indoor perimeter of the mall with a friend.

✔ Take the stairs rather than the elevator or escalator.

✔ Park your car at the back of the lot to lengthen your walk to the building.

✔ Walk around the airport while you're waiting to board.

✔ Walk your dog (or a neighbor's dog).

✔ Make an appointment at work with a coworker for a walking meeting.

Don't get discouraged if you don't have time for a 30-minute stroll. And don't get caught up in negative self-talk. If you can take 10 minutes out of your morning schedule and 10 minutes in the afternoon to walk, you've already stacked up 20 minutes for the day! Moving for 20 minutes does more than just enable you to burn calories during that particular walking session. You also raise your metabolic rate and continue to burn calories after you're done walking. You're building muscle mass, improving the strength in your joints, increasing your flexibility, promoting strong bones, and enhancing the health of your heart. Maintaining muscle during weight loss is key to helping your body burn even more calories. (See more on moving and your metabolism in Chapter 2.)

If you like to take long walks and you're an avid reader, enjoy the outdoors, *and* catch up on your reading: Try some books on tape while you're stepping. You'll want to keep walking just to find out how your book ends!

Overcoming obesity

You can help this troubled, overweight world even if you're not obese. Make a commitment to help others. If you've lost the weight you wanted to lose, share with other people how you got there. No one likes to feel alone, so here are some ideas for giving your support to others:

✔ Form small support groups at work, at church, with friends, or even among your own family members. Set up a group of carb-conscious, pedometer-stepping buddies.

✔ Give a friend or relative a pedometer as a birthday gift. Make a list of people you love and give them a pedometer for Christmas. What better way to show someone how much you really care than to say, "I want you to live longer and be healthy because I love you."

✔ Join groups online that are doing pedometer walking. You can find and give support and friendship as well as join in some interesting competition online. And you don't have to keep a notebook log of your daily steps, it's simple and easy to log your steps every day online.

Using the buddy system

Recruit one of your low-carb lifestyle friends to go pedometer walking with you. You can socialize while you're walking and stacking up steps on your pedometer. Maybe there's someone at work you'd like to get to know better. Invite him to take a walk with you during your 10-minute morning break. Careful, it could be habit forming.

Including others in your healthy and active low-carb lifestyle efforts helps make you accountable. Having someone to share your achievements with makes them even more meaningful. And having someone to share the troubling times with is uplifting and encouraging, and that person often gives you the fight you need to keep going.

Weighing in with BMI

Calculating your *body mass index*, known as BMI, is another tool for you to use on the path towards a healthy low-carb lifestyle and all-around wellness. Expert findings report that BMI provides a better assessment of whether you're overweight than you can get from simply taking a look at your scale because it's determined using a gender-neutral ratio that accounts for both height and weight. How do you determine your BMI? Just plug your numbers into this equation:

$$BMI = (W/H^2) \times 705$$

Well, a bit of translation may be in order: Take your weight (in pounds) divided by your height (in inches, squared) and multiply that by 705. Or you can take the even easier approach of visiting www.nhlbisupport.com/bmi for a handy calculator in which simply plug in a few numbers, press a button, and get your results. After you have your BMI number, you can determine where weight falls in the grand scheme of things:

BMI	Weight Status
Below 18.5	Underweight
18.5–24.9	Normal weight for your height and weight
25.0–29.9	Overweight
30.0–39.9	Obese
40 and above	Morbidly obese

Depending on where your numbers fall, you could be at a higher risk for chronic diseases such as type-2 diabetes, high blood pressure, cardiovascular disease, heart attack, stroke, and some types of cancer.

From these calculations you can make assessments as to your current state of health and consult with your doctor about a plan to start lowering your risk rates immediately. You're already on the right track pursuing your healthy low-carb active lifestyle. However, never take your own calculations or what you read in any book as gospel. Check with your doctor.

Part II
Low-Carb Cooking Made Easy

The 5th Wave   By Rich Tennant

"Do I like arugula? I _love_ arugula!! Some of the best beaches in the world are there."

In this part . . .

This part gives you low-carb recipes for every meal of the day. First, I wake you up to breakfast and help you realize how and why it's important. I even give you suggestions for breakfast on the run. Next, you find some new and healthy salad and dressing ideas that show you that greens don't have to be boring and unappetizing. Then I explain the health benefits of fish and seafood and how to shop for and prepare them before giving you some easy, delicious recipes. The next chapters include great ideas for preparing chicken and meats, including beef, pork, and lamb. You'll discover the beautiful, nutritious veggie rainbow and how important a variety of veggie color is to your dietary needs and why. Finally, I sweetly reward you with some great low-carb desserts to satisfy your low-carb sweet tooth.

Chapter 6

Waking Up to Breakfast

*B*reakfast — it's one of my favorite subjects, not to mention meals. As a former innkeeper of a country bed-and-breakfast in Branson, Missouri, I can tell you that when folks are on vacation and don't have to dash off to work, their breakfast attitude certainly changes. Everyone eats breakfast when they stay at a B&B — even folks who profess to *never* eat even a bowl of cereal or granola bar before they start their busy days. Not only do people eat breakfast at a B&B, but they even get up early enough to chat with the innkeeper while she prepares the food. It's an amazing thing, I tell you.

So now you know that I cook a really mean breakfast that brings people to the breakfast table. In this chapter, I share some of my favorite breakfast recipes that fit your low-carb lifestyle.

Prioritizing Breakfast in Your Low-Carb Lifestyle

Why eat breakfast, you ask? Think about it. The last meal you ate was the previous night's dinner. When you rise and grab your first cup of coffee of the day, you likely haven't had a morsel for at least 12 hours. Believe it or not, eating breakfast helps you lose weight or maintain your current healthy weight! Grab something to eat at least an hour after you've risen for the day. You'll find that you'll function more effectively, your concentration will be better, and you won't be as irritable and short tempered as when you skip breakfast.

Breakfast on the run!

The next time you find yourself rushing out the door on an empty stomach, grab a coffee mug and forget the coffee. Throw in 2 eggs with a pinch of salt and pepper and give them a quick whisk. Pop them in the microwave for 1 minute. If they're still a little runny, give them a quick stir and pop back in the micro for another 10 seconds, grab a fork, and run.

Or, for a quick breakfast burrito, grab a couple of low-carb, whole-wheat tortillas and pop them into the microwave for about 8 seconds. When the eggs are done, add 3 tablespoons of fresh tomato salsa and 2 tablespoons of mozzarella or cheddar cheese. Spoon the mixture into your warm tortillas, roll them up, and you're on your way. Put the breakfast tortillas in plastic wrap and pop them into the micro to warm when you get to work. It's breakfast on the run!

You say you want a quick omelet? Here's a quick omelet recipe for the microwave. Melt ½ tablespoon of butter in a small, shallow, microwave-proof dish on High in the microwave for about 15 seconds — you just want to coat the dish with butter. Place two eggs in the dish and season to taste with salt and pepper. Beat lightly with a fork. Pop the eggs in the microwave and cook on High for about 1 minute. Loosen eggs with a fork — they'll be more cooked around the edges. Return them to microwave on High for another 30 seconds. The eggs will look wet and not quite done. Let stand for 1 minute and your micro-omelet will finish cooking. Top with whatever toppings you have in the fridge.

If you want to add some extra flavor to your micro-omelet, add any of the following ingredients: cheese cubes or grated cheeses, chopped green and red peppers, chopped fresh tomatoes, sliced mushrooms, a bit of chopped green onion, leftover veggies from the night before, a dash of curry powder or some tomato salsa. Just about anything but the kitchen sink applies here.

Plus, if you eat breakfast, research shows that you're more likely to enjoy a nutritionally balanced diet overall.

Increasing your energy and metabolic rate

Overnight, your body uses energy, even while you're sleeping. Your body needs to replace some of the stores of energy it used during the night in the form of food in the morning. Whatever your lifestyle, whatever your age, wherever you live, mornings usually begin with a bang. You're out of the gate full blast and don't understand why you seem to slow down and occasionally get a headache around 10 a.m. Breakfast is the energy you need to stand up in the morning and make it to lunch.

Expecting your body to shift into full gear without stopping to refuel is like assuming your car will run on empty. Even if you try to catch up by eating a balanced lunch, you never regain the energy you would've had if you'd taken ten minutes to eat some breakfast.

A big reason to make breakfast part of your low-carb lifestyle is to kick-start your metabolic rate. Your metabolism slows down at night like everything else, and the boost of breakfast gets your body off and running again. When you increase your metabolism, you burn fat, and you know what that means — you maintain your desired body weight. (Check out Chapter 2 for the full story on increasing your metabolism.)

Avoiding cravings and increased hunger

Eating breakfast has been the mantra for many years. It's important not only to your overall health but significantly important to your low-carb healthy lifestyle. Eating breakfast will help you stave off cravings and hunger pangs. Coupled with eating healthy snacks and grazing (see Chapter 2), eating breakfast is a priority.

Eating a healthy breakfast is one way to evenly distribute your day's calories and nutrients and help maintain a steady blood-sugar level and energy level. Irregular eating habits cause a wide fluctuation in blood sugar and insulin levels that affect your energy level and give you hunger cues. Eating four or five small meals a day or snacking on good carb snacks is a great way to keep your blood sugar from spiking and sending you on a hunger roller coaster ride.

- ✔ Studies have actually linked low blood sugar levels to poor memory, concentration, and learning ability.

- ✔ Ironically, people who skip breakfast in an effort to cut carbs and calories often do more snacking later in the day and overeat at evening meals.

- ✔ Increased hunger isn't caused by eating breakfast but by other eating habits. Take a look at the foods you choose for breakfast. Sugary food, even the kind with natural sugars, such as a fruit salad or toast and jam, triggers an insulin response and raises brain levels of serotonin, leaving you hungry and sleepy within two hours.

Laying the foundation for your day

Under the breakfast banner of life I want to stress *you*. Breakfast is a very personal meal that's all about how your body works. You don't have time not to eat it. Breakfast is a huge part of any healthy lifestyle, especially your low-carb lifestyle. Experiment and figure out what works for you time-wise, palate-wise, and preparation-wise. And remember, variety is definitely the spice.

Breakfast menus vary with country, locality, and even occupation — not to mention with your healthy low-carb lifestyle of choice. Expand your horizons with common sense. If something is low in carbs and ultrahigh in fats and calories, how much of it do you think is wise for you to gobble down? Consider this rule the common sense rule. You can apply it to any food or any meal you want — not just breakfast.

And breakfast isn't just for breakfast any more. Try the Crab Scramble in this chapter for dinner. Also, see Chapter 15 for great egg crepes that are very versatile, low in carbs, and good for you.

Egging You On

Breakfast on the run tends to conjure up thoughts of foods that aren't considerations when you elect a healthy low-carb lifestyle. But eggs are a great alternative: Eggs aren't the only food on the breakfast list but because of their versatility, you can have a bunch of breakfast options if you get a bit creative. If you're not in a hurry and want some meat with your eggs, select a lean sausage. There are some incredible combinations out there these days with sun-dried tomatoes, mushrooms, various cheeses, basil, and garlic — all options that can add real spice to your breakfast. But please stay away from the fatty stuff. If you just have to have bacon, choose lean cuts, prepare it in the microwave, and blot it with paper towels to remove the excess fat instead of frying it in all that grease. (For more about good fats and bad fats see Chapter 2.)

Two eggs, please, sunny side up! That's just the beginning of the long list of ways to have your eggs. Eggs can be fried, poached, scrambled, and hard cooked. They come in wonderful disguises like omelets that can be filled with such delights as sugar-free jellies and preserves, fruit, mixed veggies, spinach, mushrooms, herbs, and more.

And then there are soufflés, meringues, and mousses made with eggs (see Chapter 13 for low-carb meringue treats). You can also add spices to change the entire egg picture. Think about curry, basil, rosemary, and any other spice — dried or fresh — that shakes or minces. Whoever thought an egg could look or taste so good!

Eggs have been referred to as nature's near-perfect food. A 1-ounce egg has only 75 calories; provides all essential amino acids (see Chapter 11 for more on amino acids), as well as lecithin and potassium; and has only 1 gram of carbohydrates. Eggs should become your new low-carb best friend. Protein is great in the mornings because it truly helps you curb cravings. If you have a boring image of eggs at this very moment, replace it with a new image that's going to help you to eat a breakfast that'll fill you up, not out.

Because eggs are almost the perfect food with some pretty impressive nutritional benefits, they are good for your general health and definitely fit in with your low-carb lifestyle. You need to take good care of this precious cargo so you can reap the most benefit from it. Here are some tips on buying and storing eggs, a couple warnings, and a bit of serving information.

- Check the sell-by date stamped on the egg carton, and use your eggs by this date. The size of the air pocket in the egg increases with age. The bigger the air pocket, the less fresh the egg is.

- Do a freshness test if you're wondering whether to use eggs on hand. Simply put the egg in a bowl of water. Stale or bad eggs float to the top, and fresh eggs sink with the rounded end pointed up.

- When you break an egg and the white spreads out very thin, throw it away even if it passes the smell test, because the egg is about to go bad or is bad.

- Store your eggs with the big round end up and the pointy end down.

- Do not use cracked eggs because they may contain harmful bacteria.

- Serve egg dishes immediately after cooking or refrigerate them.

And here are a few more egg-cellent secrets:

- The secret to cooking eggs is to be gentle and apply low heat. If eggs cook too fast or too long, they come out rubbery.

- The secret to prepping fabulous eggs? A balloon whisk is an awesome kitchen gadget to have for the best beaten eggs and especially for egg whites. For perfect egg whites, use this oversized whisk with a round-bottomed bowl and you can keep all of your egg whites in motion, simultaneously allowing tiny bubbles to form and the volume to build. This tool is a must for making successful egg dishes. See an example of a balloon whisk in Figure 6-1.

Figure 6-1:
A balloon whisk is the key to perfectly beaten eggs.

Hard-cooked heaven

"Hard-boiled" eggs can be a great part of a low-carb breakfast, and they make a fabulous snack. But eggs should never be *boiled* but should be *hard-cooked* instead. If you boil eggs too long, they get a greenish-gray look around the yolk. Did I hear an "Ah-ha! That's what causes that to happen"? Here's how to make hard-cooked eggs:

1. Put the eggs in a single layer in cold water.

2. As soon as they come to a rolling boil, remove the pan from the heat, cover tightly with the pan lid, and let the eggs sit in the pan for 15 to 20 minutes.

3. Immediately run cold water over them to cool, which makes them easier to peel too.

For the best hard-cooked eggs, use eggs that are a few days old. Really fresh eggs that are hard-cooked are more difficult to peel.

You can simplify the job of removing the shell from a hard-cooked egg if you begin by gently tapping it all over, rotating the egg as you tap. Then roll the egg between your hands to loosen the shell from the egg. Starting at the large end of the egg, begin peeling. To make it even easier for the peeling to slip off, hold the egg under cold running water while peeling or put them in a bowl of cold water.

Awesome omelets

Basically, there are two types of omelets. The French omelet can be served plain or folded over almost anything your little heart desires, and the puffy omelet is started on top of the stove and finished in the oven. Both are quick and quite easy. And now for my omelet keys to success:

- ✔ Use only fresh ingredients in your omelets.

- ✔ Make sure the eggs are at room temperature (even if you have to pop them in a little warm water to heat them up). The temperature of the egg before you start building the omelet has a profound effect on how your omelet turns out, and you want it light and fluffy.

- ✔ You can have your omelet soft or well done, but you never want to cook your omelet over high heat or it will get very tough and even burn.

- ✔ The maximum load for a successful omelet is three eggs.

- ✔ Use 1 to 2 tablespoons of water for each egg (never use milk in an omelet), plus enough butter or oil to coat the bottom of the pan. Coating the pan keeps the outside of the omelet soft.

- ✔ If you make omelets regularly, do yourself a favor and buy an omelet pan. The ideal size is a 7- or 8-inch pan with curved sides. The pan should be light enough that you can lift it with one hand and shake it as the omelet is cooking.

Plain Ol' Simple Omelet

This recipe for a very basic omelet can be a springboard for all kinds of omelet variations (see the suggestions after the recipe). Mastering omelet making is by no means difficult. Using an omelet pan gives you a finished product that's much more pleasing to the eye than just using a skillet. (See Figure 6-2 for some visual tips on how to fold an omelet.)

Preparation time: 5 minutes

Cooking time: 2 minutes or less

Yield: 1 serving

2 eggs

1 tablespoon water

¼ teaspoon salt

Pepper to taste

1 tablespoon butter

1 Break the eggs into a small bowl. Add the water, salt, and pepper. Beat until well blended but not foamy.

2 Using a small skillet or omelet pan, heat the pan and add butter making sure that the butter coats the pan evenly. You want the pan very hot but not hot enough to burn the butter. When you add the butter, it should immediately melt and begin foaming to a sizzle.

3 As the butter loses its sizzle, pour the egg mixture into the omelet pan. Holding the handle of the pan with one hand, gently shake the pan to coat the entire pan with the egg mixture. The eggs will begin to cook immediately when they hit the hot omelet pan.

4 When the omelet begins to set, tilt the pan away from you and lift the edges with a coated spatula because the edges will cook more quickly. This allows the runny mixture to flow to the bottom of the pan so it can get cooked too.

5 Place the omelet pan back on the stove, allowing it to cook until it's firm. The center will be just a tad moist, as the omelet continues to cook in the pan when you remove it from the heat. Tilt the omelet pan away from you, and gently fold one-third of the omelet over onto itself.

6 You're now holding the omelet pan up off the heat. Holding the pan firmly, you want to strike the handle of the pan two or three times, making the far side of the omelet flip back on itself over the first fold. Press the sides together to seal and, lifting the side of the omelet with your spatula, slide it off onto a plate.

7 Serve immediately.

Variation: Instead of using salt and pepper in your omelet, try Tabasco sauce. It blends very nicely with the eggs and makes the omelet much more flavorful.

Per serving: Calories 250 (From Fat 193); Fat 21g (Saturated 10g); Cholesterol 458mg; Sodium 709mg; Carbohydrate 1g; Dietary Fiber 0g (Net Carbohydrate 1g); Protein 13g.

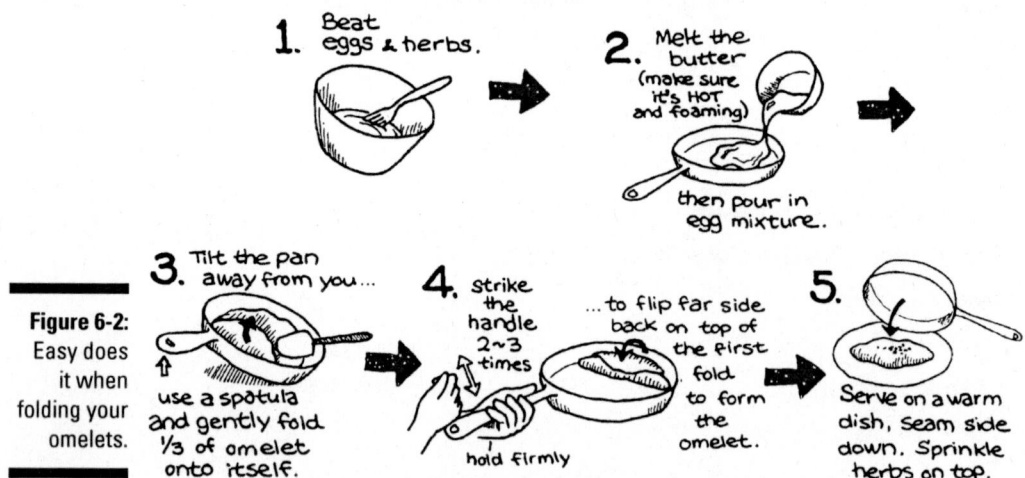

Figure 6-2:
Easy does
it when
folding your
omelets.

Whether you're using my Plain Ol' Simple Omelet recipe in this chapter or your own, consider these low-carb, easy variations:

- **Simple Farmer's Omelet:** Add ¼ cup finely grated cheese to the mixture before cooking. Sprinkle 1 tablespoon of finely chopped ham, turkey, or chicken over the omelet before folding.

- **Mexican Cheese Omelet:** Add ¼ cup Monterey Jack or pepper Jack cheese, and add 2 tablespoons bottled salsa (check the sugar content on the salsa, please). Add the cheese before folding your omelet and top with the salsa when you serve it.

- **Mushroom Omelet:** Add ¾ cup sautéed sliced mushrooms, and 1 tablespoon minced chives. Cook the eggs about 1 minute before adding mushrooms and chives. After adding, cook another 1½ to 2 minutes and then fold omelet and serve.

A general rule is the addition of 1 teaspoon of water for every egg that you plop in an omelet. Water is used because it slows down the cooking of the eggs and makes the texture of the finished omelet much lighter and fluffier.

☙ Puffy Omelet Squares with Tomato-Zucchini Sauce

Make this easy, basic puffy omelet with tomato-zucchini sauce, or try other sauces. Don't limit yourself to veggie sauces; be bold and try the omelet with some easy, fresh fruit and a dollop of whipped cream. This recipe calls for stewed tomatoes. Look for the ones with the lowest carb and sugar counts.

Preparation time: *15 minutes*

Cooking time: *40 to 45 minutes*

Yield: *4 servings*

Nonstick cooking spray

6 eggs

½ teaspoon onion powder

½ teaspoon salt

¼ teaspoon pepper, divided

14-ounce can stewed tomatoes, cut fine

½ cup quartered (lengthwise) and sliced zucchini

1 teaspoon dried basil

1 Preheat the oven to 350 degrees. Spray an 8-x-8-x-2-inch baking dish with nonstick spray and set aside. Separate the eggs, placing the whites and yolks in separate bowls.

2 Beat the egg yolks, onion powder, salt, and ⅛ teaspoon pepper for about 4 minutes or until thick and lemon-colored. Set aside.

3 Beat the egg whites until soft peaks begin to form and the tips of the peaks begin to gently fold over. Fold the whites into the egg yolks. (Dash over to Chapter 13 for a quick lesson on beating egg whites and the appearance of peaks.)

4 Spread the mixture evenly into the prepared dish. Bake for 23 to 25 minutes or until a knife inserted near the center comes out clean. Oven temperatures vary, so begin watching it after about 20 minutes.

5 While the omelet is baking, make the sauce. Combine the undrained tomatoes, zucchini, basil, and remaining pepper. Bring to boil, and reduce heat. Cover and simmer about 5 minutes or just until the zucchini is tender. Don't overcook.

6 Simmer, uncovered, for 10 more minutes or until the sauce reaches the desired consistency.

7 To serve, cut the omelet into quarters and top with sauce.

Per serving: Calories 144 (From Fat 68); Fat 8g (Saturated 2g); Cholesterol 319mg; Sodium 670mg; Carbohydrate 9g; Dietary Fiber 2g (Net Carbohydrate 7g); Protein 10g.

Scrambling skillets

Scrambled eggs are the easiest of all skillet dishes to prepare. A basic egg scramble begins with 2 eggs (more if you like) salted and peppered to your liking. Beat the eggs just until the yolks and whites are blended. Add a tablespoon of cream. Melt some butter in a pan and tilt the pan so the bottom is well coated. Depending on how you like your eggs done, you can finish your eggs by choosing from the following cooking methods:

- **Creamy and Smooth Eggs:** Cook the eggs over low heat and constantly stir them with a wooden spoon. Your scramble is finished when the eggs are moist but firm with no uncooked liquid floating about. Allow about 3 minutes cooking time for 3 to 4 eggs.

- **Large, Creamy Egg Curds:** Cook the eggs over low heat, occasionally pulling the cooked portions of the eggs to the center of the skillet allowing the uncooked portions of the scramble to run to the edges. Repeat this process until all of the eggs are cooked in large, moist curds.

- **Dry Scramble:** Cook the eggs a couple of minutes past the moist but firm stage. The eggs will look dry and crumbly.

- **Fluffy Scramble:** Beat the eggs vigorously until light and fluffy. After cooking, you can pop them in the blender for more fluff if desired. Eggs will be semi-dry (not moist) when done.

The skinny on egg substitutes

Egg substitutes are ideal for scrambled eggs, quiche, frittatas, omelets, casseroles, sauces, and other recipes that call for whole eggs. Some folks today prefer to use egg substitutes for several reasons. You don't have to worry about them going bad, and because egg substitutes are made up mostly of egg whites, they contain fewer calories and less cholesterol than fresh eggs. Egg substitutes come in refrigerated form as well as frozen. You'll find the refrigerated egg substitutes in the milk section, usually next to the cream and milk. You can find the exact substitute measurements on each carton of the particular brand that you purchase. You'll also find just egg whites that can be used for meringues and other recipes that call for just whites so you don't waste the yolks or try to figure out something to do with them. Please be sure to read the labels on egg whites to double-check whether that particular brand can be used for meringue making. (See Chapter 13 for great meringue recipes.)

⟳ *Sunday Brunch Scramble*

Sunday afternoon is a perfect time to give this recipe a whirl. The little bit of curry powder combined with the onions and sour cream give this scramble a special twist. Curry powder is a blend of rich, warm, earthy, and pungent flavors with varied overtones, always giving any dish a mysteriously warm flavor. Maybe serve this with some low-carb bagels or low-carb English muffins and just a dab of sugar-free jam or preserves. Yum! This is a quick and easy, yet filling and very low-carb, Sunday brunch.

Preparation time: 10 minutes

Cooking time: 5 to 6 minutes

Yield: 4 servings

6 eggs	*⅛ cup finely chopped green onions*
½ cup sour cream	*½ teaspoon curry powder*
2 tablespoons butter	*½ cup coarsely grated cheddar cheese*

1 Beat the eggs and sour cream together with a mixer until they're light and fluffy.

2 Melt the butter in a large skillet over medium heat. Add the green onions and cook for about 3 minutes. Add the curry powder, and stir for just a few seconds.

3 Add the egg mixture and stir gently until the eggs are cooked to desired consistency (see the bulleted list earlier in this section). Top with cheese and serve immediately.

Per serving: *Calories 284(From Fat 216); Fat 24g (Saturated 13g); Cholesterol 362mg; Sodium 200mg; Carbohydrate 3g; Dietary Fiber 0g (Net Carbohydrate 3g); Protein 14g.*

Here's a little way to test the doneness of your scrambled eggs, omelets, and frittatas: Cook them until eggs are thickened and no visible liquid egg remains.

Crab Scramble

 An almost elegant scramble, this is a great weekend brunch treat, or it can serve it as a quick main course for supper. If you take the brunch route, a portion on each plate with some colorful fresh fruit and a sprig of mint makes a lovely presentation. It's downright low-carb beautiful!

Preparation time: 5 minutes

Cooking time: 5 minutes

Yield: 4 servings

2 tablespoons butter	Salt and pepper to taste
8-ounce can lump crabmeat, chopped	½ cup grated cheddar cheese
1 teaspoon finely chopped fresh chives	8 eggs, beaten and seasoned to taste

1 Heat the butter in a nonstick frying pan over medium-high heat. When hot, turn the heat to low and add the crabmeat and chives. Cook for 2 minutes over low heat. Season with salt and pepper to taste.

2 Stir the cheese into the beaten eggs. Pour over the crabmeat in the frying pan. Cook for 3 minutes while stirring constantly.

Per Serving: Calories 313 (From Fat 190); Fat 21g (Saturated 10g); Cholesterol 506mg; Sodium 549mg; Carbohydrate 2g; Dietary Fiber 0g (Net Carbohydrate 2g); Protein 28g.

Frittata this

A *frittata* is like a flat egg cake. It's a bit thick and is cooked until it's firm but by no means dry. To make sure that you don't burn the bottom of the frittata, start it over low heat on top of the stove and then finish it under the broiler, using an ovenproof skillet. My favorite old-fashioned iron skillets are the best for frittatas. If you're a good flipper, you can flip the frittata instead of popping it under the broiler. Good luck — I, for one, don't do this very well.

Ham and Cheese Frittata

Frittatas, in my humble opinion, are even easier than omelets. Both add veggies, cheese, or meat to eggs in some manner. With an omelet, the additional ingredients are used as a filling and the finished omelet is folded over the ingredients. When making a frittata, you just throw in whatever ingredients you can find in the fridge. All of the ingredients are mixed together and poured into heated oil or butter. Most frittatas include a short trip to the broiler, so it's a good idea to start the frittata process in an ovenproof skillet.

Preparation time: *5 to 8 minutes*

Cooking time: *8 minutes*

Yield: *4 servings*

3 eggs

3 egg whites

½ teaspoon salt

½ teaspoon pepper

1¼ cups broccoli florets

6 ounces smoked deli ham, diced in ½-inch cubes

⅓ cup red bell pepper strips

Nonstick cooking spray

1 tablespoon butter

½ cup shredded sharp cheddar cheese

1 Preheat the broiler. Beat the eggs, egg whites, salt, and pepper in a large bowl until well blended. Stir in the broccoli, ham, and bell peppers.

2 Coat a 10-inch ovenproof skillet with sloping sides with nonstick cooking spray. Melt the butter over medium heat in the skillet. Pour the egg mixture into the skillet and cover. Cook for about 6 minutes or until the eggs are set around the edges. The center will be wet.

3 Uncover the skillet and sprinkle the egg mixture with cheese. Transfer the skillet to the broiler and broil 5 inches from the heat source. Watch closely, because you only need to broil for about 2 minutes, or until the eggs in the center are set and the cheese is melted.

4 Let stand for 5 minutes before serving. Cut the frittata into wedges.

Variation: You can use almost any veggie in the universe in a frittata. A few more basic ideas are red and green peppers, zucchini, cauliflower, and spinach. You can also add Canadian bacon, sausage, or ham and any kind of cheese.

Per serving: *Calories 205 (From Fat 113); Fat 13g (Saturated 6g); Cholesterol 193mg; Sodium 1,020mg; Carbohydrate 3g; Dietary Fiber 1g (Net Carbohydrate 2g); Protein 19g.*

Kickin' quiche

For a quiche to be good, you don't need the extra carbs of the crust. Quiches are actually very easy and quick to make, and I think you're are going to be quite pleased how good they are the next day for a quick breakfast or a lunch to tote.

⊙ *Crustless Mushroom Quiche*

This is a favorite quiche from my bed and breakfast in Branson and is quite like a more traditional quiche even without a crust (I never did make it with a crust at the B&B either). This is a great quiche to ensure plenty of leftovers for breakfast on the run or a great lunch (add a salad). But before you get to leftovers, enjoy this great mushroom quiche!

Preparation time: *10 minutes*

Cooking time: *35 to 40 minutes*

Yield: *6 servings*

8 ounces fresh mushrooms, cleaned and sliced

¼ cup butter, divided

1½ cups shredded Swiss cheese

¾ cup whipping cream

¼ teaspoon salt

½ teaspoon dry mustard

6 eggs

1 tablespoon Italian parsley, finely chopped

1 Preheat the oven to 325 degrees. Cook the mushrooms in 2 tablespoons of butter over medium-high heat until they're lightly browned and the excess liquid evaporates from the pan, about 3 to 4 minutes. Set aside.

2 Sprinkle the cheese in a buttered 8-x-8-inch baking dish and dot with the remaining 2 tablespoons of butter.

3 Mix the cream, salt, dry mustard, and eggs in a medium bowl. Pour the egg mixture over the cheese. Pour the mushrooms evenly on top of the egg mixture.

4 Bake at 325 degrees for 35 minutes, or until the eggs are set. Sprinkle with chopped fresh parsley. Serve immediately.

Per serving: Calories 357 (From Fat 281); Fat 31g (Saturated 18g); Cholesterol 299mg; Sodium 244mg; Carbohydrate 4g; Dietary Fiber 1g (Net Carbohydrate 3g); Protein 16g.

Crustless Quiche Lorraine

Ah my sweet Quiche Lorraine! Here's another recipe from my ol' inn in Branson that you make in the microwave. This crustless quiche recipe is a favorite of a lot of quiche lovers. Like almost all quiches, this one is good hot or cold, and it's a great portable and healthy low-carb snack. Cut the quiche in wedges, wrap it individually in plastic wrap, and you have an instant breakfast to go. If you serve this as a meal, complement your quiche with a salad of fresh greens. Feel free to experiment with this great basic quiche recipe, adding some of your favorite veggies to the mix for variety.

Preparation time: *5 minutes*

Cooking time: *15 to 20 minutes*

Yield: *6 servings*

10 slices bacon	*1½ cups half-and-half*
1½ cups shredded 3-cheese blend of mozzarella, Monterey Jack, and cheddar	*¾ teaspoon salt*
	⅛ teaspoon pepper
4 eggs	*⅛ teaspoon nutmeg*

1 Cook the bacon in the microwave by placing 2 layers of paper towels in a shallow microwave-safe dish. Place the bacon on the paper towels. Cover the bacon with a single layer of paper towels. Cook bacon on high for 5 to 7 minutes until crisp. Let the bacon cool and crumble bacon into small bits.

2 Sprinkle the bacon and the cheese in the bottom of a 9-inch glass pie plate or shallow ceramic quiche plate.

3 In a small bowl, beat together the eggs, half and half, salt, pepper, and nutmeg until well blended.

4 Pour the blended egg mixture over the bacon and cheese.

5 Bake in the microwave on high for 9 to 11 minutes. Stop the cooking after 3 minutes, and stir and then stop again after 6 minutes and stir, cooking until the quiche is set.

6 Let stand for 10 minutes before serving.

Variation: If you want to bake this in a conventional oven, simply preheat your oven to 375 degrees and bake the quiche for 40 to 45 minutes.

Variation: This is a basic quiche recipe, so feel free to add veggies, other herbs and spices, and a variety of cheeses. In place of the bacon, you can substitute chopped sautéed onions, smoked salmon, diced cooked sausage, asparagus spears, or something from the sea.

Per serving: Calories 288 (From Fat 211); Fat 23g (Saturated 12g); Cholesterol 198mg; Sodium 670mg; Carbohydrate 4g; Dietary Fiber 0g (Net Carbohydrate 4g); Protein 16g.

Quiche takes you to the land of versatility. You can eat quiche as an entrée, for lunch, breakfast, or a low-carb snack. Somehow it got a bad rap years ago, and quiche was declared a rather unmanly dish. You may remember hearing that real men don't eat quiche. This stereotyping has since disappeared, and introducing quiche to your low-carb lifestyle will add lots of variety to your menus, and will give you ways to use those leftovers — simply throw them in a quiche — all while enjoying the healthful benefits of eating eggs.

Skipping the crusts in your quiche recipes is so easy and so user friendly to your healthy low-carb lifestyle. You'll find that you can easily adapt most traditional quiche recipes to the crustless variety. Here's a little insight on low-carb crustless quiche: The finished product isn't always quite the same texture as a classic quiche because you don't use some of the binding ingredients, like hash browns for instance. If your low-carb quiches turn out to be a little fluffier and more like a scramble, it's okay. Sometimes, I'll cook my crustless quiches in a smaller size dish so the quiche is thicker – depending on whether you like it thick or thin. Experiment with a couple of these quiche recipes and it will take you about two tries to make up your mind how you like your low-carb quiche. So quiche on and do the low-carb quiche!

When you cook in the microwave, be mindful that the ingredients keep on cookin' after you remove them and set them on the counter.

Brunching with Low-Carb Treats

The flexibility of your low-carb lifestyle allows you so many wonderful food options. The days of delectable and sweet breakfast treats aren't gone; your options are just a little different. The recipes here are ideal if you're having guests over for a weekend brunch, a great excuse to get together with your low-carb friends. Your guests may be surprised to discover that these dishes are low-carb. And even if you're preparing brunch for only you and your family, these recipes are ways to treat them and eat healthy, too.

Jan's Nostalgic Pancakes

I've been flippin' pancakes for years but not the low-carb kind. I grew up on homemade buttermilk pancakes! But I gotta tell you that these come close in a big low-carb way. They're delicious and taste a little like blintzes. The trick to making these pancakes is to stay with them while they're cooking. They cook very quickly, and you can stack them up fast. Serve these with sugar-free syrup, if desired, or spread on some sugar-free jam or preserves of your choice and roll them up like a blintz. You can also sprinkle with Splenda and top with a dollop of whipped cream. Feel free to substitute fresh or frozen berries to get the real blintz effect. Use this recipe as a basic one that you can apply your sugar-free dreams to. Enjoy!

Preparation time: *10 minutes*

Cooking time: *3 to 4 minutes per pancake*

Yield: *6 pancakes*

3 eggs	*3 tablespoons white whole-wheat flour*
1 cup small-curd cottage cheese	*¼ teaspoon baking powder*
¼ teaspoon salt	*3 teaspoons butter, divided (If you're cooking the pancakes individually, you need about ½ teaspoon per pancake; if you're cooking all 6 at one time on a griddle, 2 teaspoons should be adequate)*
1 teaspoon vanilla	
1 teaspoon cinnamon	
1 packet Splenda sugar substitute	

1 Combine the eggs, cottage cheese, salt, vanilla, cinnamon, and packet of Splenda and mix well in the blender until smooth. Combine the flour and baking powder in a small dish and add to the blender. Blend again until all ingredients are well blended. The batter will be very thin.

2 Heat a nonstick skillet or griddle over medium heat. When it's hot, lightly grease with butter.

3 When the butter has melted, drop about ¼ cup of the batter onto the skillet or griddle. If necessary, spread the batter out with the back of a spoon. Let the pancake cook for about 1 minute, or until small craterlike bubbles begin to form on the top of the batter. Lift the edge of the pancake with a spatula to see if the bottom side is golden. (You may have to let it cook another 15 seconds.) Flip the pancake and brown lightly on the other side.

4 Remove the pancake from the skillet or griddle immediately and serve.

Variation: *Add ½ cup finely chopped hazelnuts (or nuts of your choice) to the batter and make nutty pancakes that are crunchy.*

Per serving: *Calories 109 (From Fat 56); Fat 6g (Saturated 3g); Cholesterol 117mg; Sodium 297mg; Carbohydrate 5g; Dietary Fiber 1g (Net Carbohydrate 4g); Protein 8g.*

Apricot-Cheddar Brunch Toast

This recipe is also from my days as an innkeeper at my country bed-and-breakfast. I've actually prepared this for guests and made extra for them to take for a breakfast on the run on a frantic Monday. Serve these toasted sandwiches with a dollop of freshly whipped cream and a sprig of mint, as well as fresh sliced strawberries on the plate, for an awesome low-carb presentation.

Preparation time: *15 minutes*

Cooking time: *6 to 8 minutes*

Yield: *4 servings*

8 slices low-carb bread of your choice	*½ cup Hood's low-carb orange juice*
¼ cup sugar-free apricot preserves	*1 teaspoon sugar-free maple syrup*
4 slices Canadian bacon	*2 tablespoons butter*
8 slices medium cheddar cheese	*Splenda sugar substitute (optional)*
3 eggs	

1 Spread four slices of bread with the preserves. Top each one with a slice of Canadian bacon and two slices of cheese. Top with the remaining slices of bread, pressing down very gently.

2 Combine the eggs, orange juice, and maple syrup in a shallow dish. (Choose a dish that is flat on the bottom and that the whole sandwich can lay flat in to make your dipping very quick and easy). Dip the sandwiches in the egg mixture, turning once with a flat spatula and allowing them to stand in the mixture for about 30 seconds per side, or until the mixture soaks in.

3 Melt the butter in a large, heavy skillet (or use your griddle) over medium heat. Cook the sandwiches for about 3 minutes on each side, monitoring the heat carefully. The cheese should be melted, and the bread should be golden brown.

4 Sprinkle with powdered Splenda, if desired, and serve with additional preserves.

Per serving: Calories 511 (From Fat 299); Fat 33g (Saturated 17g); Cholesterol 247mg; Sodium 1,117mg; Carbohydrate 23g; Dietary Fiber 6g (Net Carbohydrate 17g); Protein 31g.

Chapter 7

Soothing Your Low-Carb Soul with Soup

*A*h, soup. Close your eyes and think about how you feel on a rainy winter night when you come inside and ladle up a big bowl of hot soup. As you drink in the flavors, the feeling spreads throughout your entire body, soothing spots that ache, warming your tummy, and vibrating your very soul. For centuries soup has been used to lift spirits, satisfy, and comfort. I guarantee you're about to make a pot of old-fashioned low-carb comfort in this chapter!

Homemade soup is too often overlooked in the low carb-lifestyle. Many soups are very low in carb counts, low in calorie counts, healthy, nourishing, and preservative free — not to mention just darned good. When you become an accomplished soup maker, you're off to good living. Well, you're already well on your way to good living with a low-carb lifestyle, so it's high time you get with the soup program, too. Did I hear you mumble something about soup being a lot of trouble? Not so. You're going to find that spooning homemade soups into your low-carb lifestyle is a pleasant experience — one that'll definitely fill you up, not out. (Grab your slow cooker and take a gander at Chapter 16 for additional soup, chili, and stew recipes.)

Making Your Soup Kettle Sing

If you don't have a good stockpot, I suggest you buy one. Stockpots aren't expensive (well, they don't have to be), and a stockpot will serve you well in your soup-making adventures. Stockpots are available in different sizes, and you don't have to buy a huge one unless you plan on making big batches of soups to freeze for lunches. However, when you're making homemade soup of any kind, you want to have a fairly good-sized soup kettle.

It's great if you have the time and energy to make homemade stocks — more power to you. But pre-made stocks and broths are totally acceptable in a healthy low-carb lifestyle, and they make your soup preparations quicker and easier. But here's a tip: You can find some great quality stocks and broths in *cartons* these days to use as a base for quick homemade soups. Try them instead of taking the can route. Stocks and broth in cartons are usually lower in sodium and often more natural than their canned counterparts. Before you buy any pre-made stock or broth, check the label for sodium content and see whether the stock has a ton of preservatives. If so, walk on by and find some that have lower sodium counts and fewer preservatives. You may want to look for the word *organic* when buying pre-made stocks and broths.

Technically speaking, stock and broth are a bit different (but they're all the same to this cook)! When making stock all that's necessary is water and bones (unless it's veggie stock). Stock is usually rather bland in flavor, and it's usually an ingredient in soup. Broth is usually a bit richer than stock, and broth can be garnished and eaten by itself. Broth is prepared by simmering meat, fish, or veggies and then straining them out.

Black soybeans: A great low-carb secret

I discovered a great low-carb secret in the health-food store one day — black soybeans. These little puppies are just delicious, and I use them in chili, dips, and all sorts of food creations. They're so low in carbs, and the flavor is great in anything (see the recipe for Caribbean Style Black Soybean Soup in this chapter and check out Chapter 15 for another recipe, Spicy Black Soybean Wraps). The official count on a ½ cup of black soybeans is 8 grams of carbs and 7 grams of fiber — pretty awesome at only 1 net gram of carbs. And soybeans are so good for you. They're high in protein and fiber, low in saturated fat and cholesterol, lactose free, and a great source of omega-3 fatty acids. (Go over to Chapter 9 for more on omega-3s and their

importance to your health.) In addition to all of the nutrients in soybeans, ongoing research is proving that they reduce the risk of certain chronic diseases, including coronary heart disease.

The only black soybeans I've found are from Eden Foods. I usually have to buy them at a health-food store but have found them in a grocery store or two. Make a couple phone calls to check their stock before you make a trip across town. If you find other brands of black soybeans, please e-mail me at jan@janmccracken. com, and I'll get it out to low-carbers in my free newsletter and post it on my Web site.

Cream of Broccoflower Soup

Have you met the broccoflower? Some mad scientist has crossed the cauliflower with broccoli and created an incredible veggie. Hence, the *broccoflower.* I see it in all of the produce departments at the grocery stores, but come to think of it, broccoflowers haven't shown up at the farmer's markets. Anyway, the stuff is bursting with great nutrients like phytochemicals (see more on phytos in Chapter 12).

Preparation time: *15 minutes*

Cooking time: *30 minutes*

Yield: *4 servings*

1½ cups chicken stock	*½ teaspoon dried marjoram*
2 cups coarsely chopped broccoflower	*¼ teaspoon salt*
¼ cup chopped green onions	*⅛ teaspoon white pepper*
2 tablespoons butter	*1 cup light cream*
2 tablespoons whole-wheat pastry flour	*½ cup chopped Italian parsley*

1 Using a 3-quart, heavy saucepan, combine the chicken stock, broccoflower, and green onion. Bring to a boil. Reduce heat, cover, and simmer for 10 minutes, or just until the broccoflower is tender.

2 Remove from heat, and let the soup cool slightly. Carefully place the soup in the food processor and puree until very smooth.

3 Melt the butter in the saucepan over medium heat, and stir in the flour, marjoram, salt, and white pepper, stirring constantly to prevent lumps from forming. Gradually whisk in the light cream, whisking until the mixture is smooth.

4 Continue cooking over medium heat, stirring constantly, until the mixture begins to thicken and is bubbly (about 3 to 4 minutes). Stir in the puree of soup and heat to serving temperature. Sprinkle the parsley on top of the soup at serving time.

Tip: Optional garnishes for this soup include a dollop of sour cream, chopped Italian parsley, and green onions. You may use just one or a combination of all three.

Per serving: *Calories 217 (From Fat 172); Fat 19g (Saturated 11g); Cholesterol 57mg; Sodium 562mg; Carbohydrate 9g; Dietary Fiber 2g (Net Carbohydrate 7g); Protein 4g.*

Mozzarella Cheese Soup with Fresh Mushrooms

Hearty — that's what this soup is. Not only does it warm the cockles of your heart, but it's true old-fashioned comfort food! Combining mushrooms with mozzarella cheese in any recipe is always a sure bet, and this soup is no exception: Yep, another mouth-watering option for your low-carb lifestyle. Enjoy your soup and the cozy comfort too.

Preparation time: *20 minutes*

Cooking time: *45 minutes*

Yield: *6 servings*

1 medium onion, chopped	*2 pounds sliced fresh mushrooms*
1 carrot, quartered	*Juice of 1 lemon*
1 cup plus 3 tablespoons chopped fresh Italian parsley	*½ teaspoon salt*
	¼ teaspoon pepper
6 cups beef stock	*¾ cup grated reduced-fat mozzarella cheese*

1 In a stockpot, boil the onion, celery, carrot, and 1 cup parsley in the beef broth until tender. Remove from heat and let the vegetables cool slightly. Carefully puree the vegetables in the blender.

2 Return the pureed vegetables to the stockpot and simmer them over low heat while you prepare the mushrooms.

3 Sauté the mushrooms in the lemon juice just until tender (about 4 minutes). Add the mushrooms, salt, and pepper to the simmering broth and pureed vegetables.

4 Heat the soup to serving temperature. Ladle it into soup bowls and serve immediately sprinkled with the cheese and the remaining 3 tablespoons parsley.

Per serving: *Calories 112 (From Fat 26); Fat 3g (Saturated 2g); Cholesterol 8mg; Sodium 1,279mg; Carbohydrate 11g; Dietary Fiber 3g (Net Carbohydrate 8g); Protein 13g.*

Stopping for Soup around the World

Soup recipes that have been handed down through the ages and are an every-day menu item for folks living in a particular province or region may become a new adventure for you. Slurping as you go, discovering different staple soups from around the world is an adventure. In the world of soup, here are some places you might be off to:

- ✔ Russia or Poland for borscht
- ✔ China for its famous bird's nest soup
- ✔ West Africa for ground peanut soup
- ✔ Finland for bilberry soup
- ✔ Ireland for lamb soup
- ✔ Italy for minestrone
- ✔ Scotland for broth
- ✔ France for onion soup
- ✔ Mexico for chickpea soup
- ✔ England for mutton broth
- ✔ East India for mulligatawny
- ✔ Finally, a stop in Philly for some pepper pot soup

So grab your compass and your map, and take a little trip with me. (If Russian borscht is calling your name, see a great recipe in Chapter 16.) I include only a small sampling of the big world of soup, so I encourage you to branch out after you've made all the soup recipes in this book and begin your own inter-national recipe library. Your tummy will thank your adventuresome spirit.

German Cabbage Soup

This recipe transports you to Germany for a soup that'll warm your bones on a chilly night. Plop a dollop of sour cream on top when serving if you're so inclined. This is low-carb comfort food for sure. Serve with a side salad, and your meal is complete. I guarantee you'll be full and satisfied when you get up from the table.

Preparation time: *20 minutes*

Cooking time: *1½ hours*

Yield: *6 to 8 servings*

1 large head of green cabbage	*1 bay leaf*
2 quarts water	*3 sprigs fresh Italian parsley*
2 pounds beef chuck roast, cubed	*1 packet Splenda sugar substitute*
1 tablespoon salt	*1 tablespoon wine vinegar*
¼ teaspoon pepper	*1 sprig of fresh dill, chopped fine (or more to taste)*
1 medium yellow onion, sliced thin	
1 clove of garlic, crushed	*Sour cream for garnish (optional)*

1 Coarsely shred the cabbage. Set aside.

2 Put the water and chuck roast cubes in a large stockpot. Add the salt, pepper, onion, garlic, bay leaf, and parsley, and bring to a boil. Simmer, covered, for about 30 minutes.

3 Add the shredded cabbage, Splenda, vinegar, and dill. Cover and simmer for another 1 hour or until the meat is very tender (falling apart tender).

4 Serve piping hot with a dollop of sour cream, if desired.

Per serving: *Calories 171 (From Fat 48); Fat 5g (Saturated 2g); Cholesterol 10mg; Sodium 940mg; Carbohydrate 10g; Dietary Fiber 4g (Net Carbohydrate 6g); Protein 22g. (Analyzed for 8 servings.)*

Cold Mexican Shrimp Soup

This incredibly awesome soup is served ice cold. It's great any time but especially on a hot summer day. You can serve it as an appetizer or a main course. A friend came to my house and showed me how to make this authentic Mexican dish. For a great presentation, serve this soup in something clear and tall, like a round-bottomed beer goblet or big red wine glass. Tuck a lemon wedge on the side, and you've got elegance.

Preparation time: *30 minutes*

Cooking time: *1 minute*

Refrigeration time: *3 hours or overnight*

Yield: *6 servings*

1 pound medium shrimp

2 medium avocados

1 large lemon

1 finely chopped medium yellow onion

2 large tomatoes, diced

1 large cucumber, peeled, seeded, and diced

½ cup finely chopped cilantro

½ pound fresh crab, flaked

32-ounce jar clamato juice, chilled

Salt and pepper to taste

Lemon wedges for garnish

Additional finely chopped fresh cilantro for garnish (optional)

1 Peel and devein the shrimp and rinse well.

2 Bring about 2 quarts of water to a boil. Add the shrimp and cook for 1 minute. Drain the shrimp in a colander and run cold water over them. Set aside to cool further.

3 Dice the avocados and squeeze the juice of an entire lemon over them to prevent them from turning dark.

4 In a very large salad bowl, combine the shrimp, avocados, onion, tomatoes, cucumber, cilantro, and crab.

5 Add the clamato juice, mixing all the ingredients well. Salt and pepper to taste.

6 Refrigerate the soup for at least 3 hours before serving to allow flavors to mingle. This is better the longer it chills. If you can make it about 6 hours ahead of time, it's even more scrumptious!

7 Serve in tall, clear, round-bottomed glasses. Garnish with a lemon wedge tucked on the side of the glass and lightly sprinkle the top of each serving with cilantro if desired.

Per serving: *Calories 293 (From Fat 90); Fat 10g (Saturated 2g); Cholesterol 153mg; Sodium 925mg; Carbohydrate 28g; Dietary Fiber 7g (Net Carbohydrate 21g); Protein 25g.*

BLT Soup from the U.S.A.

An all-time favorite in the United States is the bacon, lettuce, and tomato sandwich. This great entrée soup is reminiscent of that sandwich, and it wakes up your taste buds as well as your nose. Close your eyes, and you can smell and taste the bacon, lettuce, and tomato sandwich that has been transformed into warm, wonderful soup — with no bread in sight. Serve with a side salad of your favorite greens, and you've created a masterpiece.

Preparation time: *20 minutes*

Cooking time: *50 minutes*

Yield: *6 servings*

8 slices bacon	2 tablespoons chopped fresh basil
1 large onion, chopped fine	1¼-inch by ½-inch strip orange zest
1 garlic clove, finely minced	1 teaspoon salt
2 carrots, peeled and chopped fine	1 packet Splenda sugar substitute
1 celery stalk, chopped	¼ teaspoon pepper
28-ounce can whole tomatoes in juice	6 tablespoons sour cream
3 cups beef stock	1½ cups shredded romaine lettuce

1 Using a 4-quart saucepan, cook the bacon until crispy (about 5 minutes). Drain the bacon on paper towels. Cut the bacon slices into ¼-inch strips.

2 Add the onion, garlic, carrots, and celery to the bacon drippings. Over moderate heat, cook until tender (about 8 minutes).

3 Stir in the can of tomatoes with juice, stock, basil, zest, salt, Splenda, and pepper. Bring to a boil. Reduce heat to low and simmer covered for about 30 minutes. Set aside to cool.

4 Remove the strip of orange zest. In batches, puree the mixture in the food processor until smooth. Return the pureed soup to the saucepan, and cook until heated through, approximately 5 minutes.

5 Serve in soup bowls. Top each serving with a 1-tablespoon dollop of sour cream and approximately ¼ cup of shredded lettuce. Then sprinkle each serving with crispy bacon.

Per serving: Calories 142 (From Fat 67); Fat 7g (Saturated 3g); Cholesterol 14mg; Sodium 1,249mg; Carbohydrate 13g; Dietary Fiber 3g (Net Carbohydrate 10g); Protein 7g.

↻ Caribbean Style Black Soybean Soup

I don't know about you, but I love black bean soup. Enjoy this spicy Caribbean black soybean soup. Low-carb never tasted so good.

Preparation time: *20 minutes*

Cooking time: *35 to 40 minutes*

Yield: *4 servings*

3 tablespoons olive oil

⅓ cup finely chopped yellow onion

2 cloves garlic, crushed

1 teaspoon oregano

2 teaspoons cumin

½ teaspoon dried red pepper, crushed

1 quart vegetable broth

2 cans (15 ounces each) Eden black soybeans, drained

1 bay leaf

Salt and pepper to taste

Sour cream, optional for garnish

Chopped chives, optional for garnish

1 In a small, heavy skillet, heat the olive oil over medium-high heat until hot. Add the onions, reduce the heat to medium-low and cook until soft. Don't brown the onions — you just want them transparent.

2 Transfer the onions to a large pot, adding the garlic, oregano, cumin, and red pepper. Cook over medium heat for 1 minute.

3 Add the vegetable broth, soybeans, bay leaf, and salt and pepper to taste. Simmer covered for 30 minutes. Remove the bay leaf.

4 Using your food processor, carefully puree 3 cups of the soup — it's hot. Return the puree to the stockpot and mix well. If necessary, thin with more vegetable broth.

5 If you opt for sour cream, plop it in the bottom of the soup bowl, and pour the hot black bean soup over it. Garnish with chopped chives if desired.

Per serving: Calories 227 (From Fat 119); Fat 13g (Saturated 1g); Cholesterol 0mg; Sodium 1,149mg; Carbohydrate 17g; Dietary Fiber 7g (Net Carbohydrate 10g); Protein 13g.

California Fishermen's Soup

LESS THAN **10**

California is a country, right? Okay, maybe not. But I want stop in San Francisco for some great fishermen's soup. Living in and near the fishing towns of California, I've learned that fishermen who cook their catch tend to cook it a bit differently. It's the taste of the fish they're after, not all the other stuff. This is a tomato-less fish soup, as a tomato base can cover up the true flavor of the fish at times. Enjoy this simply fish soup. (Swim over to Chapter 16 for a very different fish chowder slow cooker recipe.)

Preparation time: *25 minutes*

Cooking time: *20 minutes*

Yield: *6 generous serving*

¼ cup olive oil, divided	4 cups fish stock
2 celery stalks, diced fine	1½ cups dry white wine (not too acidic)
1 carrot, peeled and diced fine	1 pound fresh scallops
1 small leek, diced	1 teaspoon sea salt (or to taste)
2 shallots, chopped fine	2 tablespoons finely chopped fresh Italian parsley
½ pound fresh halibut, cut into 1-inch square pieces	2 tablespoons tarragon leaves
½ pound fresh haddock filets, cut into 1-inch square pieces	¼ cup minced fresh chives
½ pound fresh red snapper, cut into 1-inch square pieces	Pepper to taste
	Fresh Italian parsley for garnish (optional)

1 In a large heavy pot, heat 2 tablespoons olive oil over medium-high heat. Stir in the celery, carrot, leek, and shallots and cook until veggies are just crisp-tender, about 4 minutes.

2 Add the remaining 2 tablespoons of olive oil to the pan. Add the halibut, haddock, and snapper to the oil-and-veggie mix. Cook the fish until it's almost opaque, about 4 minutes.

3 Add the fish stock and the wine, stirring to combine the ingredients, and bring it to a slow boil. Lower the heat and let simmer for about 5 minutes.

4 Add the scallops and the salt. Cover and cook for 2 minutes. Add the parsley, tarragon, and chives. Season to taste with freshly ground black pepper.

5 Cook over medium-high heat until the soup returns to a boil. Remove from heat and serve immediately, garnishing each bowl of soup with parsley, if desired.

Per serving: Calories 332 (From Fat 114); Fat 13 (Saturated 2g); Cholesterol 86mg; Sodium 896mg; Carbohydrate 8g; Dietary Fiber 2g (Net Carbohydrate 6g); Protein 42g.

 To get the most flavored vegetable soups, use the freshest ingredients you can find. If you really want to spoil yourself, go to the farmer's market early on a Saturday or Sunday morning, buy your veggies, and go directly home and prepare your soup.

Chillin' with Soup

Soup isn't always about warming your tummy. You can serve cold soup as a dessert, as a cooling first course of a summer brunch, or even as a snack between meals. Most chilled fruit soups are purees that are sweetened and diluted with wine, fruit juice, or ice water. Many fruits, in addition to the ones I use here, can be used in soup such as strawberries, melons, peaches, pears, sour cherries, and oranges, to mention just a few.

If you're preparing cold soup to serve to guests and want it to be close to perfect, use a metal bowl when combining the ingredients and when chilling. The soup chills more quickly and more thoroughly this way.

○ Blender Blueberry Soup

This delicious cold blueberry soup is ready to serve in a few minutes. Try it as a dessert or with brunch on a hot summer day. If it's too thick for your liking, thin it with just a little white wine. The carb counts put this soup on the "treat" list. To slim down the counts further and still enjoy cold blueberry soup, skip the orange juice in this recipe and use yogurt that's as low in carb counts as possible.

Preparation time: *5 minutes*

Yield: *2 servings*

⅓ cup sour cream

1 cup plain yogurt

10-ounce package frozen blueberries, partially thawed

½ cup orange juice (use the low-carb kind if you'd like)

2 packets Splenda sugar substitute

2 thin lemon slices for garnish

Dash of cinnamon for garnish (optional)

1 Place the sour cream, yogurt, blueberries, orange juice, and Splenda in a blender. Blend on low speed until smooth.

2 Serve garnished with thin, curly lemon slices and a dash of cinnamon, if desired.

Per serving: Calories 263 (From Fat 98); Fat 11g (Saturated 6g); Cholesterol 24mg; Sodium 108mg; Carbohydrate 35g; Dietary Fiber 4g (Net Carbohydrate 31g); Protein 9g.

⏱ Chilled Raspberry Soup

Talk about a way to make an impression. After you've served your girlfriends a fantastic brunch, top it off with this Chilled Raspberry Soup for dessert. Add a delightful coffee drink, and you have yourself a winner. It's so simple, yet so divine.

Preparation time: *20 minutes*

Cooking time: *25 minutes*

Refrigeration time: *6 to 8 hours*

Yield: *About 6 1-cup servings*

2 packages (10 ounces each) frozen red raspberries, thawed

2 cups dry red wine (Burgundy works)

2½ cups water

3-inch cinnamon stick

¼ cup Splenda sugar substitute

1½ tablespoons cornstarch

Whipped cream

1 Combine the raspberries, wine, water, cinnamon, and sugar substitute in a deep, stainless steel saucepan.

2 Bring the mixture to a boil. Reduce heat and simmer over low heat for 15 minutes.

3 Press the raspberry mixture through a sieve placed over a bowl to catch the juices. Discard the seeds (if the seeds don't bother you, skip this step — I do).

4 In a small bowl, combine ¼ cup of the raspberry liquid and the cornstarch, stirring well. Bring the remaining liquid to a boil. Reducing the heat to low, stir in the cornstarch mixture.

5 Stirring constantly, cook until slightly thickened. Chill for 6 to 8 hours.

6 Serve chilled soup with a dollop of freshly whipped cream.

Per serving: *Calories 89 (From Fat 30); Fat 3g (Saturated 2g); Cholesterol 10mg; Sodium 3mg; Carbohydrate 14g; Dietary Fiber 6g (Net Carbohydrate 8g); Protein 1g.*

Chapter 8

Building More Than Just a Salad

*T*he low-carb lifestyle encourages eating generous daily amounts of leafy greens — the greener the better. But if you're like many low-carbers, you may find yourself slipping into that culinary black hole of salad boredom. You know the drill — chop lettuce, add sliced tomatoes, pour on bottled dressing, eat, and repeat. The routine gets so old that most people don't even come close to their low-carb daily allowance of greens and veggies.

But I'm here to remind you that salads don't have to be *just salads*. With the endless alternatives for building easy, fast, and great salads, you can quickly jump out of that rut and take advantage of the all the wonderful options salads present, as an essential staple of the low-carb diet.

The green leafy stuff is essential to healthy low-carb eating because it fills you up, not out. (The same can be said for other veggies as well, and I return to the garden in Chapter 12.) Greens are often overlooked and underestimated in the low-carb lifestyle. Yet most greens are so low in carbs and high in fiber that they make the almost perfect low-carb food. You'll be delightfully and healthfully surprised as you begin to build more and more greens into your eating plan. This leafy stuff is almost as good as a life insurance policy.

Building a Better Salad: Balancing Tastes, Textures, and Colors

Combining colors, flavors, ingredients, and seasonings in creative salad ways not only wakes up your taste buds, but it also provides you a beautiful rainbow of health benefits too good to pass up. Discovering lettuce in colors from bright green to red with textures ranging from almost buttery soft to peppery and crunchy is an easy assignment. I encourage you to use the freshest and finest ingredients for success in building better salads. Welcoming enticing newcomers to your familiar salad favorites is a great way to begin. (See the list of greens in the "Checking out the greens guide" section for the inside story of some greens that you may or may not be familiar with.)

Embracing the low-carb lifestyle with lots of the green stuff as a basic component puts you in a great position on the yellow brick road to wellness, which is exactly where you want to be — carb correct and healthy! Besides their carb-counting appeal, greens offer the obvious nutritional benefits of vitamins, minerals, and fiber. Plus *phytochemicals,* the new star of the nutritional stage, are everywhere in the green stuff. Experts have recently documented more than 25,000 phytos. After they're inside our bodies, this little army of phytochemicals unites as a team to fight diseases such as heart disease, certain cancers, high blood pressure, stroke, and diabetes. (Check out Chapter 12 for more info on veggies and phytos.) Leafy dark-green vegetables also supercharge your diet with vitamins A and C, riboflavin, folic acid, iron, calcium, magnesium, and potassium, along with a fine supply of antioxidants. Plus, an overlooked biggie of salad greens is that they're a source of much needed fiber in your overall healthy diet. (See more on the importance of fiber in Chapter 3.)

The darker colored parts of vegetables and fruits are known to have a higher concentration of phytochemicals and valuable nutrients. For instance, the dark green leaves of lettuce are richer in nutrients than the lighter green or whitish leaves. So pick the freshest and the darkest greens you can find!

Build meals around salads, or build salads around meals. You can choose salads to prepare in advance or salads that are quick to fix. The secret is making sure you have the necessary ingredients on hand so your salad is ready when you are. Sneaking extra healthy veggies into your salads not only adds variety and crunch to your salads, but it also results in more health benefits for you.

Turning over a new leaf

Once upon a time when you thought of salad, you may have expected an angular chunk of iceberg lettuce presented in the middle of a small salad plate with a dollop of mayonnaise on top. If you were lucky, you may have gotten a half-ripened slice of tomato, too. However, a new leaf has been turned over in low-carb salads.

The essence of low-carb salads begins with freshness and ends only with your creativity and a bit of boldness. Low-carb salads are hot and cold, pickled and marinated, side dishes or the main fare, a solid buffet presentation or a festive party snack. Low in carbs, high in health — are you sold? If so, here are a few suggestions for fitting more leafy greens into your diet:

- ✔ Make a concerted effort to double your normal daily portion of the green and leafy.

- ✔ Experiment with one new leafy green and veggie recipe every week. (See the "Checking out the greens guide: Lettuce begin" section later in this chapter for tips on introducing a variety of greens to your salad bowl.)

- ✔ Keep a variety of frozen vegetables in your freezer to add to your fresh greens just in case you don't have fresh veggies available or you're in a hurry.

- ✔ Build your spice cabinet, and experiment with different spices. You'll be amazed by what a little sprinkling can do for your salad building, and your taste buds will applaud your creativity.

- ✔ Eat more salads as entrees. Doing so may even leave a little room both carb count-wise and in your tummy for a special low-carb sweet treat. The trade-offs can be very positive (see some yummy sweets in Chapter 13).

Perhaps the best way to build salads more quickly and easily is to take advantage of all those different combinations of packaged fresh greens, veggies, and even coleslaw. With the convenience of fresh, packaged salad greens and ready-to-go veggies, building enticing low-carb salads is a snap. These mixtures make it easy to try lots of different kinds of greens and mix them with your favorite veggies without having to purchase entire bunches or heads of the leafy green stuff. Here are a few points to consider:

- ✔ When purchasing bags of mixed, prewashed lettuce and greens, pay close attention to the date stamped on the bag. Buy wise, and select the *use by* date that's as far ahead in the future as possible for added freshness.

- ✔ Although washing these packaged greens and veggies isn't necessary, I always give them a quick rinse and pop them in a plastic bag to make them a bit crisper and more alive.

Eating any of the green leafy stuff is better than not eating any at all!

Checking out the greens guide

As you begin to paint some green into your diet, you'll notice the many varieties of lettuce and greens to choose from. Remember, variety is the spice of the low-carb lifestyle, so mix it up! Here's a little lettuce lesson to help you make your decisions about which greens to buy (you can check out what some of these fine little fellas look like in Figure 8-1):

- **Arugula:** Full of bittersweet flavor, this stuff has skinny, notched leaves. Some folks like it by itself; I like to mix it with other greens.

- **Belgian or French endive:** Smooth and elongated, these endives have compact heads of slender, crisp leaves and a slightly bitter flavor that makes them taste best when mixed with other greens.

- **Bibb lettuce:** No, you don't wear this lettuce around your neck! Bibb lettuce has little heads of very tender and silky feeling leaves. It's very mild — almost sweet. You can serve this one alone or with other lettuces.

- **Boston lettuce:** Boston lettuce is similar to Bibb lettuce in texture, because it feels kind of buttery and is very tender. It's perfect all alone or mixed with other lettuce.

- **Chinese cabbage:** This cabbage consists of long, slender, tightly closed heads of wide-ribbed tender leaves. The flavor is mild, and it can be served alone or mixed.

- **Curly endive:** Leaves are curly and fringy. Endive has a very sharp, bitter taste, so you can mix it with milder greens for a pleasing combo.

- **Dandelion:** No, dandelions aren't weeds! They're actually very good for you. The leaves are jagged, a bit bitter and tangy in flavor, and rich in calcium and vitamin A. Dandelions leaves can be eaten raw in salads, or they can be steamed as a veggie dish. *Dandelion* is a French word, *dent de lion,* which means "lion's tooth."

  Be careful not to gather dandelions for consumption out of a yard that has been sprayed with chemicals and pesticides.

- **Escarole:** No, not the snails! This is big lettuce with very wide and crisp, flat leaves that curl on the edges. It's a little on the bitter side, so I vote to mix it with other types of lettuce.

- **Frisée:** Frisée is type of chicory, which is frequently used in mesclun (see more about mesclun below). The attractive pale green leaves are narrow and curly with a frizzy appearance and a slightly bitter taste.

- **Iceberg:** Good ol' iceberg lettuce is 90 percent water and has very little flavor — and almost no nutrients. Iceberg is a firmly packed head of leaves similar looking to a head of cabbage. It isn't a good choice for because you might as well eat something that's going to give you some great nutrients while you're munching.

✔ **Mesclun:** Mesclun is a somewhat expensive, mysterious mix that's available by the pound in the produce department of the grocery store. You can sometimes find it in a bag, pre-washed and ready to go. Mesclun is a dandy little mix of very young, tiny salad greens. I cheat and buy just a little for a special salad and mix it with other greens for added zest.

✔ **Parsley:** Not just another garnish, fresh parsley can add an unidentifiable bite to salads, so don't overlook it.

✔ **Radicchio:** This little, usually expensive stuff is light red to rose-colored with a slightly bitter flavor. Its texture is firm, and it brightens up the dish when it's mixed. A little goes a long way.

✔ **Red and green leaf lettuce:** Leaves are broad, tender, and loose, with a mild and delicate flavor. This lettuce may be curly and green or red-tipped and can be served alone or mixed with other greens.

✔ **Romaine:** This lettuce is the great stuff that Caesar makes his salads out of. Very firm and crisp with a hint of nutty flavor, romaine is perfect served alone or with other greens.

✔ **Savoy cabbage:** This crinkle-like leaf of green cabbage has a milder flavor than red or green cabbage.

✔ **Sorrel:** This type of green has long, crisp, arrow-shaped leaves with a sour and pungent flavor. It tastes best mixed with other lettuces.

✔ **Spinach:** Spinach salad is great by itself or as a welcome addition blended with other greens. Be sure to trim away the tough stems because they can be very bitter.

✔ **Watercress:** The stems are tough, so cut them off and throw them away. Otherwise, watercress is very crispy with a little peppery flavor. I prefer to mix it with other greens.

Use fresh, fresh greens that are as blemish-free as possible and that have been carefully washed, dried, and stored properly in the refrigerator for crispness.

A good guide when wondering how many salad greens to combine if you're not buying prepared salad mixes is to use three basic greens (and then add everything but the kitchen sink).

Figure 8-1:
It's a green, green world.

✋ Arugula, Radicchio, and Goat Cheese Salad

This salad will make your mouth sing with the combination of the robust flavors bursting with the barely bitter leaves of the radicchio gently tossed with the bittersweet arugula. The goat cheese adds an unmistakable flavor that wakes up your taste buds.

Preparation time: *12 minutes*

Yield: *6 servings*

2 shallots, peeled and sliced very thin	¼ teaspoon salt
1 garlic clove, minced fine	¼ teaspoon pepper
3 tablespoons extra virgin olive oil	10 ounces arugula
3 tablespoons red wine vinegar	2 heads radicchio
2 packets Splenda sugar substitute	4 ounces soft goat cheese
2 tablespoons fresh Italian parsley	

1 Combine the shallots, garlic, oil, vinegar, Splenda, parsley, salt, and pepper in a medium bowl. Whisk together until well combined. Set aside.

2 Combine the arugula and radicchio in a large salad bowl, tearing the greens into bite-sized pieces.

3 Pour the oil and vinegar mixture over the prepared greens, tossing gently just to coat. Allow the dish to sit and the flavors to mingle for 4 to 5 minutes. Crumble the goat cheese over the salad. Toss again.

4 Divide on six salad plates and serve immediately.

Per serving: *Calories 133 (From Fat 100); Fat 11g (Saturated 4g); Cholesterol 9mg; Sodium 185mg; Carbohydrate 4g; Dietary Fiber 1g (Net Carbohydrate 3g); Protein 5g.*

Marinated Fresh Garden Salad

 5

You can add extra zest to this salad by briefly marinating the vegetables before adding the greens. Your taste buds will ask, "What's different about this salad?" These greens have extra crunch that's sure to please salad lovers. I think this salad is especially good served with chicken as the main dish.

Preparation time: *10 minutes*

Refrigeration time: *1 hour*

Yield: *6 servings*

½ cup sliced cucumber

½ cup thinly sliced celery

½ cup thinly sliced carrots

½ cup thinly sliced red radishes

½ cup bottled Italian salad dressing

6 cups salad greens, torn into bite-sized pieces

1 Combine the cucumber, celery, carrots, and radishes in a large bowl. Add the salad dressing, and toss until coated. Refrigerate for 1 hour.

2 Just before serving, add the salad greens, and gently toss together until well mixed. Serve on cold salad plates, if desired to retain the crispy crunch of the salad.

Per serving: *Calories 110 (From Fat 87); Fat 10g (Saturated 1g); Cholesterol 0mg; Sodium 183mg; Carbohydrate 6g; Dietary Fiber 2g (Net Carbohydrate 4g); Protein 1g.*

Lettuce begin painting salads with boldness

Salads are one of the mainstays of the low-carb lifestyle and are a palette to paint whatever you desire. I say, paint with boldness. Try something new regularly, and break the mold of salad rut and routine. Remember the sky is the limit when picking enhancements for salad building.

Edible flowers

Edible flowers can make a salad very special, so experiment with tossing some around! Did you know the more fragrant the flower, the more flavorful the blossom is? You can find these lovelies in the produce section of many grocery stores. Edible flowers to look for are lavender, nasturtiums, violets, rose petals, geraniums, dianthus, and lobelia.

Salad Spinning 101

Do yourself a favor and acquire a "lettuce life-saver" — a salad spinner. This simple kitchen gadget makes drying greens quick and easy. The salad spinner is a two-part device with a large plastic bowl on the outside and a plastic basket on the inside. When shopping for your salad spinner, you choose between a few different styles — a crank, pull-cord, or push-button machine style. All of them work equally well; however, my personal preference is the crank-style.

After thoroughly washing the greens, place them in the inside basket, which is usually large enough to hold a whole head of lettuce. Let the spin begin! You'll be amazed at the high speed this little rascal spins. The water literally flies off the greens, leaving them fresh, clean, and crisp. The spinner is easy to clean and a must for the low-carb salad enthusiast. Spinners aren't expensive, and lately I've even seen them at the dollar stores. So spin on.

salad spinner

You can add just about anything — including leftovers:

- ✔ Top your salads with berries when in season (see the "Squeezing in berries and fruits" section later in the chapter)
- ✔ Sprinkle nuts on top of your salad for texture and crunch.
- ✔ Add rings of red onion for flavor and color.
- ✔ Add meats, fish, or seafood to make your salad a real meal. (Check out the Tomato and Beef Salad with Red Wine Vinaigrette recipe in the "Dressing Up Low-Carb Salads" section later in the chapter.)
- ✔ Add cheeses of all different kinds. Cheeses in your low-carb salads help fill you up, not out. And who says you can only have one kind of cheese on a salad? Simply not true.
- ✔ Experiment with homemade salad dressings. They're so easy to prepare, and I guarantee if you just give them a try, you'll take bottled dressings off your grocery list (see easy and quick dressing recipes in the "Dressing Up Low-Carb Salads" section later in this chapter).

⟡ Stir-Fried Lettuce

This is kind of a modern day form of the old-fashioned wilted lettuce, but I like it so much more. I gardened with my grandfather as a child, and wilted lettuce was one of his all-time favorites. We'd pick lettuce from the garden just before supper. Back then, it was made with bacon drippings that we saved. And if you want to pick one lettuce that's your favorite, that's dandy too. The trick to making this dish really special is to be sure not to overcook the lettuces. You want the leaves to be wilted but not droopy. You can serve this with anything your little heart desires, and I'm sure you'll get rave reviews. I like this served with anything from steak to lemon-chicken. The added touch of warming your salad plates underscores the flavors of this dish. If you want to toast the sesame seeds in this recipe, go for it by checking out the "Sesame seeds: Toast of the town" sidebar in this chapter.

Preparation time: *10 minutes*

Cooking time: *3 minutes*

Yield: *4 servings*

2 tablespoons olive oil	6 cups mixed lettuces torn into pieces
1 clove garlic, minced fine	1 tablespoon soy sauce
1-inch piece fresh gingerroot, peeled and grated	1 tablespoon sesame seeds

1 Place 4 ovenproof salad bowls in the oven at 325 degrees to warm.

2 Heat the oil in a heavy skillet over medium heat. Add the garlic and gingerroot, and stir for about 15 seconds.

3 Add the lettuce combination, quickly turning to mix with the hot oil. Continue cooking and turning constantly until the lettuce is wilted. This will take no longer than 2 minutes total, and it could be less if you use soft lettuces.

4 Divide the lettuce into the warm serving bowls. Toss with soy sauce and sprinkle with sesame seeds.

Variation: *Try this recipe using just spinach instead of a combination of lettuces if you love spinach as much as I do.*

Per serving: *Calories 89 (From Fat 71); Fat 8g (Saturated 1g); Cholesterol 0mg; Sodium 252mg; Carbohydrate 3g; Dietary Fiber 2g (Net Carbohydrate 1g); Protein 2g.*

Squeezing in berries and fruits

Adorn your low-carb salads with berries and fruits of the season. Not only do berries and fruits add a bounty of color contrast against a plate of salad greens, but they're also at their juiciest and most flavorful when in season. Along with the great flavor come great sources of Vitamin C and other nutrients — all part of the big picture of your healthy low-carb lifestyle.

Salads with berries tossed on top pique interest in the dish and add zest to the taste. Adding berries to salads has always been touted as a California thing. If that's the case, thank you California.

If your goal is to make the most perfect salad possible, begin by chilling the salad bowl that you're going to mix the ingredients in. Take it a step further and chill the serving plates for about 20 minutes in advance of serving. These steps will guarantee your salads to crackle when you eat them. If you don't have time for both steps, opt for chilling the serving plates!

Sesame seeds: Toast of the town

Sesame seeds can be used as an addition to any salad recipe. If you really want to add some more flavor, try toasting the seeds if you have time. It intensifies the flavor of this nutty little seed and makes them almost buttery. Toasting sesame seeds takes little time — you just need to stay with them. Just take a heavy, dry skillet and heat the seeds over medium heat stirring constantly until the seeds are golden brown (only about 3 to 5 minutes max). The little rascals will get really fragrant while you're toasting them. Don't leave them sit in the skillet or they'll continue to toast, and they may burn. Turn them out of the skillet as soon as they're golden brown and smelling fine. If you want to store them, place them in a tightly sealed jar at room temperature.

Berry Peachy Greens and Turkey Salad

Adding berries and nuts to any of your favorite green salads makes them come alive and become very palate pleasing. Be sure to watch for fresh berries on sale and in season, and take advantage of enjoying them in this recipe and in all your salad adventures. If fresh peaches are out of season, you can substitute thawed, frozen peaches.

Preparation time: *20 minutes*

Yield: *6 servings*

1 medium fresh peach	¼ cup olive oil
2 cups fresh strawberries	¼ cup sugar-free peach preserves
1 cup fresh blueberries	2 tablespoons balsamic vinegar
6 cups packaged mixed greens	½ cup toasted pecan pieces
2 cups cubed cooked turkey	

1 Wash the peach, strawberries, and blueberries in a colander under cold water. Slice the peach very thin, and cut the strawberries in half.

2 In a large salad bowl, combine the salad greens, turkey, blueberries, strawberries, and peach slices. Mix well.

3 To make the dressing, combine the olive oil, peach preserves, and vinegar in a small bowl. Mix well using a small whisk.

4 Pour the dressing over the salad and toss just to coat. Sprinkle with pecans.

Per serving: Calories 261 (From Fat 162); Fat 18g (Saturated 3g); Cholesterol 36mg; Sodium 49mg; Carbohydrate 12g; Dietary Fiber 3g (Net Carbohydrate 9g); Protein 16g.

Simple and quick green salad combos

Taking advantage of all the market-fresh choices at your fingertips is easy — and it doesn't even require a recipe. Use some of these ideas to get started:

- Torn Boston lettuce leaves, radicchio, arugula, walnuts, and crumbled goat cheese, tossed with your choice of vinaigrette.

- Quick Greek Salad: torn mixed green combo, minced fresh mint leaves, chopped fresh Italian parsley, crumbled feta cheese, and chopped pitted black olives. Simply drizzle with olive oil and squeeze with fresh lemon juice.

- Torn romaine lettuce, ribbon slices of turkey breast, walnuts, red onion rings, chopped fresh pear. Just add vinaigrette of your choice.

- Torn spinach leaves, sliced fresh mushrooms, thinly sliced red onion rings, finely chopped hard cooked egg, a couple thin slices of fresh orange. Add vinaigrette of your choice.

Tomato Power

Although tomatoes have had a reputation for being a little high in carb count, the health benefits far outweigh the carbs. A small tomato has approximately 3.5 net grams of carbs. You no longer have to be tomato-deprived in your low-carb lifestyle.

The luscious red color of the tomato is produced by an antioxidant called *lycopene.* This powerful nutrient plays a role in delaying cancer cells from one phase to the next, as well as protecting cell damage and assisting in the aging process. This superman of an antioxidant has been proven to reduce the risk of breast, prostate, colon, and other cancers. The citric acid in this red veggie also aids your kidneys in flushing toxins out of your body. Tomatoes are also rich in vitamin A, vitamin E, potassium, iron, and fiber. And just so you know, green tomatoes don't contain lycopene.

It turns out that tomatoes are healthier for you when they're cooked. Tomatoes contain a lot of water, and as they're cooked, the water evaporates and they become more concentrated. So if you have a half-cup of raw tomatoes versus a half-cup of cooked tomatoes in the form of tomato sauce, the sauce is a much more concentrated form of lycopene.

Cherry Tomato and Mozzarella Salad

This is a simple salad that just can't be beat, especially if you have cherry tomatoes that not only look and taste like tomatoes but smell like tomatoes too. This salad can be served with almost anything, and it's great as a snack at your desk.

Preparation time: *20 minutes*

Yield: *8 servings*

4 cups red cherry tomatoes	*2 tablespoons olive oil*
8 ounces small fresh mozzarella cheese balls	*¼ teaspoon sea salt*
½ cup fresh basil leaves, loosely packed	*Pepper to taste (optional)*

1 Rinse the cherry tomatoes. With a very sharp knife, cut the tomatoes in half and place them in a medium-sized serving bowl.

2 Carefully drain the mozzarella cheese, and cut each mozzarella ball into quarters.

3 Rinse the basil leaves under cold water and tear in very small pieces.

4 Add the mozzarella cheese pieces and the basil to the tomatoes.

5 Drizzle with olive oil and lightly sprinkle with sea salt. Top with freshly ground black pepper if desired.

Per serving: Calories 127 (From Fat 87); Fat 10g (Saturated 5g); Cholesterol 22mg; Sodium 119mg; Carbohydrate 4g; Dietary Fiber 1g (Net Carbohydrate 3g); Protein 6g.

Did you ever think that anything so delicious could be so good for you? You can find hundreds of varieties of the tomato today, all relatives of the original garden variety. Some that you'll be familiar with are the beefsteak, the Italian plum, and the sweet red cherry tomato. The tomato volunteers for the role of enhancing salads and playing a tasty part in hearty soups and great sauces. You can serve the tomato alone, sliced with salt and pepper, or you can gently stuff it with a variety of goodies and serve it as a main course. Go ahead — put fresh tomatoes in your low-carb salads, and use canned tomatoes in your cooking.

Watch for added sugar in canned tomatoes. Tomatoes have some natural sugars, but read the labels — you'll find a vast difference in various brands. You probably won't find any without some added sugars, just choose the ones with the lowest sugar possible.

Calico Tomato Salad

This is a very old recipe from my gardening days, so I've had it in my recipe collection for many years. It's a beautiful salad and easy to prepare. Be sure to use very ripe, firm, and red tomatoes for this salad, so the true homegrown tomato flavor comes out.

Preparation time: *15 minutes*

Yield: *8 servings*

5 medium tomatoes	*2 tablespoon minced fresh parsley*
1 small zucchini	*¼ teaspoon seasoned salt*
1 small sweet yellow pepper	*½ teaspoon dried basil*
¼ cup cider vinegar	*¼ teaspoon dried marjoram*
2 tablespoons olive oil	*⅛ teaspoon pepper*

1 Cut the tomatoes, zucchini, and yellow pepper in ½-inch pieces. Place them in a flat serving bowl.

2 Combine the vinegar, oil, parsley, seasoned salt, basil, marjoram, and pepper in a jar with a tight-fitting lid and shake well. Pour over the vegetables and toss. Serve immediately.

Per serving: Calories 56 (From Fat 34); Fat 4g (Saturated 1g); Cholesterol 0mg; Sodium 57mg; Carbohydrate 6g; Dietary Fiber 1g (Net Carbohydrate 5g); Protein 1g.

If you plant a garden and have an abundance of tomatoes during the season, try freezing them. When I had a huge garden in the Midwest, I picked ripe but solid tomatoes (in other words, not mushy). Rinse them well and core them like you would an apple. Then place them on waxed paper on a cookie sheet, and put them in the freezer. After they're frozen, place them in plastic bags and put them back in the freezer. They aren't good to eat sliced after they're frozen; however, they're great in soups, chili, and sauces. The skins come off during cooking, and you can take a slotted spoon and skim them off and throw them away. But be sure not to peel them: Not only do they freeze better with their skins on, but a lot of the nutrients are in the skin.

Use your nose when you buy tomatoes, whether at the grocery store or at a farmer's market. Stick your nose up to the stem end of the tomato, close your eyes, and take a sniff. Does it smell like a tomato? If not, put it down and try again. A tomato passes the good tomato test when it has great color, has taut skin, and smells like a tomato.

Beefing Up Your Salad

Check your fridge. Almost any leftover from steamed veggies to grilled steak can turn a little ol' green salad into a meal. In addition to the veggies and the meat or maybe fish, add some cubes or thin slices of cheese, sprinkle with your favorite nuts for crunch, and top with your favorite homemade dressing. Voilà — quick, easy, and filling. When you eat fresh and healthy, you'll find that staying in tune with your low-carb lifestyle is a snap. And look out for the increased energy that you'll have.

Tomato and Beef Salad with Red Wine Vinaigrette

Use this as a basic supper salad, but feel free to add more ingredients. Substitute your favorite cheese or a combination of cheeses in place of the blue cheese. And if you don't have beef in the fridge but you do have turkey, use turkey. I think you get my drift here. My purpose in giving you this recipe is for you to follow the steps as written if you want to, but also to inspire your boldness in salad building. It's an ongoing project.

Preparation time: *30 minutes*

Cooking time: *10 minutes*

Yield: *4 servings*

1 small red onion	4 ounces blue cheese
2 heads Boston lettuce	Red Wine Vinaigrette (see the following recipe)
1 bunch arugula	
½ pound thinly sliced deli roast beef	Pepper to taste
1 medium tomato, thinly sliced	

1 Slice the red onion and separate into rings.

2 Divide the lettuce onto 4 salad plates. Sprinkle the arugula over the lettuce.

3 Arrange the roast beef slices, tomato, and onions on the greens. Sprinkle with cheese.

4 Dress with Red Wine Vinaigrette, and top with black pepper.

Red Wine Vinaigrette

¼ cup olive oil	4 teaspoons red wine vinegar
1 teaspoon Dijon mustard	⅛ teaspoon salt
1 small green onion, finely chopped	Pepper to taste

Combine olive oil, mustard, onion, vinegar, salt, and pepper, mixing well with wire whisk.

Tip: *Instead of dividing the salad onto 4 salad plates, you can put it in a big salad bowl for one (maybe two). If you're having guests for dinner then double the recipe for a lovely large salad that will be a real pleaser.*

Per serving: *Calories 311 (From Fat 215); Fat 24g (Saturated 8g); Cholesterol 49mg; Sodium 1,085mg; Carbohydrate 7g; Dietary Fiber 2g (Net Carbohydrate 5g); Protein 19g.*

Dressing Up Low-Carb Salads

Tossing is an art, and dressing is the medium you use to accomplish perfect tossing. Always add the oil first, and toss just until the leaves are coated, giving the greens a bit of armor and discouraging wilting. Simply adding lemon juice or vinegar and a dash of salt and freshly ground black pepper results in a close to perfect salad.

You can quickly and easily make dressings with some tasty combos in the food processor or blender. Let's hear it for homemade salad dressings! Don't let the word *homemade* intimidate you and make you think you're going to be slaving in the kitchen for hours. You're going to love homemade salad dressings so much that you'll only have a store-bought dressing in your low-carb fridge "just in case." Bottled dressing will become your back-up, and homemade will become an everyday staple. Trust me here. Your palate is going to direct you on this one. When you think of *vinaigrette,* you may assume it's a boring combination of oil and acid, but it's so much more. The oil coats the greens to keep them from wilting, and the vinegars, herbs, and spices make your mouth sing.

The basic recipe for successful vinaigrette is a base proportion of one part vinegar to three parts oil, however — and this is a big however — adjust this to your own personal taste. You may like a little more bite so add more vinegar. You can use different types of oils, infused and flavored vinegars, and any herbs and spices to your liking. Here's a jumping off place for you to get started in creating your own special variations of basic vinaigrette. After you get started with all the great oils, vinegars, and a dash of this and a pinch of that, there won't be any stopping you. Try these variations using the one-part vinegar to three parts oil formula as your starting point.

✔ **Garlic Vinaigrette:** Just add 1 clove of garlic, finely minced.

✔ **Dried Herb Combo Vinaigrette:** Combine ½ cup of each of the following: marjoram, savory, basil, parsley, and thyme. Keep in an airtight container. Add 1 tablespoon of the mixed herbs to a new batch of vinaigrette. Let the herbs mingle and breathe for about 30 minutes before serving, or prepare several hours before and store in the fridge until serving time.

✔ **Toasted Sesame Seed Vinaigrette:** Just add 1 teaspoon of toasted sesame seeds, ½ clove minced garlic and 1 packet of Splenda sugar substitute. Try using rice vinegar in this combination. (See the "Sesame seeds: Toast of the town" sidebar for a quick toasting lesson.)

✔ **Lemon or Lime Vinaigrette:** Just add two tablespoons freshly squeezed lemon or lime.

• **Lemon Dill Vinaigrette:** Just add 2 teaspoons dill, minced fine. Let the flavors mingle for about 20 minutes before serving.

• **Lemon Thyme Vinaigrette:** Just add ½ teaspoon finely minced fresh thyme. Let the flavors mingle for about 20 minutes before serving.

In making your vinaigrette whisk together all of the ingredients except the oil, adding the oil last, slowly in a steady stream whisking as you go. If you're adding fresh herbs wait until just before dressing your salad before adding them. Or throw the ingredients in a jar with a tight-fitting lid, and shake well. You'll soon throw away the recipe and just build your own from scratch — another accomplishment for you in low-carb living.

After you find a basic vinaigrette that you like, you can begin to experiment with flavored oils (walnut or hazelnut, for example) and vinegars (like raspberry or balsamic), adding fresh-squeezed lemon or lime juice and a variety of herbs and spices. The magnifying effects of herbs and spices are probably more appreciated in a fresh salad than any other dish because a salad is so light and fresh itself. The great news about cooking with herbs and spices is that for the most part, they're all very low in both carbs and calories.

Be sure to check the labels on flavored vinegars for sugars, hidden or otherwise (see Chapter 3 on label reading). This also goes for Dijon mustards that are a great addition to vinaigrettes.

The French connection

This may come as a surprise to you but the basic dressing of the French isn't "French dressing" as you know it — red and in a bottle! The preferred salad dressing of the French is a very simple combination of good oil, great wine vinegar, freshly ground pepper, and salt. Sometimes garlic is added, especially in the South of France, and a little mustard may be thrown in as well. When fresh herbs are in season, it's whatever you want to toss in like dill, thyme, rosemary — your call.

The word *vinegar* comes from the French *vin aigre,* meaning soured wine. Vinegars have an average of about 6 percent acidity and keep for a long time if they're sealed. As a good bottle of wine reacts to the air, so does vinegar. The shelf life for vinegar to keep its bite is about 6 months.

☺ *Greens with Walnut Dressing*

Each time you make this salad, try a different mix of greens. I've added mesclun to this recipe just for fun. But it's only an option, and using another type of lettuce won't take away from the recipe. A sprinkling of edible flowers makes this salad a special occasion. (See the "Edible flowers" sidebar in this chapter for more information.)

Preparation time: 20 minutes

Yield: 4 half-cup servings

5 to 6 cups packaged mixed greens	*½ cup walnut pieces*
½ cup mesclun (optional)	*Walnut Dressing (see the following recipe)*
1 ripe pear, washed and chopped	*Edible flowers of your choice, such as nasturtiums (optional)*

1 Put the greens, mesclun, if desired, chopped pear, and walnuts in a big bowl for tossing.

2 Pour the Walnut Dressing over the salad and gently toss. Serve on clear glass plates that have been chilled in the freezer.

3 Garnish with edible flowers, if desired.

Walnut Dressing

2 tablespoons walnut oil	*1 clove garlic, crushed*
1 tablespoon extra-virgin olive oil	*¼ teaspoon dried summer savory*
2 tablespoons white wine vinegar	*¼ teaspoon salt*
1 teaspoon Dijon mustard	

Combine the walnut oil, olive oil, vinegar, mustard, garlic, savory, and salt in a jar with a very tight-fitting lid (like an old peanut butter jar). Shake until well blended. Chill until serving time.

Per serving: Calories 211 (From Fat 170); Fat 19g (Saturated 2g); Cholesterol 0mg; Sodium 196mg; Carbohydrate 11g; Dietary Fiber 4g (Net Carbohydrate 7g); Protein 3g.

You don't want to be underdressed when you go to a gala, but the ultimate embarrassment is to be overdressed for the occasion. The same goes for salad dressings — overdressing is a soggy no-no. I can't stress enough not to overdress your salad. For 8 cups of loosely packed greens, ¼–⅓ cup of dressing is adequate. You should dress your salads at serving time, because the same ingredients that perk up a salad — citrus juices and vinegars — also make the salad go limp if not eaten promptly.

Chapter 9

Living a Low-Carb Life by the Sea

In This Chapter

▶ Being aware of the healthy benefits of fish

▶ Finding out how to buy and prepare fish

▶ Discovering fun ways to cook your fish

▶ Grilling and broiling your fish

▶ Incorporating shellfish into your low-carb lifestyle

Recipes in This Chapter

▶ Lemon-Thyme Halibut en Papillote

▶ Steamed Trout

▶ Grilled Salmon Steaks

▶ Mustard-Dilled Red Snapper

▶ Sole with Lemon and Garlic Sauce

▶ Swordfish Piccata

▶ Blackened Catfish

▶ Shrimp Scampi

▶ Shrimp and Scallop Combo

*A*while back, you couldn't enjoy fresh sea fare unless you lived close to the sea. Well, my low-carb friends, this is no longer the case thanks to flash freezing of the freshest of fish from fresh and salty waters all over the globe. You can now reel in almost any type of seafood at your local grocery store.

Where you live is the criteria for how fresh fish arrives at your fish counter. Fish may be labeled *fresh,* but it may have been traveling for a while since it left the boat dock. Let's face it — when a fish is out of water, things change, so I'm going to tell you what to look for and how to shop for fish in this chapter. Then I turn my attention to simple and healthful methods to prepare all kinds of fish and seafood. If fish isn't a staple in your low-carb lifestyle, it should be. Fish is easy to prepare, and it's hard to mess it up. Fish gives you a magic combination of being high on the good-nutrition scale and very low on the carb-count scale.

You don't have to dine at one of those expensive fish-market restaurants for a great meal of fresh fish. I'm here to demystify the steps to take to make the most of just about any fish you can think of. Fish is hooked into any healthy lifestyle — and the low-carb approach is no exception.

Netting the Healthy Advantages

Many fish contain close to zero carbs, and the healthy advantages of adding fish to your menu a couple times a week are just incredible. The message here is *eat more fish*. Experts of all healthy lifestyles agree that incorporating fish into your diet is healthy to the point that it can protect against sudden cardiac death. Here are some of the healthy nutritional benefits of eating fish:

- Fish offer high-quality protein with fewer calories than a similar-sized portion of meat.

- Fish are low in sodium and are good sources of potassium, vitamins, and other minerals.

- Fish are generally low in cholesterol and saturated fats, which have been associated with high blood pressure and heart disease. They also reduce the risk factor of blood clots. (Shellfish, while low in saturated fat, are high in cholesterol.)

Fish oils are healthy for you and essential. The oils in fish may be the best source of omega-3 polyunsaturated fatty acids. Omega-3s lower your risk of heart attack and stroke. They also prevent hardening of the arteries, reduce arthritis pain, lower cholesterol, improve immune response and brain function, and help to absorb calcium into the bones. Omega-3 fatty acid also boosts the immune system's ability to respond to developing breast cancer tumors. You didn't know that the little critter with fins and a tail has a life insurance policy written on him, did you? Go fishing for omegas.

Oily, fatty fish like salmon are good sources of omega-3 fatty acids. Other good sources of omega-3s are tuna, swordfish, mackerel, sardines, herring, and halibut.

Calculating Carb Counts of Your Catch

Fish, whether they're freshwater or saltwater, weigh in at zero carbs for the most part. Some shellfish are an exception to the zero rule. It's what you have fish swimming in after you prepare it that usually drives up the carb count. So, it's "up periscope" for a closer look at some types of fish and carb counts.

The following fish and seafood have zero carb counts:

- ✔ Anchovies
- ✔ Bluefish
- ✔ Cod
- ✔ Crab
- ✔ Crayfish
- ✔ Halibut
- ✔ Mackerel

- ✔ Mahi mahi
- ✔ Salmon
- ✔ Scrod
- ✔ Snapper
- ✔ Trout
- ✔ Tuna

Lobster, prawns, and shrimp have about 1 gram of carbs per 100 grams of seafood. And here are the *approximate* carb counts per 100 grams of fish and seafood at the higher end:

- ✔ Abalone — 6 grams
- ✔ Calamari (squid) — 4 grams
- ✔ Clams — 2.5 grams
- ✔ Mussels and oysters — almost 4 grams
- ✔ Octopus — 2 grams
- ✔ Scallops — 2.5 grams

Imitation crab has very high carb counts — the real deal is always best!

Purchasing and Preparing the Catch of the Day

Fresh is what you want when it comes to fish! In this section, I help you out with a little excursion to the fish counter, giving you advice on what to look for so you can enjoy the freshest fish that's available (short of catching it yourself). And, if I had my way, I'd be catching my own — this girl loves to go fishing!

Reeling in quality

I've been lucky enough to have quite a few opportunities while living in California to step aboard albacore tuna boats in the early morning hours as they dock with their overnight catch. I've also had the pleasure of sitting and watching shellfish being unloaded on the dock while I nibbled on fresh calamari rings. I've even caught my own freshwater fish and cooked them that night over a campfire. But not many people have the time (or the opportunity) to walk down to the docks or out to a stream every time they want to enjoy these kinds of palate-pleasing experiences. But, with a few tips and tricks, you can come close to the quality — with much more convenience.

When you know what you're looking for, you can easily recognize quality fish and seafood. Whether you're buying fresh fish off the boat, at your fish market, at the grocery store, or from the frozen food aisle, following some simple guidelines will make goin' fishin' easy for you.

Buy your fresh fish from reputable fish counters in grocery stores and fish markets.

When buying fresh whole fish, here are the ways to gauge quality:

- ✔ The scales are bright and should adhere closely to the skin of the fish.

- ✔ Gill color is important. If it's red, oxygen is present, and the fish is indeed very fresh. As the fish is out of the water longer, the color of the gills begins to fade to a very light pink, then to gray, and eventually to a greenish brown. Stay away from brown fish.

- ✔ A mild, fresh, sea-like smell is good, but fish should never smell "fishy."

- ✔ Firm and elastic flesh is an excellent indication that fish is fresh. The flesh shouldn't be separating from the bones.

- ✔ Look the fish in the eye. Eyes should be bright and clear, almost transparent and bulging a bit. Sunken fish eyes aren't a good sign.

When buying cut fish steaks and fillets, look for precut signs of freshness similar to buying whole fresh fish:

- ✔ No "fishy" odor, but a mild and fresh smell.

- ✔ No traces of browning or drying around the cut edges of the fish.

- ✔ Moist and firm flesh.

- ✔ If they're in packaging, make sure it's tightly wrapped packaging such as shrink-wrap. The fish steaks or fillets should have no air space between the wrapping materials, and there shouldn't be any liquid in the package.

Proper handing of frozen fish is very important. When you're talking frozen fish, flash frozen is the way to go. *Flash frozen* refers to fish that are frozen at sea immediately after the catch, which are sometimes even fresher than buying fish off the boat at the dock. When buying your fish and seafood frozen, carry this checklist in your head (or in your pocket):

- ✔ The packaging shouldn't be damaged in any way and shouldn't have any holes.

- ✔ Look for any discoloration or freezer burn. If the slightest hint is present, find another package.

- ✔ Make sure the package doesn't have any ice crystals in it, whether it is shrink-wrapped or a bag from the frozen section. This can be an indication that the product has been previously thawed and frozen again.

- ✔ Check for an expiration date stamped on the package. You should eat the fish or seafood by this date.

Handling and storing fishies like a pro

When shopping for fish, always make your last stop the fish market or the grocery store. Please don't ever leave fish — fresh or frozen — in the car and run other errands. When you get your fish home, if it's fresh, wash it under cold water and put it in the coldest spot in your refrigerator. If you want to take really good care of your fish, ice it like the markets do. It's best to eat fresh fish within 24 hours of purchasing it.

Fishy talk

There are some interesting terms used when talking about fish. Here' are just a few so you don't get lost at sea at the fish counter. If you already have a line on these terms, swim on by:

- ✔ **Drawn fish:** No, a drawn fish isn't a fish you've sketched out with your pencil. A *drawn fish* is a whole fish with its entrails — okay, guts — removed, but with its bones and head left intact. Aren't you glad I shared this info with you?

- ✔ **Dressed fish:** All dressed up and no place to go doesn't apply here. A *dressed fish* is one that has been scaled and has had the entrails removed. It usually has the head, tail, and fins removed. Smaller fish prepared

in this way are sometimes referred to as *pan-dressed*.

- ✔ **Fillets:** This term gets tossed around all the time. Fillets are the sides of a fish cut lengthwise so they're boneless and ready to be cooked. *Butterfly fillets* are whole fish that are split lengthwise down the front of the fish so the backbone is easily removed. The fish is then opened out flat, butterfly-style.

- ✔ **Steaks:** Fish steaks are the crosscut sections of a large dressed fish. Steaks are usually cut about ¾-inch thick from the thickest part of the fish.

Thoroughly wash and rinse knives, utensils, cutting boards, and containers when handling fresh as well as cooked fish and seafood. It's possible to cross-contaminate. *Cross-contamination* can occur when cooked or ready-to-eat foods pick up bacteria from other foods, hands, cutting boards, knives, or other utensils. To avoid cross-contamination, keep raw fish and shellfish and their juices away from other foods. Place your cooked fish on a clean plate — never on the plate that was used to hold the raw fish or shellfish, unless you're a tidy cook and the plate's already been washed and dried!

Determining when your fish is done

Whatever cooking method you choose for your fish, you can estimate approximately 10 minutes of cooking time for each inch of fish. Here's how to calculate the size: Lay your whole fish, fillet, or steak flat on a counter or cutting board (for a rundown on these terms and others, see the "Fishy talk " sidebar in this chapter). Find the thickest part and measure the thickness with a plastic ruler that can be washed with warm, soapy water. If it's less than an inch, reduce the time a tad to prevent overcooking.

Fish is a delicate sort, and you cook fish to enhance its flavor, not to tenderize it like you do meat. Fish is supposed to be moist and almost translucent when it's done cooking. You can actually see the moisture of fish that's cooked to perfection.

When the recipe states that the fish should *flake* when testing for doneness, that means you can insert a fork into the fish and easily break off flakes (see Figure 9-1). Flakiness is a good sign. Overcooking fish can easily happen in just a few extra minutes. When following recipes for fish, test for doneness before the recipe tells you to. Why? Here are a couple reasons:

- All fish are not created equal. If you're cooking fish fillets or steaks, they're most likely not the exact size the recipe calls for — there's just a lot of possible variations of the weight and size of fish fillets and steaks.

- Like food from the microwave, fish continues to cook when you remove it from the oven after poaching, steaming, or baking. I like my fish really moist, so I remove it to a warm plate and let it rest for a few minutes for this specific reason — it continues to cook and by the time I serve it the doneness is perfect. Cooking fish to perfection isn't difficult, and you'll learn the technique quickly.

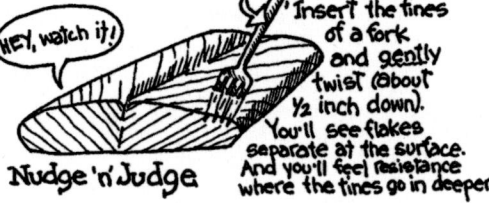

Figure 9-1:
Oh, that
flaky fish.

Cooking Methods to Fit Your Fancy

As you become skilled at cooking fish, you'll develop your own favorite ways for preparing fish. The secret to cooking any fish is to make sure that it isn't overcooked and retains its natural moisture. The spices, herbs, or liquid you use when cooking will help flavor the dish to perfection. In this section, I give you some tried and true methods of fish cookery. I suggest that you set your sails and be adventuresome and try several different methods to discover your favorite. Ahoy!

Regardless of which preparation method you choose for your fish, you can always add a little eye appeal by garnishing it with lemon halves and slices. Check out Figure 9-2 for some suggestions on some snazzy lemon peelin'.

Using parchment

En papillote is a French phrase that means *in a paper case*. Though it sounds mighty impressive, this is an exceptionally easy cooking technique for fish, and it makes an impressive presentation. Not only does the fish look pretty when you serve it, but it's also very moist because all the natural juices are locked in the individual packages.

If you don't have parchment paper in your pantry, next time you're in the grocery store, pick up a roll. As you experiment with different packet recipes for fish and other foods, be aware that some will call for you to wet the parchment, and then squeeze the water out so the paper is soft, pliable, and easy to work with. The following recipe below doesn't require that you wet the parchment paper. You can use aluminum foil in place of parchment paper, but it just isn't quite the same for this one.

Lemon-Thyme Halibut en Papillote

Simple combinations of herbs and spices combined with a touch of lemon or garlic can make fish a mouthwatering and delightful addition to your low-carb lifestyle. Grab some magical parchment paper, wrap this little fishy up, and move forward to new horizons of cooking fish.

Preparation time: *40 minutes*

Cooking time: *15 to 18 minutes*

Yield: *4 servings*

½ cup olive oil	4 lemons
12 sprigs fresh thyme, divided	8 tablespoons white wine
4 halibut fillets (approximately 8 ounces each)	1 cup diced fresh tomato

1 Preheat the oven to 425 degrees. Combine the olive oil and 8 sprigs of fresh thyme in a small saucepan. Over medium-low heat, simmer the oil and the thyme for about 20 minutes. Remove the oil from heat and allow to cool to room temperature.

2 While the oil heats and cools, check the fillets to make sure there are no bones. Cut 2 of the 4 lemons in half. Cut the remaining 2 lemons in very thin slices and set aside.

3 Cut parchment paper in 8 10-inch circles. Brush one side of each circle of parchment with some of the olive oil. Place the oiled circles oiled-side up, on a large baking sheet with sides.

4 When the oil reaches room temperature, strain it to remove the thyme.

5 Place each fillet in the middle of 4 of the oiled circles of parchment. From the fresh lemon halves, squeeze about 1 tablespoon of fresh lemon juice over each fillet.

6 Drizzle 2 tablespoons of wine over each fillet. Generously brush each fillet with the thyme-flavored oil. Distribute the diced tomatoes evenly among the 4 fillets.

7 Place a couple fresh slices of lemon and a fresh thyme sprig on top of each fillet. Carefully place a second oiled parchment circle on top of each fillet with the oil side against the fillet.

8 Fold the edges of the parchment paper together, sealing well. Place the parchment packets on a large baking sheet with sides and bake for 15 to 18 minutes.

9 Serve the fillets in their parchment paper, because they make stunning presentations. Be careful when opening each pouch, because steam will roll out along with the awesome aroma.

Variation: *Other fillets that work well en papillote are cod, monkfish, grouper, and red snapper.*

Per serving: *Calories 493 (From Fat 289); Fat 32g (Saturated 4g); Cholesterol 70mg; Sodium 122mg; Carbohydrate 4g; Dietary Fiber 1g (Net Carbohydrate 3g); Protein 46g.*

In cooking in a packet, you're wrapping the fish (and veggies if combing the two) in a tight little package of parchment paper or foil. As the fish bakes, the little paper packet fills with steam, cooking the fish and trapping all of the savory flavors that you've wrapped up so carefully. So don't open the packet until you're almost certain the fish inside is done. (For more packet cooking information and recipes, steam on over to Chapter 20.)

Figure 9-2:
Get creative
with your
lemon
garnish.

Poaching

Poaching refers to a very simple method of cooking fish. You cook the fish in a small amount of liquid just below the boiling point at a simmering temperature. This cooking method makes the fish very moist and quite tasty. Poaching is not boiling. The poaching liquid is brought to a slow simmer, cooking evenly and gently. The simmer allows just a few bubbles to break the surface of the liquid.

The liquid you use when poaching is up to you and is the central flavoring factor for the fish you're cooking. I suggest you try several different kinds of liquid until you discover the one that fits your fancy. You can use vegetable stock, fish stock, clam juice, wine with herbs, and aromatic vegetables; all are great choices for poaching fish of all kinds. Don't be bashful: Add your favorite herbs and spices, such as a bay leaf, a few sprigs of Italian parsley, and a few peppercorns.

When you're finished poaching your fish, don't waste the poaching liquid. Drain and strain it, and use it as a fantastic base for some very tasty sauces. Many chefs have become famous for their sauces made from their poaching liquids! Simple fish with simple preparation results in simply sumptuous outcomes.

When you poach fish, remove the skin before you begin the poaching process or immediately after the poaching is complete. The skin becomes very rubbery on fish when it's poached. If you're poaching fillets, it's much easier on you and the fish to remove the skin before cooking; otherwise, you may tear the flesh of the fish — the good stuff.

An old secret to poaching fish is to tie your fish in a piece of cheesecloth with long ends so you can lift the fish out easily without breaking it apart.

You can poach fish by using either of the two traditional methods: on the top of the stove or in the oven. You'll develop your favorite style of poaching fish. I suggest that you try both of the described methods here.

- **Stovetop:** Bring your poaching liquid to a boil and remove it from the heat before adding the fish. Your poaching liquid should never be boiling but should be kept at a simmer so you can attain perfect poaching. After you've added your fish to the liquid, continue to cook at a simmer, cooking for about 6 minutes per pound of fish.

- **Oven:** You can also poach in the oven. Just bring your poaching liquid to a boil in a saucepan on the stove and pour the liquid over the cheesecloth-wrapped fish in a baking pan. Cover the pan tightly with aluminum foil and place it in a preheated oven at 375 degrees. Poach for about 10 minutes per pound when oven-poaching.

Whichever poaching method you choose, you can tell when the fish is done by doing the fork flake test (refer to Figure 9-1). Insert a fork into the piece of fish, and when the fish flakes easily, it's done. Don't overcook your fish no matter which way you choose to cook it.

Steaming

I've had the pleasure of traveling to China extensively, and the food I enjoyed there was nothing short of awesome. One of the most delicious dishes I enjoyed many times during my stay was the whole steamed fish. Not only can a steamed fish be an entire meal, but it's also high on the Richter scale of healthfulness. You'll appreciate this old Chinese method of cooking fish because of the purity of flavor it develops.

Any fish likes to be steamed, so which kind of fish you steam is your choice (I opt for trout in the recipe in this chapter). Steaming fish simply involve cooking by steam that is usually generated from boiling water. The easiest way to steam fish fillets or steaks is to use the oven.

Steamed Trout

This quick and delicious Chinese-style steamed trout provides a borderline elegant presentation. You can also use other types of fish with this technique. This recipe calls for 4 wooden chopsticks, but if you don't have chopsticks, don't worry. Simply cook the fish by immersing it in the wine in a baking dish. This is more like poaching the fish instead of steaming it, but the flavors are still simple and delicious.

Preparation time: *15 minutes*

Cooking time: *20 to 25 minutes*

Yield: *2 servings*

2 whole dressed freshwater trout (8 to 9 ounces each)

2 teaspoons fermented black soybeans (see the note that follows)

1 tablespoon peeled and grated fresh ginger

1 tablespoon finely minced garlic

2 tablespoons soy sauce

1 cup dry white wine

½ cup 2-inch carrot strips

2 green onions, cut in diagonal strips

1 Preheat the oven to 400 degrees. Place your fish on a cutting board, and with a sharp knife, score the fish in a crisscross pattern. Make the cuts about ¼ inch deep and about ¾ inch apart. Set aside.

2 Drain and rinse the black soybeans.

3 Combine the black soybeans, grated ginger, and minced garlic in a small bowl, mixing well. Place 1 teaspoon of the mixture in each fish cavity.

4 Using a 13-x-9-inch baking dish, arrange 4 chopsticks across the bottom of the baking dish. Place the fish on top of the chopsticks.

5 Dribble the soy sauce over the fish. Evenly distribute the remainder of the black soybean mixture over the top of the fish.

6 Pour the wine in the bottom of the baking dish, under the fish.

7 Place the carrot and onion strips crisscross-style across the tops of the fish.

8 Cover the baking dish tightly with aluminum foil. Bake for 20 to 25 minutes. Testing fish for doneness is done a little differently with a whole fish. Press the fish with your finger; the area around the spot where you apply pressure will break into firm flakes. Also, the fish will easily pull away from the bones.

Note: *Fermented black soybeans can be purchased at Asian markets.*

Per serving: Calories 125 (From Fat 37); Fat 4g (Saturated 1g); Cholesterol 32mg; Sodium 962mg; Carbohydrate 6g; Dietary Fiber 1g (Net Carbohydrate 3g); Protein 15g.

Firing Up the Barbie and Broiler

Outdoor grilling is a great way to prepare fish. Some types of fish take better to grilling than others, however. Oily fish, such as salmon and trout, are very good candidates for the barbie. You can grill whole fish, steaks, or fillets. If you want to grill delicate fish or most freshwater fish, an easy fix is to grill the fish in aluminum foil or use a grilling basket. Preparing fish this way prevents it from sticking and falling through the cracks of the grill. It's a fish out of water, after all, and you don't want to be chasing it all over the barbie!

To prevent fish from sticking to the grill, apply cooking oil to the surface of the grill using an oiled paper towel or cooking spray *before* you light the grill. Don't be tempted to use cooking spray after it's lit. *Flames from the grill can ignite the aerosol.*

If you want to enhance the flavor of the grilled fish, place a shallow pan of soaked wood chips on the lava rocks of your gas grill. Putting the chips directly on the lava rocks may clog up your vents.

Whether it's pouring rain outside or you just prefer broiling, you can easily transform any "grill recipe" into a broiler-friendly feast. Simply use the stated grilling time as a guide when you're broiling. Remember the last thing you want to do is overcook fish. Place the fish on a broiler pan and broil 4 to 6 inches from the heat, turning it only once. Baste with a sauce mixture if your recipe says to. If not, just broil the plain ol' fish and serve with a sauce or a squeeze of lemon. For fillets or steaks that tend to dry quickly, like halibut, keep them moist while broiling by brushing on some lemon or lime juice. Check out the "Basting tasty fish" sidebar in this chapter for a number of basting suggestions.

Basting tasty fish

You can baste fish with many different kinds of liquid to seal in the natural moisture of fish while it's cooking. Most people think of butter or olive oil when they think of basting fish, but all kinds of options exist, and each imparts the fish with a different enhancing flavor. Try some of these:

✔ ½ cup water and the juice of ½ fresh lemon, cold

✔ Cold, dry, white wine

✔ Cold sour cream

✔ Cold heavy whipping cream

✔ Mixture of ½ cup white wine and ½ water, hot

Grilled Salmon Steaks

This is the simplest preparation of salmon and possibly the very best — grilled with a squeeze of fresh lemon and some melted butter. It's an entrée fit for a king, yet so carb-conscious and so full of those great omega 3s. I suggest that you don't salt and pepper the salmon before cooking; just have the shakers on the table in case someone would like to season the cooked fish. If you're cooking for just yourself, or yourself plus one, this recipe is easily scaled down to fit your portion needs. The easy formula to cut this recipe back is to figure 1 tablespoon of melted butter and a half of a lemon wedge per salmon steak.

Preparation time: *10 minutes*

Cooking time: *6 to 8 minutes*

Yield: *6 servings*

6 fresh salmon steaks (approximately 6 ounces each)

Olive oil for brushing

3 lemons, halved

6 tablespoons melted butter

1 Preheat your gas grill on high heat. Rinse salmon quickly under cold running water and pat dry with a paper towel. Brush the fish with olive oil.

2 When the grill is hot, place the salmon on the grill. Don't close the grill cover. Turn the salmon only once, cooking about 3 minutes on each side (depending on the thickness of your salmon steak).

3 Baste the salmon a few times with the olive oil while cooking. The salmon will be opaque when done.

4 Remove the steaks from the grill. Drizzle each salmon steak with 1 tablespoon of melted butter, and place ½ lemon on each plate. Serve immediately. If desired, serve more melted butter on the side.

Variation: After initially brushing the salmon with olive oil, before placing the fish on the grill, use a combination of sprigs of fresh dill, sage, rosemary, lovage, fennel, or other herbs of your choice, and surround the fish with the fresh herbs, creating bundles. Tie the herbs around the fresh salmon with kitchen twine you've soaked in water, and grill the bundled salmon for a fantastic flavor. Let the flavor of the herbs and salmon take center stage: Serve with just a bit of fresh squeezed lemon.

Per serving: *Calories 243 (From Fat 78); Fat 9g (Saturated 1g); Cholesterol 97mg; Sodium 127mg; Carbohydrate 3g; Dietary Fiber 1g (Net Carbohydrate 2g); Protein 37g.*

Mustard-Dilled Red Snapper

Red snapper is a very flavorful and lean fish. The color of this fish varies from shimmering pink to almost red. This recipe brings out just how delicate and delicious snapper can be. All the snapper needs is a bit of enhancing with fresh dill, a little lemon juice, and a touch of Dijon mustard, and you have an outstanding low-carb meal.

Preparation time: *5 minutes*

Cooking time: *6 to 10 minutes*

Yield: *4 servings*

Nonstick cooking spray	2 ½ tablespoons mayonnaise
1 tablespoon freshly grated Parmesan cheese	½ teaspoon pepper
1 tablespoon fresh minced dill	1 pound fresh red snapper fillets
2 teaspoons freshly squeezed lemon juice	4 lemon wedges
1½ teaspoons Dijon mustard	

1 Preheat the broiler. Line the broiler pan with aluminum foil and spray the foil with non-stick cooking spray. In a small bowl, mix the Parmesan cheese, dill, lemon juice, mustard, mayonnaise, and pepper.

2 Place the fish fillets on the broiler pan and spread the mayonnaise mixture over the tops and sides of the fillets, coating the fish evenly.

3 Place the fish 4 to 6 inches under broiler for about 6 minutes. The topping will begin to brown, and the fish will begin to flake when tested with a fork. Watch that the topping doesn't get too brown.

4 Serve with fresh lemon wedges.

Per serving: Calories 184 (From Fat 80); Fat 9g (Saturated 2g); Cholesterol 46mg; Sodium 170mg; Carbohydrate 2g; Dietary Fiber 0g (Net Carbohydrate 2g); Protein 23g.

Sole with Lemon and Garlic Sauce

This lemon and garlic sauce is fresh and lively. Use the leftover sauce to complement veggies served on the side of this great dish for a how-low-can-you-go carb count meal. Sole is a member of the huge flatfish family, which is a very confusing fish family. Commercial fishermen in the United States reel in more than a dozen different species of flatfish. Some are called flounder, some are called sole, and some are called both. These fish are thin, flat fish with both of their eyes located on the side of their head that faces up. Whatever these fish are called, they all share a delightful sweet and delicate white flesh, so enjoy!

Preparation time: *15 minutes*

Cooking time: *5 to 10 minutes*

Yield: *4 servings*

½ teaspoon white pepper	1 shallot, minced fine
¾ teaspoon garlic powder	2 tablespoons fresh lemon juice
¾ teaspoon onion powder	1 clove garlic, minced fine
1 pound fillets of sole	1 tablespoon finely minced fresh Italian parsley
4 teaspoons melted butter	

1 Preheat the broiler. Combine the white pepper, garlic powder, and onion powder and sprinkle over the fillets.

2 Lay fish in an 8-x-12-inch baking pan.

3 Combine the butter, shallot, lemon juice, garlic, and parsley and spoon over the fish.

4 Broil the fish 4 to 6 inches from broiler for about 3 to 5 minutes. Fish will become opaque quickly and will cook very quickly. Monitor the fish as it cooks because each of the fillets has a mind of its own. One fillet may be done in 5 minutes, and it may take a total of about 10 minutes for all of the fillets to be done.

5 As each fillet gets done, remove it from the broiler pan, transfer to a warmed plate, and cover with foil to keep warm until all fillets are done and ready to serve.

Tip: *Always watch your cooking times and baby-sit fish when you're cooking it. There's nothing worse than overdone, dry, and rubbery fish.*

Per serving: *Calories 136 (From Fat 45); Fat 5g (Saturated 3g); Cholesterol 63mg; Sodium 84mg; Carbohydrate 3g; Dietary Fiber 0g (Net Carbohydrate 3g); Protein 19g.*

Swordfish Piccata

If you haven't experienced swordfish, you're in for a tasty low-carb surprise — you'll be amazed at the carb counts. The texture of swordfish appears to be meaty, but don't let that fool you into thinking it's hardy and needs long cooking times. Treat it with a little tender love and care to preserve its natural moisture.

Preparation time: *5 minutes*

Cooking time: *4 to 5 minutes*

Yield: *4 servings*

4 swordfish steaks (about 8 ounces and ½-inch thick each)

2 tablespoons olive oil

½ teaspoon pepper

1 tablespoon fresh lemon juice

2 tablespoons capers

1 tablespoon finely chopped fresh Italian parsley

1 lemon, sliced very thin

1 Preheat the broiler. Rub both sides of the fish steaks with the olive oil. Grind fresh pepper over both sides of the swordfish steaks and place them on the broiler pan.

2 Broil fish on each side for about 2 minutes, turning only once. Fish will turn almost opaque.

3 Place fish on warmed plates for a nice touch. Sprinkle with fresh lemon juice, capers, and fresh parsley. Garnish with lemon slices.

Variation: *Try a simple olive oil and fresh lemon juice marinade for swordfish steaks. Use ¼ cup fresh lemon juice and 1 tablespoon of extra-virgin olive oil. Combine with 2 minced garlic cloves. Marinate the fish for about 20 minutes. Top each fillet with a slice of purple onion and pop them under the broiler or on the grill. Sprinkle some fresh feta cheese on top before serving.*

Variation: *Marinate chunks of swordfish in herbed vinaigrette for 15 to 20 minutes. Skewer the marinated chunks and cook under the broiler or on the grill.*

Per serving: *Calories 323 (From Fat 138); Fat 15g (Saturated 3g); Cholesterol 83mg; Sodium 320mg; Carbohydrate 2g; Dietary Fiber 1g (Net Carbohydrate 1g); Protein 42g.*

Blackened Catfish

The recipe for this blackening seasoning can be made hotter by adding more pepper. You can make a large amount of seasoning and store it in a tightly covered jar. Just about any fish takes to blackening. I've reeled in a catfish by his whiskers here for you to blacken and enjoy. You can't beat the flavor of this guy on a platter! I'll never forget coming home from work one day when we lived at the lake in Iowa. My daughter Katie had been on the dock fishing and had caught a huge catfish that was so big she couldn't get it off the hook by herself. So there it was in the bathtub — Katie had cut her line, taken it in the house, and plopped it in the tub to keep him fresh. Supper was great that night!

Preparation time: *10 minutes*

Cooking time: *4 minutes*

Yield: *6 servings*

2 ½ teaspoons salt	*½ teaspoon dried oregano leaves*
1 teaspoon onion powder	*½ teaspoon crushed dried thyme leaves*
1 teaspoon cayenne (adjust to taste)	*1 tablespoon butter*
¾ teaspoon white pepper (adjust to taste)	*1 tablespoon olive oil*
¾ teaspoon black pepper (adjust to taste)	*2 pounds fresh catfish (approximately*
1 tablespoon paprika	*6 6-ounce pieces)*

1 Combine the salt, onion powder, cayenne, white pepper, black pepper, paprika, oregano leaves, and thyme leaves, and mix or shake well. Place seasoning in a pie plate or shallow bowl.

2 Preheat a heavy skillet, preferably cast iron, over medium high heat until it's hot but not smoking. Melt the butter and add the oil. The skillet should be hot before adding the fish.

3 Dredge both sides of each piece of fish in seasoning mixture.

4 Drop the fish into the skillet and cook for 2 minutes on each side. The fish will be firm and opaque. Catfish is done when it just starts to flake.

Per serving: Calories 233 (From Fat 149); Fat 17g (Saturated 4g); Cholesterol 73mg; Sodium 1,024mg; Carbohydrate 2g; Dietary Fiber 1g (Net Carbohydrate 1g); Protein 23g.

Sailing Around with Shellfish

Holy mackerel, I almost forgot about the shellfish. Some shellfish are a bit higher in carbs than all the fishes in the sea. Scallops, oysters, and clams are on the higher end of the spectrum. But if you're a shrimp and crab lover, you'll be delighted to know they hold down the low end when it comes to carb counts (see the "Calculating Carb Counts of Your Catch" section earlier in this chapter).

Just take a quick gander at the carb counts and make the shellfish with lower carb counts part of your low-carb healthy lifestyle starting right now. Save those with higher counts for special occasions because, despite the higher carb counts, the health benefits are a positive trade-off, so you don't have to deny yourself these shellfish entirely. But don't forget that how you prepare any seafood also affects the carb count. Does it get any better? Eating fantastic seafood can help you maintain your optimal weight and make you healthier at the same time.

Seafood stir by the seat of your pants

I sometimes make a delicious stir-fry with shrimp, scallops, and calamari rings — all of which are waiting for me in my freezer. I also peek in the freezer and see what kinds of veggies I have on hand. On any given day, they may include broccoli; green string beans; maybe a few wax beans; a combo of red, green; and yellow peppers; edamame; skinny asparagus spears; or a host of other great veggies. And I always try to keep frozen garlic, parsley, and basil on hand too. My skillet of choice is a very old cast-iron skillet. I pour some olive oil in the skillet and throw in some garlic, basil, and parsley, giving it a quick stir. Then I add my frozen veggies, stirring until everything is well mixed.

(A couple dashes of soy sauce enhance the flavors even more.) I start with the veggies and cook them a little bit to give them a head start before I add the seafood because seafood cooks very quickly. Cook this conglomeration until the shrimp turns pink, the veggies are crisp-tender, and the scallops and calamari are cooked through. I actually make a skillet-full and have it for a quick supper and put the rest in the fridge. It's great cold the next day for lunch, or you can pop it in the microwave. And one of my favorite ways to eat it is wrapped up in a low-carb tortilla! Cook this once and eat it two or three times!

Shrimp Scampi

Shrimp Scampi is a simple recipe, but it's always a favorite. Seafood can make your everyday low-carb lifestyle feel like fine dining a couple times a week. You may want to throw a tablecloth, some cloth napkins, and maybe even a couple candles on the table for this one. But then again, it's ready in minutes, so it's also a candidate when you're in a rush to get out the door. This is delightful served over a bed of steamed zucchini or squash strips.

Preparation time: *5 minutes*

Cooking time: *3 to 4 minutes*

Yield: *4 servings*

1 teaspoon butter	*Juice of 1 lemon*
2 teaspoons olive oil	*¼ teaspoon salt*
2 cloves garlic, minced fine	*¼ teaspoon pepper*
1 pound medium peeled shrimp	*¼ cup finely chopped fresh Italian parsley*
¼ cup dry white wine	*1 lemon cut in wedges for garnish*

1 Melt the butter in a sauté pan and add the olive oil. Add the garlic and sauté for 1 minute. Be careful not to let the garlic burn. If it does, toss it and start again.

2 Add the shrimp and sauté for one minute.

3 Add the wine, lemon juice, salt, and pepper and continue to sauté until the shrimp turns pink. Don't overcook.

4 Sprinkle with fresh parsley and garnish with lemon wedges. Serve immediately.

Per serving: Calories 126 (From Fat 38); Fat 4g (Saturated 1g); Cholesterol 171mg; Sodium 342mg; Carbohydrate 3g; Dietary Fiber 1g (Net Carbohydrate 2g); Protein 18g.

Shrimp and Scallop Combo

Here's a great combo of shrimp and scallops that weighs in at around 9 grams of carbs per serving. A combination of shrimp and scallops with a rich and creamy sauce, this dish is sure to become a one of your low-carb favorites when you're in the mood for something special. If you have those cute little ovenproof individual scallop shells, they make a very impressive presentation for this recipe.

Preparation time: *20 minutes*

Cooking time: *30 to 35 minutes*

Yield: *4 servings*

3 tablespoons butter, divided	*Salt and pepper to taste*
8 large tiger shrimp, peeled, deveined, and cut into thirds	*2 tablespoons flour*
1 pound fresh scallops	*1¼ cups light cream, heated*
1 tablespoon finely chopped fresh Italian parsley, divided	*1 cup grated Gruyère cheese, divided*
1 cup dry white wine	*¼ teaspoon nutmeg*
	1 lemon, cut in 4 wedges for garnish

1 Melt 1 tablespoon of the butter in a large saucepan. Add the shrimp, scallops, half of the fresh parsley, and the wine. Season to taste with salt and pepper. Cover and bring to a boil over medium-high heat. Remove from heat and let sit covered for 3 or 4 minutes.

2 Remove the seafood from the pan and place it in a medium bowl. Set the seafood aside. Strain the liquid into another bowl and set the liquid aside.

3 Melt the remaining 2 tablespoons butter in the saucepan over medium-low heat. When the butter is hot, quickly stir in the flour and whisk until well blended. Cook for only 1 minute over reduced heat.

4 Slowly add the strained poaching liquid into the flour mixture, stirring constantly.

5 Add the cream and the rest of the parsley, mixing all ingredients well. Over very low heat, cook for 8 to 10 minutes. Preheat the broiler while you finish cooking the sauce.

6 Stir in half of the Gruyère cheese and all of the nutmeg into the sauce. Cook over low heat for 2 more minutes.

7 Place the seafood in the sauce and stir well. Remove from the heat.

8 Spoon the seafood mixture into individual ovenproof serving dishes. Sprinkle with the remaining cheese. Broil in the oven for 3 to 4 minutes, just until the cheese is melted. Watch carefully so the cheese doesn't brown or burn.

Per serving: *Calories 489 (From Fat 297); Fat 33g (Saturated 20g); Cholesterol 179mg; Sodium 557mg; Carbohydrate 9g; Dietary Fiber 0g (Net Carbohydrate 9g); Protein 35g.*

Chapter 10

Stickin' with Chicken in Your Low-Carb Lifestyle

In This Chapter

▶ Reading over the bird's impressive résumé

▶ Preparing and cooking chicken safely

▶ Picking apart a whole chicken

▶ Jazzing up your chicken the low-carb way

▶ Cooking chicken a different way — every day

▶ Transforming your chicken into comfort food and classy fare

Recipes in This Chapter

▶ Grilled Ginger Chicken Strips

▶ Cheese and Spinach–Stuffed Chicken

▶ Southern Fried Chicken

↻ Cheese and Spinach Dumplings

▶ Chicken Spoon Bread

▶ Roast Chicken and Gravy

▶ Orange Chicken Veronique

▶ Chicken and Zucchini in Dijon Sauce

The pause in the daily toil is known as the dinner hour. *Hour* you say — who has time for a whole hour for dinner? I understand. Your healthy low-carb lifestyle advocates that you eat a great dinner. You're tired and hungry after a long day, and the dinner temptations are more abundant than you can shake a proverbial resolution at. Have no fear — it's chicken to the rescue.

You think chicken is boring? Only if you want it to be. Don't let your chicken fall into ho-hum boredom. Preparing chicken that works with your low-carb lifestyle can be a very tasty and satisfying adventure. Dressing chicken up with spices, squeezes of fresh lemon and lime, sugar-free preserves, marinades and sauces, and other goodies makes chicken a whole new chapter in your low-carb life. You can create a family dish that's cozy and wholesome, or you can dress your chicken to the nines with all kinds of delicacies in an elaborate gourmet dish. Experimenting with a food that's so low in carbs is great, and what's even better is that you can usually find chicken on sale.

The Skinny on Chicken

Chicken has quite an impressive résumé. For starters, chicken has almost zero carbs. But the low-carb angle is just the beginning of the nutritional benefits. Chicken provides a generous helping of protein (which provides energy), iron, B vitamins, phosphorous, and calcium, and without the skin, chicken is skinny on fat, calories, and cholesterol too!

In the scheme of simple economics, chicken gives your budget a break when you compare it with other meats. And if you really want to save some dough, buy whole fryers on sale and learn how to cut them up, which I conveniently cover in the "Wholly Chicken" section later in the chapter if you don't already have it mastered.

If you're looking for variety in your overall low-carb diet, chicken is a great place to start. Chicken gets rave reviews in versatility: You can bake it, poach it, grill it, broil it, roast it, and microwave it, just for starters (see the "Fixin' Chicken: Let Me Count the Ways" section later in the chapter). Plus, a potpourri of herbs and spices can change the looks of a chicken and enhance the flavor in many different directions. All you need is a sense of culinary adventure.

Practicing Safe Chicken

Be safe with chicken rather than sorry, and handle raw chicken accordingly. Research shows that properly handling chicken prevents food-borne illness from salmonella and other bacteria associated with undercooked or raw chicken.

Practicing safe chicken begins at the grocery store or the meat market. Pay attention to what you're putting in your shopping cart. If chicken doesn't look fresh or looks like it has freezer burn, leave it alone. Be sure to check the sell-by date on the package labels of the chicken before you purchase it. And don't go grocery shopping and leave chicken in the car while you make a few stops and run a few errands. You're asking for trouble — raw chicken needs to be refrigerated immediately.

It's a myth that keeping chicken moist when storing is best. In fact, it's one of the worst things you can do, because bacteria grow in moisture. You can safely store chicken in the shrink-wrapped package that you purchase it in for several days. Personally, I don't keep chicken in the fridge more than two days after buying it before using it or freezing it.

Handling with care

Obeying the rules of the chicken road is relatively simple. The following list contains the basics for keeping you and yours safe when handling, cooking, and serving chicken. I hope that I pop into your head if you start to take a short cut next time you're barbecuing chicken — I'll be there smiling at you saying, "I don't think so."

✔ Before preparing any chicken, always rinse it under cold water, and then pat it dry with paper towels. If you're roasting a whole chicken, patting the inside cavity of the chicken with paper towels is also important.

✔ After handling raw chicken, wash your hands, sink, countertops, and any utensils you've used in the process with hot, soapy water.

✔ Don't let raw meat or its juices touch other food. So don't lay your raw corn on the cob next to your raw chicken. And don't place raw chicken directly on your countertop to avoid leaving lingering bacteria that could contaminate other foods.

✔ Always marinate chicken in the refrigerator, not outside on the counter-top or picnic table. Marinating chicken at room temperature isn't safe. It's also wise to place the marinating chicken on the lower shelf of your fridge just in case it leaks. If you're marinating in plastic bags, then do yourself a favor and place the marinating bags in a large glass dish. You'll prevent some sticky cleanups.

✔ Never use a platter you had the raw chicken on as a serving platter. Either wash the platter in hot, sudsy water, and then use it, or get out another serving dish. If you're a grill master, avoid using the pans you took the chicken to the grill in until they're washed thoroughly.

✔ Wooden cutting boards and chicken are a no no. They harbor bacteria and can cause you some very unpleasant problems. If you've used a wooden cutting board, use a bleach solution to clean it. Best-case scenario: Toss the wooden cutting board, and buy yourself a new plastic one that cleans up in a jiffy. I use a dedicated cutting board for chicken.

If you purchase frozen chicken, the ideal way to thaw it is to place it in the refrigerator and thaw it gradually. Never thaw chicken at room temperature. To speed up the thaw if you're in a hurry, you can run cold water over the chicken.

Don't refreeze cooked chicken that has thawed or raw chicken that has been previously frozen.

For the full story on storing and preparing chicken safely, go the U.S. Department of Agriculture's Food Safety and Inspection Service Website at www.fsis.usda.gov/Fact_Sheets.

Turning up the heat

Always cook chicken thoroughly. Heat destroys bacteria. Do a chicken check, and pierce the chicken with a fork. The juices of the chicken are clear when the chicken is done. There isn't even a hint of pink in the juice of done chicken. And when testing a whole chicken for doneness, the leg should move freely when twisted or lifted. But, no bones about it, the best way to tell if your chicken is done is to take its temperature with your trusty meat thermometer. Actually, bones do come into play:

✔ If you're cooking chicken with bones, the internal temperature should register at 180 degrees for it to be done. When taking the bird's temperature for doneness, insert a meat thermometer at the thickest part of the thigh taking care not to hit a bone.

✔ Boneless parts should be cooked to an internal temperature of 170 degrees.

Be sure to check for doneness, even when you've set the timer according to a recipes stated cook time. All ovens and stoves aren't created equal, and cooking on medium may mean something entirely different to you than it does to Mary Jane. The size of a whole chicken or even a chicken breast can vary a lot as well. And, if you're cooking both white meat and dark meat pieces in a baking dish or on the barbie, be sure to test both the dark meat and the white meat pieces with your thermometer, because the dark meat takes longer to cook.

Wholly Chicken!

When working with any whole chicken, remove the giblets from the cavity of the chicken. If you want to keep the giblets for later use, either refrigerate or freeze them immediately. Remove any loose fat on the chicken and discard it. After rinsing the chicken thoroughly, pat it dry with paper towels. If you'd like to freshen the skin of the chicken if it's a bit dry, rub it inside and out with fresh lemon. Be sure to season the cavity of the chicken with salt and pepper.

Cutting up a whole chicken

Cutting up a chicken is a great technique to master and add to your kitchen tricks. You'll be pleasantly surprised at the dollars you'll save in your food budget by buying whole fryers rather than chicken parts. Cutting up a whole chicken is a bit intimidating but is by no means difficult. The first step is to understand that you're in charge, not the chicken. Check out Figure 10-1, which outlines the process in a few simple steps.

CUTTING A CHICKEN INTO PARTS

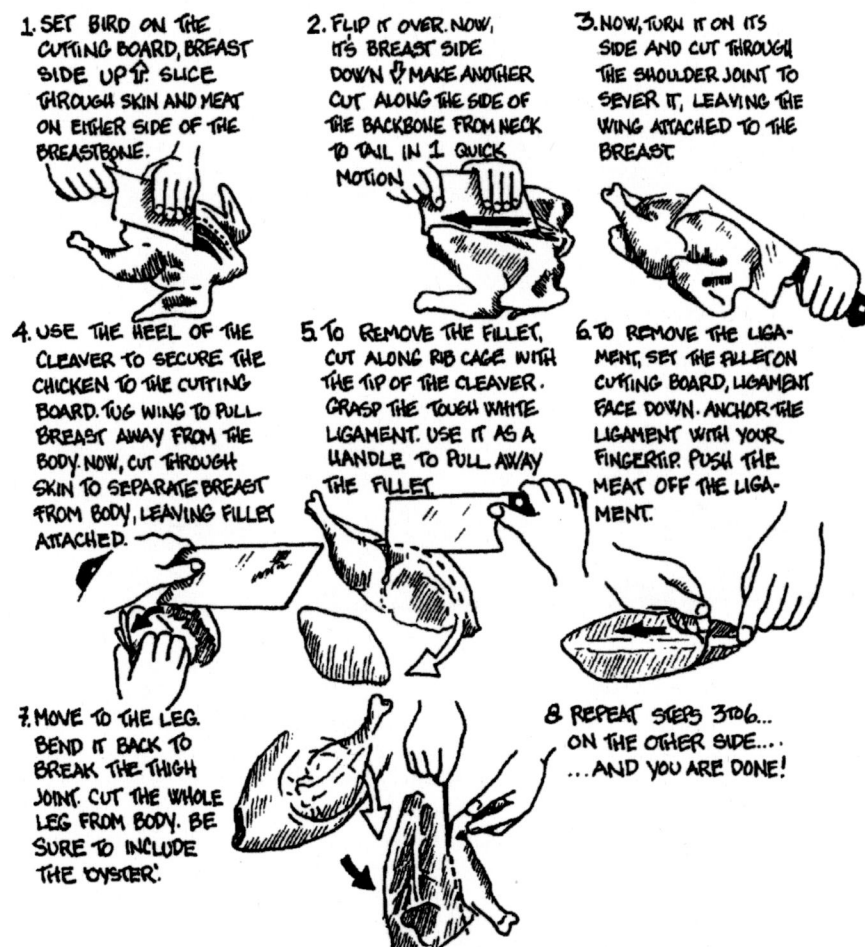

1. SET BIRD ON THE CUTTING BOARD, BREAST SIDE UP T. SLICE THROUGH SKIN AND MEAT ON EITHER SIDE OF THE BREASTBONE.

2. FLIP IT OVER. NOW, IT'S BREAST SIDE DOWN & MAKE ANOTHER CUT ALONG THE SIDE OF THE BACKBONE FROM NECK TO TAIL IN 1 QUICK MOTION.

3. NOW, TURN IT ON ITS SIDE AND CUT THROUGH THE SHOULDER JOINT TO SEVER IT, LEAVING THE WING ATTACHED TO THE BREAST

4. USE THE HEEL OF THE CLEAVER TO SECURE THE CHICKEN TO THE CUTTING BOARD. TUG WING TO PULL BREAST AWAY FROM THE BODY. NOW, CUT THROUGH SKIN TO SEPARATE BREAST FROM BODY, LEAVING FILLET ATTACHED.

5. TO REMOVE THE FILLET, CUT ALONG RIB CAGE WITH THE TIP OF THE CLEAVER. GRASP THE TOUGH WHITE LIGAMENT. USE IT AS A HANDLE TO PULL AWAY THE FILLET.

6. TO REMOVE THE LIGA-MENT, SET THE FILLET ON CUTTING BOARD, LIGAMENT FACE DOWN. ANCHOR THE LIGAMENT WITH YOUR FINGERTIP. PUSH THE MEAT OFF THE LIGA-MENT.

7. MOVE TO THE LEG. BEND IT BACK TO BREAK THE THIGH JOINT. CUT THE WHOLE LEG FROM BODY. BE SURE TO INCLUDE THE 'OYSTER'.

8. REPEAT STEPS 3 TO 6... ON THE OTHER SIDE... ...AND YOU ARE DONE!

Figure 10-1: How to cut up a whole chicken.

Making a substitution

If you prefer the white meat of chicken and don't care at all for the dark meat or you prefer dark to white meat and a recipe calls for a cut-up frying chicken, just do a little substitution of parts. Keep in mind that the number of servings in the recipe doesn't change, but the nutritional information may change. If the recipe calls for a 2½- pound to 3-pound frying chicken, the following parts can be substituted:

- 8 to 10 chicken wings
- 8 to 10 chicken thighs
- 8 to 10 chicken drumsticks
- 4 to 5 whole chicken legs
- 4 to 5 chicken breast halves with ribs

When you have a recipe for cubed chicken, and you don't have a clue how much chicken it equates to before it's cubed, this info should help you:

- If you have a 2½- to 3- pound fryer, the yield is 2½ to 3 cups of cubed chicken.
- Two whole boneless chicken breasts yield about 2 cups of cubed chicken.

Finger Lickin' Low-Carb Good: New Flavors in Chicken

Chicken is so susceptible to absorbing flavors that the sky is the limit with chicken dishes packed with flavor. You can rub chicken with delightful dry or wet rubs, leave it resting in marinade, or infuse whole chickens or your favorite pieces of chicken with yummy flavors under their skin. A chicken doesn't care if it has its skin on or not when you're doctoring it up with scrumptious flavors, so the choice is yours. In the following sections, I cover a couple of ways to transform chicken from another plain ol' chicken dinner to tasty low-carb stuff. Have some fun with chicken and experiment!

Rubbing chicken the right way

Savory rubs are a quick, easy way to add complex flavors to grilled chicken. You can use rubs on chicken with or without skin. But only use the rub on the skin if you plan to eat the skin; if you remove the skin after the chicken is cooked, you're going to lose the flavor. Decisions, decisions! Here are a couple of rubs to get you started in the right rub direction:

- **Dry rubs:** These rubs can include dried herbs and spices, such as curry powder, garlic powder, onion powder, rosemary, thyme, oregano, and chili powder, which can be applied directly onto the skin or meat of the chicken. There's also a tomato powder on the market that's pretty awesome for getting a touch of tomato flavor in a rub if you like. You can prepare your favorite spice combinations in advance so your chicken doesn't have to wait for his rub down. I put my dry-rub mix in a large shaker and shake it over the bird, instead of rubbing it in with my hands or fingers — but hey, it's your barbeque! You make the call.

✔ **Wet rubs:** You can magically transform a dry rub into a wet rub that's full of herbs and spices by just adding a little liquid such as any vinegar, citrus juice, or wine that you enjoy cooking with. Wet rubs can also begin with wet ingredients, such as various mustards or fresh garlic. Some wet rubs end up like a paste, and you can spread them on with a knife if you like. If you come up with more of a marinade than a rub by adding quite a bit of liquid, it's no problem: Just grab your basting brush and go to town.

Marrying the chicken and the marinade

A *marinade* is a seasoned liquid containing an acid such as vinegar, wine, or lemon juice, usually some oil, and herbs or spices. When you marinate chicken, meat, or fish, you're actually soaking it in the liquid, and the goal is to have the food absorb the flavors before cooking. Sometimes, a marinade is also used as a tenderizer for tougher cuts of meats.

Always use a non-metal shallow bowl for marinades. You can also use a heavy-duty plastic self-sealing bag. Check out Figure 10-2 for a breakdown of good and bad marinating equipment.

Figure 10-2: Choose one of the good guys.

The flavorful liquids of marinade can contain very few carbs. Marinades add big flavor to chicken, along with moisture. Be sure to mix your marinades in a glass dish or bowl, because they don't do well in metal. Here are a few examples of marinade inspiration to get your creative juices flowing:

- ✔ Minced garlic, fresh rosemary, fresh chopped thyme, grated orange peel and lemon peel, lemon juice, and freshly ground black pepper
- ✔ Yogurt and freshly chopped mint
- ✔ Curry powder with garlic and yogurt
- ✔ Five-spice powder, chicken stock, soy sauce, freshly grated ginger, and a touch of orange juice

An easy and quick marinade is a good quality Italian dressing and maybe even Italian dressing with garlic and cheese. Just be sure to check the carb counts and look for hidden sugars (see Chapter 3).

There are a lot of premixed marinades on the market, but I caution you to turn to the label and check not only the carb counts but also the calories. Plus, look for hidden sugars and MSG. Some of the prepackaged marinades are laden with sugar, and your low-carb self will suffer the consequences.

After you mix your favorite marinade, add the chicken pieces of your choice, and roll them about so they're well coated. Refrigerate the pieces of chicken in the marinade for an hour before cooking unless a recipe directs you otherwise (some recipes call for short marinating times). Then just remove the pieces from the dish, and broil them or pop them on the grill. You can also marinate chicken (and meats) in large resealable plastic bags (see Figure 10-3). In fact, taking this approach is even easier because you cut down on your cleaning time.

Using a Plastic Bag to Marinate Food

Figure 10-3:
Marinating made easy.

Place food in a plastic bag.

Pour marinade into the bag.

Press all of the air out of the bag.

Seal shut, making sure the food is surrounded by the marinade, folding over if necessary.

If you're going to use sauce for basting and also serve it on the side of your chicken dish, do it wisely. While basting chicken, you risk the possibility of contaminating the sauce with microorganisms from the uncooked chicken. Don't take any chances. Simply separate your sauce in two bowls from the beginning. If you've prepared the sauce from scratch, be a little stingy and start small with the sauce in the basting bowl. If you have leftover marinade, do yourself a favor and toss it because nasty bacteria can be lurking in it from the raw chicken.

Grilled Ginger Chicken Strips

The fresh chopped ginger in this marinade gives these chicken strips a great flavor. You can cook these strips on the grill outside, as I do here, but use a veggie grate or you may lose them between the cracks. You can also use your electric indoor grill or a cast-iron grill pan. They're delicious when hot off the grill and also great for lunch the next day. You may want to consider doubling or tripling this recipe so you'll have leftovers.

Preparation time: *1 hour and 15 minutes*

Cooking time: *6 to 8 minutes*

Yield: *4 servings*

4 boneless skinless chicken breast halves	*¼ cup fresh lemon juice*
2 cloves garlic, minced fine	*½ teaspoon hot pepper sauce (more if desired)*
2 tablespoons peeled and chopped fresh ginger	*1 tablespoon white wine vinegar*
	¼ cup olive oil
2 tablespoons soy sauce	*¼ teaspoon pepper*

1 Cut the chicken breasts in wide strips (see the tip in this section for easy chicken-breast stripping). Preheat your barbecue grill to medium.

2 Combine the garlic, ginger, soy sauce, lemon juice, hot sauce, vinegar, olive oil, and pepper in a jar with a tight fitting lid. Shake until well blended.

3 Place the chicken strips in a shallow dish, and pour part of the mixture over top (be sure to save some for basting). Refrigerate for an hour.

4 Remove the chicken strips from the marinade, place them on the barbecue grill in a veggie grate and cook for 6 to 8 minutes (depending on the size of the strips). Baste frequently with the marinade while cooking, turning the chicken at least 3 times. Make sure chicken strips are done by inserting a fork in one and checking that the juices run clear.

Per serving: Calories 255 (From Fat 146); Fat 16g (Saturated 3g); Cholesterol 63mg; Sodium 531mg; Carbohydrate 2g; Dietary Fiber 0g (Net Carbohydrate 2g); Protein 24g.

Want to thinly slice chicken into strips with a little control? Pop the chicken in the freezer for about an hour or until it's almost frozen. With a very sharp knife, cut across the grain of the meat. This method is great if you want to slice boneless chicken breast for stir-fry or other recipes.

Want pretty chickens? Well, glaze them. Set the chicken on the rack in the roasting pan breast side up, and brush with a glaze. While the chicken is roasting, brush with the glaze again. Your chicken will come out a shiny golden brown. It's the prettiest chicken you've ever seen.

Getting under a chicken's skin

If you want to create an incredible low-carb chicken dish, getting under the skin of a whole chicken, chicken breasts, or thighs is an easy way to infuse chicken with subtle flavors. If you're a garlic lover, you can get under the skin of a chicken with as much garlic as you can handle for a garlic infusion. Fresh herbs, such as rosemary, when placed under the chicken's skin with some butter, will also really wake up your taste buds, and the chicken just pulls in the flavor. Follow these simple steps to flavor the chicken under the skin:

1. Rinse the chicken well with cold water, and pat it dry (inside and out). Work on a counter top with a disposable or washable plastic cutting board placed under the chicken.

2. Loosen the membrane on the breast, legs, and thighs of the chicken by running your fingers carefully under the chicken's skin to separate it from the flesh. Be gentle so you don't tear the skin off the bird — you're just lifting it up for access to add various ingredients.

3. Carefully place spoonfuls of delicious stuffing ingredients — cheese, butter, herbs, or a combination of ingredients — under the skin. Placing these spoonfuls will make your chicken look like it has a bad case of the mumps because you'll have little mounds sticking up.

4. Now you can rub the cheese, butter, or herbs with your hand to spread it evenly. The idea here is to plop your mixture of choice under the skin and then even it out, spreading the little mounds of ingredients as evenly under the chicken's skin as possible. This need not be perfectly smooth as your goal is flavoring the chicken not a chef's award for chicken of the month.

5. The bird is headed for the roasting pan. When the chicken comes out of the oven it will be a bit puffy looking from the stuffing and a beautiful golden brown. I suggest that you serve on individual plates with complimentary vegetables that are colorful and you have a beautiful and delicious presentation. The result is a tender, moist chicken that's packed full of flavors. With each bite, you get a forkful of moist meat, fragrantly spiced stuffing, and crispy skin.

Fat in the skin of the chicken doesn't migrate into the meat of the chicken as it cooks. If you like to cook chicken with the skin on to keep it moist, please do. Your chicken will be more flavorful, moist, and tender. If you remove the skin before you eat it, keep in mind that some of the seasoning as well as some of the flavor disappears.

Cheese and Spinach–Stuffed Chicken

If you find that roasting a whole chicken is too time consuming or just too much fuss, these fabulous stuffed breasts will likely prove more adaptable to your specific low-carb lifestyle. This recipe allows you to enjoy the wonderful flavor infusion you get from roasting a bird.

Preparation time: *10 minutes*

Cooking time: *40 to 45 minutes*

Yield: *8 servings*

½ of a 10-ounce package of frozen spinach, thawed and squeezed dry

2 tablespoons reduced-fat cream cheese, softened

½ cup lowfat ricotta cheese

2 tablespoons minced scallion

1 egg white

1 teaspoon grated lemon zest

⅛ teaspoon pepper

Pinch of ground nutmeg

¼ teaspoon salt

8 boned chicken breast halves (about 1¾ pounds)

1 Preheat the oven to 400 degrees. In a medium bowl, combine the spinach, cream cheese, ricotta cheese, scallion, egg white, lemon zest, pepper, nutmeg, and salt. Stir the mixture until well blended.

2 Very carefully loosen the skin from the chicken with your fingers (see my tips in this section on how to pull this off), being careful not to tear the skin completely away from the meat of the bird. Spread 2 tablespoons of the mixture under the skin of each breast half.

3 Place the chicken on a rack in a medium-sized baking pan. Bake the breasts for 40 minutes or until the chicken is done (a meat thermometer inserted into the chicken reads 180 degrees).

4 Remove the skin from the chicken before eating if you prefer.

Per serving: Calories 172 (From Fat 64); Fat 7g (Saturated 3g); Cholesterol 67mg; Sodium 172mg; Carbohydrate 2g; Dietary Fiber 1g (Net Carbohydrate 1g); Protein 24g.

Fixin' Chicken: Let Me Count the Ways

In this section, I present the easiest and quickest ways for preparing chicken so you can begin to fit the real versatility of chicken into your low-carb lifestyle and not have to spend all day cooking. Get serious about cooking chicken quickly. You'll be glad you did. Here are some options for your next chicken dinner:

- **Oven-fried:** This is a way to get a tasty and crispy crust on your chicken without the fat from frying. You can also experiment with all kinds of spices and herbs that work well for oven-fried chicken. There's no need to miss out on old-fashioned chicken when you can have something more flavorful and carb conscious. You can have your low-carb oven-fried chicken and your low-carb gravy too. For an oven-fried idea, check out the Southern Fried Chicken recipe in the section in this chapter.

- **Grilled:** Grilling and chicken are close enough to a perfect combination. The delicate flavor of chicken is enhanced when you cook it on the grill. When you use marinades when grilling chicken, not only is additional flavor infused into the chicken but the marinade also tenderizes the chicken. Grilling doesn't have to mean taking a trip outside, you can use your handy dandy inside tabletop grill too. Try the Grilled Ginger Chicken Strips recipe earlier in this chapter.

- **Roasted:** If you roast your chicken (and turkey too for that matter) try turning them over — yep, roast them breast side down. Think about it: When the breast is up and the bird is resting on its back, all of those juices are flowing downward during the cooking process. Reverse the process for more moistness and less escape of juices.

  And here's another tip: Begin roasting your chicken at a higher heat for just a short period of time. This will make the skin crispy and seal the juices in. I usually roast my bird for about 15 minutes at 450 degrees and then reduce the oven heat to 375 degrees until it's done. As always, the times and temperatures vary according to the recipe that you're preparing and the size of the bird you're cooking. For a tasty roasted chicken dish, try the Roast Chicken and Gravy recipe in this chapter.

Don't rush your chicken off to the table when it has finished roasting. It has had hot time in the oven, so let the poor bird rest for 10 to 15 minutes before serving her up so the juices will settle in. Your roasted chicken eating experience will be much tastier, and the meat will be moister. If you let it rest breast-side down, gravity will do its job, and the juices will give you more flavorful and moist white meat.

When you want a very fast and tasty meal, just poach your chicken breasts in the microwave and top them with a low-carb sauce or something as simple as lemon-pepper-herb spice. You'll be surprised how chicken soaks up flavors in a hurry. Just add a quick green side salad, and you have a better-than-average low-carb meal in minutes.

Turning Back the Clock with Comfort Food

At one time, chicken was reserved for Sunday dinner. Oh, how times have changed. One thing has not changed over the years, though, and that's our desire and need to be comforted by some of the food we eat. After living the low-carb lifestyle for ten years now, there are times I just want to roll in mashed potatoes. Well, at least have a bite of them. These food desires aren't out of the ordinary, which is why not depriving yourself of certain textures and types of food — like comfort food — is so important in developing your healthy low-carb lifestyle.

The recipes in this section may not be mashed potatoes, but there are some awesome recipes that fill that comfort-food void and don't take a ton of time to prepare. The old-fashioned Midwest cook in me has worked hard to bring you what I hope will be some good ol' comfort food low-carb recipes. Not only do you have a lot of variety with food in your healthy low-carb lifestyle, but you also can discover ways to your old-fashioned favorites that are low in carb counts.

A kitchen gadget that may just delight you is a vertical stainless-steel roaster. If you stop by the grocery store and pay way too much for a freshly roasted chicken, invest in one of these gadgets and make your own just like you'd find in the deli. To use this great kitchen tool, simply slip the prepared chicken over it with the neck end of the chicken up. Here's the magic of the gadget — as the steel heats up, the chicken actually cooks from within, and the skin browns evenly on all sides. When you cook the bird in this manner, all the fat drips into the roasting pan.

You can't have fried chicken without breadcrumbs, and making your own low-carb breads crumbs to use in my Southern Fried Chicken recipe is a snap. Check out Figure 10-4 for a step-by-step how-to to having your low-carb crumbs in a jiffy. Just use your favorite choice of low-carb bread and let it get stale. I have a small pan in my oven that I pop bread in that's past freshness, and when I'm ready for breadcrumbs, it's all dried out the natural way. If you want to season the little darlings, just add dried herbs and spices like rosemary, thyme, parsley, basil, and so on.

Southern Fried Chicken

No, I'm not kidding. You're going to have southern fried chicken without straying from your low-carb lifestyle. Isn't it just grand? If you want gravy to go with your low-carb fried chicken, check out the Roast Chicken and Gravy recipe in this section. Enjoy this old-time favorite, de-carbed.

Preparation time: *10 minutes*

Cooking time: *50 minutes to 1 hour and 15 minutes*

Yield: *8 servings*

½ cup plain low-carb breadcrumbs	⅛ teaspoon pepper
½ teaspoon paprika	2 frying chickens (about 2 pounds each), cut up
¼ teaspoon salt	2 tablespoons melted butter
¼ teaspoon celery salt	
¼ teaspoon celery seed	

1 Preheat your oven to 375 degrees. Combine the breadcrumbs, paprika, salt, celery salt, celery seed, and pepper in a large, self-sealing plastic bag. Shake to mix.

2 Place the chicken pieces side by side in a large glass baking dish with the legs and thighs on the outside since dark meat takes longer to cook. Make sure you pack the pieces in tightly, right up against one another.

3 Brush the chicken pieces with the melted butter to moisten and make a base for the seasoned crumbs to stick to. Sprinkle the breadcrumb mixture over the chicken pieces.

4 Bake uncovered for about 50 minutes to 1 hour and 15 minutes or until crisp and a meat thermometer inserted into the chicken reads 180 degrees.

Per serving: Calories 205 (From Fat 85); Fat 9g (Saturated 4g); Cholesterol 85mg; Sodium 268mg; Carbohydrate 2g; Dietary Fiber 1g (Net Carbohydrate 1g); Protein 27g.

Making Your Own Bread Crumbs

Figure 10-4: Low-carb bread-crumbs in a snap.

🍎 *Cheese and Spinach Dumplings*

Dumplings are comfort food that you may think have disappeared from your low-carb lifestyle. But deprivation isn't part of this lifestyle, so you have to find new ways to satisfy your cravings without the carbs. I think these dumplings are bound to tickle your taste buds. You can serve them with the chicken recipes in this chapter. Yes, chicken *and* dumplings. Or add a salad on the side and you have a very quick and hearty meal.

Preparation time: *15 minutes*

Cooking time: *3 to 5 minutes*

Yield: *16 1-dumpling servings*

1 cup frozen chopped spinach, thawed	⅛ teaspoon pepper
1 cup lowfat ricotta cheese	1 tablespoon melted butter
1 egg	6 tablespoons white whole-wheat flour (be sure to use this type of flour to make this recipe work)
4 tablespoons freshly grated Parmesan cheese	
¼ teaspoon garlic salt with parsley flakes	¼ cup flour for rolling the dumplings
2 teaspoons crushed dried rosemary	½ cup freshly shredded Parmesan cheese

1 Squeeze thawed spinach in paper towels until almost all of the moisture is removed. Measure the 1 cup of spinach *after* squeezing moisture out. Set aside.

2 In a medium saucepan, bring about 2 quarts of salted water to a boil.

3 In a medium bowl, combine the ricotta cheese and egg, mixing well. Add the spinach, grated Parmesan cheese, garlic salt, rosemary, pepper, and melted butter combining ingredients until well blended. Add the flour last and blend into the mixture evenly.

4 Place the ¼ cup flour in a little mound on waxed paper.

5 Roll enough of the mixture in the palms of your hands until round and the size of a golf ball. Roll each dumpling ball in the flour mound on the waxed paper and, if necessary, sprinkle flour on top to hurry the process a little. Set each dumpling aside on the waxed paper until all have been rolled and floured.

6 Drop the dumplings into the boiling water one at a time. Cook the dumplings for about 3 minutes (set your timer). As the dumplings begin to cook through, you'll see them rolling through the water.

7 Remove the dumplings with a slotted spoon into a microwave-safe baking dish. (I place my dumplings close together in a round serving bowl for presentation purposes.) Sprinkle the freshly shredded Parmesan cheese over the top of the dumplings and microwave on high for one minute until cheese is melted. Serve at once.

Variation: *Cook the dumplings in chicken broth to give them a richer flavor.*

Per serving: *Calories 62 (From Fat 26); Fat 3g (Saturated 2g); Cholesterol 22mg; Sodium 124mg; Carbohydrate 5g; Dietary Fiber 1g (Net Carbohydrate 4g); Protein 4g.*

Chicken Spoon Bread

You're going to be pleasantly surprised at the carb count on this little dish I whipped up. You can't eat spoon bread for every meal with your low-carb lifestyle, but it sure is a great low-carb treat from time to time. This recipe certainly adds to the comfort food list, and I know you're gonna love it.

Preparation time: *30 minutes*

Cooking time: *About 1 hour*

Yield: *8 servings*

Nonstick cooking spray	3 eggs, separated
⅓ cup shredded carrots	½ teaspoon baking powder
¼ cup chopped mushrooms	⅛ teaspoon salt
¼ cup finely chopped onion	¼ teaspoon pepper
1 cup light cream	2 cups cooked and chopped chicken breast
1 cup water	1 tablespoon finely chopped fresh Italian parsley
1 teaspoon chicken-flavored bouillon granules	
½ cup yellow cornmeal	½ cup shredded mild cheddar cheese

1 Coat a large, heavy skillet with nonstick cooking spray. Heat the skillet over medium high heat. Add the carrots, mushrooms, and onion, and sauté until the mushrooms are just tender, about 3 to 5 minutes depending on the mushrooms you choose. Set aside.

2 Preheat the oven at 350 degrees. Combine the cream, water, and bouillon in a large saucepan and cook over medium heat until it begins to boil. Stir in the cornmeal, reduce the heat, and cook, stirring occasionally, until thickened, about 15 to 20 minutes. Remove from heat.

3 Beat the egg yolks with a hand mixer until they're light and lemon colored. Stir the baking powder, salt, and pepper into the egg yolks.

4 In a large bowl, combine the sautéed vegetables, cornmeal mixture, egg yolk mixture, chicken, and parsley, stirring until well blended.

5 In a clean bowl with clean beaters, beat the egg whites until they're stiff, and fold them into the chicken mixture. Spoon the mixture into a 2-quart casserole dish that has been sprayed with nonstick cooking spray.

6 Bake for 40 minutes, uncovered. Sprinkle with cheese and bake for about 4 more minutes or until the cheese melts.

Per serving: *Calories 211 (From Fat 103); Fat 12g (Saturated 6g); Cholesterol 137mg; Sodium 312mg; Carbohydrate 9g; Dietary Fiber 1g (Net Carbohydrate 8g); Protein 17g.*

Roast Chicken and Gravy

Yep, I said gravy. Are you hungry yet? Well, I told you I'm an old-fashioned cook gone low-carb. This Roast Chicken and Gravy will remind you of old times gone by. Served with old-fashioned sides of veggies (see the recipes in the Chapter 12), this meal will delight you — and your guests.

Preparation time: *10 minutes*

Cooking time: *About 2 hours*

Yield: *6 servings*

1 roasting chicken, 3 to 4 pounds	*3 cups chicken stock, divided*
1 teaspoon sea salt	*3 tablespoons whole-wheat pastry flour*
½ teaspoon pepper	*Salt and pepper to taste*
2 tablespoons melted butter	

1 Preheat the oven to 400 degrees. Season the chicken both inside and out with salt and pepper. Brush the entire chicken with butter.

2 Place the chicken on a rack in a shallow roasting pan, breast side up. Pour 1 cup chicken broth in the bottom of the roasting pan. Roast, uncovered for about 30 minutes.

3 Baste the chicken with pan drippings and broth in the roasting pan. Reduce the oven temperature to 350 degrees, and roast for an additional hour to 1 hour and 20 minutes, depending on your oven and the size of your chicken. Continue to baste the chicken every 20 minutes or so with the drippings and broth in the roasting pan. Test the chicken for doneness with your meat thermometer, which should read 180 degrees with the thermometer placed in the fleshiest part of the thigh of the chicken.

4 When done, place the chicken on a serving platter, and let it rest while you make the gravy. Keep the bird nice and warm by making a loose tent of heavy aluminum foil and placing it over the chicken to hold in the heat.

5 Skim the fat from the roasting pan. Add ½ cup chicken broth to the drippings and stir over a hot burner to loosen the browned bits in the roasting pan. This only takes about 1 to 2 minutes. Transfer the mixture to a heavy skillet.

6 Blend the flour into ¼ cup chicken broth in a small container using a fork to stir and blend well. Make sure there are no lumps. Slowly pour the mixture into the skillet with drippings, and place the skillet over medium heat, stirring constantly with a wooden spoon or whisk.

7 Gradually add the remaining 1¼ cups of chicken broth, continuing to cook and stirring constantly until the mixture comes to a boil and begins to thicken. This will take only about 3 to 4 minutes. Salt and pepper to taste.

Per serving: Calories 233 (From Fat 111); Fat 12g (Saturated 5g); Cholesterol 90mg; Sodium 1,055mg; Carbohydrate 3g; Dietary Fiber 0g (Net Carbohydrate 3g); Protein 26g.

Introducing a Little Uptown Flair

Dress rehearsal is over, and now you're going to cook chicken like they do uptown. This little ditty (or section) shows you how you can easily turn chicken into an elegant presentation. This dish has been known to make just another day an occasion.

Orange Chicken Veronique

Veronique? Not to worry — it just means to garnish with grapes. This easy chicken dish is also elegant. So when you're expecting guests, this recipe is a surefire hit.

Preparation time: *15 minutes*

Cooking time: *25 to 30 minutes*

Yield: *6 servings*

1 tablespoon light olive oil or vegetable oil	¼ teaspoon dried marjoram leaves
6 skinless, boneless chicken breast halves	1 teaspoon cornstarch mixed with 1 tablespoon water
½ cup orange juice (preferably low-carb)	½ cup halved seedless green grapes
½ cup dry white wine	½ cup halved seedless red grapes
2 packets Splenda sugar substitute	1 teaspoon grated orange peel
¼ teaspoon salt	6 very thin orange slices for garnish (optional)
⅛ teaspoon white pepper	

1 Place a 12-inch nonstick skillet on medium high heat and add the oil. Add the chicken, and brown on both sides, cooking for about 5 to 6 minutes only. Remove the chicken from the skillet. Drain the excess oil from the skillet, and wipe the skillet with a paper towel. Place the chicken back in the skillet.

2 Add the orange juice, white wine, Splenda, salt, pepper, and marjoram leaves to the skillet. Reduce the heat to low and simmer, covered, for 12 to 15 minutes. Be sure the juices from the chicken are running clear, not pink. Remove the chicken from the skillet, and place on a warmed serving platter. Cover with aluminum foil to keep warm.

3 Dissolve the cornstarch in the tablespoon of water. (I like to do this by using a small jar and combining the cornstarch with the water and shaking it up instead of trying to stir the lumps out.) Stir the thickening mixture into the orange and wine mixture in the skillet, stirring constantly. Add the grapes and orange peel.

4 Cook for only 2 to 3 minutes until the sauce is slightly thickened and translucent. Spoon over chicken and serve immediately. Garnish with orange slices, if desired.

Per serving: Calories 175 (From Fat 47); Fat 5g (Saturated 1g); Cholesterol 63mg; Sodium 152mg; Carbohydrate 8g; Dietary Fiber 0g (Net Carbohydrate 8g); Protein 23g.

Chicken and Zucchini in Dijon Sauce

Talk about quick, easy, and yummy. This is a great low-carb staple that you can add to your list of go-to recipes, while the Dijon sauce gives it a bit of an out-of-the-ordinary flair. The best part: It works well with whatever veggies you have on hand. I call for low-fat yogurt to serve as the base of the sauce here. You can use low-carb yogurt if you choose. Just check the carb and calorie counts on any yogurt you select. Don't be fooled; read those labels (see Chapter 3).

Preparation time: *15 minutes*

Cooking time: *10 to 12 minutes*

Yield: *4 servings*

½ cup plain lowfat yogurt	1 garlic clove, minced fine
2 tablespoons Dijon mustard	2 medium zucchinis cut into thin strips
¼ teaspoon crushed dried tarragon	1 tablespoon olive oil
Nonstick cooking spray	12 ounces boneless, skinless chicken breasts, cut into bite-size pieces
1 medium carrot, cut in very thin strips	

1 In a small bowl, stir together the yogurt, mustard, and tarragon. Set aside.

2 Spray a large heavy skillet (or wok) with nonstick cooking spray. Heat the skillet over medium heat. Stir-fry the carrot and garlic for one minute.

3 Add the zucchini, and stir-fry for about 3 minutes or until the veggies are crisp-tender. Remove the contents from the skillet and set aside.

4 Add the olive oil to the skillet, and stir-fry the chicken for 5 to 7 minutes until the pieces are no longer pink.

5 Return the veggies to the skillet, and add the yogurt mixture. Toss to coat all the ingredients with the sauce. Cook, stirring constantly, for 1 minute or until all the ingredients are thoroughly heated.

Variation: Don't limit yourself to this great basic recipe for a very quick and tasty meal. If you have broccoli in the refrigerator, go ahead and add it. If you have sugar snap peas, be my guest. Some other tasty veggies that make a lovely presentation with the cream sauce are red, yellow, and green bell pepper strips (you can buy them precut in the frozen section), fresh mushrooms, chopped broccoli florets, and asparagus spears. Just keep in mind that your choices of veggies will vary the carb count somewhat.

Tip: Sometimes I take a recipe like this and just keep adding a variety of veggies that I love and/or have on hand in the freezer. Double the sauce portion of the recipe and you have a great lunch to take to work the next day or to nosh at home.

Per serving: *Calories 174 (From Fat 60); Fat 7g (Saturated 1g); Cholesterol 49mg; Sodium 265mg; Carbohydrate 8g; Dietary Fiber 2g (Net Carbohydrate 6g); Protein 21g.*

Chapter 11

Visiting the Meat Counter

*I*n this chapter, I get right to the heart of the matter — great recipes for beef, pork, and lamb. Along the way, I provide you with pointers on selecting lean cuts of meat and using the best cooking techniques to make sure your meal comes out just right, regardless of the cut of meat you're preparing. So, grab your wallet — it's off to the butcher with you!

Bringing Lean Meats to the Table

Some low-carb diets — notice I referenced "diets" and not "lifestyle" — call for lots of meat and as much fat as you care to gobble up. In my opinion, this approach is one of the myths of the low-carb diet, because diets high in saturated fats can contribute to heart disease.

What's the real beef about meat and the low-carb lifestyle? Healthy lifestyles are all about moderation, not deprivation. And the fact is that meat is a source of a number of essential nutrients. So, in this section, I discuss the essential nutrients found in meat, provide some insight on watching fats and calories, and give you some suggestions on choosing lean cuts of meat.

The essentials: Protein

Feeling full and satisfied is important to the success of the healthy low-carb lifestyle that you've chosen, and protein fills the bill. Protein fills you up very quickly and helps stave off hunger. It's a star in producing a slower and steadier increase in blood glucose levels (go to Chapter 2 for an extensive discussion on glycemic index and glycemic load).

Protein is an essential nutrient that your body needs. Protein helps fight disease and is essential to your metabolism. Your internal organs, skin, nerves, muscles, tendons, bones, brain, hair, and nails are largely made up of fibrous proteins. And guess what? You need protein to replace the tissue in your body that continuously breaks down.

The great thing about meat is that it's a *complete protein* food, meaning it supplies each of the *amino acids* (think of these as protein building blocks) that your body can't make on its own. Other foods are incomplete sources of protein. When you eat these foods, you need to combine them in ways that ensure you're getting all the amino acids you need. So including some lean meat in your low-carb lifestyle is about eating *complete protein foods* — foods that are protein-efficient, supplying not just some of the essential amino acids but *all* of them.

I'm not telling you to eat meat three times a day, so please don't think that this is an eat-a-lot-of-meat section. I'm simply providing you with the upside of the nutrition and protein-efficiency lean meats can provide. If you don't get protein from eating meats, then you simply need to substitute other protein-rich foods such as eggs, dried beans, and soy foods in combinations that ensure you're getting all the amino acids you need.

Everything in moderation: Fats

As you approach your favorite meat counter, keep in mind that consuming some fat is an essential component to any diet:

- ✔ Fats not only add to the flavor of your food, but they also give you a full feeling and a quick energy source.

- ✔ Fats provide your body with protective cushions for vital organs and supply the fatty acids for many chemical processes that regulate the passage of nutrients in and out of cells.

- ✔ Fats also transport and aid in your body's absorption of fat-soluble vitamins A, D, E, and K.

But, as you can read in Chapter 2, you need to think about consuming more healthy unsaturated fats and less artery-clogging saturated and trans fats.

When it comes to making choices about which meats to choose, go for *lean* cuts of meat. If you opt for a healthy low-carb lifestyle, your focus is about the right balance for your body and what works for you. I'll simply state that moderation and balance are always the keys to anything in life. Just as I don't feel the all-the-meat-you-can-eat approach to low-carb dieting represents a healthy nutritional balance, I don't think deprivation is necessarily the answer either.

Lean cuts of meat are another very tasty, healthy alternative for your low-carb lifestyle. They're rich in B vitamins, zinc, and iron, and they add variety to your low-carb lifestyle. Just don't forget about the importance of fish, seafood, and poultry as well. (See Chapter 9 for more about fish, Chapter 10 for all your poultry needs, and either chapter for bunches of great recipes.)

Calories still count. Whether you consume excess calories from carbohydrates, fat, or protein, the body converts the excess calories to fat storage in your body.

Cutting up

When you're scoping out which cuts of meats to buy, look for meat that doesn't have big chunks of fat and heavy marbling. *Marbling* is the intermingling of fat within the meat. Beef is the most popular meat among Americans, with pork coming in second, followed by lamb. Table 11-1 lists the three most popular meats and provides you with some suggestions for cuts that are the least fatty.

Table 11-1	Least Fatty Cuts for Three Popular Meats	
Beef	*Pork*	*Lamb*
Tenderloin	Pork loin	Loin chops
Sirloin	Tenderloin	Whole leg
Top loin	Sirloin	Sirloin roast
Top round	Rib chops	Blade chops
Bottom round	Boneless ham	
Eye of round	Canadian bacon	
Flank, skirt, and London broil		

Because you're selecting less fatty meats, keep in mind that the cooking time speeds up and leaner cuts of meats tend to dry out more quickly in the cooking process. You only need to experiment preparing lean meats a couple times to master it.

Steaking Out a Low-Carb Favorite

Beef is perceived as being high in saturated fats, but if you choose lean cuts and trim them of all visible fat, you can remove almost all of the saturated fat. Just trim it off with a very sharp knife before cooking (see Figure 11-1).

Steak Diane

This entrée is often served in some of the finest restaurants, and there's no reason why you can't make it in your very own kitchen. It comes together so quickly that you can prepare any night of the week. Add a little ambiance to the evening by making it special. How about a tablecloth and some cloth napkins? And a little red wine with your Steak Diane? This is low-carb dining at its finest!

Preparation time: *10 minutes*

Cooking time: *12 to 14 minutes*

Yield: *2 servings*

2 6-ounce filet mignons

⅛ teaspoon salt

⅛ teaspoon pepper

3 tablespoons butter, divided

2 tablespoons finely minced shallots

1 teaspoon Dijon mustard

1 tablespoon fresh lemon juice

1 tablespoon finely chopped fresh chives

1 teaspoon Worcestershire sauce

1 teaspoon brandy

1 tablespoon finely minced fresh Italian parsley

1 Season both sides of the meat with salt and pepper.

2 Using a heavy skillet, melt 1 tablespoon butter over medium heat. Add the steaks to the skillet, and cook for about 3 minutes on each side for medium-rare meat.

3 Move the steaks from the skillet to serving plates to keep them warm.

4 Add 2 tablespoons butter, the shallots, and the mustard to the drippings in the skillet (still over medium heat), and cook for only 1 minute.

5 Add the lemon juice, chives, and Worcestershire sauce to the skillet. Cook, stirring constantly, for 2 minutes.

6 Remove from heat, then add the brandy to the mixture, and pour immediately over the steaks. Garnish by sprinkling the minced parsley on top of the steaks.

Per serving: *Calories 524 (From Fat 380); Fat 42g (Saturated 20g); Cholesterol 152mg; Sodium 313mg; Carbohydrate 3g; Dietary Fiber 0g (Net Carbohydrate 3g); Protein 32g.*

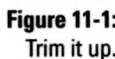

Figure 11-1:
Trim it up.

Try some of these variations as toppers to melt on your already deliciously cooked steaks:

- **Parisienne:** Add finely chopped fresh Italian parsley to butter.
- **Herbed:** Add tarragon and some chopped watercress to butter.
- **Olive butter:** Blend chopped fresh green (or dark) olives with butter.

Sampling a Wide Range of Recipes and Techniques

Meats are a valuable part of a healthy low-carb lifestyle. In choosing lean cuts of meat, you may want to complement the meat with more herbs and spices, because the lack of fat takes away some of the flavor of the finished dish. Because you're going to trim excess fat, less cooking time is required. Keep your meat thermometer handy so your meats aren't undercooked. But by the same token, you don't want them overcooked, because they'll be dry and stringy. Most recipes tell you the minimum degree of doneness to test for.

Do yourself a favor, and invest in a meat thermometer if you don't have one. To test for doneness of beef and lamb, insert the thermometer in the thickest part of the meat, being sure not to hit the bone. Current guidelines from the U.S. Department of Agriculture advise to cook meat to at least 145 degrees to kill all bacteria. Here are the basics of temperatures for doneness from the USDA:

- Medium rare: 145 degrees
- Medium: 160 degrees
- Well done: 170 degrees

Cook your pork and ground meat to a reading of at least 160 degrees to assure that it's done. For more information on preparing and storing meats and other foods safely, go the U.S. Department of Agriculture's Food Safety and Inspection Service Website at www.fsis.usda.gov/Fact_Sheets.

Baked Ham and Sauerkraut Rolls

Calling sauerkraut lovers everywhere! This recipe is quick and easy, and the carb count is way low. These rolls are good leftover for lunch the next day, too.

Preparation time: *10 minutes*

Cooking time: *20 minutes*

Yield: *2 servings*

8-ounce can sauerkraut, rinsed and drained

½ teaspoon caraway seed

2 tablespoons thinly sliced green onions

8 thick slices cooked deli ham

¼ cup mayonnaise

2 tablespoons plus 1 teaspoon light cream

2 teaspoons Dijon mustard

1 Preheat the oven to 375 degrees. Combine the sauerkraut, caraway seed, and onion in a medium bowl. Chop 2 slices of the ham very fine. Stir the ham into the sauerkraut mixture, combining well.

2 In a small bowl, combine the mayonnaise, 2 tablespoons of the light cream, and the mustard to make mustard sauce for the rolls. Add ¼ cup mustard sauce to the sauerkraut mixture, stirring together until well combined. Set the remainder of the mustard sauce aside.

3 Divide the sauerkraut mixture into six equal amounts.

4 Spread the sauerkraut mixture down the long side of each of the 6 remaining ham slices. Roll up each slice of ham, and place the seam side down in a 6-x-10-x-2-inch baking dish. Cover with aluminum foil. Bake for 18 to 20 minutes until heated thoroughly.

5 Stir the remaining teaspoon cream into the remaining mustard sauce, and spoon it over the ham rolls right before serving.

Per serving: Calories 365 (From Fat 273); Fat 30g (Saturated 7g); Cholesterol 82mg; Sodium 2,112mg; Carbohydrate 6g; Dietary Fiber 2g (Net Carbohydrate 4g); Protein 22g.

There are no hard and fast rules for cooking meat, because each cut lends itself to a variety of preparations. In following your healthy low-carb lifestyle, roasting, broiling, and grilling are the preferred ways to prepare meat. But don't forget about using your slow cooker (see Chapter 16) and stir-frying.

You can tenderize and add flavor to any meat by marinating it in a store-bought Italian dressing or homemade vinaigrette. If you have the time, London broil, tri-tip, and round steak are especially good when marinated overnight (see the "Marinating meats" sidebar for more information).

Marinating meats

Marinating is covered extensively in Chapter 10. But there are some specifics to marinating meats that I'd like to give you to tuck in your chef hat. So fire up the grill!

✔ Marinades make a world of difference to less tender cuts of meat such as London broil, flank steaks, and sirloin tips. Vinaigrettes, lemon juice, and wine, which are all acidic ingredients, tend to increase the juiciness of meats as well as tenderize.

✔ Always place meats that you're marinating in the refrigerator. A minimum of 4 hours is usually a good rule of thumb for marinating, and overnight is great. This is personal preference and if you want to marinate your meat for an hour and throw it on the grill then, hey, it's your choice. I personally like for the meat to really soak up those marinade flavors so I plan ahead and go for the longer marinade time.

Slow cooking

A slow cooker is a great way to cook a roast and have dinner ready when you come through the door after a long day. You can use less expensive and slightly tougher cuts of meat for cooking in the slow cooker. Because of the long cooking time and the way the slow cooker works, the meat tenderizes as it cooks (see Chapter 16 for more info on low-carb slow cooking and some fabulous recipes).

Roasting

Oven roasting is a traditional way of preparing meat — usually roasts or large pieces of meat. Slow oven roasting is done over a longer period of time and at a lower oven temperature, with the result being tender and juicy meat. If the roast has the bone in it, it cooks faster, because the bone actually acts as a heat conductor. Some cooks choose roasts with bone because they believe the end result is better flavor than boneless roast.

Rolled and boned roasts should be set on a rack for roasting. Don't cover the roast, and don't add water, because the meat will steam rather than roast.

 After you remove your roast from the oven, let it rest for about 15 minutes (set it on the countertop in the pan) unless the recipe specifically states otherwise. The meat actually continues to cook, and its juices settle into the meat, making it easier to carve and juicier.

Apricot-Glazed Pork Roast

This entrée will make you smile. The combination of the apricot preserves with the Dijon mustard and the fresh rosemary fills the kitchen with a fabulous aroma while it's cooking. Plus, I think you'll enjoy the distinctive flavor of the glaze. The juices should run when you slice the roast, because the glaze holds them all inside.

Preparation time: *10 minutes*

Cooking time: *About 1 hour*

Yield: *6 servings*

½ cup sugar-free apricot preserves	*Salt and pepper to taste*
1 tablespoon Dijon mustard	*3-pound lean pork roast*
1 tablespoon finely chopped fresh rosemary	

1 Preheat the oven to 325 degrees. Line a shallow baking pan with foil to aid in clean up.

2 Microwave the sugar-free apricot preserves for about 45 seconds to 1 minute on high to melt (depending on the microwave, you may have to heat for another 30 seconds).

3 In a small bowl, combine the melted preserves, mustard, rosemary, salt, and pepper. Divide the glaze in half in two separate bowls. Brush half of the glaze on the roast. Set the other half of the glaze aside.

4 Place the pork roast in the pan, and roast it in the oven for 1 hour or until the meat ther-mometer registers between 150 and 155 degrees as it will continue to cook after you remove it from the oven. Remove the meat from the oven, and cover with foil to keep it warm. Let it stand for 15 minutes.

5 Slice the roast, and drizzle with the pan juices. Serve with the remaining glaze.

Per serving: Calories 348 (From Fat 139); Fat 16g (Saturated 6g); Cholesterol 128mg; Sodium 252mg; Carbohydrate 7g; Dietary Fiber 0g (Net Carbohydrate 7g); Protein 46g.

Broiling

Broiling is a great method for quickly cooking smaller cuts and more tender cuts like chops and steaks. Spray the broiler rack on the broiler pan with non-stick cooking spray to prevent the meat from sticking to the rack. Be sure to preheat the broiler before starting to cook your meat. When you broil, it's important to only turn the meat one time to maintain the juices. If there's a band of thin fat around the pork chops or steaks after trimming, score the fat at one-inch intervals so the chops won't curl up on you.

Herb-Rubbed Pork Chops
with Tomato-Arugula Salsa

If you prefer to cook these pork chops on the grill, be my guest. Whether they're grilled or broiled, be sure not to overcook them so the chops don't become dry. Use your meat thermometer for perfect doneness.

Preparation time: *15 minutes*

Cooking time: *10 to 15 minutes*

Yield: *4 servings*

2 teaspoons olive oil	*Salt and pepper to taste*
1 tablespoon finely chopped fresh sage	*4 5-ounce loin pork chops, bone in (about 1 inch thick)*
¼ teaspoon dried thyme	*Tomato-Arugula Salsa (see the following recipe)*
1 bay leaf	
1 tablespoon finely chopped fresh rosemary	

1 Combine the olive oil, sage, thyme, bay leaf, rosemary, salt, and pepper in a small bowl, whisking together to combine. Rub the mixture on the pork chops, and place the meat on a platter.

2 Preheat the broiler, and bring the chops to room temperature on the platter while broiler is preheating.

3 Prepare the Tomato-Arugula Salsa.

4 Broil the pork chops close to heat for 5 to 7 minutes on each side.

5 Serve with the Tomato-Arugula Salsa, topping each pork chop.

Tomato-Arugula Salsa

1 clove garlic, chopped fine	*Salt and pepper to taste*
2 teaspoons olive oil	*2 cups torn arugula*
1 tablespoon fresh lemon juice	*1 medium tomato, diced*

1 In a small bowl, combine the garlic, olive oil, lemon juice, and salt and pepper to taste.

2 Place the arugula and tomato in a medium bowl. Pour the oil mixture over and toss.

3 Refrigerate until serving time.

Per serving: *Calories 219 (From Fat 117); Fat 13g (Saturated 3g); Cholesterol 61mg; Sodium 201mg; Carbohydrate 3g; Dietary Fiber 1g (Net Carbohydrate 2g); Protein 22g.*

Parmesan-Garlic Lamb Chops with Zucchini Relish

I use store-bought Parmesan-Garlic Italian dressing a lot for marinating and basting meats — it's almost magical. If you can't find Parmesan-Garlic Italian dressing, your favorite bottled Italian will work fine — just watch the carbs in all store-bought dressings. It tenderizes and flavors all at the same time. If you're an avid fan of garlic, add fresh garlic to these chops for an even more intense flavor.

Preparation time: *10 minutes*

Cooking time: *20 minutes*

Yield: *4 servings*

1 red onion, peeled and sliced thin	*¼ teaspoon salt*
1 tablespoon olive oil	*8 4-ounce lamb chops*
1 zucchini, chopped	*3 tablespoons Parmesan-Garlic Italian dressing (store-bought)*
1 tablespoon chopped sun-dried tomatoes	
1 teaspoon finely chopped fresh rosemary	

1 Preheat the broiler. To prepare the Zucchini Relish, cook the onion in the olive oil in a small skillet over medium-high heat for 4 to 5 minutes until translucent.

2 Add the zucchini, sun-dried tomatoes, fresh rosemary, and salt. Cook for 5 minutes until the zucchini is tender. Set the Zucchini Relish aside and keep warm.

3 Arrange the pork chops in a broiler pan, and baste them on both sides with the Italian dressing. Broil for about 4 minutes per side for medium rare chops and about 5 minutes per side for medium to medium-well chops, turning once.

4 Serve immediately with the Zucchini Relish on the side or on top of the chops.

Per serving: *Calories 326 (From Fat 176); Fat 20g (Saturated 5g); Cholesterol 100mg; Sodium 365mg; Carbohydrate 5g; Dietary Fiber 1g (Net Carbohydrate 4g); Protein 31g.*

If you use the broiler in your oven for broiling meat, place a slice of bread in the drip pan. It soaks up the fat drippings and helps prevent a fire from flaring in the oven.

Making pockets in meats, especially pork chops, is a yummy variation and isn't as difficult as it looks. When you're at the meat counter, make sure to select chops that are about 1¼ inches thick. With a sharp knife, cut from the outside of the chop towards the bone. Cut almost to the bone, and you have your pocket ready for stuffing.

Grilling

Grilling, in my estimation, is the best. And it isn't just for summer any more — it's become a year round sport, even if you have to scrape the snow off the barbie. Each individual has his or her specific ways of grilling, but here are a couple of my tips for striving for perfection when grilling steaks and chops:

- ✔ Let the meat reach almost room temperature before grilling. It cooks better.
- ✔ Don't salt the meat before grilling; salt it after you've cooked it instead. Salt pulls the juices out of the meat.
- ✔ If you use tongs instead of a fork for turning, you preserve more of the meat juices.
- ✔ Make sure excess fat is trimmed to avoid flare-ups while grilling and to keep the meat from curling during cooking.
- ✔ Be sure to test for just the right doneness to the individual's liking (see the "Sampling a Wide Range of Recipes and Techniques" text earlier in the chapter).

Brush the grill with some olive oil before cooking your meat to prevent it from sticking to the grill.

Stir-frying

Stir-frying is a very healthy low-carb way of cooking up a whole meal. You can begin with thin pieces of meat and add your favorite vegetables. If you're especially hungry, grab a whole-wheat low-carb tortilla, and fill it with your stir-fry mixture.

Beef and Asparagus Stir-Fry

This easy and quick recipe is sure to please. Use frozen asparagus if the fresh stuff isn't available — some of the frozen asparagus these days is actually a better grade than the fresh. And make sure you don't overcook the asparagus. You want it crisp-tender.

Preparation time: *20 minutes*

Refrigeration time: *1 hour*

Cooking time: *6 to 10 minutes*

Yield: *4 servings*

10 ounces boneless beef tenderloin	*1 teaspoon cornstarch*
2 tablespoons dry sherry	*2 teaspoons olive oil*
1 tablespoon finely chopped ginger root	*24 fresh asparagus spears (a little over 1 pound) cut diagonally into 2-inch pieces*
2 garlic cloves, chopped fine	
2 teaspoons soy sauce	*¼ cup thinly sliced scallions*
1 tablespoon dark sesame oil	*1 tablespoon toasted sesame seeds (see the note that follows)*
Zest from 1 orange	

1 Cut the beef tenderloin into thin strips and set aside. In a large bowl, combine the sherry, ginger root, garlic, soy sauce, sesame oil, and orange zest, mixing well.

2 Place the strips of tenderloin in a large plastic zipper bag. Pour the marinade over the meat, and seal the bag. Refrigerate for 1 hour, turning 2 or 3 times to make sure all the pieces are marinating.

3 Strain the marinade into a measuring cup, and add enough water to make ⅓ cup liquid. Add the cornstarch, stirring to dissolve.

4 Use a wok if you have one, but if you don't, a large, heavy skillet will do just fine. Add the olive oil and the beef to the skillet, stir-frying for about 1 minute. Remove the beef from the skillet with a slotted spoon, and set aside.

5 Reduce the heat, and add the asparagus pieces, stir-frying for only 2 to 3 minutes. Return the reserved marinade and beef to the skillet, and cook on high, stirring constantly for 2 minutes or until the sauce thickens and the beef is cooked through.

6 Sprinkle with scallions and sesame seeds, and serve immediately.

Note: *Toasting sesame seeds provides tremendous flavor, and it's really simple to do. Just heat a dry skillet over medium heat. Add the sesame seeds, and cook them for a few minutes, shaking the skillet occasionally. When the aroma becomes pronounced and the seeds start to darken, remove the skillet from the heat and transfer the seeds to another container.*

Per serving: Calories 188 (From Fat 101); Fat 11g (Saturated 2g); Cholesterol 36mg; Sodium 192mg; Carbohydrate 7g; Dietary Fiber 2g (Net Carbohydrate 5g); Protein 15g.

 If you want to be able to very easily cut your meat thin for stir-frying, slice it when it's still slightly frozen. If your meat is fresh, pop it in the freezer for a bit. Freezing the meat gives it more body and makes it easier to hold onto. Make sure that the oil in your skillet or wok for your stir-fry is hot before you add the meat. Stir-frying about 10 ounces of meat at one time is about the load limit. If you're going to make a bigger batch of stir-fry, then do it in two stirrings. Another trick to stir-frying is to have all your ingredients ready when you begin, because you don't have a moment to go digging in the fridge or the spice rack.

 Cutting boards are an important part of meat preparation. Whatever type of cutting board you choose, make sure to wash it with hot, soapy water immediately after using it. Research has shown that using a light bleach solution on your cutting boards from time to time is a good idea. If your cutting board is dishwasher safe, by all means pop it in the dishwasher, but clean it before.

Making Ground Beef More Than a Burger

You can dress ground beef up so much that you may not even recognize it! It's very versatile for your low-carb lifestyle and I could write a whole cookbook just on ground beef and its many guises. The basics are ground sirloin, ground chuck, ground round, and just plain ol' ground beef. The prices differ from leanest to fattest with ground sirloin being the leanest and the most expensive and ground beef having the highest fat content and being the least expensive.

Ground beef shouldn't be kept in the fridge for more than a couple of days. If you're not going to use it in that amount of time then pop it in the freezer. Don't refreeze ground beef after you've thawed it out. And don't add seasonings to your ground beef before freezing it as the flavors of the seasonings can be affected by freezing.

Be sure to drain any excess fat from ground beef after browning. You can use a wire mesh strainer to accomplish this or a metal colander. Don't put the fat drippings down your garbage disposal though — yikes!

 When you're making regular meatloaf, make several individual meat loaves rather than one big one. They take less time to cook. You can bake them in a shallow baking dish or even in muffin tins sprayed with nonstick cooking spray. Keep in mind that individual meatloaves aren't recommended for the Roma Meat Loaf recipe.

Roma Meat Loaf

This is an old recipe I used to make when my kids were little. I'd prepare it the night before and then pop it in the oven when I got home from work. Serve with some steamed veggies and a side salad. You'll be simply delighted when you slice this like a jellyroll and the cheese oozes. It's so yummy! You need low-carb breadcrumbs for this recipe, so check out Chapter 10 for the scoop on how to make your own.

Preparation time: *20 minutes*

Cooking time: *1 hour and 15 minutes*

Yield: *8 servings*

2 pounds ground beef

2 eggs, slightly beaten

¼ cup low-carb breadcrumbs

¼ cup finely chopped yellow onion

¼ teaspoon dried oregano

Salt and pepper to taste

½ teaspoon garlic salt

1 can (15 ounces) tomato sauce (the lowest carb count you can find)

½ cup shredded mozzarella cheese

1 can (4 ounces) mushrooms

¼ teaspoon garlic salt

1 packet Splenda sugar substitute

1 teaspoon oregano

1 teaspoon dried parsley flakes

1 Preheat the oven to 350 degrees. In a large bowl, mix the ground beef, eggs, breadcrumbs, onion, oregano, salt, pepper, and garlic salt. Use 2 tablespoons of the tomato sauce to further moisten the mixture.

2 Tear off a good-sized piece of waxed paper, and place it on the countertop. Place the meat mixture in the middle of the waxed paper. Flatten the meat mixture into a 9-x-12-inch rectangle (no, it doesn't have to be perfect). Sprinkle with cheese and mushrooms.

3 Using the 12-inch side, roll as you would a jellyroll, and place it in a 9-x-5-inch baking pan. Bake for 1 hour.

4 To prepare the sauce: Combine the can of tomato sauce (minus the 2 tablespoons), garlic salt, Splenda, oregano, and parsley in a small saucepan.

5 Cook the ingredients over medium-low heat for 15 minutes before removing the meat loaf from the oven.

6 Remove the meat loaf from the oven and drain. Pour the sauce over the meat and bake for an additional 15 minutes.

7 Slice immediately before serving, and the cheese will deliciously ooze from the center of the meatloaf.

Per serving: *Calories 283 (From Fat 153); Fat 17g (Saturated 7g); Cholesterol 129mg; Sodium 639mg; Carbohydrate 6g; Dietary Fiber 2g (Net Carbohydrate 4g); Protein 26g.*

Cheese-Stuffed Ground Round Patties

These stuffed patties are like an entrée with a surprise tucked inside. I'm a sucker for melted and oozing cheese, and if you are too, then you're going to love this recipe. You may want to put a bib on and have the hose handy as these are delicious but a bit messy in the eating department. The combination of the hot, oozing stuffed patty with the crisp lettuce wakes up your taste buds. Just don't wear your favorite shirt when you eat these! If these cheese combinations aren't your favorites, just change them. Check out Figure 11-2 for some tips on stuffing technique.

Preparation time: *20 minutes*

Cooking time: *13 to 15 minutes*

Yield: *4 servings*

1½ pounds ground round	*¼ cup finely chopped fresh Italian parsley*
½ cup shredded mild cheddar cheese	*1 teaspoon Worcestershire sauce*
¼ cup crumbled blue cheese	*2 teaspoons olive oil*
1 clove garlic, minced fine	*1 medium red bell pepper, cut into thin strips*
½ teaspoon sea salt	*8 large iceberg lettuce leaves, washed and crispy cold*
2 teaspoons Dijon mustard	

1 Shape the ground round into 8 patties that are about ¼-inch thick and 4 inches in diameter.

2 In a small bowl, combine the cheddar cheese, blue cheese, garlic, sea salt, mustard, parsley, and Worcestershire sauce. Blend by gently tossing the mixture.

3 Mound about 3 tablespoons of the cheese mixture in the middle of 4 of the patties. Top the patties with the remaining 4 patties, pinching the edges together and completely sealing the cheese mixture in the middle.

4 Heat the olive oil in a large, nonstick skillet over medium-high heat until the skillet is hot. Add the pepper strips, stirring as they cook, about 3 to 5 minutes. Don't let the pepper strips brown. Sprinkle them with salt before removing them from the skillet.

5 Cook the beef patties in the same skillet over medium-high heat for about 5 minutes. Turn the patties over, top them with the pepper strips, and cook another 4 to 5 minutes, or until centers aren't pink.

6 Immediately wrap each patty between 2 large iceberg lettuce leaves and serve.

Per serving: Calories 350 (From Fat 165); Fat 18g (Saturated 8g); Cholesterol 113mg; Sodium 650mg; Carbohydrate 4g; Dietary Fiber 1g (Net Carbohydrate 3g); Protein 41g.

HOW TO STUFF A BURGER

1.
START WITH 2
THIN BEEF PATTIES

2.
PLACE FILLING
ON 1 PATTY.

3.
PRESS THE 2
PATTIES TOGETHER.

4.
NO FILLING
SHOWS.

5.
PRESS AND SHAPE
TO AN EVEN THICKNESS.

Chapter 12

Serving Up Veggies Galore

I think veggie power — I'm talking taste, variety, and health benefits — is sorely overlooked. Non-starchy vegetables are so low in carbs and so high in nutrients that they should be pillars of your low-carb lifestyle.

When you think about vegetables, you may think *boring,* but I'm here to shake you out of the doldrums. Getting a handle on the possibilities that vegetables offer can reinvigorate your low-carb lifestyle with tremendous tastes and variety. Plus, the nutrients in these little rascals are proven to prevent disease and help slow the appearance of aging. Add in all that fiber in raw plant foods that can lower cholesterol, reduce the risk of diabetes, and reduce the risk of many types of cancer, and you have a recipe for a tasty and healthy food source.

In this chapter, I cover some of the low-carb advantages vegetables offer and their health benefits. Then I move onto helping you choose some new selections from the produce section, prepare delicious main-dish veggie meals and sides, and spice up standard — and quick — vegetable preparations.

Moving Veggies to the Forefront of Your Low-Carb Lifestyle

After you realize all the benefits of veggies, they'll be movin' on up on your low-carb list. Colorful vegetables provide a wide range of essential vitamins, minerals, fiber, and phytochemicals your body needs to maintain good health and energy levels. Eat plenty of different vegetables (and fruits; see Chapter 3 for more on fruits that are lower in carbs). Non-starchy vegetables are very low in carbs (I include whole list of low-carb veggies in Chapter 3). Do yourself a favor and eat more veggies — not only are they good for you, but they might just prove to be a lifesaver for you. The risk of chronic diseases and some cancers is reduced just by upping your veggie intake.

Your low-carb lifestyle should include generous portions of the rainbow of veggies available to you. Make your meals colorful. Not only is the presentation more appealing that way, but the variety is also pleasing to your taste buds. More importantly, brightly colored plant foods contain antioxidants and phytochemicals (see the "Focusing on antioxidants and phytochemicals" sidebar in this chapter for an explanation of these disease-fighting substances found in veggies and fruits). Every color in a veggie or fruit is associated with a different phytochemical. The more colors in your daily veggie rainbow, the more powerful the punch.

Focusing on antioxidants and photochemicals

One of the goals of your low-carb lifestyle is to burn fat more quickly and more efficiently, resulting in weight loss and weight maintenance (see Chapter 2 for the details). Burning fat in your body is referred to as your metabolic burn. When you burn something, it causes *oxidation*, a chemical process that in turn produces highly reactive compounds called *free radicals.*

Free radical production is a normal part of life as simple as breathing in oxygen. Your body's natural defense systems normally neutralize the free radicals that develop. Unfortunately, it isn't quite this simple. Pollutants in the air of all kinds, UV radiation, and other environmental assaults and even excessive use of alcohol can be overpowering factors decreasing the ability of your body to neutralize these free radicals. As a result, the free radicals run rampant, causing damage to your body's cell function and structure. This is serious damage that not only can contribute to the aging process but leads to serious illnesses such as heart disease and cancer. The good news? Vegetables (and fruits) can play a large role in combating these

problems. Plant food is somewhat magical in that it has the amazing ability to produce an army of phytochemicals and antioxidants that charge forth and neutralize the free radicals in your body, keeping your body healthier and helping to oust chronic disease.

Antioxidants are chemical substances that convert the free radical to a harmless molecule. There are thousands of antioxidants in fresh vegetables, as well as phytochemicals. *Phytochemicals* are plant chemicals that are neither vitamins nor minerals, yet they are health enhancers. The study of phytochemicals is relatively new and one of the hot topics in the health field.

So, the simple solution to a very complex process that's taking place in your body 24/7 is to eat plenty of fresh, multicolored vegetables in a wide variety. And a relatively simple explanation as to why people are much more vulnerable to disease today is because these vital defenses found only in a rich plant food diet have been eliminated from our diets. And so, veggies to the rescue!

🍑 Oven-Roasted Vegetable Medley

You can substitute or switch around any of the vegetables in this recipe. I offer this recipe as a method of preparing vegetables. When you're deciding on your choices of veggies, make the dish look like a rainbow medley. Not only do the colors make the dish more attractive, but the health benefits are much greater as well. Experiment with some of your favorite herbs and spices with this recipe. I added rosemary as an option, but I sprinkle rosemary into just about anything I can. Serve this dish with a side of one of your new favorite veggie sauces (see the "Veggies on the Side" section later in the chapter to discover these delectable sauces). Happy and colorful roasting!

Preparation time: *20 minutes*

Cooking time: *30 minutes*

Yield: *4 servings*

1 pound asparagus	*1 medium red onion*
1 medium summer squash	*3 tablespoons olive oil*
1 medium zucchini	*1 teaspoon salt*
1 medium yellow bell pepper	*½ teaspoon pepper*
1 medium red bell pepper	*1 teaspoon dried rosemary (optional)*

1 Preheat the oven to 450 degrees. Cut the asparagus, squash, zucchini, yellow bell pepper, red bell pepper, and red onion into fairly uniform, bite-sized pieces.

2 Using a large roasting pan, toss the vegetables with the olive oil, salt, pepper, and rosemary, if desired, mixing and coating evenly.

3 Spread the veggies in the roasting pan in a single layer and roast for 30 minutes. Stir a couple times during the roasting. Vegetables should brown lightly and be crisp-tender (not limp).

Per serving: *Calories 144 (From Fat 94); Fat 10g (Saturated 1g); Cholesterol 0mg; Sodium 589mg; Carbohydrate 11g; Dietary Fiber 4g (Net Carbohydrate 7g); Protein 3g.*

Aim for a minimum of five to seven servings of veggies per day, some of which should be raw snacks. When you eat veggies raw, the nutrient quotient stays way up there because they're fresh and *raw* — you haven't cooked out any of the nutrition. The fresher the better.

Disease fighting antioxidants and phytochemicals are found in all vegetables and fruits. But the real stars of the vegetable world are the *crucifers*. The name *crucifer* comes from the cross-shaped flowers these vegetables produce. Crucifer vegetables include cabbage, cauliflower, broccoli, and dark, leafy greens such as spinach. Although cabbage and broccoli are the best-known crucifers, other members in the family include kale, collard greens, mustard greens, rutabaga, kohlrabi, and turnips. (Check out Chapter 8 for more on greens.)

Add slivered or sliced almonds to asparagus and broccoli dishes for texture and crunch. If you're a walnut lover, add ½ cup walnut halves to a veggie combo.

Introducing Variety: A Veggie Buying Handbook

Preparation of tasty veggies takes little time and effort for spectacular results (see the "Cooking Them Just Right" section later in the chapter), all it takes is a little imagination and getting to know your veggies. If you're not familiar with certain veggies and find yourself cooking the same old vegetables the same old way, step up to a new choice. I first introduce low-carb vegetables in Chapter 3 with the other components of a low-carb shopping list. Here I make trying new vegetables a bit easier by providing a few hints on how to choose the pick of the crop. Some may be old friends of yours, and some may be new to your neighborhood. So pick out some new veggie friends.

- **Artichokes:** Select firm, compact artichokes that have no brown blemishes. They should be fleshy with good green color and tightly closed leaf scales. Cut them 1 inch from the top and cut the stem close to the base. Remove the lower outer leaves that tend to be tough. Cut the thorny tip from each leaf with kitchen scissors. Your artichokes are now ready for a great new recipe experience.

- **Asparagus:** The greener the asparagus, the better. Stalks should be firm with compact tips, and they shouldn't be woody or flat or have blemishes. When preparing asparagus, either break off the woody end of the stalk or cut it at an angle.

- **Avocados:** You want your avocados to be plump and slightly firm yet yield to gentle pressure. Most avocados are hard and not ripened when they're picked. Ripen them at room temperature in a paper bag on the counter. Don't pick bruised or shriveled avocados, because it's an indication that they're overripe.

- **Bell peppers:** Brightly colored with a shiny sheen means peppers are at their peak. Red, green, orange, and yellow varieties of peppers should be thick-fleshed and crisp. Avoid peppers that are wrinkled, shriveled, and dull. Red, yellow, and orange peppers are sweeter than green peppers.

- **Beets:** Meet beets, the first cousins to spinach (yes, really). Look for young beets with fresh green tops. Not only can you cook the beet root, but you can also cook the tops, which are loaded with healthy nutrients.

- **Broccoli:** Pick broccoli with bright green stems and leaves and tightly closed dark green florets. Try to avoid stems that are too thick, florets that have begun to yellow, or leaves that are wilted.

✔ **Cabbage:** When I say cabbage, I'm talking about a whole family here. In this cruciferous family, there are red heads and green heads, which should be solid and firm. Brussels sprouts are in the cabbage family, too, and their small heads should be tight and solid.

✔ **Carrots:** You want carrots that are well-shaped and smooth with bright orange color. Don't select carrots that have cracks or are flabby and wilted. Small to medium carrots are more likely to be more tender and sweeter. Don't be fooled by carrots that are packaged in orange cello bags, because they can be deceptive and look fresher and more orange than they actually are.

✔ **Cauliflower:** Avoid bruises or brown spots on cauliflower. Pick compact heads with white florets and green, crispy leaves. Store cauliflower in the fridge wrapped in plastic wrap and wash just before cooking.

✔ **Eggplant:** Try to select firm eggplants that are small rather than large because the smaller ones tend to be more tender. Check that the stems and the little cape-like bracts are intact and green. If the bracts are loose, the eggplant is likely older and may have begun to spoil, so pick another one.

✔ **Green beans:** Buy young, crisp, bright green beans that snap. To prepare, break off the ends and remove strings if necessary.

✔ **Green onions (scallions):** Choose green onions/scallions with small bulb bottoms and fresh green tops. Avoid any with wilting leaves.

✔ **Leeks:** Try to choose leeks that are young, firm, and straight and have bright green leaves. If the root end is enlarged, they may be tough and not as sweet. Avoid leeks with yellow leaves.

✔ **Mushrooms:** Although mushrooms are technically in the fungi family, I include them in this chapter because, while you're in the produce section buying veggies, you'll buy mushrooms, too, not even considering what family they belong to! Select mushrooms that are firm, plump, and unblemished. Check out different mushrooms — from button to shiitake, cremini to brown — for a different look, texture and taste. Don't wash before refrigerating because they'll keep longer that way.

✔ **Onions:** Carefully select onions that are clean with dry and papery skins. Make sure they feel firm and solid with no soft spots. Avoid onions that are beginning to sprout.

✔ **Parsnips:** Look for smooth, firm, well-shaped parsnips. Stay away from parsnips that are shriveled and soft or too large. Parsnips have good nutritive value and are very tasty.

✔ **Spinach:** Look for crisp and very dark green leaves — the greener the better. Purchased in its natural state, spinach is usually very sandy and needs a lot of preparation in cleaning and removing the sand. I opt for prewashed myself.

✔ **Turnips:** Shop for crisp, solid turnips. The turnip actually contains 92 percent water and no starch or sugar, but it has a pungent essential oil. Turnips are very nutritious and can be very tasty when prepared using a good recipe.

✔ **Water chestnuts:** These little wonders, usually bought in a can, aren't vegetables but are actually fruits of a water plant. I won't hold this against them, though. They add such wonderful crunch to veggie dishes that we can invite them into the family in this chapter. Be sure to rinse canned water chestnuts in cold water before using because doing so makes them crisper and removes any of the tinny flavor resulting from being canned.

✔ **Zucchini:** Buy small and medium, dark green zucchini. When you pick them up, they should be heavy for their size and free from blemishes, with thin, tender skin. Zucchini is a member of the summer squash family that also includes yellow squash.

☜ No-Pasta Lasagna

Are you wondering what the heck lasagna is doing in the veggies chapter? Well, this dish is made with eggplant. And this stuff is so good that you won't even know the pasta isn't there! You have to try it to believe it. I call for 2 cups of tomato juice in this recipe. Simply use the product with the lowest carb counts you can find.

Preparation time: 30 minutes

Cooking time: 2 to 3 hours

Yield: 6 servings

½ cup Merlot	2½ cups cottage cheese
14.5-ounce can diced tomatoes	½ cup grated mozzarella cheese
2 cups tomato juice	2 eggs
1 medium green pepper, chopped	¼ cup chopped fresh Italian parsley
½ medium yellow onion, chopped fine	½ cup green onion
5 black olives, minced	2 to 3 medium zucchini
1 teaspoon dried oregano	1 large eggplant
1 teaspoon dried basil	Sea salt to taste
1 teaspoon pepper	¼ cup freshly grated Parmesan cheese (add more if desired)

1 Combine the Merlot, diced tomatoes, tomato juice, green pepper, onion, olives, oregano, basil, and pepper in a large saucepan. Let it simmer for 1 to 2 hours.

2 While the sauce is cooking and making the kitchen smell wonderful, make the cheese filling. In a medium bowl, combine the cottage cheese, mozzarella cheese, eggs, parsley, and green onion. Blend thoroughly with a large wooden spoon.

3 Peel the zucchini and the eggplant, and slice them lengthwise in thin strips to resemble lasagna noodles. You may want to blot the strips with paper towels to remove any excess moisture. Salt lightly to taste with sea salt (not iodized salt).

4 Preheat the oven to 350 degrees about 10 minutes before the sauce is done and you're ready to assemble the lasagna. Put a thin layer of sauce in the bottom of a clear oven-proof dish or a ceramic lasagna dish. Then, using the eggplant and the zucchini in place of pasta, make a layer of the zucchini and eggplant, alternating them in the same layer. Next, add a layer of cheese filling and then a layer of sauce. You know the rest of the routine — repeat.

5 Sprinkle with the fresh Parmesan cheese and bake for 1 hour.

Per serving: *Calories 221 (From Fat 70); Fat 8g (Saturated 5g); Cholesterol 31mg; Sodium 1,004mg; Carbohydrate 19g; Dietary Fiber 5g (Net Carbohydrate 14g); Protein 18g.*

Cooking Them Just Right

Water is public enemy number one when it comes to retaining all the natural nutrients in vegetables. So don't plop your veggies in a pan of water and boil the heck out of them until they're pale in the face and look like they're about to faint. Cooked veggies are the most appetizing when they retain their original bright color. That's why the techniques I cover in this section — steaming and blanching and stir-frying are the best ways to prepare veggies. My favorite is steaming when I'm preparing them as an entrée or a side dish. If I'm preparing veggies to include in another dish, such as stuffed green peppers, then blanching is what I like to do. Stir-frying veggies at my house is almost a daily occurrence for one meal — it's so quick and easy, and those fresh veggies are so bright and colorful when they're stir-fried.

Likewise, when preparing vegetables for cooking, don't soak them in water because important vitamins and minerals dissolve in the soaking process. Wash veggies quickly, and drain and cook them immediately.

If you frequent farmer's markets to buy your vegetables, you may find that these vegetables need a bit less cooking time than the ones you buy in the grocery stores. The reason for this difference is because the store-bought produce is older and has traveled a farther distance to get to you. Because farmer's market produce comes almost directly from the fields, you'll find it to be a tad more tender than the produce that's been on a truck for several days to get from the field to the produce department in your grocery store.

If you want your veggies to cook evenly, and you're not cooking them whole, cut them in uniform sizes.

Steaming and blanching

The most recommended way to cook vegetables is to steam them in a steamer basket or in a microwave in a small amount of water until they're crisp-tender. *Crisp-tender* means cooking them just long enough to be a bit soft but to maintain their crunch. Cooking veggies until they're crisp-tender helps to maintain their important nutrients, texture, and bright colors.

A steamer basket is just what the doctor ordered for steaming veggies, and you can use it in about any size pan. This inexpensive little lifesaver is merely an expandable fanlike device. The microwave works fine too for steaming, and you can find plastic steamers for microwave use. You'll find both types of steamers in kitchen specialty stores, discount stores, and even the dollar store from time to time. If you're really into veggie steaming, there are some great electric steamers with built-in timers.

☙ Bell Peppers Stuffed with Spinach

I love stuffed peppers, but most recipes include white rice. My colorful and tasty solution is to use spinach for the stuffing. This recipe calls for green, red, and yellow bell peppers. I like to mix them up because they make a beautiful presentation, but you use whichever color or colors you prefer. This recipe calls for low-carb breadcrumbs, so check out Chapter 10 for tips on making your own.

Preparation time: *25 minutes*

Cooking time: *40 to 45 minutes*

Yield: *6 servings*

1 medium green bell pepper	*1 teaspoon dried basil*
1 medium red bell pepper	*½ teaspoon dried oregano*
1 medium yellow bell pepper	*½ teaspoon salt*
8 cups water	*½ teaspoon pepper*
10-ounce package of frozen spinach	*¼ teaspoon garlic powder*
½ cup finely chopped yellow onion	*⅓ cup shredded mozzarella cheese*
⅓ cup low-carb whole-wheat breadcrumbs	

1 Cut the peppers in half lengthwise and remove all the seeds.

2 Using a large stockpot, bring 8 cups of water to a boil over high heat. Add the peppers. You're blanching the peppers (just a quick plunge into boiling water), and you don't want them to lose their vibrant color, so about 3 or 4 minutes is sufficient.

3 After blanching the peppers, rinse them with cold water to stop them from cooking further, and drain. Place the peppers side by side in a 10-inch square baking dish and set aside.

4 Preheat the oven to 350 degrees. Following the directions on the package of spinach, cook it, and then drain and press it against a colander with the back of a wooden spoon to remove excess moisture.

5 In a small mixing bowl, combine the spinach, onion, breadcrumbs, basil, oregano, salt, pepper, and garlic powder.

6 Stuff each pepper half with ⅙ of the mixture and bake for 20 minutes. Remove the dish from the oven and sprinkle the tops of the peppers with the mozzarella cheese. Return the dish to the oven, and continue baking for another 5 to 10 minutes or until the peppers are hot through the center and the cheese is melted.

Per serving: Calories 63 (From Fat 15); Fat 2g (Saturated 1g); Cholesterol 5mg; Sodium 315mg; Carbohydrate 9g; Dietary Fiber 4g (Net Carbohydrate 5g); Protein 5g.

Sometimes, you just need to blanch veggies. *Blanching* is a cooking method in which you plunge veggies into boiling water to firm the flesh and to heighten and set color and flavor. You usually blanch when you're going to continue cooking the vegetables by baking or grilling them, such as when you're preparing stuffed bell peppers (see the recipe for Bell Peppers Stuffed with Spinach in this chapter). Blanching is a very quick process — the veggies are in and out!

As soon as your veggies are cooked to crisp-tender, put them in a colander to drain and place them in a hot serving bowl. Don't put cooked veggies back into a hot pan to keep them warm, because they'll continue to cook from the heat retained in the pan and will wilt, lose their color, and lose their flavor.

Stir-frying veggies

Stir-frying is a great cooking method for vegetables. *Stir-frying* is quickly cooking food in a hot skillet or wok over medium-high heat, stirring constantly, using a small amount of oil. This quick cooking seals in moisture and allows the food to retain much of its flavor, nutrients, color, and texture. You can stir up a meal in minutes that's totally low-carb.

To ensure even and quick cooking, prepare your vegetables in small, uniform shapes. But different types of stir-fry-friendly veggies require different cooking times. So just start your stir-fry with the slowest-cooking veggies, and add your other choices as you go. Here's a breakdown of some common stir-fry ingredients, in order of longest cooking time (add these first) to shortest (add these last):

- Cauliflower and carrots
- Broccoli, asparagus, and snow peas
- Red, yellow and green bell peppers
- Pea pods and edamame
- Long green string beans, wax beans
- Mushrooms and summer squash
- Coarsely shredded cabbage
- Water chestnuts

Finally, after all your veggies are in the skillet or wok, you can add fresh herbs, soy sauces of various varieties, hoisin sauce, chili sauce, peanut sauce, and oyster sauce.

Use a spatula or a long-handled spoon to gently lift and turn the veggies with a folding motion so the food cooks evenly. The trick to stir-frying is to keep the food moving at all times.

If you can't serve your stir-fried veggies immediately, don't cover them, because the retention of heat creates a moist steam that softens the crisp texture of the veggies you just achieved by stir-frying. Not only does the crisp texture disappear, but the color also fades, and the veggies become limp and very unattractive.

A great addition to any stir-fry is a bit of fresh gingerroot. Remember that a little goes a long way. You can add gingerroot by grating it with a paring knife. Gingerroot keeps forever in the freezer. You don't have to defrost it to add it to your stir-fry. You can peel it while it's frozen and just scrape some off, grating the ginger into your stir-fry mix.

Vegetables for stir-frying are readily available in the frozen food section of your grocery store. They are already precut and just begging for you to stir fry 'em!

○ *Stir-Fried Asian Veggies*

A nice change from your ordinary stir-fry, this recipe gives your low-carb lifestyle a sweet and sour smack without interrupting your low-carb flow. Most vegetables are candidates for stir-frying, so feel free to experiment, using this recipe as a guide.

Preparation time: *15 minutes*

Cooking time: *5 to 6 minutes*

Yield: *6 servings*

1 tablespoon soy sauce	*1 cup diagonally sliced green onions*
1 tablespoon white wine vinegar	*6-ounce package frozen Chinese pea pods*
1 teaspoon grated fresh gingerroot	*2 cups shredded cabbage*
1 tablespoon sugar-free maple syrup	*1 cup fresh bean sprouts, rinsed well*
Nonstick cooking spray	*1 cup bite-size sweet red bell pepper strips*

1 Make the sauce first by combining the soy sauce, vinegar, ginger, and maple syrup in a small bowl. Set aside.

2 Spray a large, heavy skillet or wok with nonstick cooking spray. Heat the skillet over medium-high heat. When the skillet is hot, add the green onions, stir-frying for 1 minute. Add the cabbage and the Chinese pea pods, stir-frying for 2 minutes. Add the bean sprouts and the red pepper, stir-frying for 1 more minute. All veggies should be crisp-tender.

3 Pour the sauce over all the ingredients, toss to coat in the skillet, and heat thoroughly.

Per serving: *Calories 37 (From Fat 2); Fat 0g (Saturated 0g); Cholesterol 0mg; Sodium 167mg; Carbohydrate 7g; Dietary Fiber 2g (Net Carbohydrate 5g); Protein 3g.*

Bean bundles

If you want to impress guests with a simple side dish, try this: Take 30 fresh green beans and cut off each end squarely. Divide the beans into 6 groups (5 in each group), and tie each group into a "bundle" of beans by using a fresh chive.

For extra pizzazz and a splash of color, place a slice of red bell pepper under the tie of the chive. Steam the bundles until they're crisp-tender. Squeeze fresh lemon over the bean bundle as you're serving your guests.

Veggies on the Side

There's no need to invest hours in the kitchen, work from a recipe, and dirty a couple hundred pots and pans when you want to whip up a quick carb-friendly side dish. In this section, I share my favorite seasoning and sauce secrets that will get a side on your table quickly with little fuss and muss. Simply steam, blanch, or sauté your favorite veggie (see the "Steaming and blanching" section earlier in the chapter), and then check out the following suggestions. Plus, I throw in a few easy — and fabulous — recipes that are great when you're in the mood for something just a bit more involved.

Adding zip with seasonings and sauces

Most veggies perk right up when you quickly season them with simple ingredients like fresh herbs, lemon juice, freshly ground pepper, or some nice sea salt. Many veggies also take kindly to garlic butter. In the following list, I present some all-time veggie favorites and some seasonings and sauces that complement them nicely:

- **Asparagus:** Nutmeg, lemon peel, lemon pepper, basil, hollandaise sauce, freshly grated Parmesan cheese, various vinaigrette dressings, herb butters, lemon juice

- **Broccoli:** Oregano, marjoram, hollandaise sauces, garlic, herb butters, freshly grated Parmesan cheese, vinaigrette dressings

- **Brussels sprouts:** Cheese sauces, mustard and mustard sauces, dill, chestnuts, freshly grated Parmesan cheese, herb butters

- **Carrots:** Freshly grated ginger root, mint, nutmeg, tarragon, cinnamon, chives, Italian parsley, dill, chervil, orange zest, lemon, herb sauces

- **Cauliflower:** Curry powder, cheese sauces, mustard sauces, freshly grated Parmesan cheese, nutmeg, rosemary, basil, caraway seed, dill weed, tarragon

- **Summer squash:** Oregano, marjoram, dill weed, nutmeg, ginger, allspice, rosemary, lemon pepper, parsley, freshly grated Parmesan cheese

- **Turnips:** Thyme, yogurt, mace, nutmeg, white sauce variations, cheese sauces, orange zest.

Making mushrooms sing with Marsala

Here's a quick suggestion that tastes great as a side with that juicy steak you just cooked on the grill. Using a large skillet, sauté 1 cup fresh sliced mushrooms of your choice in 2 tablespoons butter, 2 tablespoons olive oil, and 1 clove minced fresh garlic. Add 2 tablespoons Marsala wine and simmer for 10 minutes.

There are a ton of low-carb sauces that you can make quickly and have on hand for quick and delicious cooked-veggie platters as an entrée or a side dish. Veggies platters aren't just for appetizers any more! If you get into grilling veggies, these sauces are also great dips for the grilled veggies, or you can make it easy and just pour the sauce all over them:

- **Lemon-herb butter:** Combine ½ cup soft butter, 1 tablespoon lemon zest, ½ teaspoon dried basil, 1 teaspoon snipped fresh Italian parsley, and ½ teaspoon snipped fresh chives.

- **Quick and easy cheese sauce:** Melt ½ pound cheddar cheese in a double boiler; gradually stir in ½ cup light cream; add a dash of cayenne pepper.

- **Chive-parsley sauce:** Melt ¼ cup butter and stir in 1 tablespoon minced fresh chives and 1 tablespoon minced fresh Italian parsley.

- **Mustard-horseradish dressing:** Mix ¼ cup mayonnaise, 2 tablespoons Dijon mustard, and 2 teaspoons prepared horseradish.

- **Dill sauce:** Melt ½ cup butter and stir in 1 tablespoon chopped fresh dill.

Give your veggies on the side a hint of meaty flavor when you serve them with chops or roast by adding half of a chicken or beef bouillon cube to the cooking water. You don't need to salt them. Be sure not to overcook your veggies — cook them till just tender-crisp.

⟲ Brussels Sprouts and Mushrooms with Rosemary

This great combination of Brussels sprouts and fresh mushrooms with the aroma and flavor of fresh rosemary makes a delightful side dish that's sure to please. I'm a big fan of rosemary, and if you haven't tried it in your cooking, you just have to. Not only does rosemary wake up your taste buds, but it also makes the entire kitchen smell great. This dish is high on the healthy side and very low on the carb side.

Preparation time: *10 minutes*

Cooking time: *8 to 10 minutes*

Yield: *5 servings*

2 cups small, fresh Brussels sprouts	⅛ teaspoon pepper
3 tablespoons butter	½ teaspoon grated lemon peel
1 crushed clove of garlic	1 cup halved fresh mushrooms
2 teaspoons fresh rosemary	5 fresh sprigs rosemary for garnish (optional)

1 In a medium saucepan, boil the Brussels sprouts in about an inch of water. Cook for about 6 minutes — just until crisp-tender. Drain.

2 Melt the butter in a large skillet over medium heat. Stir in the garlic, rosemary, pepper, and lemon peel.

3 Add the mushrooms and cook over medium heat just until the mushrooms are softened (about 3 minutes). Stir in the Brussels sprouts and continue cooking only until thoroughly heated, about 2 to 3 minutes.

4 Garnish each serving with a sprig of fresh rosemary, if desired.

> *Tip!* *Store mushrooms in a brown paper bag in the refrigerator rather than in a plastic bag or plastic container.*
>
> *Variation:* *Add crisp, crumbled bacon or chopped toasted almonds.*
>
> *Variation:* *Top the cooked Brussels sprouts and mushrooms with homemade tomato sauce (see Chapter 17 for a great recipe) and grated cheese of your choice. Bake for 15 minutes at 350 degrees.*

Per serving: Calories 80 (From Fat 64); Fat 7g (Saturated 4g); Cholesterol 18mg; Sodium 10mg; Carbohydrate 4g; Dietary Fiber 1g (Net Carbohydrate 3g); Protein 2g.

☼ *Creamy Whole Cauliflower*

Our good friend the cauliflower is the star low-carb veggie that gets a bit of a presentation makeover in this recipe — you cook and serve the whole thing. This side dish wows guests and families alike.

Preparation time: *10 minutes*

Cooking time: *25 minutes*

Yield: *8 servings*

1 small cauliflower head	*2 tablespoons lemon juice*
⅔ cup lowfat sour cream	*3 scallions, chopped fine*
¼ cup cream cheese, room temperature	*Salt and pepper to taste*

1 Trim the outside green leaves from the cauliflower and wash well. Fill a large stockpot with enough water to cover the cauliflower. Add salt to the water and bring to a boil.

2 When the water is boiling, put the cauliflower in and reduce to simmer. Simmer for about 15 minutes or until crisp-tender (you don't want soggy cauliflower).

3 Drain the cauliflower and place it in a warmed serving bowl (something pretty and colorful is nice). Keep the cauliflower warm by covering the bowl with foil.

4 Place the softened cream cheese and sour cream in a heavy-bottomed saucepan over low heat. Stirring constantly, heat until the cream cheese is melted, about 3 or 4 minutes. Add the lemon juice, scallions, and salt and pepper to taste.

5 Spoon the sauce over the cauliflower and serve immediately.

Tip: Don't overcook vegetables. Cook them the very shortest time possible and only until crisp-tender. Watch them carefully, because it usually takes just a matter of minutes. They'll taste better, look better, and be better for you. The fresher the vegetables are, the better they are for you.

Variation: Introduce a bit more flavor by adding some Dijon mustard in your sauce.

Per serving: *Calories 59 (From Fat 35); Fat 4g (Saturated 3g); Cholesterol 15mg; Sodium 125mg; Carbohydrate 5g; Dietary Fiber 1g (Net Carbohydrate 4g); Protein 2g.*

☞ *Artichoke Heart Casserole*

Artichokes are loved by many and are strangers to many. So don't be a stranger. The combinations of flavors in this dish are sure to tickle your taste buds, and if you already love artichokes, then this dish is really for you. Check out Chapter 10 for tips on how to make your own low-carb breadcrumbs for this recipe.

Preparation time: *15 minutes*

Cooking time: *40 minutes*

Yield: *6 servings*

Nonstick cooking spray	¼ teaspoon salt
¼ cup chopped yellow onion	⅛ teaspoon ground red pepper
2 cloves garlic, minced fine	9-ounce package frozen artichoke hearts, thawed and chopped
⅓ cup chopped sweet red pepper	
1 cup chopped fresh mushrooms	¼ cup soft low-carb whole-wheat breadcrumbs
1 cup part-skim ricotta cheese	
⅓ cup shredded mild cheddar cheese	1 tablespoon minced fresh Italian parsley
1 egg, beaten	1 tablespoon freshly grated Parmesan cheese
1 teaspoon lemon juice	1 teaspoon melted butter

1 Preheat the oven to 350 degrees. Spray a 1-quart casserole dish with nonstick cooking spray and set aside.

2 Coat a large, heavy skillet with nonstick cooking spray and place over medium-high heat until the skillet is hot. Add the onion, garlic, sweet red pepper, and mushrooms, and sauté until tender, about 8 minutes. Don't overcook. Set aside.

3 In a large bowl, combine the ricotta cheese, cheddar cheese, egg, lemon juice, salt, and ground red pepper, stirring well. Stir in chopped artichokes and the sautéed vegetable mixture. Spoon into the casserole dish.

4 In a small bowl, combine the breadcrumbs with the parsley, Parmesan cheese, and butter, mixing well. Sprinkle the breadcrumb mixture over the casserole. Bake uncovered for 30 minutes.

Tip: *Give your low-carb breadcrumbs a taste of Italy by adding a little garlic powder and onion powder and a dash of dried Italian seasoning.*

Per serving: *Calories 139 (From Fat 67); Fat 7g (Saturated 4g); Cholesterol 57mg; Sodium 284mg; Carbohydrate 9g; Dietary Fiber 3g (Net Carbohydrate 6g); Protein110g.*

➔ *Marinated Veggies in Living Color*

This recipe is another way to experience a rainbow of color in your veggies. This is a great side dish and can be a great lunch to go because it makes a big batch. You can even grab a low-carb whole-wheat tortilla and make a roll-up for lunch at your desk. Feel free to add your favorite vegetables to this recipe or just remember that color is important.

Preparation time: *20 minutes*

Cooking time: *5 minutes*

Refrigeration time: *6 hours*

Yield: *12 servings*

3 medium zucchini (about 5 cups)

2 medium carrots (about 1 cup)

½ cup coarsely chopped red pepper

½ cup sliced red onion rings

½ cup water

¼ cup spicy vegetable juice

2 tablespoons fresh lemon juice

2 tablespoons white wine vinegar

1 clove garlic, minced fine

1 tablespoon minced fresh Italian parsley

1 packet Splenda sugar substitute

¼ teaspoon celery seed

¼ teaspoon salt

1 Cut the zucchini into ½-inch slices. Peel the carrots and cut them into ¼-inch slices.

2 In a 3-quart saucepan, combine the zucchini, carrots, red pepper, red onion, and water. Cover and cook over high heat for about 5 minutes, only until the veggies are crisp-tender. Stir occasionally to make sure the veggies are cooking evenly. Drain and set aside.

3 In a small mixing bowl, combine the vegetable juice, lemon juice, vinegar, garlic, parsley, Splenda, celery seed, and salt. Whisk the ingredients, mixing well.

4 Place the veggies in a large serving bowl and pour the juice mixture over the vegetables. Toss, coating evenly. Cover tightly with plastic wrap.

5 Refrigerate for at least 6 hours before serving to allow flavors to mingle. Stir a few times. Use a slotted spoon to serve the marinated veggies.

Per serving: Calories 18 (From Fat 0); Fat 0g (Saturated 0g); Cholesterol 0mg; Sodium 74mg; Carbohydrate 4g; Dietary Fiber 1g (Net Carbohydrate 3g); Protein 1g.

Experiencing the tasty textures of puree

Do you miss mashed potatoes? Pureed veggies have the same texture of mashed potatoes, so try them to satisfy your low-carb lifestyle palate. Your food processor comes in handy here. You can serve these purees as side dishes with meats, chicken, or fish. Comfort food a la veggies! Try the following recipes — I think you'll like 'em:

- **Broccoli puree:** Puree 2 cups cooked fresh broccoli florets with ½ teaspoon salt, ¼ teaspoon marjoram, and 1½ tablespoons butter.

- **Cauliflower puree:** Puree 2 cups cooked fresh cauliflower florets with ½ teaspoon salt, ¼ teaspoon rosemary, and 1½ tablespoons butter.

- **Green bean puree:** Puree 2 cups cooked fresh green beans with 3 scallions (white part only), 3 tablespoons freshly snipped dill, 1½ tablespoons butter, 2 tablespoon heavy cream, ¼ cup chicken broth, and salt and pepper to taste.

Chapter 13

Dazzling Low-Carb Desserts

In This Chapter

▶ Indulging in sweets within the low-carb limit

▶ Fitting fruits into your dessert repertoire

▶ Becoming a master of sweet meringues

▶ Puffing along with low-carb French pastries

▶ Chomping on chocolate in the low-carb life

*T*he word *dessert* doesn't have to instantly introduce thoughts of deprivation and sacrifice in your low-carb healthy lifestyle! There are very creative and healthful ways to satisfy your sweet tooth without experiencing the dreaded guilt that comes with that last bite of a carb-laden dessert. In this chapter, I provide you with tips on selecting and preparing low-carb desserts. I introduce you to one of my personal low-carb favorites, the meringue, I take some of the guilt out of old-fashioned favorites like cobbler and bread pudding, and I help you indulge in your desire for the good stuff — chocolate.

Fitting desserts into your low-carb lifestyle can take some creativity. But in this chapter, I take a lot of the guesswork out of the process. Now, I know all about the infamous time factor in today's lives. But if you can make mouthwatering and delightful low-carb desserts at home — and many rather quickly — does that get your attention? I thought so.

Satisfying Your Sweet Tooth

The secret to low-carb dessert success is replacing most of the refined sugars in your sweet creations. With that slight of hand, desserts can be light on the carbs but still sinfully sweet and delicious. You can have your low-carb cake and eat it too! But keep one little thing in mind — variety, balance, and moderation are the keys to success in all healthy lifestyles.

- ✔ **Choose your sweets wisely:** Just because a dessert is lower in carbs doesn't mean eating a ton of the stuff is a healthy choice. *Remember:* Calories count too. Also, beware of sugar alcohols because they can cause weight loss to stall for some folks and also create bloaty and uncomfortable tummies for others (see Chapter 2).

- ✔ **Eat sweets as dessert after your meal:** After a healthy, low-carb meal, you're no longer experiencing pangs of hunger, and you've consumed tons of good-for-you nutrients. Therefore, the urge to throw caution and moderation to the wind isn't as strong. Try to avoid eating sweets as a snack. I know this isn't going to always happen when you're having a craving for something sweet. Just be selective when you give into those cravings. (And check out Chapter 14 where I present all kinds of other low-carb snacking options.)

- ✔ **Drink tea or coffee with your sweets:** I've found that drinking a cup of hot tea or coffee when I want something sweet helps me not want so much of the sweet food.

There are a gazillion low-carb sweet products, including prepackaged brownies and cheesecakes, cookies, muffin mixes, candy bars, and ice cream out there. Always read the labels on these sweets (see Chapter 3 for a label-reading lesson). Sometimes these products are very high in calories and are loaded with sugar alcohols and nasty additives. Just because it says low-carb doesn't make it friendly to a healthy lifestyle.

Sugar is more than sweet

Sugar can be a huge contributor to obesity, chronic diseases, everyday weight gain, and a bunch of other maladies. Sugar is high in calories, and it has absolutely no nutritional benefits. Those are the facts. But it's also a fact that most folks, including yours truly, enjoy the sweet stuff. But sugar also does so much more than just sweeten and enhance the flavor in cooking. Especially in baking, sugar performs a number of what I consider important "mechanical" or "technical" functions:

- ✔ Under heat, sugar caramelizes, which makes your food a pretty golden brown and makes it smell wonderful while it's cooking and baking.

- ✔ Sugar makes your cookies and cakes tender, moist, light, and airy.

- ✔ Sugar produces structure in baked goodies by interacting with proteins and starches during the baking process.

- ✔ Sugar provides nourishment to yeast and therefore speeds up the growth of the yeast.

✓ Sugar acts as a preservative in jams and jellies.

✓ Sugar not only enhances the flavor of ice cream but also adds to the smoothness and texture of ice cream.

✓ Sugar provides you with a *mouth-feel* that's difficult to duplicate. Mouth-feel is about the texture of food. With your low-carb lifestyle, you may miss that certain crispness that you used to get from a potato chip or a pickle, the chewiness of soft candies, or the fresh soft feel of cakes and crunchiness of cookies. The texture or *mouth-feel* of the foods that are baked with sugar is one that you may certainly miss — it's what makes certain foods (especially sweets) so appealing and satisfying.

White sugar isn't included in a healthy low-carb lifestyle. As an old-fashioned Midwest cook, I'm the first to admit that baking without sugar is especially challenging. I have certainly had my share of flops of sweet treats made with artificial sweeteners that ended up in the trashcan! But sweet help is here!

Choosing a sweetener that fits your needs

Artificial sweeteners have come a long way, and I'm sure that you have your favorite. In the recipes in this book, I call for Splenda (either in packets or in granular form) or Splenda Sugar Blend for Baking. They work well for me in my cooking and baking, and they agree with my low-carb life. Just for the record, I'm a Splenda advocate, but in no way do I profit from your purchase of Splenda. It just works for me, and sharing what has worked for me in my low-carb lifestyle over the past ten-plus years is what a lot of this book is about.

Splenda works well for baking and cooking fruits and desserts because it has the capacity to stand up to high temperatures — it doesn't break down. The recipes in this dessert chapter call for Splenda Sugar Blend for Baking because it works so well. Splenda Sugar Blend for Baking contains sugar. But ½ cup of Splenda Sugar Blend for Baking replaces a full cup of sugar. So don't be mistaken that Splenda Sugar Blend for Baking doesn't contain any carbs. Check out the comparison:

Ingredient	Calories	Carbs
Sugar (1 cup)	768	192
Splenda Sugar Blend for Baking (½ cup replaces 1 cup sugar)	384	96

If you'd like to know all more about Splenda, check out Chapter 4, or for the complete story, visit www.splenda.com.

You can use any artificial sweetener as a substitute for any of the artificial sweetener ingredients the recipes in this chapter call for. I believe that artificial sweeteners are a personal choice in your low-carb lifestyle (get the scoop on artificial sweeteners in Chapter 2). But keep in mind that different artificial sweeteners react differently — especially in baking — so if you substitute suggested ingredients in the recipes in this chapter, the outcome may not be the same. I personally prefer not to cook with polyols and sugar alcohols. But I'm not here to try to convince you to do it my way. As the old saying goes, "If it ain't broke, don't fix it!" If it's working for you, keep cookin'!

Some artificial sweeteners don't hold up well in cooking and baking when heated and may actually be dangerous to your health. Aspartame is one of these artificial sweeteners. I encourage you to do your homework and research to make sure you're using safe sweeteners. And, yes, there's a huge controversy over artificial sweeteners and sugar alcohols/polyols (see Chapter 2 for more on this controversy).

Picking the Finest Fruit Desserts

Have a look in Mother Nature's recipe box, and you'll find sweet treats sweetened with natural sugar. Mother Nature is clever in her packing methods of fruits, which contain no preservatives and are brimming with nutrients and vitamins. As a special added benefit, she bulks fresh fruits with fiber that fills you up and not out. The fiber factor is important to your low-carb healthy lifestyle not only for the health benefits but also for its help in lowering the net carb counts (see Chapter 2 for more on net carbs). Clever lady, Mother Nature!

While some fruits are higher in carb counts, such as pineapple and bananas, opt for a seed fruit like blackberries and raspberries, and the fiber count goes way up. When you subtract the fiber count from the carb count for these sweet berries, the net carb counts are very reasonable in your low-carb lifestyle. (See Chapter 3 for more on fruits that work in a low-carb diet.)

If you use canned fruits, you can reduce the carb counts even more if you drain the fruit and rinse it.

Choosing light desserts to end meals if you're already full makes so much sense. There are a lot of wonderful fresh fruit recipes that can satisfy your sweet tooth after a great meal. One way to dress up fresh fruits and create scrumptious desserts is with low-carb sauces made from yogurts, sour cream, mascarpone, and cream cheese (see Chapter 14 for some specific suggestions). So get into fruit design and create some beautiful and healthy fruit plates for desserts.

○ Fruit Kabobs with Pineapple Dip

This fruit dessert is simple and refreshing, and the pineapple dip makes it shine. Feel free to include other fruits on your bamboo skewers; just remember that carb counts will vary. Did you ever think that something so pretty could be so good for your low-carb lifestyle? This dessert is a great dish to take to a summer barbecue. The pineapple dip here calls for plain yogurt. As always, look for the lowest sugar and carb counts you can find. And heads up: You need bamboo skewers for this one.

Preparation time: *15 minutes*

Cooking time: *12 to 14 minutes*

Cooling time: *About 1 hour*

Yield: *6 servings*

¼ cup low-sugar apple juice

1 cup fresh pineapple, chopped

¼ cup plain yogurt

1 cup small fresh strawberries

1 cup fresh blackberries

1 cup cubed cantaloupe

2 kiwis, peeled and cut into ½-inch thick slices

2 nectarines, with peel, cut into ¼-inch thick slices

1 To make the pineapple dip, combine the apple juice and pineapple in a small saucepan, and bring to a quick boil over medium-high heat. Reduce the heat to low, cover, and let simmer for 10 minutes, stirring occasionally. Remove the pineapple mixture from the heat and let it stand until cool (about ½ hour).

2 Place the cooled pineapple mixture in your blender, adding the yogurt. Blend the pineapple mixture and yogurt until smooth. Cover and refrigerate until serving time.

3 Place pieces of fruit — strawberry, blackberry, cantaloupe, kiwi, and nectarine — alternating the fruits on the bamboo skewers and filling the kabobs.

4 Serve the fruit kabobs with the pineapple dip.

Tip: You can find frozen pineapple chunks very reasonably priced in the frozen section of your grocery store. That way you don't have to attack a whole pineapple for this recipe. The produce section has fresh pineapple already cut up and sold in little clear boxes, but it's very pricey.

Per serving: Calories 94 (From Fat 8); Fat 1g (Saturated 0g); Cholesterol 1mg; Sodium 10mg; Carbohydrate 22g; Dietary Fiber 4g (Net Carbohydrate 18g); Protein 2g.

⟡ Old-Fashioned Blueberry Cobbler

If you love berry pies and cobblers, you may think you can't enjoy them with your low-carb lifestyle. Well, not with this old-fashioned Midwest cook at the low-carb helm! I've developed this incredible low-carb version of an old blueberry cobbler recipe I made years ago. It's sure to please your cravings for cobbler. If you want to substitute peaches or a mixture of raspberries and blueberries, go for it — it's your cobbler!

Preparation time: 15 minutes

Cooking time: 30 to 35 minutes

Yield: 9 servings

Nonstick cooking spray	¼ cup Splenda Sugar Blend for Baking
4 cups frozen blueberries, unsweetened	4 tablespoons cold butter, cut into 6 pieces
¼ cup Splenda Sugar Blend for Baking	2 tablespoons half-and-half
2 tablespoons whole-wheat pastry flour	1½ teaspoons whole-wheat pastry flour
1 cup whole-wheat pastry flour	1½ teaspoons Splenda Sugar Blend for Baking
1 teaspoon baking powder	¼ teaspoon cinnamon
¼ teaspoon salt	

1 Preheat the oven to 375 degrees. Coat an 8-x-8-inch square baking dish with nonstick cooking spray. In a large bowl, mix the blueberries, ¼ cup Splenda Sugar Blend for Baking, and 2 tablespoons pastry flour. Place the mixture in prepared baking dish.

2 In a medium bowl, combine 1 cup pastry flour, baking powder, salt, and ¼ cup Splenda Sugar Blend for Baking. Stir to combine dry ingredients.

3 Cut the butter into the dry ingredients using a pastry blender (3 to 4 minutes) or a few quick pulses in your food processor until the mixture resembles coarse meal.

4 Add the half-and-half, and stir until the ingredients are moistened. Mold the mixture into a ball with your hands (flour your hands a little if dough is a bit sticky).

5 Tear off a piece of wax paper about 18 inches long, so you have room to work, and sprinkle 1½ teaspoons of pastry flour on it, spreading it out evenly with your hand. Place the dough on top of the floured wax paper.

6 Place another piece of wax paper on top, and roll the dough out to the size of the 8-x-8-inch baking dish. It doesn't matter if the edges of the dough aren't even. You simply want it to cover *most* of the fruit that's waiting in the dish for the crowning glory of the dough topping. Use your baking dish as a guide by placing it over the top of the dough when it's rolled out in a creative semi-square.

7 Pick up the piece of wax paper with the dough on it, and turn it over on top of the blueberries in the baking dish. Peel off the wax paper.

8 Combine 1½ teaspoons Splenda Sugar Blend for Baking and ¼ teaspoon cinnamon. Spray the top of the dough lightly with cooking spray and sprinkle the mixture evenly over the top of the dough (the cooking spray will help the cinnamon mixture to stick to the dough). Bake for 30 to 35 minutes. The topping will be semi-golden brown, but watch it, because you don't want to overbake it.

Variation: Serve with a dollop of whipped cream or low-carb vanilla ice cream.

Variation: Instead of using the entire dough rolled out for the topping of the cobbler, use cookie cutters and cut out shapes if you're celebrating something — Christmas tree shapes or hearts for example. Cut out 9 shapes, so each individual serving has a cutout.

Tip: If you haven't used whole-wheat pastry flour, it's so smooth it's almost like silk, so you sometimes have to work with it a little differently. You need to be the judge of how mixtures feel. Sometimes you have to add just a tad more pastry flour, because it's such a soft flour. You'll get the hang of it after a couple times baking with it and will love it. It's healthy, and it brings great light and airy results to your low-carb cooking and baking. You can combine whole-wheat pastry flour with white whole-wheat flour when you need a more substantial flour (not as soft a flour).

Per serving: Calories 137 (From Fat 53); Fat 6g (Saturated 3g); Cholesterol 15mg; Sodium 110mg; Carbohydrate 21g; Dietary Fiber 2g (Net Carbohydrate 19g); Protein 1g.

 For a quick dessert, slice up some fruit, such as apples, peaches, and nectarines, and add artificial sweetener, lemon juice, and cinnamon to taste. Pop it in the microwave to warm. Add a small scoop of low-carb vanilla ice cream and enjoy the decadence as the ice cream melts into the warm fruit.

Red, red wine and nectarines

Nectarines are a winner for a spirited treat. Allow one large, ripe nectarine for each person. Leave the skins on the nectarines and, right before dinner, slice them in a shallow bowl of red, red wine that's been chilling all day (use the wine of your choice; a light red table wine works, as does Merlot). By dessert time, you have a chilled, spirited treat. Serve in something tall, clear, and stemmed for an elegant presentation. Add a sprinkling of fresh red raspberries on the top and maybe a dollop of whipped cream.

Dancing the Meringue in the Kitchen

You can do so much with meringue, and I guarantee it'll bring sweet sunshine to your low-carb lifestyle. The beauty of meringue is that it's mostly egg whites and no-calorie, no-carb air! You can make all kinds of cookies, cakes, ice cream cakes, pies, piecrusts, and simple shells. The list of fillings begins with fresh fruits, fruit purees, and fruit sauces and continues with all kinds of puddings and low-carb ice creams, to mention a few. You can make puddings from scratch, or you can use sugar-free pudding mixes. You can buy a bag of frozen mixed fruits and make a quick sauce. In a snap, you've created a delicious and beautiful dessert. If you're having guests, meringue shells with mouthwatering, luscious fillings are sure to be a showstopper.

Whipping together a few ingredients

Regardless of what final form your marvelous meringue takes, all meringues start with the same basic ingredients and a few simple steps. Meringue is simply beaten egg whites that are stiffened with sugar or sugar substitute, cream of tartar and/or salt to stabilize the egg whites, and some flavoring, which is usually vanilla (of course, you can get creative with your flavoring).

It's best to separate the whites of eggs from the yolks when the eggs are cold. But the secret to increased volume and finer texture of your whipped egg whites is to start whipping them at room temperature. So separate and wait. The volume of your whites can be increased 6 to 8 times if you leave them at room temperature for no longer than 30 minutes before you begin beating.

Here's the basic two-step approach and some explanation that should provide you with a firm foundation for your meringue mixing and serve you well as you tackle any meringue recipe. See Figure 13-1 for how meringue peaks should look.

1. **Beat/whip your eggs until they form soft peaks and then add cream of tartar.**

   Soft peaks refers to egg whites that are beginning to foam and are cloudy looking. Don't begin on high speed when you're beating your whites. Start at medium-low to medium speed, making them foamy. If you start out with your mixer in high gear, large bubbles are likely to form, which isn't what you want. You're after lots of tiny air bubbles for great texture. Cream of tartar is added at the stage when the whites begin to foam. Cream of tartar is a mild acid salt. It plays a huge role in successful meringues because the acidic nature of cream of tartar acts as a stabilizer in the whites. When you stop the mixer and lift the beaters, the soft peaks should be a little droopy.

2. **Add sugar substitute and beat/whip your eggs to stiff peaks.**

   When beating your egg whites for meringues, it's best to wait until soft peaks begin to form before adding the sweetener. Crank your mixer up on high, and as the foamy whites become moist and shiny, it's time to add your sweetener. So as not to deflate the whites, add the sweetener at the side of the bowl instead of pouring it in the middle. To get the whites to the stiff peak stage, keep your mixer on high and beat until the whites are glossy. Stop your mixer when the tips of the peaks stand up straight when you lift the beaters. This is a critical stage to your success in meringue building. A matter of less than one minute can turn your wonderful stiff peaks dull and dry, and then they're useless.

Now you can build your meringue castles and shape them any way you want. One of my favorites that's so easy is meringue shells — like the one on the front of the book. (That's why we put it there — because it's my favorite!) Meringue shells are versatile and can make an elegant presentation. In the "Mastering meringue shells" section, I show you how to build meringue shells step by step. But I also give you some recipes that include meringue piecrust and cookie options.

Figure 13-1:
Reaching
the peaks.

Here are some tips to help you get the hang of making marvelous meringue:

- ✔ Make sure your egg whites are at room temperature. You get more fluff this way because the volume of the egg white increases when warm.

- ✔ When you're beating the egg whites, use a squeaky clean and dry bowl that's preferably stainless steel, glass, or copper — never plastic. Egg whites just don't cooperate in a plastic bowl because, even though plastic appears to be clean, it still can retain some grease that you can't see. Also make sure the eggbeaters and the spatula are free of grease. To be sure your utensils are squeaky clean, wipe them with fresh lemon juice, rinse in warm water, and dry them thoroughly.

- ✔ Make sure your hands are very clean and free of oil or butter when you crack your eggs. I'm not kidding here — grease interferes with beating the whites in the bowl, and greasy hands do the same thing!

- ✔ If you drop a speck of the yolk into the egg white when separating the two, take the speck of yolk out with a broken eggshell. Again, this is about not getting any grease or fat in the egg white. If there's a tiny speck of egg yolk in the whites, they won't whip up to a high volume. That's why you use a broken eggshell — so you don't mess up the whites with a utensil that could have some residue on it.

✔ Get a weather report before making meringues — I'm serious! If it's raining outside or if the humidity is really high, getting volume with your egg whites is tough. No, I can't explain it — it just is. Trust me.

✋ Raspberry Ribbon Pie with Meringue Crust

I've had this recipe in my recipe box since I was in my 20s, so you know it's a very old favorite. Back then, it was full of sugar and high in carb counts. But I've successfully brought this favorite back to low-carb life. This pie isn't only delicious and very different, but it's also very pretty.

Preparation time: 30 minutes

Cooking time: 1 hour and 35 minutes

Refrigeration time: 3 hours

Yield: 6 servings

Nonstick cooking spray

4 egg whites

¼ teaspoon cream of tartar

2½ tablespoons Splenda Sugar Blend for Baking

1 4-serving package sugar-free raspberry gelatin

2 tablespoons Splenda Sugar Blend for Baking

1¼ cups boiling water

10-ounce package frozen red raspberries, unsweetened

1 tablespoon lemon juice

3 ounces cream cheese, softened

2 tablespoons Splenda Sugar Blend for Baking

1 teaspoon vanilla

Dash of salt

1 cup heavy cream, whipped

1 Preheat the oven to 275 degrees. Spray a 9-inch glass pie plate with nonstick cooking spray. Set aside.

2 Bring the egg whites to room temperature for no longer than 30 minutes and beat them until they're foamy. Add the cream of tartar and continue beating until the whites begin to form soft peaks.

3 Gradually add 2½ tablespoons Splenda Sugar Blend for Baking until the whites form stiff glossy peaks.

4 Spread the meringue with the back of a large tablespoon evenly in the bottom of the pie plate, and swirl it up the sides. Smooth it out. Bake for 1 hour and 10 minutes at 275 degrees. Turn the oven up to 300 degrees, and bake an additional 20 minutes. Remove from oven and cool.

5 Dissolve the gelatin and 2 tablespoons Splenda Sugar Blend for Baking in 1¼ cups boiling water. Add the frozen raspberries and lemon juice, stirring until the berries are thawed. Chill until partially set.

6 Blend the cream cheese, 2 tablespoons Splenda Sugar Blend for Baking, vanilla, and salt, using a mixer. Fold in a small amount (about ⅛ cup) of whipped cream, and then gently fold in the remaining whipped cream.

7 Spread half of the white cream cheese mixture over the bottom of the cooled meringue pie shell. Cover with half of the red gelatin mixture. Repeat layers. Chill until set.

Variation: Add ½ teaspoon vanilla and ½ cup chopped pecans to the meringue. Bake the meringue crust at 300 degrees for 1 hour. Cool and fill with a whipped cream filling such as the Chocolate-Strawberry Whipping Cream Filling in this section or one of your own favorites out of your recipe box.

Tip: For perfect whipped cream, chill your bowl and your beaters for about 15 minutes before whipping the cream. Beat whipping cream on low to medium speed just until soft peaks form. If you whip it too much, you'll have butter.

Per serving: Calories 290 (From Fat 177); Fat 20g (Saturated 12g); Cholesterol 70mg; Sodium 246mg; Carbohydrate 19g; Dietary Fiber 1g (Net Carbohydrate 18g); Protein 7g.

 The easiest way to make anything meringue these days is to use the egg white product found in your dairy case. These liquid egg whites aren't expensive, and they let you avoid trying to figure out what to do with all those yolks. You can measure the whites by the cup or tablespoon, and the guide is right on the carton. Even though you're using the egg whites in a carton, be sure to bring them to room temperature before you start beating them with your mixer. It makes all the difference in the world in the way they whip up.

 Don't even think about trying to make meringue on a rainy or foggy day. You'll end up with a sticky mess. The humidity in the air makes meringue lose its crispness.

Meringue trivia

A bit of meringue trivia: A Swiss pastry chef in the early 18th century created the very first meringues. "Chef Meringue" was also known as Gasparni. As the story goes, Gasparni lived in a small town known as Mehryngen, and he named his elegant new dessert after his hometown.

☙ Chocolate Cinnamon-Walnut Meringue Cookies

These low-carb cookies are great to tuck in your lunch bag. They're also great served with your favorite low-carb ice cream. Make this treat extra-special by serving your ice cream in an old-fashioned sundae glass on a dessert plate with a couple cookies on the side. You can find these sundae glasses at the dollar store.

Preparation time: *15 minutes*

Cooking time: *20 minutes*

Yield: *14 cookies (1 per serving)*

¼ cup Splenda Sugar Blend for Baking	⅛ teaspoon salt
¼ teaspoon cinnamon	⅛ teaspoon cream of tartar
4 teaspoons cocoa powder	⅓ cup chopped walnut pieces
2 egg whites, room temperature	

1 Preheat the oven to 300 degrees. Line two baking sheets with parchment paper and set aside.

2 Sift together the Splenda Sugar Blend for Baking, cinnamon, and cocoa on a sheet of wax paper. Set aside.

3 In a small bowl, beat the egg whites until foamy. Add the salt and cream of tartar, and beat into stiff, shiny peaks. Gently fold in the cocoa mixture. Fold the nuts in last.

4 Drop generous teaspoons of the batter onto the baking sheets. You may want to use the old two-spoon method, using one spoon to dip the mixture out of the bowl and then the second spoon to push the meringue mixture onto the baking sheet. Give the cookies room, spacing them about 1-inch apart on the baking sheet.

5 Bake about 20 minutes or until set. Remove the cookies from the oven and transfer to a wire rack to cool completely. Store in an airtight metal container at room temperature.

Tip: Meringue cookies don't freeze well — the meringue becomes tough. Guess you'll just have to eat them!

Per serving: *Calories 36 (From Fat 17); Fat 2g (Saturated 0g); Cholesterol 0mg; Sodium 29mg; Carbohydrate 4g; Dietary Fiber 0g (Net Carbohydrate 4g); Protein 1g.*

Mastering meringue shells

Did that beautiful meringue shell filled with sweet yummy-looking fruit on the cover of the book get your attention? Did it make your mouth water for something sweet? You too can make great low-carb meringue sweet treats. I've dedicated quite a bit of time and energy in this section to help you master the basics of meringue making, and then you'll dream up all kinds of scrumptious fillings for them. Meringue shells are my favorite low-carb sweet. They're unique and like eating sweet crunchy air.

You need to make sure to have parchment paper on hand when making meringue shells. You can make the shells either by placing mounds on the baking sheet or by using a pastry bag. It just depends on how fancy you want to be. I make mine in mounds like this:

1. **Line your baking sheet with the parchment paper.**

   This stuff is magical because the meringues don't stick to it, and you just peel it off.

2. **Place equal mounds of meringue on the parchment paper. You can do this with a tablespoon, or if you're a precise person, you can actually measure each meringue (about ½ cup).**

   If you want to be really precise, draw 3- to 3¼-inch circles on the parchment paper for uniformity. If you'd rather wing it, be my guest.

3. **Hollow out the center of the mound of each meringue with the back of a tablespoon.**

   This hole is where you're going to put your filling when the meringues are baked. It's kind of like a little meringue bowl.

If you prefer the fancy way of doing things to recreate that look found on the cover of this book, use a pastry bag instead. If so, follow these steps:

1. **Use a size 6 star tip on your pastry bag, and fill it with meringue.**

2. **Begin piping the meringue until you have six coiled circles (see Figure 13-2).**

   This should take up a space of about 3 to 3½ inches.

3. **Add one more piping around the outer edge of your meringue circle.**

☝ *Basic Meringue Shells with Berry Filling*

This recipe is the beautiful meringue shell on the cover of this book, and it's just as delicious as it looks! I'm giving you a very simple and basic meringue recipe here that you can use for shells and for tortes with fillings. You can even make meringue ice cream sandwiches (find out how later in the recipe). After you master basic meringue, you'll have so many scrumptious low-carb options you just won't know where to start.
Remember: *The basic meringues have only 8 grams of net carbs each;* it's what you put in the middle that make the carb counts go up. Because this basic meringue recipe has a hint of vanilla flavoring coupled with a bit of sweetness, your sweet tooth cravings will be oh so satisfied. Let the meringue madness begin!

Preparation time: *15 to 20 minutes*

Cooking time: *35 minutes*

Drying time: *1 hour*

Yield: *6 servings*

2 egg whites	*¼ cup Splenda Sugar Blend for Baking*
¼ teaspoon cream of tartar	*Berry Filling (see the following recipe)*
Pinch of salt	*6 sprigs fresh mint (optional)*
¼ teaspoon vanilla	

1 Preheat the oven to 300 degrees. Line a baking sheet with parchment paper and set aside.

2 Bring the egg whites to room temperature. Beat the whites until foamy in a squeaky-clean aluminum or glass bowl (not plastic) with very clean beaters. Add the cream of tartar, salt, and vanilla, and continue beating until the whites begin to form soft peaks.

3 Gradually add the Splenda Sugar Blend for Baking as you continue to beat until the whites form stiff peaks. Whites should remain glossy.

4 Spoon the meringue into 6 equal mounds on the baking sheet (see the text earlier in this section for tips and tricks).

5 Shape the mounds of meringue into nest-like cups. You can do this easily with the back of a small tablespoon, working from the center out and then smoothing around the edge of the meringue cup.

6 Bake for 35 minutes, and don't open the oven door. You can take a peek to see if they're done and turn off the oven, close the door again and let the meringue dry for 1 hour in the oven. Then transfer them to a cooling rack to air dry until you're ready to fill the cups when you're ready to serve. While the meringue is baking and drying, you can prepare the Berry Filling and chill it.

7 When ready to serve, spoon the Berry Filling into the meringue shells. Garnish with fresh mint, if desired.

Berry Filling

Preparation time: *5 minutes*

Cooking time: *12 minutes*

Refrigeration time: *2 hours*

Yield: *6 servings*

1 teaspoon fresh lemon juice	*½ pint fresh blueberries*
1 tablespoon blackberry fresh fruit spread (no sugar added, preferably organic)	*½ pint fresh raspberries*
1 tablespoon Splenda Sugar Blend for Baking	*2 cups strawberries, hulled and halved*

1 Combine the lemon juice, blackberry fresh fruit spread, and Splenda Sugar Blend for Baking in a small bowl, and mix with a teaspoon.

2 Combine the blueberries, raspberries, and strawberries in a bowl. Pour the blackberry liquid over the berries, and stir the berries all together. Let the berries stand until juices form, probably about 2 hours in the fridge. Stir occasionally.

Variation: Fill the meringue shells with sugar-free vanilla pudding mix. Spoon ¼ cup pudding into each meringue, and top with fresh blackberries.

Variation: Make plain, chocolate, or flavored basic meringue. Spread meringue in 3-inch flat rounds and bake. When dry, spread with your favorite low-carb ice cream (like chocolate chip). Pop another meringue on top, wrap it in wax paper, and freeze it in a self-sealing plastic bag. It's a very crunchy sweet treat.

Tip: Trying to get your parchment to lie down on your baking sheet? After you whip your egg whites, plop a few small dabs of them on the baking sheet. Put your parchment paper on top, and smooth it down.

Per serving: Calories 91 (From Fat 3); Fat 0g (Saturated 0g); Cholesterol 0mg; Sodium 44mg; Carbohydrate 21g; Dietary Fiber 3g (Net Carbohydrate 18g); Protein 2g.

Figure 13-2: Piping meringue.

☞ *Meringues with Chocolate-Strawberry Whipped Cream Filling*

This recipe is quick, easy, and elegant. It just doesn't get much better than this! Whip up the Basic Meringue Shells recipe I provide in this section. Save this for a very special occasion or indulge in some low-carb decadence. No you can't roll in this stuff and you can't eat the whole thing!

Preparation time: *15 minutes*

Yield: *6 servings*

8 ounces cream cheese, softened

¼ cup baking cocoa

½ cup plus 1 tablespoon Splenda Sugar Blend for Baking

1 cup heavy cream, whipped

1 pint fresh strawberries, halved

6 Basic Meringue Shells (see the recipe earlier)

Additional whipped cream for garnish (6 small tablespoons to hold strawberry garnish in place)

6 whole strawberries for garnish

1 Combine the cream cheese and cocoa and beat until blended. Add ½ cup Splenda Sugar Blend for Baking and beat until fluffy. Gently fold in 1 cup whipped cream.

2 Place 1 pint of the strawberries and 1 tablespoon Splenda Sugar Blend for Baking in the blender, and blend until it's almost a puree (don't over blend).

3 Spoon the chocolate cream cheese filling into the meringue shells. Top with the pureed strawberries.

4 Add a small dollop of whipped cream to each shell and garnish each one with a whole strawberry.

Per serving: Calories 433 (From Fat 282); Fat 31g (Saturated 20g); Cholesterol 106mg; Sodium 173mg; Carbohydrate 35g; Dietary Fiber 3g (Net Carbohydrate 32g); Protein 6g.

If your meringues get stubborn when it's time for them to come off the parchment paper, try using a very thin pancake turner to help coax them off without breaking them.

Storing meringues is a bit tricky but you can do it. If you're planning to use them for guests or a party make them no earlier than two days in advance. To store, make sure that they're completely cool and store in an airtight container separated by waxed paper at room temperature for up to two days.

Puffin' Pastries Gone Low-Carb

What a treat — a specialty French pastry gone low-carb. I call them puffies, but the real name for this French delight is *choux pastry*. Puffies can be the beginnings of low-carb cream puffs, chocolate éclairs, and profiteroles. The variations are endless and left only to your sweet low-carb imagination.

You'll be delightfully surprised at how quick these little puffies come together. You can even freeze them and pop them out when your sweet tooth is hollering at you. Puffies have a very low carb count, so the carb count of the finished puffy only depends on what you decide to fill or stuff it with.

Use these tips to master the recipe for Puffies in this chapter:

✔ Heat the butter and the liquid in a small, heavy saucepan, heating slowly. You want the butter to be melted before the boiling point is reached.

✔ You can simply drop the puffies on a cookie sheet and bake them, or you can get fancy and pop them in a pastry bag and pipe out the dough.

✔ Place the puffies in a very hot oven first so they puff up, and then reduce the heat so they don't get too brown while they're drying.

✔ The secret to not having your puffies collapse on you is to make sure they're cooked and dry all the way through.

✔ If you're making round puffs, make a little hole or a slit in them as soon as you remove them from the oven to allow the steam to escape. If you're making éclairs, make the éclair slit in them.

✔ If you want more room inside your puffies for filling, or if they're not quite dry in the middle, hollow them out while they're still warm from the oven. Split them with a knife, and gently remove any soft dough from the inside. Fill them when they're cooled and pop their tops on. Serve with a sauce and maybe a dollop of whipped cream.

⚬ Puffies

This is a quick and easy recipe for cream puffs that can be filled with everything from whipped cream fillings to tuna salad to fruits and berries to ice cream to sugar-free puddings — the list is endless. And so your low-carb puff imagination begins. If you can resist, puffies freeze well.

Preparation time: *15 minutes*

Cooking time: *30 minutes*

Drying time: *5 minutes*

Yield: *8 servings*

Nonstick cooking spray

3 tablespoons butter

⅓ cup water

¼ teaspoon salt

¼ cup plus 1 tablespoon whole-wheat pastry flour

1 large egg

1 large egg white

1 Preheat the oven to 300 degrees. Spray a large baking sheet with nonstick cooking spray.

2 In a heavy pan, combine the butter, water, and salt. Bring to a boil and reduce the heat to low.

3 Add all the flour at once, and stir until the globby mix begins to pull away from the sides of the pan and form a ball (film will begin to form in the bottom of the saucepan).

4 Remove the pan from the heat and let cool for about 3 minutes. Add the whole egg and then the one egg white, one at a time, beating vigorously after each addition. The mixture will become smooth and shiny.

5 While the pastry is still warm, use a tablespoon to spoon the dough onto the prepared baking sheet, making 8 mounds.

6 Turn the oven up to 450 degrees, and place the baking pan in the lower third of the oven. Bake for 15 minutes, and the dough will be well puffed and lightly browned.

7 Quickly turn the oven back to 300 degrees, and bake 15 minutes longer until golden.

8 Carefully cut a small slit in the side of each puffy, and allow the steam to escape. Turn off the oven, and leave the puffs in the oven to dry for 5 minutes. Remove and place on the racks to cool. Slice the puffs in half, and if there's damp dough inside, hollow it out with a spoon.

9 Fill with your filling of choice and pop the top back on to complete your puffy.

Per serving: *Calories 59 (From Fat 39); Fat 4g (Saturated 3g); Cholesterol 12mg; Sodium 87mg; Carbohydrate 4g; Dietary Fiber 1g (Net Carbohydrate 3g); Protein 1g.*

Don't get bored with your puffies. Try the following variations:

✔ For chocolate puffies, add 1 tablespoon of baking cocoa and 1 teaspoon Splenda Sugar Blend for Baking to basic dough mixture. Fill with vanilla ice cream. Top with low-carb chocolate topping and low-carb caramel topping. Place four pecan halves for feet, and you have a low-carb chocolate turtle cream puff!

✔ Fill a puffy with chilled sugar-free white chocolate pudding. For a quick low-carb topping, combine 2 tablespoons Splenda Sugar Blend for Baking and ⅛ teaspoon cornstarch. Add 2 teaspoons unsweetened cocoa and blend together. Stir in 1 tablespoon hot coffee. Drizzle over your filled puffy.

✔ Low-carb ice cream makes a quick and tasty puffy filling. Choose from mint chocolate chip, butter pecan, chocolate, strawberry, vanilla bean, chocolate chip, or your personal favorite.

✔ Prepare a small package of instant sugar-free vanilla, chocolate, or pistachio pudding mix. Prepare as the label directs, but use only 1¼ cups milk. Whip 1 cup of heavy cream, and fold it into the pudding. If you're using vanilla pudding, you can add all kinds of extracts such as peppermint, almond, orange, or one of your favorites.

Dabbling in Chocolate Decadence

I can't dedicate an entire chapter to low-carb desserts without offering a few chocolate recipes. Well, I guess I could, but I'm sure I'd be leaving out a lot of chocoholics out there. I once read that the original chocolate cake was called "devil's food" — fitting, isn't it?

When you're making a low-carb chocolate treat and you need to flour the pan, use baking cocoa instead of flour.

The Chocolate Bread Pudding recipe in this section is made in a ramekin. If you're unfamiliar with these baking dishes, check out Figure 13-3.

Figure 13-3:
A ramekin
for your
Chocolate
Bread
Pudding.

✐ Chocolate Fruit Pizza

This was a high-carb, high-sugar treat I made for my guests at my bed-and-breakfast in Branson, Missouri, and they raved about it. I've since made the recipe chocolaty low-carb and covered it with healthy fresh fruits. The crust is a pat and bake crust, so it's super quick and easy. The combination of the chocolate and the light filling with the fruit and glaze is sure to make your low-carb heart smile. If you skip the glaze, you knock off a bunch of carbs. And if this carb count looks a tad high to you, look at a normal recipe for this dessert: The carb counts are up at around 70 or 80 per slice! I've specified fruits for the recipe but you can ignore me and use your favorites, just be sure to watch the carb counts.

Preparation time: *25 minutes*

Cooking time: *17 to 22 minutes*

Yield: *8 servings*

Nonstick cooking spray	¾ cup pineapple juice
1 cup whole-wheat pastry flour	1 teaspoon Splenda Sugar Blend for Baking
¼ cup Splenda Sugar Blend for Baking	2 teaspoons cornstarch
2 tablespoons baking cocoa	½ cup sliced kiwi
½ cup butter, softened to room temperature	1 cup sliced strawberries
¼ cup sour cream	1 cup blueberries
¼ cup plain yogurt	½ cup red raspberries
2 teaspoons Splenda Sugar Blend for Baking	1 cup blackberries
¼ teaspoon vanilla	1 nectarine, cut in thin slices for garnish
1 tablespoon lemon juice	

1 Preheat the oven to 400 degrees. Spray a 9-x-1¼-inch quiche dish lightly with nonstick cooking spray (you can also use a glass pie plate; just don't use metal).

2 Combine the flour, ¼ cup Splenda Sugar Blend for Baking, and cocoa. Add the softened butter, and mix until a soft dough forms (I use my hands to mix).

3 Press the dough firmly and evenly against the bottom of your quiche dish. Bring it up just slightly along the sides of your dish because it will shrink when you're baking it.

4 Bake for 12 to 15 minutes or until set. Don't over bake! Let it cool completely before preparing the toppings for the pizza.

5 Combine the sour cream, yogurt, 2 teaspoons Splenda Sugar Blend for Baking, and vanilla well. Spread the mixture over the cooled chocolate crust, and refrigerate.

6 In a small saucepan, combine the lemon juice, pineapple juice, 1 teaspoon Splenda Sugar Blend for Baking, and cornstarch. Stirring constantly, cook until the mixture is bubbly and begins to thicken. Continue cooking, still stirring constantly for 2 more minutes. Let the mixture cool until completely cool.

7 Arrange the fruit on top of the pizza, saving the nectarine slices until last for garnishing. Spoon the cooled glaze over the fruit. Cover tightly with plastic wrap, and chill until serving time.

Variation: Skip the glaze if you're really in a hurry as the chocolate pizza still tastes yummy and it's quick, quick without the glaze. The glaze is tasty too, but its purpose is more to hold the fruit in place and prevent it from drying out and turning brown.

Variation: You can also use individual tart pans for a special party and really impress your low-carb guests. Just be sure to watch the pat and bake crust, because it bakes very quickly in the tart pans. Set your timer and check them often!

Variation: This recipe makes a great chocolate crust for any type of pudding, chiffon, or ice cream pie. So get creative. Try filling this pat-and-bake chocolate crust with sugar-free pistachio pudding. Top it with freshly whipped cream and chocolate curls.

Per serving: Calories 270 (From Fat 124); Fat 14g (Saturated 8g); Cholesterol 34mg; Sodium 13mg; Carbohydrate 35g; Dietary Fiber 5g (Net Carbohydrate 30g); Protein 3g.

ᗒ *Chocolate Bread Pudding*

Talk about to die for — this stuff is the ultimate in chocolate decadence. The recipe tells you to make it in 1 cup ramekins, but you can easily make it in ½ cup ramekins and make 12 rather than 6. If you don't have ramekins, use ovenproof custard dishes. You can serve this bread pudding hot from the oven, lukewarm, or right from the fridge. It's a great decadent treat, but this isn't an everyday low-carb snack. I guarantee it's like no bread pudding you've ever tasted!

Preparation time: *15 minutes*

Cooking time: *15 minutes*

Yield: *6 servings*

Nonstick cooking spray

6 ounces semi-sweet chocolate chips

4 tablespoons Splenda Sugar Blend for Baking

⅛ teaspoon ground cinnamon

¼ teaspoon salt

2½ cups cubed soft, fresh, low-carb bread (about 4 slices of bread)

1 cup heavy cream

½ cup water

1 egg, at room temperature

Splenda for garnish (optional)

1 Preheat the oven to 400 degrees, and place the rack in the middle of the oven.

2 Spray the ramekins (or custard dishes) with nonstick cooking spray, and place them on a baking sheet, spaced evenly. Melt the chocolate chips in the microwave. Start off at 45 seconds on HIGH and then stir them. If necessary, pop them back in for another 15 seconds. The chocolate doesn't have to be super runny, just melted.

3 Combine the Splenda Sugar Blend for Baking, cinnamon, salt, and bread cubes in a medium bowl.

4 In a large measuring cup, combine the heavy cream with the water. Whisk the egg into the heavy cream mixture and add the melted chocolate, stirring until well blended.

5 Pour the chocolate mixture over bread mixture. Using a large spoon, stir vigorously until well blended.

6 Use a ½-cup measuring cup to pour the mixture into each ramekin. They'll be slightly more than half full and won't raise much during baking.

7 Bake for 15 minutes or until the tops of the pudding are just barely firm to the touch. Sprinkle the tops with a light dusting of Splenda, if desired.

Tip: *The success of this awesome bread pudding depends on the freshness of the bread you use. I use very fresh low-carb white bread with no more than 9 grams of carbs per slice. If you're serving to guests, create an elegant presentation by placing a couple fresh red raspberries and a fresh mint sprig on the side of the dessert dish with a dusting of Splenda on top.*

Per serving: *Calories 358 (From Fat 225); Fat 25g (Saturated 14g); Cholesterol 90mg; Sodium 239mg; Carbohydrate 33g; Dietary Fiber 4g (Net Carbohydrate 29g); Protein 5g.*

◌ Dirt Cake

Did you ever think that Dirt Cake would go low-carb? It seems that all your favorites are getting smarter and following a low-carb healthy lifestyle — even Dirt Cake! This recipe is great fun if you're going to a garden party, a barbecue, or a shower — it makes a great centerpiece as well as a tasty dessert. I call for it to be assembled in a new plastic flowerpot and decorated with silk flowers, but you can also use a large, clear glass bowl like a salad or trifle bowl. You can use a regular terra cotta–looking new flowerpot or a clear plastic one. This is a very thoughtful treat to take to a friend that's convalescing from an illness at home. If you're going to a barbecue, you can freeze your dirt cake and let it thaw out when you get there. For even more fun, serve with a new, small garden spade.

Preparation time: 20 to 25 minutes

Yield: 10 to 12 servings

2 packages CarbWell Oreo cookies, frozen

½ stick butter, softened

8 ounces cream cheese, softened

¼ cup Splenda Sugar Blend for Baking

2 small packages sugar-free vanilla pudding (the 4-serving size)

3½ cups low-carb milk

1 cup heavy cream, whipped

1 Buy a new 8-inch pretty plastic flowerpot. Wash it out really well with hot, soapy water. Line the flowerpot with aluminum foil.

2 Crush the frozen cookies in your blender or food processor until they look like potting soil.

3 Using your mixer, cream together the butter, cream cheese, and Splenda Sugar Blend for Baking.

4 Prepare the pudding with the low-carb milk. Fold in the whipped cream.

5 Fold the whipped cream mixture into the cream cheese mixture.

6 Beginning at the bottom of the flowerpot (or bowl) layer your ingredients beginning with crushed cookies then the cream cheese/pudding mix, alternating layers. Be sure you end with the crushed cookies as the top layer, so your sunflower will blossom in the "dirt."

7 Refrigerate until ready to serve, or freeze if you're taking it to a gathering. When you're ready to serve, wrap the stem of a silk flower in aluminum foil, and stick the flower in the middle of the cake.

Variation: You can also prepare this dessert layered in a cake pan. I've even seen this dessert served in a child's plastic sand bucket served with a plastic shovel.

Per serving: Calories 419 (From Fat 274); Fat 31g (Saturated 17g); Cholesterol 79mg; Sodium 291mg; Carbohydrate 35g; Dietary Fiber 4g (Net Carbohydrate 22g); Protein 8g.

Part III
Expanding Everyday Low-Carb Cooking

The 5th Wave   By Rich Tennant

"Don't use that excuse on me, Wayne. Ain't no good reason why a man following a low-carb lifestyle can't help himself to some of Earl's grilled mealworms."

In this part . . .

The chapters in this part help you expand your low-carb cooking experience. Snacking is an important part of your healthy low-carb lifestyle, so I invite you to venture into snacking and dipping with variations. Restaurants everywhere are serving low-carb wraps, so if you'd like to wrap up some great low-carb stuff in your own kitchen, I show you how. If you're looking for comfort food, you've come to the right place. If you don't already have a slow cooker, you may want to consider buying one so that you can have a low-carb comfort-food meal ready and waiting for you after a long day at work. Finally, I give you some mouthwatering recipes with 5 net carbs or less, which are pretty much low-carb heaven for me. If you see an angel, then you'll know that they're heavenly for you, too!

Chapter 14

Outsmarting Cravings with Low-Carb Snacks and Dips

In This Chapter

▶ Snacking your way to a healthy lifestyle

▶ Putting nuts and veggies on the top of your snack list

▶ Dreaming up delicious low-carb dips

Score another point for the low-carb lifestyle. Taking a low-carb approach to life not only means you *can* snack but that you're actually *encouraged* to snack. If you're a veteran of the diet wars and are familiar with their many taboos against snacking, this news is likely as shocking as it is exciting.

Not just any snack will do, however. And that's where this chapter comes in. In it, I stress that the question isn't to snack or not to snack but how and when to snack. Snacking unwisely with your low-carb lifestyle can be a disaster, while snacking wisely can actually help you burn calories, helping you lose or maintain your weight.

Snacking Smart

One of the low-carb lifestyle mantras is don't get too hungry — eat something. One of the secrets of low-carb success is to keep your gylcemic index (GI) level even and prevent spikes in blood sugar levels. Spikes in your blood sugar level compare to sugar highs when you get that surge of energy — but then those sugar levels dip, and so does your energy. The GI is a system that rates and measures how quickly food raises your blood sugar level. Snacking keeps those blood sugar peaks and valleys evened out, which evens out your flow of energy, making you more alert and energized. (To find out more about the glycemic index, see Chapter 2.)

While snacking is keeping your GI level even, it's doing double duty and feeding your metabolic fire to keep it burning those calories and fat. Woo hoo! Just as you throw another log on the fire to keep that campfire burning, you need to feed your internal furnace, known as your metabolism, to stoke your metabolic burn. Your furnace (or metabolism) turns your food into fuel for your body while it's burning up calories and fat.

Give your metabolism a little boost and some encouragement to keep its burn going. Eat a healthy snack when you have a snack attack, or eat one before the craving hits. Regular snacking is a desirable and rewarding part of the low-carb lifestyle.

Snacking more is better

Bodies are quirky rascals and sometimes they have a mind of their own! Research has proven that eating less to lose weight confuses your body. Your body says, "Hey, when are you going to feed me again?" It then decides that it had better store some sugar and fat just in case you don't feed it for a while. So opting for starvation diets or cutting way back on food intake simply doesn't work. When you get your body accustomed to eating healthy low-carb meals and snacking smartly in between, your body begins to relax, and your more apt burn those calories and fat up right away. Because you've become consistent in smart snacking, your body knows that more food is on the way. The weird thing is that you can eat more smart snacks along with your smart carb meals and lose more weight. (Check out Chapter 2 for more information on eating more frequently to lose weight.) The big jackpot comes when you fold in some exercise like walking (see Chapter 5), and your chances of maintaining your healthy weight go way up in your favor.

Snacking better is great

Eating healthy snacks helps you to maintain your weight instead of causing you to stall your weight loss or, worse yet, pack on pounds. Choosing smart snacks is thinking about fiber and protein foods that are a *good* double-edged sword. Fiber and protein fill you up, giving you a satisfied feeling, and the fiber gives you tons of nutrients and doesn't budge the scales upward. (Find out more about fiber and protein in Chapter 2.)

I'm an advocate of snacks of fresh veggies and fruits, cheeses, and nuts, with the keyword being *fresh*. This doesn't mean that there aren't some prepared foods out there that are low-carb snack acceptable. One of my favorite store-bought snacks is sugar-free freezer pops. Prepackaged nuts are another good snack idea. Yes, I know what you want me talk about — all of the cookies and candies and bars that are labeled *low-carb* with low, low carb counts plastered on the front of the package. Am I going to tell you that I never eat a low-carb chocolate chip cookie or a low-carb bar? Nope, not this lady — you may come to one of my book signings, and I'll be busted! I just want to caution you that a lot of the prepacked low-carb snack material that's out there isn't healthy for you and has been known to create some major weight stalls. They're no different than the every day All-American super snacks of potato chips, cheese curls, cookies, candy, kettle corn, and soda. The United States is an obese nation because of some of these foods. So if you load up on the low-carb prepared snacks, you're just trading one bad habit for another. Be good to your body and eat with smart low-carb thinking in mind, which translates into moderation.

A secret to snacking is to eat your snack slowly and pace yourself — don't gobble. Eating slowly helps satisfy your hunger or your craving much better, and taking your time gives you an opportunity to enjoy a little break from the simple everyday stresses of life. Stop, have a snack, take a deep breath, and maybe even go for a 5-minute walk.

Managing snacking is key

In low-carb snack management, the key is to try to plan your snacks for the entire day either the night before or at least before you head out the door to go to work, run errands, or whatever it is you're off to do. Part of the success of the low-carb lifestyle is to be just a tiny bit ahead of the game. Think of yourself as the manager of your healthy lifestyle, and your job is to outwit your appetite. This way of thinking becomes somewhat of a game, and you do like to win, don't you?

I usually carry some raw almonds with me wherever I go. Baby carrots are another frequent companion of mine. Don't let your appetite or cravings pop up and catch you off guard with nothing healthy in the fridge, the cupboard, the car, your workplace, or even your purse. It'll help you stay away from those nasty vending machines and drive-thrus. *Always* have something low-carb healthy available to pop in your mouth to make your tummy happy. A happy tummy becomes a healthy weight-controlled body. (Find out more about planning foods and meals in Chapter 20.)

Just how easy — and tasty — can it be to assemble low-carb snacks? I want you to get a feeling for the vastness of the great food combinations just waiting to be discovered. If you play your cards right, you'll never get bored with food in your low-carb life. Just keep on smart snacking! Check out the following list to get started snacking now.

- ¼ cup cottage cheese and 3 or 4 almonds
- ¼ cup of your choice of fresh or frozen strawberries, blueberries, raspberries, or green grapes
- ½ cup plain yogurt, ½ packet Splenda, and 1 teaspoon toasted almonds
- ½ cup blackberries and 1 stick string cheese
- A cup of bouillon
- 4 slices very thin deli turkey breast and half an apple (cut in slices)
- 4 slices very thin deli turkey or ham spread with cream cheese and sprinkled with fresh chives, rolled up
- Up to 10 green or black olives
- Stalk of celery filled with natural peanut butter, cream cheese, or homemade nut butter
- An ounce of hard cheese wrapped in an ounce of hard salami
- Low-carb tortillas with all kinds of easy fillings, such as mayonnaise, half an avocado (chopped fine), and salt and pepper to taste (see the suggestion in the Ricotta Dip for Fruits recipe later in the chapter)
- Hard-cooked eggs with salt and pepper

If you want to make a special snack that's a bit out of the ordinary, try toast cups. Trim the crusts from sliced, low-carb whole-wheat bread, brush the bread with butter, press into muffin tins, and toast until golden at 350 degrees. Fill with tuna salad, chicken salad, or another favorite of your low-carb recipes.

Surviving the Munchies with Low-Carb Treats

The keys to successful healthy snacking with your low-carb lifestyle are to not get ravenous and to always have something healthy with you to munch on at all times. Your pre-planning will pay off in the long term.

One way to improve your odds of healthy snacking is to use lots of resealable plastic bags. For example, when you come home from shopping with your big bag of nuts, you can measure them out in individual bags to take with you, thus reducing the temptation to eat more than you need by dipping into the big bag. You can do the same thing with your fresh veggies. When I come in with a big bag of baby carrots, I throw them in a colander, give them a quick swish (even though the package tells me they're prewashed), and put them in individual snack bags. If I'm out the door on errands or a shopping spree, I don't have to stop and fill a bag with fresh snacks — I just grab one and go.

Going nuts

Well, nuts! Yes, nuts are a great answer to low-carb snacking. For starters, they're portable: They're easy to tote, they're not messy, and you can eat them literally anywhere. When you get that little twinge of hunger, eat a few nuts. You'll be amazed when your hunger magically disappears. Here's a bit of nutty health news to urge you to make nuts part of your snacking routine:

✔ Recent studies have shown that consuming 1 to 2 ounces of nuts a day can actually help you lose weight and even help you to keep it off. Although some nuts are higher in carbs than others, no nut is a bad low-carb choice. It appears that nuts may very well keep that metabolic burn going, so burn, baby, burn.

✔ Even though nuts are high in fat, they contain 90 percent heart-healthy fats — unsaturated fats that don't have an impact on raising your cholesterol. These little rascals can help reduce your risk of heart attack while you soothe your cravings.

✔ Nuts are also a great source of fiber and protein. Both fiber and protein are great components for high nutrient low-carb foods and snacks. They fill you up and not out.

Even better, nuts are versatile. In addition to eating them as a snack, you can use them in place of croutons on your salad and even use them to give extra crunch to your favorite veggie recipes.

But what about the carbs, you ask? Consider the following breakdown for ¼ cup of each kind of nuts. I subtracted the fiber counts for you, so these are net carb counts. (Find more on net carbs in Chapter 2.) I only caution you to be aware of calorie counts in nuts such as cashews because the calorie counts run pretty high. I'm not saying don't eat cashews. Just be aware that calories count too in an overall healthy low-carb lifestyle. Here are the net carb counts for ¼ cup nuts (check out Figure 14-1 to see what these guys look like):

✔ Almonds: 2.8 net grams

✔ Brazil nuts: 2.6 net grams

✔ Cashews: 2.8 net grams

✔ Hazelnuts: 2.4 net grams

- Macadamia nuts: 1.8 net grams

- Peanuts: 3.6 net grams

- Pecans: 1.2 net grams

- Pistachios: 6.2 net grams

- Walnuts: 2.2 net grams

 Here's an idea for a quick treat: Roast some raw almonds. Lightly coat a shallow, nonstick baking pan with some light olive oil and toss them. Sprinkle them with an herb or spice of your choice, like a little curry powder, chili powder, or even some dried basil to liven things up. Bake at 350 degrees for 9 to12 minutes until slightly darkened. Watch 'em so they don't burn. Enjoy them warm!

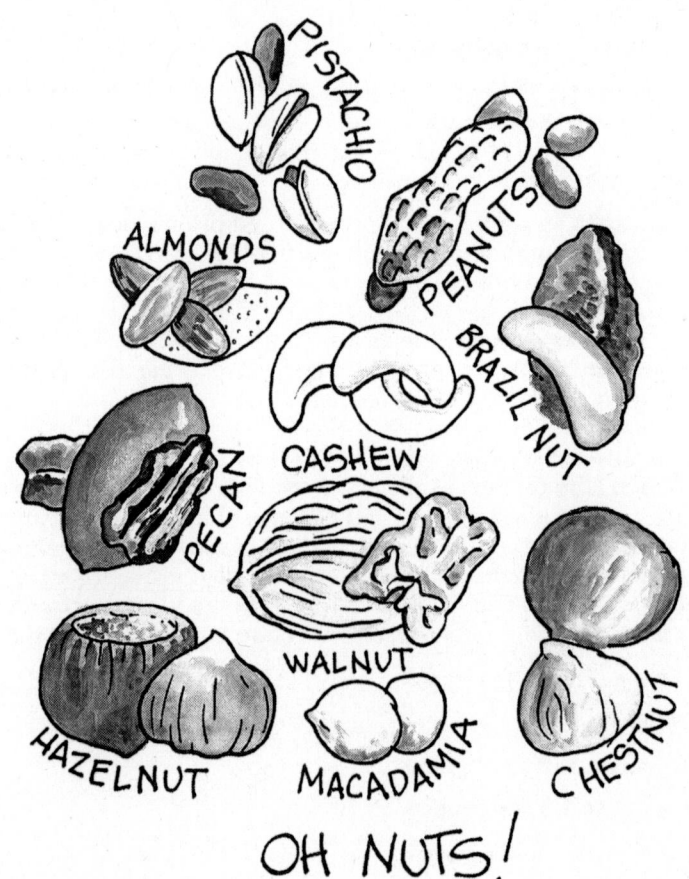

Figure 14-1:
Go nuts!

⌁ Spiced Pecans

These are sure to please and are guaranteed to wake up your taste buds in addition to satisfying that annoying hunger pang. These are best served warm. You can store them in an airtight container for a day or so but no longer than that.

Preparation time: *5 minutes*

Cooking time: *20 minutes*

Yield: *8 ¼-cup servings*

⅛ stick butter	*½ teaspoon hot pepper sauce*
1 tablespoon Worcestershire sauce	*2 cups large whole pecans*
1 tablespoon finely minced garlic	*Salt (optional)*

1 Preheat the oven to 375 degrees. Melt the butter and combine it with the Worcestershire sauce, garlic, and hot pepper sauce in a small bowl. In a medium bowl, pour the butter mixture over the nuts and toss until coated.

2 Place nuts on a jellyroll pan and toast for about 20 minutes or until browned. Shake the pan occasionally to be sure the nuts are toasting evenly.

3 Drain on paper towels before serving. Do a taste test and add salt, if desired. Store in an airtight container at room temperature.

Per serving: *Calories 245 (From Fat 225); Fat 25g (Saturated 5g); Cholesterol 15mg; Sodium 30mg; Carbohydrate 4g; Dietary Fiber 2g (Net Carbohydrate 2g); Protein 3g.*

Why not water?

Have you ever thought of water as a snack? Did you know that by the time your brain tells you that you're thirsty, your body is already beginning to be dehydrated? I'm talking about lack of hydration — not lost-in-the-desert dehydrated. Keeping your body well hydrated and your low-carb lifestyle in tow is even more achievable if you drink plenty of water.

If you have a craving mid-morning, grab that water bottle and gulp down some of the clear, revitalizing stuff, and then have your low-carb snack. Drinking water will soon become a habit for you, and you'll be amazed what it does to the scales. Guess you'd better "just add water" to the snack list.

☾ Nutty Popcorn

Popcorn is a bit of a strange bird. Some folks can eat it and not gain an ounce, and some people (like me) gain a pound just looking at the stuff. So pay attention for bloating and watch the scale after you eat this stuff even though this recipe has a measly 5 net grams of carbs. Whatever your personal experience, it sure is acceptable for a special treat. The popcorn in this recipe is especially satisfying and especially crunchy with the addition of nuts. I'm sure that after just reading the recipe, you're going to think of all kinds of variations of this basic low-carb munchie. You can save dollars if you air-pop your own popcorn. It's so easy, and it isn't even messy, so give it a whirl. The upside is the freshest of fresh popcorn without preservatives.

Preparation time: *5 minutes*

Cooking time: *10 minutes*

Yield: *9 servings (1 cup each)*

2 tablespoons butter	*8 cups popped popcorn*
1 teaspoon curry powder	*1 cup pecan pieces*
½ teaspoon salt	

1 In a small skillet, melt the butter until it bubbles, being careful not to let it brown or burn. Add the curry powder and salt and stir.

2 With popcorn in a large bowl, add the nuts and drizzle the butter mixture over the popcorn and pecan pieces. Toss until well coated.

Variation: *For seasoned popcorn of a different flavor, try substituting the curry powder and the nuts with 2 teaspoons of freshly chopped chives, 2 teaspoons of fresh dill weed, 2 teaspoons of freshly grated Parmesan cheese, and 1 teaspoon of celery salt.*

Per serving: *Calories 133 (From Fat 103); Fat 12g (Saturated 2g); Cholesterol 7mg; Sodium 130mg; Carbohydrate 7g; Dietary Fiber 2g (Net Carbohydrate 5g); Protein 2g.*

☜ *Maple-Cinnamon Almond Snack*

This snack is quick to fix and is pleasing to your sweet tooth. When you have a sweet craving, grab a few of these tasty nuts for a special treat that's almost like a low-carb candy. Indulge in this snack, because the carb counts are on your side. A word of warning, though: Don't eat all the nuts in one sitting just because this recipe is labeled low-carb and sugar free. If you want to have a stash of these almonds, simply double the recipe.

Preparation time: *5 minutes*

Baking time: *12 minutes*

Yield: *4 ¼-cup servings*

1 cup raw almonds	*3 tablespoons sugar-free maple syrup*	*½ teaspoon cinnamon*

1 Preheat the oven to 350 degrees.

2 In a medium mixing bowl, stir together the almonds, syrup, and cinnamon until the almonds are well coated.

3 Line a shallow pan with parchment paper. Bake the almonds in the pan for 10 to 12 minutes, stirring a couple times. The glaze will dry on the nuts during baking.

4 Let the almonds cool and break apart, if necessary. (If there's high humidity, they may be a bit sticky, but if it's very dry day, they'll be almost perfect.) Store in an airtight container at room temperature if they make it that far!

Per serving: *Calories 217 (From Fat 165); Fat 18g (Saturated 1g); Cholesterol 0mg; Sodium 28mg; Carbohydrate 10g; Dietary Fiber 4g (Net Carbohydrate 6g); Protein 8g.*

Vegging out

It's the most incredible thing I've ever experienced: When you eat more green stuff, you crave more green stuff. I know that sounds bizarre, and if you've never experienced it, you're probably shaking your head in disbelief. But it's true. If you get in the habit of snacking on broccoli and green leafy stuff, your cravings will shift to actually wanting some fresh veggies for a snack. Try it, and you'll be amazed. This shift in cravings won't happen overnight, but stick with it, and you'll be longing for veggies in no time. I double dare you to try it.

Celery Stick Tuna Delight

The results here are delightful to look at and munch into. The combination of ingredients is so colorful that you'll want to party on with your low-carb lifestyle and enjoy the low carb count in this festive treat. If you want to tote this snack along with you, just carry the celery in a resealable plastic bag and the tuna combo in a little plastic container, and put everything together when you're ready to munch. This recipe calls for shredded cabbage, carrots, and zucchini. Make sure you shred them very fine. I have a little 2½ cup mini food processor that I use to shred them into shape.

Preparation time: *12 minutes*

Yield: *12 servings*

3-ounce package cream cheese, room temperature	3-ounce pouch albacore tuna
1 tablespoon plain yogurt	½ cup finely shredded red cabbage
½ teaspoon dried basil	½ cup finely shredded carrot
½ teaspoon garlic salt with parsley	¼ cup finely shredded zucchini, unpeeled
Salt and pepper to taste	12 celery sticks (4 inches long)

1 In a small bowl, combine the cream cheese, yogurt, basil, garlic salt, salt, and pepper, mixing until well blended.

2 In a second small bowl, toss the tuna, cabbage, carrot, and zucchini until well combined.

3 Stir the cream cheese mixture into the tuna mixture.

4 Heap the tuna mixture into and onto the celery sticks — there's a bunch of filling here. You can serve immediately or refrigerate the prepared sticks for about a half hour so the mixture chills and is even crunchier with the crispy celery combination. If you prefer, store the tuna mixture separately and heap it into the celery when you're ready to serve and snack.

Per serving: Calories 43 (From Fat 25); Fat 3g (Saturated 2g); Cholesterol 11mg; Sodium 164mg; Carbohydrate 2g; Dietary Fiber 1g (Net Carbohydrate 1g); Protein 3g.

○ *Veggie Wedgie Crisps*

This snack is great hot, but I love it cold as well. You can take wedgies along as leftovers for a snack at work. Or you can prepare everything in advance and keep them in the fridge until you crave a snack at home. Just pop them in the oven. Veggie Wedgie Crisps are like a mini snack pizza (only better)!

Preparation time: *15 minutes*

Cooking time: *15 to 18 minutes*

Yield: *2 servings*

1 cup small fresh broccoli florets

1 package (3 ounces) cream cheese, room temperature

½ teaspoon dried basil leaves

½ teaspoon garlic powder with parsley flakes

2 8-inch low-carb whole-wheat tortillas

½ cup fresh chopped mushrooms

½ cup thin strips red, yellow, and green bell pepper

½ cup shredded mozzarella cheese

1 Preheat the oven to 350 degrees.

2 Trim off the bottoms of broccoli florets. Cut the florets into quarters and place them in a mini food processor. Chop the broccoli until it reaches a very fine consistency — like broccoli sand! You should have about ½ cup of broccoli at this point.

3 In a small bowl, combine the softened cream cheese, basil, and garlic powder, mixing well with a fork. Spread the mixture evenly on both tortillas. Place the tortillas on a heavy cookie sheet.

4 Sprinkle the broccoli on top of the cream cheese mixture, spreading it evenly. Add the mushrooms and strips of pepper on top of the tortillas. Bake for 10 minutes.

5 Increase oven temperature to 400 degrees and remove the cookie sheet from the oven. Divide the cheese evenly, sprinkling on both tortillas.

6 Return the tortillas to the oven for another 5 minutes. The cheese should be oozing and melted. Cut the tortilla into wedges and serve immediately.

Variation: *Add fresh sliced Roma tomatoes on top after removing the tortillas from the oven, drizzle them with a little olive oil, and sprinkle on some freshly chopped basil. Talk about waking up your taste buds!*

Per serving: *Calories 301 (From Fat 208); Fat 23g (Saturated 13g); Cholesterol 69mg; Sodium 421mg; Carbohydrate 18g; Dietary Fiber 10g (Net Carbohydrate 8g); Protein 16g.*

Skinny Dipping

The possible combinations of low-carb dips are limited only by your wildest culinary notions. You can take a base of yogurt, cottage cheese, sour cream, or cream cheese and mix it with a variety of soft cheeses, herbs, and spices in dips that could fill an entire cookbook. You can choose fruit dips, veggie dips, hot dips, or cold dips — dips for parties or dips for snacking. Dips are for more than potato chips! Dippin' fresh fruits and veggies is so much better.

Quick slim dippin'

You don't need a recipe with a list of 12 ingredients and a lengthy preparation time for the end result to taste really good. Slim ingredients can make mighty tasty stuff. Try some of the following quick combinations, and feel free to experiment using these base ingredients:

- **Yogurt**
  - With grated horseradish and fresh chopped Italian parsley
  - With finely chopped cucumber and a little dill
  - With a little fresh orange juice, some lemon zest, and a packet of Splenda sugar substitute (this dip can also be made with sour cream rather than yogurt)
- **Sour cream**
  - With dill weed and chopped garlic
  - With fresh, crisp bacon crumbles
  - With apricot sugar-free preserves
- **Cottage cheese**
  - With leftover sauces, seasoned to taste
  - With a spot of Dijon mustard and some minced fresh chives
- **Cream cheese**
  - With a splash of whipped cream to thin just a tad and some chopped pecans
  - With finely chopped fresh green onions chopped fine

My favorite accompaniments for these concoctions are — you guessed it, veggies. Celery, carrot sticks, zucchini sticks, cucumbers, blanched asparagus, cauliflower, radishes, snow peas, yellow squash, Brussels sprouts, broccoli, and broccoflower all work great.

☺ *Three-Cheese Roasted Garlic Dip*

This dip is just awesome with fresh veggies. Feel free to substitute any of your favorite cheeses for one or all of the ones I list here. No matter what you substitute, you just can't go wrong with this recipe.

Preparation time: *20 minutes*

Cooking time: *45 minutes*

Refrigeration time: *4 hours*

Yield: *20 servings*

2 medium heads of garlic

3½ ounces goat cheese

2 packages (8 ounces each) cream cheese, room temperature

2 tablespoons crumbled blue cheese

1 teaspoon dried thyme leaves

1 Preheat the oven to 400 degrees. Cut off the tops of the garlic heads, exposing the tops of the cloves. Place the garlic in a small baking pan and bake for 45 minutes, or until garlic is very tender.

2 Remove the garlic from the pan and cool completely. Squeeze the garlic into a small bowl and then mash with a fork.

3 Combine the goat cheese and cream cheese in a medium mixing bowl and beat until smooth. (You can also use a food processor for this step.) Stir in the blue cheese, garlic, and thyme.

4 Cover and refrigerate for at least 4 hours or overnight to let the flavors mingle.

5 Serve the cheese dip with crispy fresh vegetables. This dip is especially nice served with red and yellow bell pepper strips, cucumber slices, zucchini, and broccoli.

Per serving: Calories 105 (From Fat 87); Fat 10g (Saturated 6g); Cholesterol 30mg; Sodium 105mg; Carbohydrate 2g; Dietary Fiber 0g (Net Carbohydrate 2g); Protein 3g.

I love to make this for a quick sweet snack when a craving hits me and just won't give up. If you close your eyes, you'll think you're eating cheesecake! Take ½ of an 8-ounce package of cream cheese. Add 1 packet of Splenda and a couple drops of pure vanilla extract. Take a fork and stir it all up (it'll be hard at first). If you want to really jazz it up, add a tad of sugar-free preserves. It's a great quick sweet-tooth fix.

⌒ *Broccolomole Dip*

Spell check had a really tough time as I was writing this one, but you're going to love this recipe regardless of its crazy name. This dip is a sister in looks to guacamole, but its color is a little brighter green. Broccoli is the ultimate veggie and has a rave rating in the low-carb lifestyle. So whip up this skinny recipe and dip in with fresh veggies, or treat yourself to some low-carb tortilla chips.

Preparation time: *10 minutes*

Cooking time: *5 minutes*

Refrigeration time: *3 to 4 hours*

Yield: *8 servings*

2 cups precut fresh broccoli	*1 tablespoon mayonnaise*
¼ cup sour cream	*3 tablespoon lemon juice*
1 tablespoon minced onion	*¼ teaspoon chili powder (more to taste)*

1 Cook the fresh broccoli to crisp-tender in your steamer basket. Run cold water over it and place the broccoli in the refrigerator to chill for about 30 minutes.

2 Combine the broccoli, sour cream, onion, mayonnaise, lemon juice, and chili powder in your food processor and blend until smooth.

3 Refrigerate for several hours or overnight.

4 Serve with fresh, crisp veggies.

Per serving: *Calories 35 (From Fat 27); Fat 3g (Saturated 1g); Cholesterol 4mg; Sodium 19mg; Carbohydrate 2g; Dietary Fiber 1g (Net Carbohydrate 1g); Protein 1g.*

Here's another quick dip: Combine and beat until smooth 12 ounces cottage cheese, 2 tablespoons mayonnaise, 1 tablespoon lemon juice, ¾ teaspoon garlic salt, and a dash of freshly ground black pepper. Dip in with any of your favorite veggies.

For a very cool presentation, serve your homemade dips in a hollow green or red pepper or in a couple red cabbage leaves. If you're having guests, you can make individual dishes out of large red cabbage leaves, serving raw vegetables in one and dip in the other. Experiment and come up with your own creative serving dish.

Fruity choices

Fruits have been controversial in some low-carb lifestyles. Living low-carb for life is all about balance and not depriving yourself of foods that are proven to be good for you, such as fruit. However, some fruits are loaded with carbs, so you can be selective in choosing fruits that work for you. You can choose what fruits to eat according to what fits the healthy low-carb lifestyle that works for you. If you're eating fruit every day and the scale starts creeping up, then cut back to every other day or maybe three times a week. If you're highly sugar sensitive, then the natural sugar will have a bit of an effect on you, and it could come about in weight gain. I encourage you, however, for the ultimate healthy low-carb lifestyle to eat fruit! Here are some raw fruits that are lower in carbs than others and are thus lower on the glycemic index (refer to Chapter 2 for an explanation of how the GI fits into your low-carb lifestyle).

- ✔ Apples
- ✔ Apricots
- ✔ Blackberries
- ✔ Blueberries
- ✔ Cantaloupe
- ✔ Cherries
- ✔ Figs
- ✔ Grapes
- ✔ Honeydew
- ✔ Nectarines
- ✔ Oranges
- ✔ Peaches
- ✔ Pears
- ✔ Plums
- ✔ Raspberries
- ✔ Rhubarb
- ✔ Strawberries
- ✔ Tangerines

🍑 Ricotta Dip for Fruits

This dip is so delicious that it may be difficult to keep yourself from sitting by the bowl and eating the whole thing, but please restrain yourself. Be a dainty dipper and eat just the right amount. Make sure that it's well chilled before you serve it (if you can keep your fingers out of it). You can even prepare it the night before and take it with you to work to snack on during the day. Expect some rave reviews on this recipe if you serve it to guests — but you may not want to share! Heartier fruits like apples, pears, nectarines, and pineapple work well with this.

Preparation time: *8 minutes*

Refrigeration time: *1 hour*

Yield: *1¾ cups (14 servings of 2 tablespoons each)*

15 ounces ricotta cheese	1½ teaspoons grated orange peel
2 packets Splenda sugar substitute	¾ teaspoon ground cinnamon
½ teaspoon vanilla extract	

1 Combine the ricotta, Splenda, vanilla extract, orange peel, and cinnamon in your food processor and puree until very smooth.

2 Transfer the mixture to a bowl, cover tightly, and refrigerate until serving or snacking time.

Variation: *You can also spread this dip on a low-carb tortilla. Sprinkle some red raspberries or strawberries in the middle of the tortilla, roll it up, and you have a great snack. Use any fruit you want to enhance this low-carb tortilla snack.*

Per serving: *Calories 54 (From Fat 36); Fat 4g (Saturated 3g); Cholesterol 16mg; Sodium 26mg; Carbohydrate 1g; Dietary Fiber 0g (Net Carbohydrate 1g); Protein 3g.*

Chapter 15

Wrapping It Up, Low-Carb Style

*T*hey're everywhere! You'll find very few restaurants and fast food establishments where you can't get a wrap, and a lot of these restaurants offer specific, low-carb wraps as alternatives to sandwiches that are packed with carbs. Call them trendy if you want, but I think wraps are brilliant — not to mention delicious. You can build an entire low-carb meal that's satisfying *and* easy to prepare around tasty, nutritional wraps. And did I mention versatility? Wraps cater to no specific mealtime — you can enjoy them for breakfast, lunch, dinner, as a snack, or on the run.

Wrapping Your Taste Buds Around a Low-Carb Favorite

If you can roll it up, it's a wrap! Depending on what you're wrapping, you have myriad choices for the "wrapper." Low-carb tortillas are probably the most popular, most accessible, and quickest option for a wrapper. Makers of tortillas have jumped on the low-carb bandwagon and created some delicious low-carb tortillas, many with 3 grams of carbs or less. Tortillas are a great staple to have on hand if you're in a hurry or want a quick, healthy snack.

Tortillas are always best warm. Just pop them in the microwave on high for about 10 seconds. They'll be warm and ready to roll!

But tortillas aren't the only medium for making wraps, so now it's time to think outside the box. You'll forever be "en-wraptured" by all your low-carb wrapper options:

- **Egg crepes:** These wrappers are light as a feather, and they complement any filling you wish to use. Wrap them up with veggies or use them as dessert wraps (see the "Raising the Wrap Bar with Egg Crepes" section later in the chapter).

- **Leafy green or red lettuce:** Because leaf lettuce is pliable, yet fresh and crisp, it makes a great wrap. If you aren't accustomed to using different lettuces as wrappers, leaf is a great place to start.

- **Romaine lettuce:** This lettuce takes on its own robust flavor, so be sure to use it with something that tends to be a bit spicy so the romaine doesn't overwhelm the filling. Also, make sure that you cut off the rigid spine at the bottom of the romaine. You'll find that romaine is a less bendable lettuce, but get over it because its flavor with fillings is worth this wrap being a bit messy.

- **Iceberg lettuce:** It isn't the most nutritious lettuce, but the carb counts are great. If you have a hot ground meat filling you want to corral in a wrap, the cool crispness of iceberg is a sure fit. (Check out the Cheese-Stuffed Ground Round Patties recipe in Chapter 11.)

- **Boston lettuce:** With its round shape, this lettuce is perfect for wraps.

- **Radicchio:** Some people absolutely adore this stuff, and some turn up their noses and run the other way due its slightly bitter flavor. (You can read more about radicchio and other greens in Chapter 8.) Radicchio complements grilled fillings nicely.

- **Napa cabbage:** This type of cabbage has very broad leaves but is a little on the thin side. Napa can make a great wrap, but use two leaves to prevent your wrap from breaking apart.

- **Red and green cabbage:** The wide, round leaves make red and green cabbage perfect for rolling up fillings. Both cabbages have distinctive flavors all their own, so the choice is yours. The red cabbage can make a great presentation for guests.

- **Cheese:** You can use any kind of sliceable cheese as a wrapper — and a great wrapper at that. The trick with cheeses is to have them almost room temperature to make the slices more pliable and easier to handle so they don't crack on you.

- **Sliced ham, turkey, chicken, prosciutto, and salami:** These sliced meats make great wraps that give you endless combinations for wrapping it up. If you use thinly-sliced deli meat, go with two or three slices to make sure your filling stays in place and makes it to your mouth. See the Sushi Under (Low-Carb) Wraps recipe in this section for one example.

Sushi Under (Low-Carb) Wraps

These clever little wraps are soooo tasty — and portable! They're perfect when you're having a craving or it's still 45 minutes until lunchtime. You can substitute all kinds of ingredients in these simple sushi wraps (check out my suggestions at the end of the recipe), and it's quick. You'll get accustomed to healthy low-carb snacks in no time when they're this yummy and easy.

Preparation time: *10 minutes*

Yield: *4 servings*

4 slices deli ham	*4 tablespoons whipped cream cheese*	*1 small cucumber, quartered lengthwise and seeded*

1 Remove any excess moisture from the ham with a paper towel. Carefully spread each ham slice with 1 tablespoon cream cheese right up to the edges.

2 Remove any excess moisture from the cucumber slices with a paper towel. Place a cucumber slice at the edge of a ham slice, and roll it up tightly. Gently press the edge of the ham to seal. Repeat the process with each of the remaining ham and cucumber slices.

3 Wrap each roll in plastic wrap, and place them in the fridge until it's time to munch. Then cut the roll in slices resembling sushi.

Variation: *In place of the ham, you can use slices of turkey breast or chicken breast. You can also try rolling up slices of your favorite cheeses with fillings. Try adding fresh chives, any herb or spice that you love, or even a tad of sugar-free apricot jam to the sour cream. The veggies you choose can be crispy red peppers, a couple pieces of blanched asparagus (it's great cold), or leftover long green beans with some chopped red pepper. And the spread can change from cream cheese to homemade mayonnaise (see recipes later) or bottled or homemade dressings!*

Per serving: Calories 53 (From Fat 37); Fat 4g (Saturated 2g); Cholesterol 17mg; Sodium 186mg; Carbohydrate 2g; Dietary Fiber 0g (Net Carbohydrate 2g); Protein 3g.

If you're taking the lettuce route for your wraps, rinse and spin it ahead of time and pop it in a zipper-type plastic bag to make sure that the lettuce is very crisp. No one likes limp lettuce. I've done this forever, and it seems that the little bit of moisture that's left on the lettuce after spinning and zipping makes it extra crispy as it sits in the fridge.

If you're taking the tortilla route, and the wrap is going to sit for several hours (say you're taking them for lunch), the trick to keeping your low-carb tortilla from getting soggy is to put a layer of lettuce on top of the tortilla and then add your fillings.

Filling in the Wraps

Making top-notch wraps depends on more than just the wrapper. What's inside is left only to your imagination, what's in your pantry, or what you have left over in the fridge. Here are some tips to keep in mind as you fantasize about your fillings:

✔ **Opt for variety in texture:** Using ingredients with different textures tends to wake up your taste buds and leave you more satisfied.

✔ **Balance things out:** You don't want your wrap to taste like dry cardboard, so balance things out by adding some moist stuff in with that left-over turkey.

✔ **Develop theme wraps:** In other words, pursue a main flavor and enhance from there. Like most things in life, you need a base to build from, and wrap building is no exception.

Time to get your brain thinking about all the foods you can wrap up. It's a quick four-part process:

1. **Just start with one or more main ingredient from this list:**

    • Chopped, hard-cooked eggs

    • Albacore tuna in a pouch

    • Salmon in a sealed bag

    • Canned shrimp

    • Smoked ham

    • Turkey strips

    • Chicken strips

    • Deli roast beef

    • Veggies galore

    • Salad mixes

    • Fruits

2. **Add a dressing or dressing combo:**

    • Plain yogurt

    • Mayonnaise

    • Cream cheese

    • Sour cream

- Italian or ranch dressing

- Dijon mustard

- Horseradish

- Peanut butter

- Yogurt and sour cream combo

- Caesar dressing

- Sweetened cream cheese (use a sugar substitute of your choice)

3. **Select some crunchy stir-ins and sprinkle-ons:**

- Alfalfa sprouts

- Sliced bell peppers

- Chopped cucumber

- Chopped green onions

- Crumbled and shredded cheeses

- Crispy bacon

- Water chestnuts

- Pears and apples

- Herbs and spices

- Nuts

- Whipped cream

4. **Grab a low-carb, whole-wheat tortilla and wrap it up.**

Voilà — you're a wrap star!

Be a copycat. When you're out and about in restaurants — whether they're of the sit-down or fast-food variety — check out what's on the menu (besides what you're ordering). You can learn a lot and possibly discover some awesome wrap ideas. Lots of eateries have low-carb wraps on the menu. Just because the presentations are gorgeous doesn't mean the preparation is difficult. And if low-carb wraps aren't on the menu, then use your carb smarts and copycat a low-carb version. You can do it!

Wraps are so quick and easy that they work well as appetizers if you have surprise guests. Just roll them up and cut them in bite-sized pieces. Use a combination of fillings, and you can put together an awesome appetizer tray in no time.

 **Peanut Butter and Cream Cheese Wraps**

Is your sweet tooth talking to you? Here's a delightfully refreshing little treat that'll make you smile. If you don't indulge too often, it's a great sweet fix that's really easy on the carb counts. If you prefer, please leave out the sugar substitute: These wraps are perfectly delightful without it. Cut diagonally in bite-size pieces to savor it and make the treat last longer.

Preparation time: *10 minutes*

Yield: *4 wraps*

1 packet Splenda sugar substitute	*½ cup natural crunchy peanut butter*
¼ cup cream cheese, softened	*4 low-carb whole-wheat tortilla wraps*
½ teaspoon pure vanilla extract	*1 cup thinly sliced fresh strawberries*

1 In a small bowl or cup, mix the Splenda with the cream cheese and vanilla until well blended.

2 Add the peanut butter and swirl together (this doesn't have to be mixed well — just swirly).

3 Spread one-fourth of the mixture evenly on 4 low-carb whole-wheat tortillas. Sprinkle with ¼ cup strawberries each.

4 Roll the tortillas burrito-style (see the "Shaping Up Your Tortillas" section, later in this chapter).

Variation: *This cream cheese, Splenda, and vanilla mixture (without the peanut butter) can be used for many treat wraps. You can add a little sugar-free jam or preserves to give it a special hidden flavor or just add a dash of your favorite sugar-free syrup (in place of the vanilla). If you want a maple flavor, use sugar-free maple syrup. I've been known to mix plain cream cheese with vanilla and Splenda and indulge in a couple teaspoons to ward off a sweet attack. If you close your eyes, you think you're eating cheesecake.*

Recipe Per Serving: *Calories 315 (From Fat 209); Fat 23g (Saturated 5g); Cholesterol 16mg; Sodium 343mg; Carbohydrate 22g; Dietary Fiber 11g (Net Carbohydrate 11g); Protein 13g.*

If you stuff your wrap so much that you can't roll it, how are you going to get it to your mouth? If you're on the go, you better pack an extra shirt. Don't be stingy on your wrap stuffings — just insightful. The more wraps you create, the better stuffer you'll become — especially after you've sent a few tops to the dry cleaners. You may have a second wrap, you know, because they're low-carb healthy after all.

Tossing salad into the wrap mix

Salad wraps are great, the variety is unending, and they're quick and easy. Next time you're at the grocery store, pick up a combo bag of prewashed lettuces (see Chapter 8), a bag of shredded cabbage or brocco-cabbage, Italian dressing, and some feta cheese. Put the lettuce, cabbage, and cheese in a bowl and toss with the Italian dressing. Warm your low-carb whole-wheat tortilla and fill it with your salad combo. You've just made a healthy, low-carb meal in a matter of minutes.

You can choose a different kind of mix every time you pick up a new bag of prewashed greens — Caesar salad, spinach, mesclun mix, baby greens, and the list goes on. Spend a little time in that section of the produce department, and you'll be amazed at the ingredients that jump out at you.

Cheeses in salad wraps are like the icing on the cake. You can enjoy so many flavors of cheeses all at once. Experiment with a delightful Italian blend of shredded cheeses that includes combos of mozzarella, Romano, provolone, Parmesan, and Asiago cheeses. Wake up your taste buds.

Securing wraps in style

Want to roll up your wraps so they don't come undone? A creative way to do so, especially if you're entertaining company, is to wrap the green part of a green onion around the wrap a couple times, tying the binding in knots. Place your wraps on a platter, add some colored kale for garnish, and you have a very special presentation.

Wraps to go are the best. Make sure to roll them tightly and secure them in plastic wrap so that they hold their shape and they're ready to go into the microwave at the office or wherever you're headed. Be sure to remove them from the plastic wrap before heating in the microwave. To ensure safe travel for your wrap, you may want to add an overcoat of aluminum foil to hold it all together.

Pay attention when you're heating or reheating wraps in your microwave. Plastic wrap is great stuff to hold a wrap securely while storing in the fridge or toting in your lunch box. But before popping your wrap in the microwave, undress it and get rid of that plastic wrap. The U.S. Department of Agriculture warns not to let plastic wrap touch any food during microwaving. It seems there are some little rascals called *adipates* that make the plastic wrap stick to bowls. Controversy over one particular adipate found in the plastic has been bubbling for decades. So better to be safe than sorry: Don't let plastic wrap touch foods during microwaving.

Shaping Up Your Tortillas

There are a few little tricks to tuck away for when you shape your wraps. I know the image of a rolled tortilla is the most common, but you may have some fillings that you don't want oozing out the ends. Get a sample tortilla and have a wrap-folding practice session with the following methods:

- **Roll-up wrap:** This method is the most common. Put your filling down the middle of the tortilla and spread it from top to bottom to form a long line. Don't take it all the way to the edge. Start at one side of the tortilla and fold the tortilla over the filling, tucking it in a little to secure the filling. After tucking, gently pull the filling toward you with the tortilla and begin rolling. It's a wrap — time to eat!

- **Half-moon wrap:** Spread your filling in a half-moon shape over half of the tortilla. Don't spread the filling all the way to the edges, or you'll experience oozing. Then just fold the empty side over the filled side — like a quesadilla. This type of wrap is a bit tricky to pick up sometimes, so you may want to keep it on your plate and eat it with a fork.

- **Burrito wrap:** Put your filling down the middle of the tortilla. Spread it out so it's like a thick line but not touching either side of the tortilla. Take the bottom third of the tortilla, and fold it up over the filling. Take the left side of the tortilla and fold it to the middle; then do the same with the right side. The top of the wrap is open. See Figure 15-1.

WRAPPING FILLINGS IN TORTILLAS

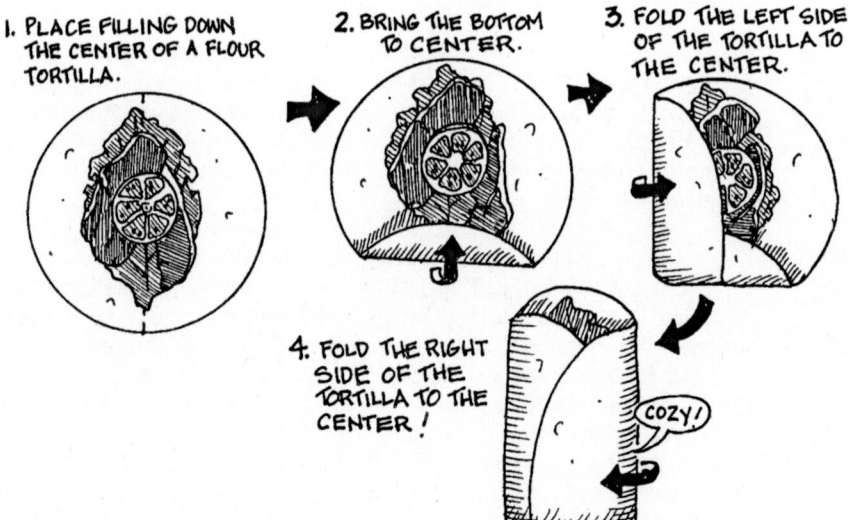

1. PLACE FILLING DOWN THE CENTER OF A FLOUR TORTILLA.

2. BRING THE BOTTOM TO CENTER.

3. FOLD THE LEFT SIDE OF THE TORTILLA TO THE CENTER.

4. FOLD THE RIGHT SIDE OF THE TORTILLA TO THE CENTER!

COZY!

Figure 15-1: That's a wrap — a leakproof wrap.

Cheesy Hot Steak Wraps

The original cheese-steak sandwich is believed to have its roots in 1930s Philadelphia. That sandwich recipe just doesn't fit in the low-carb genre, but because I love it, I made a few adjustments. Now it's carb friendly and even easier to eat because it's a wrap.

Preparation time: *10 minutes*

Cooking time: *8 minutes*

Yield: *4 wraps*

1 tablespoon olive oil	*2 cups green pepper slices*
½ clove garlic, minced fine	*½ pound deli roast beef, cut in thin slices*
¼ teaspoon salt	*¼ cup Italian salad dressing*
¼ teaspoon pepper	*4 low-carb whole-wheat tortillas*
¼ cup chopped yellow onion	*1 cup shredded Monterey Jack cheese*

1 Place the olive oil in a heavy skillet. Over medium heat, add the garlic, salt, and pepper, stirring to mingle the spices with the olive oil. Add the onions and peppers. Cook until the peppers are crisp-tender. This should take no longer than 5 minutes.

2 Add the roast beef and salad dressing to the skillet, mixing well, and cook until the roast beef is heated through, about 3 minutes.

3 Spoon one-fourth of the beef mixture evenly down the middle of each tortilla. Sprinkle each tortilla with ¼ cup cheese and roll them up. Make sure to work rather quickly, because the heat from the beef mixture makes the cheese melt inside your wrap.

Per serving: Calories 335 (From Fat 206); Fat 23g (Saturated 8g); Cholesterol 52mg; Sodium 1,167mg; Carbohydrate 18g; Dietary Fiber 9g (Net Carbohydrate 9g); Protein 24g.

If you like salsa, splash some in your wrap. Be sure to wrap it burrito style so you don't end up with it all over your shirt.

Hot Salami Wraps

This hot wrap is sure to please, with its combination of cheeses and salami. Feel free to substitute the meats of your choice or combine a couple different kinds of meat.

Preparation time: *10 minutes*

Cooking time: *10 to 12 minutes*

Yield: *4 wraps*

¼ cup butter, room temperature

4 low-carb whole-wheat tortillas

8 tablespoons freshly shredded Parmesan cheese

4 ounces thinly sliced provolone cheese

4 ounces thinly sliced salami

¼ cup roasted red bell peppers, drained and cut in small pieces

4 ounces shredded mozzarella cheese

1 Preheat your oven to 400 degrees. Spread butter on only one side of each of the tortillas (buttered side up). Sprinkle with Parmesan cheese.

2 In the center of each tortilla, layer one-fourth of the provolone, salami, and peppers. Then sprinkle one-fourth of the mozzarella on top of each. Bake 10 to 12 minutes, or until the tortillas turn golden brown. Serve open-faced or fold them like a quesadilla.

Per serving: Calories 501 (From Fat 265); Fat 41g (Saturated 21g); Cholesterol 103mg; Sodium 1,286mg; Carbohydrate 15g; Dietary Fiber 8g (Net Carbohydrate 7g); Protein 28g.

Pizza Wraps

For all you pizza lovers, you're going to love these Pizza Wraps. They're guaranteed to soothe your hankering for pizza and keep your carbs in check. This is just a very basic recipe to give you an idea of where to start. You can have a grand time adding the carb-friendly toppings of your choice. If you're in a hurry, pop these in the microwave, and you'll be eating in no time.

Preparation time: *10 minutes*

Cooking time: *10 to 12 minutes*

Yield: *4 wraps*

½ cup pizza sauce (choose the one with the least carbs and lowest sugar content)

4 low-carb whole-wheat tortillas

1 cup mozzarella cheese

24 small pepperoni slices

1 Preheat your oven to 350 degrees. Spread the pizza sauce evenly over the tortillas to within 1 inch of the edges. Sprinkle each tortilla evenly with ¼ cup mozzarella cheese.

2 Place 6 pepperoni slices down the center of each tortilla and roll them up. After all the tortillas are rolled, wrap them individually in aluminum foil.

3 Place the wraps in a baking dish and bake for 10 to 12 minutes. Make sure the wraps are heated all the way through and the cheese is melted.

Variation: *In place of the pepperoni, add your favorite veggies, like fresh sliced mushrooms, chopped bell peppers, broccoli, or fresh tomatoes. Or go with Canadian bacon and anything else that's on the low-carb list.*

Per serving: Calories 303 (From Fat 203); Fat 23g (Saturated 9g); Cholesterol 48mg; Sodium 1,043mg; Carbohydrate 15g; Dietary Fiber 9g (Net Carbohydrate 6g); Protein 18g.

Pesto Salmon Wraps

I love pesto, and I love salmon, so this is one of my favorite recipes. I tend to load up on the salmon, making this a fat wrap, so if it's too much for you, just cut back a little on your salmon.

Preparation time: *15 minutes*

Yield: *6 wraps*

¼ cup pesto	6 low-carb whole-wheat tortillas
3 ounces cream cheese, softened	1 pound thinly sliced smoked salmon (cold)

1 Mix the pesto and cream cheese until well blended.

2 Divide the mixture evenly and plop it on top of each of the 6 tortillas. Spread evenly. Top each tortilla with cold smoked salmon, and roll.

Per serving: Calories 240 (From Fat 135); Fat 15g (Saturated 5g); Cholesterol 36mg; Sodium 1,813mg; Carbohydrate 12g; Dietary Fiber 8g (Net Carbohydrate 4g); Protein 22g.

🍅 Spicy Black Soybean Wraps

Black soybeans are one of the greatest foods you'll discover in your low-carb life. For a ½ cup of black soybeans, the net carb count is a whopping *1 gram*. Plus they're very nutritious and full of fiber. Here's a great spicy wrap that you can easily adjust to your liking.

Preparation time: *10 minutes*

Cooking time: *15 minutes*

Yield: *6 wraps*

15-ounce can Eden black soybeans, rinsed and drained	¼ to ½ teaspoon crushed red pepper flakes	6 low-carb whole-wheat tortillas
1 small yellow onion, chopped fine	2 teaspoons tomato paste	3 cups finely shredded lettuce
1 clove garlic, minced	2 tablespoons chopped mild green chiles	4 ripe Roma tomatoes, diced
	2 tablespoons tomato juice	1 cup shredded cheddar cheese

1 In a large, heavy skillet combine the beans, onion, garlic, red pepper flakes, tomato paste, chiles, and tomato juice. Stirring constantly, bring the ingredients to a simmer.

2 Cover and cook over low heat for about 10 minutes. Check often and make sure there's enough liquid so the mixture doesn't burn. If in doubt, add a couple teaspoons of water to keep from sticking. During the last few minutes of cooking, uncover and let all the juices evaporate.

3 Remove the skillet from the heat and mash the beans to a chunky texture with a fork.

4 Heat the tortillas in the microwave on high for about 10 seconds per tortilla. I heat them individually.

5 Spoon 2 heaping tablespoons of filling onto each tortilla and top with the lettuce, tomatoes, and cheese. Roll 'em up and serve.

Per serving: Calories 180 (From Fat 81); Fat 9g (Saturated 4g); Cholesterol 20mg; Sodium 348mg; Carbohydrate 19g; Dietary Fiber 11g (Net Carbohydrate 8g); Protein 14g.

Raising the Wrap Bar with Crepes

Egg crepes for wraps — are you shaking your head? Well, stop. After you get the hang of whipping up these easy and light creations, you'll be wrapping them around everything. They take only minutes to make, and you can enjoy egg crepe wraps either hot or cold. Expand your wrap horizon and treat your taste buds to variety.

Kick-start your low-carb day with egg crepes filled with Canadian bacon and a variety of cheeses with sprinkles of green onion. Egg crepes are so versatile that you can even spread them with sugar-free preserves and a dollop of whipped cream for a sweet treat. The carb count is low on low-carb tortillas, but it drops to almost zero for egg crepe wraps — try that one on for size.

If you research crepe batters, you'll find all kinds of variations. The reason I've created this basic egg crepe recipe for you is because the tasty crepes are so low in carb counts that they allow you to spend your carb budget with your choice of fillings — breakfast, lunch, dinner, great snacks, and sinfully delicious desserts, all wrapped up in this low-carb crepe.

Kicking out egg crepes

Crepes can be tricky to get the hang of at first, but with just a little practice, you'll have tons of new low-carb wraps at your fingertips. And when you're living the low-carb lifestyle, variety is definitely the spice. Don't let crepe batter scare you. It's just a bunch of eggs. Uncharted courses are always a tad intimidating, but jump right in and you'll be creating all kinds of great low-carb crepe variations — and smiling as you go.

A few things to keep in mind when making the basic low-carb egg crepe recipe I include in this chapter:

- ✔ **Make sure that your crepe pan is *hot* before adding the batter.** Since the pan is hot, the crepe will begin to cook instantly even though the pan is off the stove for a few seconds to start things off.

- ✔ **Perfect your swirling motion.** To make a crepe, you pour your batter in the middle of your crepe pan, take the pan off the heat source, and *swirl* the crepe batter to cover the bottom of the pan. See Figure 15-2.

- ✔ **Work on your spatula skills.** While the crepe is back on the burner, setting up and cooking, take a nonstick spatula and carefully begin working around the outside of the crepe, lifting the edges all the way around. The crepe will set up from the outside in, so you want to simply lift the edge a bit, until you meet sticky resistance. At that point, move the spatula around the crepe and repeat. Eventually, you'll be able to gently free the entire crepe. You'll be working quickly as the total time to cook an egg crepe is one minute or less.

- ✔ **Stack away!** When you're done cooking both sides of the crepe (the second side will only take 10 to 15 seconds), slide the crepe off the pan onto a plate. Continue making as many crepes as you wish and stack them one on top of each other. Since the egg crepes have no flour in them, you don't have to worry about them sticking together as many other crepe variations tend to do.

Basic Egg Crepes with Veggies

I present veggies with this basic egg crepe recipe, but get creative and enjoy another layer of low-carb food. Remember that each of these egg crepes has only *1 gram of net carbs*. Your choice of fillings is what determines how much the carb counts increase from there. Here, I've whipped up a sweet-and-spicy sauce with a few veggies as one idea of a tasty filling with respectable carb counts. Use this basic recipe to strike out in all directions of wrapping it up with egg crepes. The sky is pretty well the limit with egg crepes because they're so low-carb user friendly. I think you'll be delighted with this new addition to your low-carb lifestyle.

Preparation time: *5 minutes*

Cooking time: *10 to 12 minutes*

Yield: *4 crepe wraps*

12 fresh asparagus spears	5 eggs
2 medium carrots	1 tablespoon heavy cream
2 green onions	⅛ teaspoon cream of tartar
1 teaspoon grated fresh ginger	⅛ teaspoon salt
1 tablespoon soy sauce	Nonstick cooking spray
3 tablespoons sugar-free orange marmalade	

1 Cut the asparagus spears into 3-inch pieces. Cut the carrots into thin strips and then into 3-inch pieces. Cut the green onions into 2-inch pieces.

2 Using a vegetable steamer, steam the asparagus, carrots, and green onions for 5 to 7 minutes. Don't overcook; you want the veggies to be crisp-tender.

3 In a small bowl, stir together the ginger, soy sauce, and marmalade and set aside.

4 Beat the eggs, heavy cream, cream of tartar, and salt together until blended, but you don't want them to froth.

5 Spray your crepe pan with nonstick cooking spray. Heat the crepe pan until hot.

6 Measure ¼ cup of the egg mixture and pour it into the center of the pan. Lift the pan and swirl the egg mixture for even distribution.

7 Place the crepe pan back on stove and cook over medium heat — you don't want the crepes to cook too quickly or to burn.

8 Cook until the egg mixture starts to set around the edges and on the bottom. As it's setting, lift gently the crepe around the edges using your nonstick spatula. This helps form the crepe and enhance even cooking. You'll have to cook the crepe on the first side for only 45 seconds to 1 minute.

9 Flip the crepe over to the other side and let it sit over the heat for just 10 to 15 seconds. Slide it out of the crepe pan and onto a plate and do it all over again for the next crepe.

10 Be sure to spray your crepe pan each time with nonstick cooking spray. You'll have egg crepes in one minute or less per crepe!

11 When all your crepes are cooked, spread about 2 teaspoons of the sweet-and-spicy sauce down the center of each egg crepe. Place a combination of the veggies on the crepe and fold it burrito style with one end open (see the section, "Shaping Up Your Tortillas," earlier in the chapter). Serve with the remaining sauce on the side.

Tip: You may get 5 crepes out of this recipe, so don't be surprised. It all depends on the size of the eggs that you're using. If you get an extra crepe, save it and fill it with some leftovers for lunch the next day or make it a dessert crepe.

Per serving: Calories 147 (From Fat 70); Fat 8g (Saturated 3g); Cholesterol 271mg; Sodium 409mg; Carbohydrate 11g; Dietary Fiber 2g (Net Carbohydrate 9g); Protein 10g.

Pouring Crêpe Batter into a Pan

Figure 15-2: Pouring crepe batter.

Pour the batter into the crêpe pan with a ladle or measuring cup.

Swirl the pan around so the batter runs to the edges and covers the bottom of the pan.

If you want sweet egg crepes, simply add some sugar substitute to the basic egg crepe batter I outline in this chapter. You can make a ton of delicious desserts and sweet treats with egg crepes. Here's one idea: Spread the sweet crepes with sugar-free apricot jam and roll them up. Place them under the broiler long enough to just heat them through and brown ever so lightly. Heat about ¼ cup brandy in a small pan and pour over the crepes. Carefully ignite, and when you're sure all flames are out, serve immediately with a dollop of freshly whipped cream.

Taking crepe making seriously

Get serious about making egg crepes. They're a real treat to your low-carb healthy lifestyle. You can find quality crepe pans at your local cookware store or on the Internet (see Figure 15-3). A crepe pan makes things easier because of its perfect shape and size. Also, the design of the crepe pan allows the heat to be distributed more evenly while cooking your crepe. As you know, any specialty item or gadget in your kitchen makes your job easier and more fun.

Figure 15-3:
Crepe pan.

Chapter 16

Coming Home to Slow-Cooked Comfort Foods

Slow cooking and low-carbing are an awesome and underappreciated combination. Life is hectic, and if you're like many folks, your schedule is out of control. You love home-cooked meals, and your low-carb lifestyle is very important to you. But you're tired after a long day at home or at the office. Slow cooking can help put your life in s-l-o-w m-o-t-i-o-n — or at least slower motion. Slow food is comfort food (which can be right at home in a low carb-lifestyle). You're going to get very spoiled when you use your slow cooker on a regular basis. It can provide you with a meal that's ready when you walk through the door, and it gives you a ton of flexibility. Coming home after a long day to the wonderful smells of crockery cooking is like having a gremlin in the kitchen. I'm so hooked that I even use my slow cooker on the weekends when I'm off for a day of shopping.

Just a little self-discipline and pre-planning when it comes to preparing meals in your slow cooker can make your low-carb lifestyle even more enjoyable in multiple ways — from enjoying tasty meals to having more time for other activities. Try using the slow cooker. I think you'll like it. And in this chapter, I make it easy to get started.

Don't forget that slow cooking isn't just for the daytime. If you're off to Aunt Martha's for a family gathering the next day, you can let something cook all night and just take the slow cooker with you. Some slow cooker carriers are made especially for such occasions.

A Quick and Simple Guide to Low-Carb Slow Cooking

Because slow cooking is so kind to meats and vegetables, your choices of what to cook are almost unlimited. Many of the great foods you can enjoy with your low-carb lifestyle take on a new dimension with slow cooking.

You can prepare a great entrée in your slow cooker, whip up a quick salad, and you have a meal in minutes because your little silent chef has been cooking all day. Or, you can add the veggies in with your meat and cook them altogether. Another option that you may laugh at but will understand when you become a low-carb slow-cooking fan is to consider being the proud owner of two slow cookers — a small one and a large one. That way, you can simmer soup while you cook an entrée, or you can cook a meat dish in one slow cooker and cook a vegetable in another. Options are always nice.

Profiling slow cookers

The slow cooker's resumé indicates a profile with many fine qualities:

✔ A slow cooker works very well completely unsupervised, and it's safe to leave home alone.

✔ Not only is it a silent chef, but it also makes your house smell cozy and homey.

✔ Years of testing indicate that a slow cooker has a great track record in proven reliability.

✔ Slow cookers don't mind waiting for you to get accustomed to using them. They know that after you get in the groove of slow cooking, you're hooked.

✔ Unlike stove cooking, slow cookers don't overcook meats and veggies. But you have to steer the timing. If you leave it cooking for 20 hours, and your food is all shriveled up, don't blame the slow cooker! This is where a slow cooker with a timer shines. (See the next section, "Sizing up the crockery cooker crew," for more about hardware options.)

✔ A slow cooker can magically make less tender cuts of meat melt in your mouth. Fact is, slow cookers prefer less tender cuts so they can excel in their jobs.

✔ Slow cookers don't ask much — just that you leave the lid on.

✔ Slow cookers prefer not to be interrupted with a lot of stirring.

✔ A slow cooker is very efficient — when you're cooking on low, you're using less energy than most light bulbs.

Sizing up the crockery cooker crew

You can find a slew of slow cookers on the market, and whether you choose one because you like the color or the little flowers on the crock, or because chrome goes with your kitchen (all fine criteria that I too have used), I want you to know one thing: Size matters in a choosing a slow cooker.

Slow cookers come in a number of sizes, and the one that works best for you depends on whether you're cooking for one, two, or an entire family. If you've ever tried to shove a 5-pound roast into a small slow cooker, then you can relate. For optimum results, don't fill your slow cooker more than three-quarters full. If you're cramming your slow cooker to the top, it may be time to look into buying a larger one.

The world of slow cookers is changing all the time, with vast improvements over the old models. You may want to develop a "slow cooker wish list" to have handy for those special occasions when no one knows what to buy you for a gift. Here's a little list of shapes, sizes, and bells and whistles that are available and that you may want to check out depending on what you want your slow cooker to do (no, it won't clean the house):

- ✔ **Size:** Slow-cooker capacities start as small as 16 ounces. More standard sizes are 3.5 quart, 5.3 quart, 6 quart, 6.5 quart, and 7 quart. A middle-of-the-road size that you may want to start out with is a 5.3-quart capacity, which will cook a meal for four. I recommend a 6.5-quart oval cooker for large family meals. This setup allows you to cook large cuts of meats and add veggies too, or cook a large casserole.

- ✔ **Shape:** Shape is important. Ovals let you cook larger cuts of meat. Some cook 2 chickens at one time! In my estimation, ovals are the way to go.

- ✔ **Heat settings:** Older models and some of the less expensive ones still have just high and low settings. Newer and more expensive models have a third setting of warm or medium. Three settings definitely put you in cooker control.

- ✔ **Bells and whistles:** The options available nowadays are just incredible. Some have retractable cords. Some have an auto-cook feature that can start the cooking off with a bang on high and then automatically and gradually shift down to low. Then it goes to warm to keep the food perfect until serving time. I recommend the ones that automatically shift into warm mode after the cooking time is complete. That way, if you run late getting home, your meal won't be overcooked — just on hold.

- ✔ **Construction:** The crocks and the lids in the newer models are dishwasher safe. Easy cleanup is very nice.

If you have an older model and don't want to buy a new slow cooker, there's a little specialty gadget out there called a *programmable module*. You plug your slow cooker into the module and plug the module into the wall outlet. You then use your handy-dandy little module to program your cooking time and temperature. It will even shift the heat down to warm mode for you. These are available online.

Wondering what size cooker to use for a new recipe? If you have a 3½-quart or 4-quart slow cooker, the total ingredients shouldn't exceed 2 to 2½ quarts. If they do, you need to step up a notch in cookers.

Any recipe that fits in a 4-quart slow cooker can easily be doubled to cook in a larger cooker. Think about this fact when you purchase your new slow cooker, because it may mean that you can slow cook dinner *and* tomorrow's lunch.

Turning to cooking times and temperatures

Most slow cookers have heating coils that encircle the crockery insert, which is what allows the food to cook evenly. This is by far the most efficient and dependable method of slow cookery, and in this chapter, I assume that it's the type of slow cooker you're using. (Check out Figure 16-1 for a breakdown of slow cooker components.)

The settings and temperatures vary on slow cookers, but a pretty good rule of thumb is that the low setting is about 200 degrees, and the high setting is about 300 degrees. If you want to hurry your cooking up a bit, keep in mind that 2 to 2½ hours on low is equal to about an hour on high. If you come home and your food isn't done to your liking, and it has been cooking on low all day, just crank it up to high to finish.

Keeping the lid on your slow cooker is the secret to its success. It takes this little wonder a matter of 15 to 20 minutes to recover when you're nosy and remove the lid. The lids are clear so you can look through them, so keep your mitts off, okay? If condensation is built up on the lid, just give it a spin on the cooker, and you'll have a quick, clear view of what's cooking.

Testing the waters and surveying food safety

Want to take your slow cooker's temperature and see just how fast it's cooking and at what temperature? The bottom line on the performance of your slow cooker comes down to food safety. As cookers age, they may not be able to achieve and maintain high enough temperatures, and it may be time to invest in a new one. This is a great Saturday project when you're hanging around the house all day. Let the test begin:

1. **Fill your slow cooker with 2 quarts of water (yes, please measure it).**

2. **Cover and heat the water on the low setting for 8 hours.**

Figure 16-1:
Decon-
structing
the slow
cooker.

Don't take the lid off during the test.

3. **After 8 hours, lift the lid and pop a thermometer in the water immediately (the water temperature drops quickly with the lid off).**

   The temperature of the water should be in the 185-degree range after heating on low for 8 hours. If the temperature is considerably higher than 185 degrees, your slow cooker has revved up cooking coils, and you may want to reduce the cooking time of your dishes to prevent over-cooking.

   If the temperature is lower than 185 degrees, then your food isn't likely reaching a safe temperature quickly enough in your slow cooker, and therefore the food may not be safe. It's time for a new slow cooker.

Following are a couple don'ts to remember for keeping food safe in your slow cooker:

- Don't store cooked food in the slow cooker in the fridge (I know, it's the easiest thing to do). Don't give bacteria any chance to grow in your food. It's always safer to store food in the fridge in a container other than what it was cooked in. Take the extra 3 minutes to start soaking the cooker and transfer the leftovers to a plastic storage container.

- Don't reheat food in a slow cooker. If you have leftovers, reheat them in the usual manner — either on top of the stove or in the microwave — but please don't put the food through slow cooking a second time.

Converting low-carb favorites into slow-cooker classics

You say you have a favorite low-carb recipe, but you didn't get it in a slow-cooker recipe book. Never fear, Table 16-1 contains a conversion chart to help you convert your favorite recipes to slow cooking.

Table 16-1	Cooking Time Conversion Chart for Slow Cooking	
Recipe's Cooking Time	*Slow Cook on Low*	*Slow Cook on High*
30 minutes	4 to 6 hours	2 to 3 hours
60 minutes	6 to 8 hours	3 to 4 hours
2 to 3 hours	10 to 14 hours	4 to 7 hours

Taking in a few tips on technique

There are always tricks to any trade, and slow cooking is no different. Here are a few little inside tips for you to make the most out of your slow cooking experiences:

- ✔ Bright green veggies, like broccoli, tend to lose their color as well as some of their nutrients and flavor if cooped up in a slow cooker all day. The solution is to cook your favorite bright green veggies in the microwave until crisp-tender and add them to your crockery meal right before serving.

- ✔ Surprise — meats cook more quickly than vegetables in a slow cooker (a little role reversal here). Therefore, cut your veggies somewhat evenly for even cooking and place them in the bottom of the crock with the meat on top of the veggies.

- ✔ In crockery cooking, using whole-leaf herbs and spices is better than using ground ones, because you'll end up with better flavor in the dishes you're preparing. Extended cooking at low temperatures can sometimes cause some spices to become bitter. (Pepper appears to head the list, so use freshly ground pepper when possible.) Experiment, because the flavor of some herbs and spices tends to disappear in slow cooking. You'll get the hang of what suits your taste buds very quickly.

- ✔ Don't add such ingredients as sour cream, milk, or whipping cream at the beginning of cooking anything in your slow cooker and let it cook all day. Any dairy products should be added at the last minute and stirred into whatever you're preparing. Curdling cuisine isn't what you're after.

✔ Don't dump a package of frozen vegetables or frozen meat into your crock. Doing really slows your cooking time down. Also, because some ingredients are frozen and some are not, it makes for inconsistent cooking, and consistent slow cooking is what this is all about. Be sure the food is defrosted thoroughly before leaving it home alone in your slow cooker all day.

Cleanup can be a snap:

✔ An easy way to clean your slow cooker after using it is to simply fill it with hot, soapy water and let it stand. Be careful when trying to clean a hot slow cooker. If you add cold water, it may cause your crock to crack. Don't use harsh abrasives to clean your slow cooker. One of those net sponge pads works really well.

✔ If you want an easy cleanup after using your slow cooker, simply spray it with nonstick cooking spray before using it.

✔ Some of the newer models can be popped into the dishwasher, but I still recommend that you do a little precleaning of your crock.

Hearty Low-Carb Meals

Slow Cookers For Dummies, by Tom Lacalamita and Glenna Vance (published by Wiley), is a great place to start if you want to practice converting regular slow-cooking recipes into low-carb culinary fare. The recipe need not say "low-carb" for it to fit the low-carb lifestyle (with a little tweaking that is). Check those carb counts and your carb smarts for those perfect low-carb dishes. If you get stumped, just e-mail me at jan@janmccracken.com, and I'll be glad to help you out. Adjusting a recipe so that it's low-carb isn't as difficult as you may think. Refer to Table 16-1, earlier in this chapter, for a conversion chart for converting your favorite recipes to slow cooking and just go for it.

Key West Ribs

5

If you watch for sales, you can get incredible meaty, country-style pork loin ribs (which are also called picnic ribs or simply country-style ribs in some areas) at a great price — as low as 99 cents a pound. In addition to being easy on the budget, this particular recipe is low in carbs and a real treat. You can save those dollars for a rib-eye steak on the grill another day.

Preparation time: *10 minutes*

Cooking time: *8 to 9 hours*

Yield: *4 servings*

2½ pounds pork loin ribs	*2 tablespoons lime juice*	*1 teaspoon grated orange peel*
¼ cup barbecue sauce	*½ teaspoon salt*	
¼ cup finely chopped onion	*1 teaspoon grated lime peel*	*¼ cup orange juice*

1 Place the ribs in a 4-quart slow cooker. You may have to cut the ribs to get them to fit into the slow cooker, depending on how they're packaged.

2 In a small bowl, combine the barbecue sauce, onion, lime juice, salt, lime peel, orange peel, and orange juice, and pour over the ribs. Cover and cook on low for 8 to 9 hours.

3 Spoon the sauce over the ribs before serving.

Tip: *Make the sauce the night before. The next morning, all you have to do is put your meat in the slow cooker and pour in the sauce, and you're out the door.*

Per serving: *Calories 318 (From Fat 156); Fat 17g (Saturated 6g); Cholesterol 108mg; Sodium 498mg; Carbohydrate 5g; Dietary Fiber 1g (Net Carbohydrate 4g); Protein 33g.*

One of my favorite slow-cooking meals

I buy whatever roast is on sale, and when I say on sale, I mean *really* on sale. Sometimes you can score a whole roast for $5. Take a large, yellow onion and slice it from top to bottom (not in rings), and place it in the bottom of the slow cooker. Peel a few carrots, cut them in half, then cut them lengthwise, and lay the carrots on top of the onions. Pour about a ½ inch of water over the onions and carrots. If you like mushrooms and celery with your roast, add them too. Remove the roast from the packaging and make about six slits on each side of it. Slice fresh garlic cloves in half and insert the pieces of garlic deep into the slits. Salt and pepper the roast well on both sides. Put the roast on top of the onions and carrots. Slow cook the roast (depending on the size) for about 9 hours on low or about 6 hours on high. My grandmother used this technique to cook roast for Sunday dinner. However, that was before the day of slow cookers, so she did it in the old Dutch oven. But you can't leave Dutch ovens home alone!

Herb-Roasted Lemon Chicken

Instead of paying $6 to $8 for a lemon-roasted chicken at the deli on your way home from work, with just a tad of preplanning, you can have it waiting for you when you walk through the door. You can cook two chickens for the price of one in your slow cooker, and your house will smell yummy. Not to mention the fact that you'll save a half hour or more by not making the stop at the deli. I suggest you plan this meal for a Monday night dinner. Make sure that chicken and the ingredients for any side dishes that you want are on your weekend grocery list. Mondays are hectic for everyone, so wouldn't it be nice to come home to this comforting entrée waiting for you?

Preparation time: *8 minutes*

Cooking time: *7 to 10 hours*

Yield: *4 servings*

1 fryer, about 4 pounds	½ teaspoon sea salt
Nonstick cooking spray	½ teaspoon pepper
3 lemons	1 tablespoon finely chopped fresh Italian parsley
2 tablespoons olive oil	¼ teaspoon leaf thyme

1 Remove the giblets from the chicken and reserve them for another use. Rinse the chicken and pat dry. Remove any excess fat from the chicken.

2 Coat the crock with nonstick cooking spray for easy cleanup.

3 Wash the lemons. Using a very sharp knife, make tiny slits in 2 of the lemons. This will allow the flavors of the lemon to escape while cooking. Cut all 3 of the lemons in half.

4 Rub the skin of the chicken with the olive oil and sprinkle the salt and pepper on the outside of the bird.

5 Put 4 of the lemon halves in the cavity of the chicken. Place the chicken in the slow cooker with the breast side down. Squeeze the juice of the remaining lemon halves over the chicken. Then sprinkle on the parsley and thyme.

6 Cover and cook on low for 7 to 10 hours. Test for doneness by inserting a meat thermometer into the thickest part of the thigh without touching the bone. The thermometer should register 170 degrees.

Tip: *The liquid from cooking this delightful dish can be used as a very lemony gravy. Better yet, it makes a great sauce for asparagus, broccoli, and green beans. Yum.*

Per serving: *Calories 336 (From Fat 116); Fat 13g (Saturated 4g); Cholesterol 155mg; Sodium 438mg; Carbohydrate 2g; Dietary Fiber 0g (Net Carbohydrate 2g); Protein 50g.*

Corned Beef with Vegetables

With a name like McCracken, I had to include corned beef somewhere in my book. Slow cooking is kind to corned beef because it makes the meat so tender and juicy. You can have this meal waiting for you when you get home and then have leftovers for lunch the next day or for snacks. (See the sidebar "Reuben wraps," later in the chapter, for a great lunch and snack idea). Watch for frequent sales on corned beef. This meal is kind to your budget with no sacrifice to taste, and it's a great fit with your low-carb lifestyle.

Preparation time: *10 minutes*

Cooking time: *8 to 9 hours*

Yield: *8 to 10 servings*

1 corned beef brisket, about 4 pounds	*¾ cup dry white wine*
3 carrots, cut in 3-inch pieces and halved	*1 cup canned beef broth*
2 stalks celery, cut in 2-inch pieces	*1 bay leaf*
2 medium yellow onions, quartered	*3 whole cloves*

1 Wash the brisket under cold running water and pat dry.

2 Add the carrots, celery, onions, wine, broth, bay leaf, and cloves to the slow cooker. Place the brisket on top of the vegetables. If necessary, cut your brisket in half so that it fits well in the slow cooker.

3 Cover and cook on low for 8 to 9 hours, until very tender.

4 Serve the meat and vegetables with broth ladled over the top.

Per serving (based on 10 servings): Calories 362 (From Fat 233); Fat 26g (Saturated 9g); Cholesterol 133mg; Sodium 1,666mg; Carbohydrate 5g; Dietary Fiber 1g (Net Carbohydrate 4g); Protein 26g.

When cooking chicken in the slow cooker, you may want to remove the skin before you start cooking. The skin tends to curl up and isn't very pretty. My solution is to work with boneless and skinless chicken. The exception to this chicken rule is when you're cooking a whole chicken; then you want to leave the skin on to hold in the juices.

If you have a recipe that says to cook an hour on high and then reduce to low, set your timer to remind you so that you don't walk out the door and leave the cooker on high all day. You'll be much happier when you come through the door if your creation has cooked all day on low.

Casserole of Chicken, Artichokes, and Mushrooms

This is a low-carb casserole at its finest. Serve this hearty casserole with a crisp side salad and get ready for rave reviews and requests for a repeat performance. Artichoke hearts are very low in carbs, but be sure to check the labels and do a little comparing when shopping to be sure you get the best quality, as well as the lowest carb counts.

Preparation time: *10 minutes*

Cooking time: *8 to 8½ hours*

Yield: *6 servings*

3 pounds skinless, boneless chicken breasts	*2 tablespoons butter*
2 tablespoons olive oil	*½ pound fresh mushrooms, washed and sliced*
1 teaspoon kosher salt	*1 tablespoon cornstarch*
Pepper	*1 tablespoon cool water*
¼ cup chicken broth	*1 can (15 ounces) artichoke hearts, drained*
¼ cup white wine	*½ cup slivered almonds*
1 teaspoon fresh tarragon	*½ cup shredded Asiago cheese*

1 Wash the chicken breasts and pat dry. Rub the chicken breasts with olive oil and season them with the salt and pepper to taste.

2 Pour the chicken broth and wine into the slow cooker. Place the chicken breasts in the liquid. Sprinkle the tarragon over the chicken breasts.

3 Cover and cook on low for 8 to 8½ hours, or until the chicken is done — when tested with a meat thermometer, it should register at 180 degrees.

4 In a skillet, melt the butter and quickly sauté the mushrooms, being careful not to over-cook. This will only take about 4 minutes.

5 Turn the slow cooker on high and bring the sauce to a simmer. Meanwhile, combine the cornstarch and water in a small cup, mixing well. Stir the cornstarch mixture into the simmering sauce and cook until slightly thickened (about 4 minutes).

6 Stir in the sautéed mushrooms and drained artichoke hearts and heat thoroughly. Sprinkle with the slivered almonds and cheese and serve immediately.

Per serving: Calories 448 (From Fat 193); Fat 21g (Saturated 7g); Cholesterol 144mg; Sodium 844mg; Carbohydrate 10g; Dietary Fiber 3g (Net Carbohydrate 7g); Protein 53g.

Slowing Soups and Stews to a Simmer

Slow cookers and soups are a marriage made in heaven. You'll find that cooking times vary for soups and stews — some are suited for all-day cooking, and some aren't. When a soup or stew recipe calls for stock or broth (refer to Chapter 7 for soup recipes), don't feel compelled to use homemade. You're trying to save yourself some time here. If you have frozen stock on hand, that's great. If not, break out a can or carton of the stuff and slow cook away. Using prepared stock or broth is okay for your low-carb lifestyle.

Russian Borscht

This is a great Sunday treat to have cooking all day while you're doing things around the house or watching football. Borscht is a rich Eastern European soup that contains beets or cabbage. Other ingredients may include potatoes, beans, meat, or sausage. You may know of the cold version of borscht, but hot versions are also common. According to old cooking folklore, a wooden spoon will stand upright when stuck into the pot of borscht if it's done correctly. I think you'll enjoy this recipe on a lazy weekend day.

Preparation time: *10 to15 minutes*

Cooking time: *8 to 9 hours*

Yield: *12 servings*

4 cups thinly sliced green cabbage	*1 cup finely chopped yellow onion*	*3 cans (15 ounces each) beef broth*
1 pound fresh beets, shredded	*4 cloves garlic, minced fine*	*¼ cup lemon juice*
5 carrots, peeled and sliced thin	*1 pound beef chuck, cut into small cubes*	*1 packet Splenda sugar substitute*
1 parsnip, peeled and sliced thin	*1 can (14 ounces) diced tomatoes, undrained*	*1 teaspoon pepper*
		12 heaping tablespoons sour cream

1 Using a large slow cooker, layer, in order, the cabbage, beets, carrots, parsnip, onion, garlic, beef, tomatoes, beef broth, lemon juice, Splenda, and pepper.

2 Cover and cook on low for 8 to 9 hours. Vegetables should be crisp-tender.

3 Make sure the seasonings are to your liking. Add more lemon juice or Splenda as your palate desires.

4 Serve with a dollop of sour cream.

Per serving: *Calories 140 (From Fat 44); Fat 5g (Saturated 3g); Cholesterol 26mg; Sodium 556mg; Carbohydrate 14g; Dietary Fiber 4g (Net Carbohydrate 10g); Protein 11g.*

Kettle of Fish Stew

This is a hearty and delightful meal to come home to — and the flavors, oh my, the flavors. The combination of the fresh veggies, the herbs and spices, and the fresh fish are a great beginning. Add slow cooking to the ingredient combo, and it's gonna make your mouth sing. To top it off, this is a beautiful dish. Try it out, and I'm sure you'll want to serve it to guests. Your slow cooker will make it look like you've been slaving in the kitchen all day with this one — not!

Preparation time: *20 minutes*

Cooking time: *6 to 8 hours*

Yield: *4 servings*

1½ pounds flounder or halibut, cut in 1-inch pieces	½ cup finely chopped yellow onion	3 tablespoons melted butter
1 can (16 ounces) whole Roma tomatoes, mashed	½ cup chopped celery	3 tablespoons flour
½ cup dry white wine	½ cup peeled and finely chopped carrots	⅓ cup light cream
1 bottle (8 ounces) clam juice	¼ cup chopped Italian parsley	⅓ cup freshly grated Parmesan cheese (optional)
1 teaspoon salt	¼ teaspoon dried rosemary	

1 Combine the fish, tomatoes, wine, clam juice, salt, onion, celery, carrots, parsley, and rosemary in your slow cooker.

2 Cover and cook on low for 6 to 8 hours.

3 Combine the melted butter, flour, and cream, whisking until well combined. Stir into the fish mixture.

4 Continue cooking until the mixture is slightly thickened, about 5 minutes.

5 Serve in wide soup bowls for the ultimate presentation and sprinkle with freshly grated Parmesan cheese, if desired.

Tip: *For a thicker stew, leave the cover off your cooker for the last hour of cooking.*

Variation: *If you want to finish this up on the stove, just remove about 1 cup of the broth from the slow cooker with a ladle. Then, in a small saucepan, melt the butter and flour together on the stove. Add the cream and the cup of broth. Cook 2 minutes, until it begins to thicken. Then stir the whole mixture back into the stew and let it simmer and thicken for about 20 to 40 minutes.*

Per serving: Calories 312 (From Fat 129); Fat 14g (Saturated 8g); Cholesterol 118mg; Sodium 1,062mg; Carbohydrate 13g; Dietary Fiber 1g (Net Carbohydrate 12g); Protein 31g.

☜ Black Bean and Veggie Chili

This slow cookin' meal is perfect for a cold and rainy day. It's great to make a big batch, so you have plenty left over for lunches or snacks. This chili freezes really well, and you can freeze it in individual containers ready to grab to pack in your lunch bag.

Preparation time: *10 minutes*

Cooking time: *7 to 8 hours*

Yield: *6 servings*

1 small zucchini, quartered lengthwise and sliced	*1 packet Splenda sugar substitute*	*½ teaspoon cumin*
2 cloves garlic, minced	*1 can (16 ounces) whole Roma tomatoes with juice, chopped fine*	*½ teaspoon dried oregano leaves*
1 celery stalk, chopped		*¼ teaspoon dried basil*
1 small yellow onion, chopped	*1 can (14 ounces) puréed tomatoes, undrained*	*½ teaspoon sea salt*
1 tablespoon chili powder (more if desired)	*½ cup vegetable stock*	*¼ teaspoon pepper*
1 tablespoon unsweetened Dutch cocoa powder	*2 cans (15 ounces each) Eden black soybeans, drained and rinsed*	*1½ cups grated cheddar cheese (¼ cup per serving for garnish)*

1 Combine the zucchini, garlic, celery, onion, chili powder, cocoa powder, Splenda, Roma tomatoes, puréed tomatoes, vegetable stock, beans, cumin, oregano, basil, sea salt, and pepper in the slow cooker.

2 Cover and cook on low for 7 to 8 hours. The chili will be bubbling.

3 Ladle the chili into individual deep chili or soup bowls. Top with the cheddar cheese.

Per serving: Calories 237 (From Fat 100); Fat 11g (Saturated 6g); Cholesterol 30mg; Sodium 875mg; Carbohydrate 20g; Dietary Fiber 6g (Net Carbohydrate 14g); Protein 16g.

Reuben wraps

Leftover corned beef brisket makes tasty wraps for snacks or lunch to tote. Keep low-carb whole-wheat tortillas on hand for occasions such as this. Simply take a couple low-carb whole-wheat tortillas and spread some bottled creamy Russian dressing (be sure to check the carb counts and the sugar content when purchasing) on each one. Layer the tortillas with thinly sliced corned beef, Swiss cheese, and sauerkraut. Roll them up and pop them in the microwave separately for about 15 to 20 seconds, or until the cheese just begins to melt. Microwave temperatures vary, so don't overcook — you don't want crispy brisket roll-ups.

Chapter 17

Even More Delightful Dishes with 5 Net Grams of Carbs or Less

All of the recipes that I include in this chapter are less than 5 net grams of carbs (the *net* part means that the fiber counts have been subtracted for you; see more on net carbs in Chapter 2). Though many of the recipes I include throughout this book contain less then 5 net grams of carbs, I thought I'd include a bonus chapter of sorts to shoehorn just a few more dishes in that are super skinny on the carbs. And just because the carb counts are in the basement, that doesn't mean that the quality and taste of the dishes are down there with the carb counts! So if the recipe has zero to five carbs, you can eat a ton, right? No — you can eat until you're satisfied and smile a lot while you're savoring every bite, knowing how low the carb counts are that you're consuming. You can prepare sumptuous meals that I bet you never dreamed were so low in carb counts. Remember that moderation in all things in life is still the key. You're striving for balance in your low-carb lifestyle, and it's achievable and awaiting you. So let's get cookin'!

How Low Can You Go? Incredible Entrees

Yes, we're dancing the low-carb limbo here — how low can you go? Well, shimmying under 5 grams of net carbs in delicious entrees rocks; it helps put you well under the low-carb bar for your daily carb counts! Wisely build menus with the myriad of whole fresh foods that miraculously fall into the zero- to five-gram category, and you'll never be bored with your low-carb lifestyle. In so doing, you can also make room for special treats, still staying within your daily carb intakes. It's a magical combination.

Most fish, poultry, and meats hover around the almost zero carb count, so they're always candidates for a low-carb building block. And talk about choices! Consider poultry, which includes all types of fowl, such as duck, goose, quail, pheasant, chicken, turkey, and Cornish hens. Remember that some meats and fish are all-around healthier for you than others, so be sure to check those calorie counts and the saturated fat contents too (see Chapter 2 for more on fats and calories) and factor that into your plans (see Chapters 9, 10, and 11, for all your fish, fowl, and meat needs, respectively).

Salmon Steaks in Wine Marinade

Hold on to your hat! This awesome recipe has less than 1 gram of carbs per serving. These salmon steaks are awesome on the grill, or you can cook them in the broiler or in the toaster oven on broil . . . ah, choices! (Check out additional low-carb fish recipes in Chapter 9.) And you don't have to break the bank when you buy white wine for this recipe — the inexpensive stuff works just fine.

Preparation time: *20 minutes*

Cooking time: *12 minutes*

Yield: *4 servings*

2 tablespoons light olive oil	1 teaspoon lemon juice
¼ cup dry white wine	Dash of hot pepper sauce (optional)
1 tablespoon grated fresh ginger	Salt and pepper
1 teaspoon soy sauce	4 salmon steaks (about ¾-inch thick)

1 To prepare the marinade, combine the oil, wine, ginger, soy sauce, lemon juice, and hot sauce, if desired, in a large bowl. Season with salt and pepper to taste.

2 Place the salmon steaks in the marinade (in a flat dish) and refrigerate for 15 minutes.

3 Cook the salmon on the grill or under the broiler for about 12 minutes, turning twice and basting occasionally. To test for doneness, do the flaky fish test — insert a fork and if it flakes, it's done. You don't want to overcook salmon. Serve with fresh lemon.

Per serving: Calories 207 (From Fat 99); Fat 11g (Saturated 2g); Cholesterol 65mg; Sodium 305mg; Carbohydrate 0g; Dietary Fiber 0g (Net Carbohydrate 0g); Protein 25g.

Chicken on the Barbie

This is pretty unbelievable — chicken quarters dripping in delicious sauce with a carb count so low! It doesn't get much better. So crank up the barbie and pick a salad in Chapter 8 to serve with this great chicken dish. Get ready for rave reviews and, if you're dining with fellow low-carbers, get out your recipe cards because they'll want to write this one down.

Preparation time: *10 minutes*

Cooking time: *35 to 50 minutes*

Yield: *4 servings*

3 tablespoons olive oil	2 garlic cloves, minced fine	Juice of 1 lime
1 tablespoon soy sauce	¼ cup heated chicken stock	1 whole fryer chicken, 3 pounds, quartered
1 tablespoon tomato paste (or use homemade tomato sauce; see the recipe in the following section)	3 drops Worcestershire sauce (more if desired)	Salt and pepper

1 Preheat the grill to medium (you can use your indoor tabletop grill too if you want to). Combine the olive oil, soy sauce, tomato paste, garlic cloves, chicken stock, Worcestershire sauce, and lime juice in a small bowl. Place the chicken quarters in a ceramic baking dish and baste with the marinade. Salt and pepper to taste.

2 Place the chicken quarters on the barbie and cook on medium for about 8 minutes. Turn the chicken over, baste with marinade, and cook an additional 8 minutes.

3 Baste the chicken again with marinade and turn again to finish cooking. Depending on the size of the bird, cooking will take 20 to 35 minutes. Insert the meat thermometer into the thickest part of the chicken quarter to check doneness. The thermometer should register an internal temperature of 180 degrees.

Per serving: Calories 492 (From Fat 293); Fat 33g (Saturated 8g); Cholesterol 179mg; Sodium 429mg; Carbohydrate 2g; Dietary Fiber 0g (Net Carbohydrate 2g); Protein 46g.

Just because meat, poultry, and fish are minuscule on the carb front, don't think you're totally in the clear. The culprits so many times are in the sauces and marinades that you slather on the meat. Always check for those hidden sugars and hidden carbs, especially in store-bought sauces and marinades. (Meander over to Chapter 10 for more on marinades.)

Spinach and Flounder Pinwheels

These are so good, not to mention quick — it's a microwave recipe. The combination of the white flounder against the green of the spinach makes an enticing presentation. For a change, serve on a bed of fresh baby greens and drizzle your favorite dressing over all.

Preparation time: *20 minutes*

Cooking time: *5 to 7 minutes*

Yield: *4 servings*

½ cup frozen spinach, thawed with the water squeezed out	*1 tablespoon finely chopped pecans*	*4 flounder fillets, 4 ounces each*
½ cup soft low-carb breadcrumbs	*1 teaspoon lemon juice*	*¼ cup dry white wine*
1 jar (2 ounces) sliced pimientos, drained (optional)	*½ teaspoon dried whole marjoram*	*1 teaspoon grated lemon rind*
2 tablespoons grated onion	*¼ teaspoon salt*	*12 fresh spinach leaves (optional)*
	¼ teaspoon pepper	*4 lemon wedges*

1 Combine the spinach, breadcrumbs, pimientos (if desired), onion, pecans, lemon juice, marjoram, salt, and pepper in a medium bowl, mixing well.

2 Spoon 3 tablespoons of the spinach mixture in the center of each fillet and spread it out evenly over each fillet. Roll up like a jelly roll (begin at the skinny end!). Secure the roll-up with a wooden toothpick.

3 Place the rolls, seam side down, in an 11-x-7-x-2-inch microwave-safe baking dish.

4 Combine the wine and the lemon rind and pour over the rolls. Cover the dish with heavy-duty plastic wrap and vent on one corner.

5 Microwave on high for 5 to 7 minutes, or until fish easily flakes when tested with a fork. Do not overcook.

6 Let stand for 1 minute. Remove from the dish and be sure to remove the wooden picks before eating these pinwheels. If serving as appetizers, arrange them on a platter. If serving as a main course, transfer to individual plates.

7 Use fresh spinach for garnish, if desired, and serve with lemon wedges.

Tip: *When using frozen spinach, if you want to make sure all the moisture is out, thaw it quickly in the microwave. Then wrap it in a couple layers of paper towels and just squeeze it over the sink. This technique isn't fancy, but it works very well.*

Per serving: *Calories 144 (From Fat 26); Fat 3g (Saturated 0g); Cholesterol 53mg; Sodium 391mg; Carbohydrate 6g; Dietary Fiber 4g (Net Carbohydrate 2g); Protein 23g.*

Turkey Cheese Pockets

These turkey cheese pockets are great served with a simple fresh spinach salad that's sprinkled with chopped hard-boiled egg, a couple cherry tomatoes, and a basic vinaigrette dressing. You can pop these pockets in the microwave for a snack or lunch the next day, and I've been known to eat them cold. If you need a little help from your friends on making pockets in meats, jump on over to Chapter 11 for a quick pocket-making lesson and then come back and make this recipe.

Preparation time: *15 minutes*

Cooking time: *20 to 30 minutes*

Yield: *4 servings*

4 boneless turkey breast pieces (approximately 8 ounces each)	*4 fresh sage leaves*
	8 strips bacon
Salt and pepper	*4 teaspoons olive oil*
4 thick slices deli-style mozzarella cheese	*2 tablespoons fresh lemon juice*

1 Preheat the gas grill or inside grill to medium heat. With a sharp knife, moving across the width of the turkey breasts, cut a pocket in each breast. Season inside the pocket carefully with salt and pepper to taste.

2 Place a piece of cheese into each pocket and tuck a sage leaf in with the cheese.

3 Taking each piece of bacon in turn, hold down the end of the bacon strip and stretch it out, using the back of a large knife or a rolling pin. You want the bacon stretched out to the point that you can wrap it around the turkey breast pieces. Wrap 2 pieces of bacon around each turkey breast piece, covering and securing the pocket. Secure the bacon strips to the turkey with wooden toothpicks. The bacon strips help keep the cheese filling intact when cooking.

4 In a small bowl, whisk the oil and lemon juice together.

5 Grill the turkey pockets for about 10 minutes on each side. Baste frequently with the lemon and oil mixture. Test the turkey breasts for doneness with a meat thermometer. The thermometer should register 180 degrees when inserted into the thickest part of the breast piece.

Per serving: *Calories 437 (From Fat 164); Fat 18g (Saturated 7g); Cholesterol 182mg; Sodium 547mg; Carbohydrate 1g; Dietary Fiber 0g (Net Carbohydrate 1g); Protein 63g.*

Serving Up Zero to Five in the Sauce and on the Side

Side dishes are important to all of your low-carb meals. Great sides can be very low in carbs and high in the flavor department. Sides can include salads, veggies, a combination of the two, and even fruit sides. (See Chapter 8 for some great side salad recipes.) Veggies are a mainstay of a healthy low-carb lifestyle (for more veggie info and recipes, check out Chapter 12). Low-carb veggie sides can be quick and easy when you steam, roast, microwave, or cook them on top of the stove. What sets them apart from bland and boring is jazzing them up a little bit with a splash of citrus, some freshly chopped herbs, some crunchy nuts, caraway seeds, or sprinkles of shredded cheese — the list really is endless. And all this jazz adds very few carbs to these healthy sides. Your challenge is to see how many different recipes you can come up with in the zero-to-five net carb count category.

Cauliflower and Broccoli with Cheese and Bacon

Dietary fiber has never tasted so good as in this recipe! Talk about a low-carber's dream dish! And it's squarely in the *yum* category too.

Preparation time: 10 minutes

Cooking time: 8 to 10 minutes

Yield: 4 servings

1 pound fresh broccoli	1 tablespoon sour cream
1 pound fresh cauliflower	2 tablespoons grated cheddar cheese
2 strips thick-cut bacon	

1 Trim the broccoli and cauliflower into florets. Place them in a steamer and steam over boiling water for about 4 minutes until crisp-tender. Don't overcook.

2 Microwave the bacon on paper towels until crispy. Drain on fresh paper towels. Cut the bacon into thin strips or crumble.

3 In a large serving dish, combine the cauliflower, broccoli, and bacon. Top with the sour cream and grated cheddar cheese.

Per serving: Calories 102 (From Fat 43); Fat 5g (Saturated 2g); Cholesterol 10mg; Sodium 194mg; Carbohydrate 10g; Dietary Fiber 6g (Net Carbohydrate 4g); Protein 7g.

Homemade Tomato Sauce

This is a great homemade tomato sauce that comes in under the banner of 10 grams of carbs or less. And because you're making it from scratch, you don't have to worry about the added sugars and those sneaky additives. If you can buy the tomatoes at a farmer's market so they taste as good as they smell, your sauce will be even better (see Chapter 8 for more tomato info). You can use tomato sauce in a variety of different recipes, and using the homemade stuff is sure to spoil your taste buds. You can serve this terrific sauce over a medley of veggies of your choice, such as zucchini and fresh green beans, meatballs, or maybe spinach dumplings (go to Chapter 10 for recipe), just to give you a few ideas.

Preparation time: *25 minutes*

Cooking time: *2 hours and 20 minutes*

Yield: *Approximately 6 cups (serving size is ¼ cup)*

4 slices thick-cut bacon, diced large	½ teaspoon oregano	1 chile pepper, seeded and sliced
1 medium yellow onion, chopped fine	1 packet Splenda sugar substitute	1 can (6 ounces) tomato paste
1 medium carrot, peeled and diced	1 tablespoon finely chopped fresh Italian parsley	1 cup chicken broth
½ celery stalk, diced	12 large ripe tomatoes, peeled, cut in half, and seeded	Salt and pepper
1 teaspoon basil		

1 Heat a large deep and heavy-bottomed saucepan until hot. Add the bacon and cook for about 4 minutes.

2 Add the onion, carrot, celery, basil, oregano, and Splenda to the saucepan. Mix and cook for 5 to 6 minutes, until the vegetables begin to brown.

3 Add the parsley, tomatoes, pepper, tomato paste, and chicken broth and season with salt and pepper to taste. Cook for 2 hours over low heat, stirring frequently.

4 Serve, or cover and refrigerate.

Tip: *Freeze the tomato sauce in serving-size plastic containers that meet your needs to ensure you always have great, homemade tomato sauce at your fingertips.*

Per serving: *Calories 66 (From Fat 37); Fat 4g (Saturated 1g); Cholesterol 5mg; Sodium 128mg; Carbohydrate 6g; Dietary Fiber 1g (Net Carbohydrate 5g); Protein 2g.*

To peel a tomato easily and efficiently, spear it in the stem end with a fork, and plunge it into boiling water for 30 seconds or until the skin splits. Immediately dip the tomato into very cold water. Then use a sharp paring knife and simply pull the skin off the tomato. To save more nutrients and flavors when you cook whole tomatoes, cook them with the skins on. They float to the top, and you can just skim them off with a slotted spoon as they separate from the tomato. (Chapter 12 has more info and tomato recipes.)

An old-fashioned secret when making anything with tomatoes is to add some sugar, because it brings out the flavor of the tomato in an undetectable fashion. So with your low-carb lifestyle, instead add a packet of Splenda sugar substitute to your chili, tomato sauces, and other tomato dishes.

Fighting the Snack Attack

In a low-carb lifestyle, you don't want to let yourself get voraciously hungry (see Chapter 5 for more on why this is true). I have a habit of carrying a little bag of raw almonds with me in my purse no matter where I go. If my energy takes a dip, I know I need a little protein, and I have a few almonds available to give me an energy boost.

Research has shown that women who eat a few ounces of nuts a day as a snack lose twice as much weight and gain more trim muscle than those women who don't include nuts in their everyday diets. As for all the guys out there, I don't have the research to back it up, but I can't see why it wouldn't be the same for you. Losing weight is all about burning fat, and nuts contain hormones that produce a metabolism booster. So get nuts!

The low-carb lowdown on cheese

Cheeses are a bountiful low-carb staple. Most cheeses have few carbs — if not zero carbs. All of your everyday cheeses, such as goat cheese, cream cheese, Swiss, cheddar, mozzarella, Parmesan, provolone, and even cottage cheese, are dandy. And they make up just the tip of the proverbial cheese iceberg. Because cheese is full of protein and calcium, it makes a great snack when you feel that starvation pang. Venture out and try some new combinations.

Just a few words of caution in your low-carb cheese world, when it comes to specialty cheeses. Watch for specialty cheeses that may have some additional ingredients that make the carb counts spike. For instance, I keep lusting after a soft goat cheese log at a local specialty store that has cranberries in it. Not only are there cranberries marbled through the beautiful cheese, but there are added sugars as well. Sometimes it takes a little willpower to succeed in the low-carb lifestyle. Also, take a peek at the calorie counts because some specialty cheeses have higher calorie counts, so you may want to use them sparingly.

Eggplant Sandwiches Extraordinaire

If you're an eggplant lover, this sandwich will be a dream come true. Not only can you serve it as a main-course sandwich, but it's also a great snack treat, cut in bite-size pieces for grazing. The net carb count for the entire sandwich is 2 grams, so enjoy!

Preparation time: *40 minutes*

Cooking time: *15 to 18 minutes*

Yield: *8 servings*

2 eggplants, 1 pound each	*4 slices prosciutto, halved*
½ tablespoon kosher salt	*8 large fresh basil leaves*
Nonstick cooking spray	*⅛ cup shredded mozzarella cheese*

1 Cut the eggplants into sixteen ¼-inch slices out of the middle or the largest part of the eggplant. Reserve the remainder for use in a stir-fry. Salt and set aside for 30 minutes.

2 Spray a heavy skillet with the nonstick spray. Over high heat, place the eggplant slices in the hot skillet and cook for about 10 minutes, turning once. The eggplant will become soft.

3 Remove the eggplant slices from the heat onto a platter or large plate.

4 Now build your eggplant sandwiches. Layer 8 slices of the eggplant with a piece of prosciutto, a fresh basil leaf, and 2 teaspoons mozzarella cheese. Top with a second eggplant slice, sandwich-style.

5 Heat the skillet again over medium-high heat and spray with the nonstick spray. Return the sandwiches to the skillet and cook for about 3 minutes on each side, or until the cheese begins to melt.

6 Remove the sandwiches and let them rest for about 2 minutes. Cut in half and serve.

Tip: *Never use iodized salt when salting eggplant, because the iodine content can actually give the eggplant a bitter after-taste. Be sure to use sea salt or coarse kosher salt instead.*

Per serving: *Calories 42 (From Fat 18); Fat 2g (Saturated 1g); Cholesterol 10mg; Sodium 508mg; Carbohydrate 3g; Dietary Fiber 1g (Net Carbohydrate 2g); Protein 3g.*

☞ Stuffed Mushrooms

Stuffed Mushrooms make a satisfying snack or a great appetizer for a low-carb party. The recipe makes about 20 servings, so at only 2 net grams of carbs per stuffed mushroom, you can eat more than one. This recipe calls for low-carb breadcrumbs, and you'll need to make your own out of your favorite low-carb bread. I make them ahead of time and store them in a tightly sealed container in the fridge. (Hop over to Chapter 10 for a quick breadcrumb-making lesson.)

Preparation time: *15 minutes*

Cooking time: *30 minutes*

Yield: *20 servings*

1 package (10 ounces) frozen chopped spinach, thawed and squeezed dry	1 tablespoon butter	¼ cup finely chopped pimiento
Nonstick cooking spray	¼ cup finely chopped yellow onion	½ teaspoon dried crushed oregano
1½ pounds large fresh mushrooms with stems (about 20)	2 cloves garlic, minced fine	½ teaspoon dried crushed basil
1 tablespoon olive oil	¼ cup freshly grated Parmesan cheese	¼ teaspoon salt
	¼ cup dry, fine low-carb breadcrumbs	Pepper

1 Preheat the oven to 425 degrees. Thaw the frozen spinach. Place it in a paper towel and squeeze out all the excess liquid.

2 Spray a 10-x-15-x-1-inch baking dish with the nonstick cooking spray and set aside.

3 Wash the mushrooms in a colander, removing the stems. Rub the mushroom tops with the olive oil and set aside. Finely chop the mushroom stems to make 2 cups of stems.

4 In a heavy 10-inch skillet, melt the butter and cook the chopped mushroom stems, onion, and garlic over medium-high heat. Cook only until the onion is tender and clear; don't allow the onion to brown.

5 Add the drained spinach and cook over low heat until the moisture has evaporated (about 3 minutes, depending on how well you've squeezed the spinach). Stir in the Parmesan cheese, breadcrumbs, chopped pimiento, oregano, basil, salt, and pepper to taste. Stir the spinach mixture until well blended.

6 Spoon the spinach mixture into the oiled mushroom tops. Place them in the baking dish. Bake for 30 minutes, until the mushrooms are tender (not soggy).

Tip: *Using freshly grated hard cheeses can make a dish sing. Use a regular grater or one of those fancy cheese devices that require you to insert different blades and turn the handle (like the ones in the restaurant).*

Per serving: *Calories 32 (From Fat 15); Fat 2g (Saturated 1g); Cholesterol 2mg; Sodium 73mg; Carbohydrate 3g; Dietary Fiber 1g (Net Carbohydrate 2g); Protein 2g.*

Chinese Chicken Wings

These wings are a special treat. One-and-a-half pounds makes 8 servings, so the size of the wings will depend on how many are in a serving. Although honey isn't on the low-carb list, I've left it in this recipe because it makes the sauce so sweet and the wings taste great. However, if you want to substitute sugar-free maple syrup, please do so.

Preparation time: *30 minutes*

Refrigeration time: *4 hours*

Cooking time: *30 minutes*

Yield: *8 servings*

1½ pounds chicken wings	1 tablespoon honey
1 tablespoon light olive oil	1 teaspoon minced garlic
¼ cup soy sauce	1 teaspoon finely minced fresh gingerroot
⅓ cup pineapple juice	2 tablespoons water

1 Using a 9-x-13-inch baking pan, place the wings side by side, forming only one layer.

2 In a small bowl, combine the olive oil, soy sauce, pineapple juice, honey, garlic, ginger-root, and water and pour over the chicken wings. Toss to coat the wings evenly. (If you prefer to use a large zipper-type plastic bag to coat the wings, please do so.) Cover tightly and refrigerate for about 4 hours.

3 Preheat the oven to 350 degrees. Drain the marinade from the wings. Bake the wings for about 30 minutes, or until browned.

4 Serve with warm, wet towels so you can eat the wings with your fingers. Yum.

Per serving: *Calories 128 (From Fat 73); Fat 8g (Saturated 2g); Cholesterol 28mg; Sodium 487mg; Carbohydrate 3g; Dietary Fiber 0g (Net Carbohydrate 3g); Protein 10g.*

Sweet Indulgence

Just because it satisfies your sweet tooth doesn't mean that the carb counts have to be off the charts. There are some simple sweet indulgences that will surprise you (be sure to check out the recipes in Chapter 13 for a variety of sweet things that are lower in carb counts that I'm sure you'll enjoy).

◌ Lemon Cloud

This sweet offering is so elegant, light, and airy. And the carb count is so low that you can even sprinkle a few red raspberries for garnish and still be under your 5 grams of carbs. What a treat! This recipe is kind of a *faux soufflé*. By that, I mean that you build it like you do a soufflé, and it acts like a soufflé when cooking, but it doesn't hold up like one. Don't be disappointed when it deflates on you very quickly. It's okay because the flavor and taste are what you're after in this recipe — like airy, sweet, and lemony eggs! You bake this lemony cloud in a soufflé dish.

Preparation time: *15 minutes*

Cooking time: *30 minutes*

Yield: *4 servings*

4 eggs, separated	¼ teaspoon lemon zest	¼ teaspoon cream of tartar
½ teaspoon pure vanilla extract	6 packets Splenda sugar substitute	Nonstick cooking spray
1 teaspoon lemon extract		

1 Preheat the oven to 350 degrees. In a large bowl, using an electric mixer, beat the egg yolks on medium speed for 1 minute. Add the vanilla, lemon extract, lemon zest, and 3 packets of the Splenda. Turn the mixer up to high and beat for 2 minutes.

2 In a medium bowl (not plastic), beat the egg whites with the cream of tartar on high until soft peaks begin to form. Add the remaining 3 packets of Splenda and beat until the egg whites are stiff.

3 Taking the egg white mixture one-third at a time, fold gently into the yolk mixture until the two mixtures are just blended.

4 Spray a 1½-quart soufflé dish with the cooking spray and pour the mixture into the dish. Place the soufflé dish in a shallow pan. Pour hot water into the pan until it's 1 inch high. Put the lemon cloud in the oven immediately after you put it in the soufflé pan to keep the air in the lemon mixture for baking.

5 Bake for 30 minutes and don't open the oven door while the lemon cloud is baking (it'll cause it to fall before you take it out of the oven). Serve immediately. Red raspberries are an optional garnish.

Variation: Prepare your favorite low-carb chocolate sauce or buy some low-carb syrup or sauce. Warm the sauce or syrup in the microwave and pour it over the lemon cloud. Spritz each serving with some whipped cream. This total package won't come in under the 5-grams carb count, but you now have a low-carb splurge treat.

Per serving: Calories 85 (From Fat 45); Fat 5g (Saturated 2g); Cholesterol 213mg; Sodium 63mg; Carbohydrate 2g; Dietary Fiber 0g (Net Carbohydrate 2g); Protein 6g.

Part IV
Eating Low-Carb on the Town and on the Run

The 5th Wave   By Rich Tennant

"Of course you're better off eating fish and vegetables, but for St. Valentine's Day, we've never been very successful with, 'Say it with trout'."

In this part . . .

On your mark, get ready, get set, go! Is that the way you feel every morning? In this part, I try to help you out with your low-carb, healthy lifestyle by giving you tips on eating out and cooking in a hurry. I encourage you to pack your own lunch by giving you brown-bagging options, as well as options from the frozen food section of your grocery store. I set the timer to see if you can beat me in the delicious meal options that you can prepare in a flash. With all these ideas, you'll probably agree with me that low-carb never tasted so good!

Chapter 18

Taking the Low-Carb Road to Restaurants

Don't let dining out with your low-carb lifestyle intimidate you or make you feel guilty. You deserve to dine out and enjoy yourself. Restaurants are making a huge effort toward offering healthful options on their menus. At this writing, fast food chains are offering low-carb meals, and so are many of the fine restaurants and large hotel chains. Low-carb cruises are even available.

The freedom of the low-carb lifestyle is simply astounding when you prioritize low-carb living and make smart choices. You have no reason to stop making these smart choices when you dine out. After all, you don't leave your low-carb lifestyle at home when you go to a restaurant. This is your way of life, so it follows you everywhere!

In this chapter, I give you a bunch of great tips and tricks for ordering with confidence, navigating menus, and choosing standard restaurant dishes that work in your low-carb lifestyle. Then I take it one step further, with an eye toward maximizing your options, by covering the low-carb options at a variety of ethnic restaurants.

If you have a vote in where you're dining, choose a restaurant that you know provides a delicious and satisfying meal that fits your low-carb lifestyle. This doesn't mean you have to eat at the same restaurant all the time, though. Be adventuresome and try new places, but do try to stay away from home-style buffets. And if you're dining with friends and they ask where you'd like to go, speak up. Vocalize what works for you instead of saying, "Oh, anywhere is fine."

The Art of Placing Your Low-Carb Order

Don't set yourself up to get up from what should be a pleasant dining experience feeling guilty. It just isn't necessary. You're always in the driver's seat of what goes in your mouth, no matter where you are. When you're at a restaurant, be very specific when you place your order: Ask the server for details on the dishes you're considering (How's it prepared? What's in that sauce? Are the veggies fresh or canned?), and ask for exactly what you want. Just because something isn't on the menu doesn't mean it isn't available.

When it comes to ordering, the key is to *ask*. The following may be some common requests you find yourself making:

✔ May I substitute mixed veggies or cottage cheese for the french fries?

✔ Is fresh fruit in season but not shown on the menu as an option?

✔ Because I get two sides dishes, can I have two orders of veggies?

✔ Instead of having the fresh catch of the day drowned in that fancy schmancy sauce, can I simply have it grilled with a squeeze of lemon?

Good restaurants enjoy making their guests happy and meeting their cuisine desires because they want to build repeat customers in the process of pleasing you. So make the restaurant folks happy by asking for what you want.

Taking precautionary dining measures

For goodness' sake, don't starve yourself before you go out. You set yourself up for a big fall and risk disappointing yourself as soon as the bread basket arrives. Going into a fine restaurant with the delicious smells and beckoning menu is a very scary low-carb move on an empty stomach.

Before you leave the house or work, grab a handful of nuts and munch on them on the way to the restaurant to take the hunger edge off. Drink some water to wash down the nuts, and you're set.

When you arrive at the restaurant and are seated, if you're really hungry, order a hot cup of tea. And how about that bread basket? If you're dining with someone who wants bread, ask if he'd mind putting his bread on his bread plate and sending the basket away from the table. It's the old out-of-sight, out-of-mind trick at work. If you're dining with a table full of friends, make sure the bread is out of your immediate reach. Across the table is a good place for it.

Scanning the menu: Keyword traps and treats

In restaurant lingo, there are some trap words and phrases that describe dishes that are off the charts in carbs and promise to upset your low-carb apple cart. As you look at the menu, look for the words that may be the enemy in disguise. Avoid ordering anything with these words in the description:

- ✔ All you can eat
- ✔ Batter-fried
- ✔ Breaded
- ✔ Covered in sauce
- ✔ Crispy
- ✔ Decadent desserts
- ✔ Deep-fried
- ✔ Dipped in batter
- ✔ Extra-large
- ✔ Glazed
- ✔ Jumbo
- ✔ Loaded
- ✔ Pan-fried
- ✔ Smothered
- ✔ Tempura

But don't let that list get ya' down. There are still so many delightful dishes you can indulge in when eating out. Here are some words you can eat by:

- ✔ Baked
- ✔ Braised
- ✔ Broasted
- ✔ Charbroiled
- ✔ Fresh
- ✔ Grilled
- ✔ Herb stuffed
- ✔ Poached
- ✔ Roasted
- ✔ Steamed
- ✔ Stir-fried

Always check out any sauces to be sure that they're not loaded with hidden sugars or high carb counts. Sometimes it will be hit and miss because, even if you ask, you're not going to get a great answer about ingredients. When in doubt, ask for your sauces on the side, and that way you can use it as a dipping sauce instead of saturating your entree with the sauce.

Indulging in guilt-free, low-carb cuisine

Here's a good rule of thumb: Food that's prepared simply, such as grilled fresh fish, is usually a healthy entree.

Look at these mouthwatering, low-carb entrees that you can indulge in with no guilt whatsoever:

- Grilled or broiled fish of any kind
- Lobster with drawn butter on the side
- Fresh crab legs with drawn butter on the side
- Steamers and mussels
- Prime rib specials
- Steak
- Broiled, grilled, or baked chicken or turkey
- Grilled pork chops
- Grilled lamb chops
- Shrimp cocktail

Go easy on the cocktail sauce that comes with your shrimp, because it can be loaded with sugar. You don't have to submerge your shrimp in the sauce to enjoy it.

And don't forget the cheeseburger. Yes, that's right. Go ahead and order a big, thick cheeseburger — just make a few modifications. Ask your server to give you some iceberg lettuce on the side, and skip the bun. When your burger arrives, wrap it in the lettuce (see Chapter 11 for a great stuffed burger to make at home). Or you can order a burger with Swiss cheese and a double order of mushrooms on top of the burger. Skipping the bun and eating it open-faced with mushrooms tumbling down and Swiss cheese oozing out is sure to be a treat. It's politically correct to eat that big, fat burger low-carb style with a fork and knife.

When you order a burger, ask the server to leave off the special sauce and substitute condiments on the side. Ketchup can be loaded with sugar, so just go easy. Mustard, mayo, and dill pickles are fine, however. Ask for extra lettuce and tomatoes too because they give you more to wrap your mouth around.

Salads are always great restaurant choices as well. Add these to your ordering options:

- ✔ **Caesar salads of all kinds (minus the croutons):** Add chicken, shrimp, salmon, or steak to make this salad a full meal.

- ✔ **Marinated vegetable salads:** Make sure to ask what the veggies have been marinated in so you don't get stuck with a sugar-laden marinade.

- ✔ **Chef salads and salad bars:** Skip the bacon bits and the croutons, please. And just because you order the salad bar, you don't have rights to the potato salad and all those other starchy carb salads at the bar. However, if you find a really fresh salad bar that serves soup as well, you've just found a diamond in the rough because it can be a great low-carb place for lunch too.

Reviewing some restaurant survival tips

With a few survival tips, you'll be armed and ready to dine anywhere in the world at any meal. Not only can you eat healthy when eating out, but you can most definitely enjoy it as well. Deprivation is not on the menu — healthy choices on your part are what are on your menu. Smile at the waiter, order, and *bon appétit!*

- ✔ **Order first:** After you carefully inspect the menu options and grill the server, place your order. Don't wait to hear the choices of the folks you're dining with. Your food decisions are personal and shouldn't depend on what anyone else at the table is ordering. It's your lifestyle, remember?

- ✔ **Stick with water:** Diet sodas are full of caffeine and may increase your appetite, as well as trigger carb cravings Order water with a slice of lemon or, better yet, order sparkling water in a wine glass. I do it all the time. It makes the meal feel even more special, and if your dining mates are drinking wine, you have a wine glass to lift too. Here's a toast to you for respecting your low-carb lifestyle while dining out!

- ✔ **Ask for the to-go container early:** If the portions are huge, you don't have to eat everything on your plate. Maybe you ordered your favorite salad, and it's enough for three. Before you douse it with salad dressing, ask for a to-go container and put half of the salad in the container. Ask for some salad dressing to go if you especially like the one served with the salad. You have tomorrow's lunch already figured out.

- ✔ **Ask for dressings and sauces to be served on the side** *always***:** Some restaurants tend to drown the salad and use more sauce than necessary. Don't let it spoil your meal when you can simply avoid it by ordering your dressings and sauces on the side to begin with. By doing so, you're where you're supposed to be — in the low-carb driver's seat! (See the suggestion in the earlier section "Scanning the menu: Keyword traps and treats" for more about sauces on the side.)

✔ **Start with a cup of soup:** Order a cup of soup and eat it slowly. This low-carb choice will begin to fill you up. According to some research, eating soup at the beginning of the meal slows your rate of eating. The soup begins to fill your stomach, which signals the brain and curtails your appetite. As a result, you eat less later.

✔ **Consider constructing your own meal:** Where is there a rule that says you have to order an entree? Order a carb-friendly appetizer with a side salad or order two of your favorite appetizers.

✔ **When you're done, get rid of your plate:** Ask the waiter to take your plate as soon as you finish eating, especially if any food is left on it. You can't continue to pick at your food after you feel full if it's gone.

Cruising the Low-Carb World of Ethnic Dining

Ethnic restaurants aren't off the low-carb map by any means. In fact, some of them are great choices. Come with me on a little trip around the world and explore some low-carb suggestions specific to various ethnic cuisines.

Chinese

Chinese restaurants always have plenty of tasty stir-fried veggies on their menus. Try different dishes like Chinese cabbage or different combinations of meat, chicken, and seafood with veggies. Sit-down Chinese restaurants usually make each dish to order, so if you want certain vegetables with shrimp, for instance, and this dish isn't on the menu, ask if the chef can stir it up for you. More than likely, the restaurant is glad to comply with your wishes. Of course, stay away from the white rice and the sweet-and-sour dishes. If it tastes sweet in a Chinese restaurant, you better believe it is *loaded* with sugar. And drink plenty of tea — tea somehow always tastes better in a Chinese restaurant.

Greek

When I say Greek food, do you immediately think of gyros, baklava, and high carbs? Interestingly enough, Greek food is mostly cooked with olive oil, and the food is grilled. On the Greek restaurant menu, you'll probably find grilled shish kabobs of lamb and veggies or fish and veggies. Other entrees offered may be grilled seafood or grilled vegetables and possibly a baked fish dish. Greek salads are always tasty, too, and feel free to eat my share of olives.

Italian

I know you immediately think of pasta when you think of Italian food. However, some good Italian restaurants have dishes to die for that fit into your low-carb lifestyle. Try a delicious vegetable antipasto and a side salad. You can actually make a meal out of that combination. I've had some awesome specialty salads in Italian restaurants, so check them out.

If the restaurant offers a Marsala entree, it's probably low-carb safe because it's broth-based and cooked with Marsala wine. Also very Italian are veal piccata and chicken piccata, which are made with white wine and capers. You may run into some great red fish stew, cioppino, which has many different kinds of seafood and fish in it. Cioppino is an entire meal in itself. Also, be sure to ask about the specials when you're eating Italian because restaurants sometimes have fresh fish prepared in a very palate-pleasing manner.

Japanese

The best Japanese restaurants with the freshest ingredients are the ones where you can watch them cook the meal. These restaurants have lots of fresh ingredients available, as well as fresh seafood and meats. You can pick and choose what you want from the menu, and they usually cater to special requests, so don't be shy. I've found that a lot of these types of restaurants have early-bird specials in the evening, so watch for them so you can have a tasty low-carb meal that's easy on the pocketbook as well. If you've never had this dining experience, it's a treat, so try it at least once.

Nouvelle

Nouvelle cuisine is a style of French cooking that became popular in the 1970s. If you want to eat French food, go with nouvelle because the menu tends to include garden-fresh ingredients, which fit well with your low-carb lifestyle. The philosophy of Nouvelle cuisine includes veggies cooked crispy fresh and fruit-based sauces rather than heavy sauces loaded with cream and flour. If you're feeling Frenchly adventuresome, you can opt for a menu item called *prix-fixe,* which is very simply a bunch of courses in very small servings, which can be a real treat if you haven't tried it. Although the French are known for their sauces, some of them are lighter fare and wine-based, so ask questions about sauces. If you must indulge in something a little heavier, ask your server to please serve it on the side and maybe serve only half a portion. On the menu, you also may find some delightful soufflés and ratatouille, a vegetable dish cooked in olive oil, which are great options. If you're lucky, a poached fresh catch of the day may be available.

Mexican

A taco salad is a great choice for your low-carb lifestyle. I'm talking about the one that comes in a big taco bowl with meat and tomatoes on top. But the secret to this dish is to *not* eat the bowl. You can add fresh salsa and guacamole to your taco salad, too. These salads are usually huge, so make a decision before you dive into your salad to get a to-go container. Guess what? You have lunch for the next day. Another great choice is tasty Mexican fajitas without the wraps that are usually served on the side. Just ask your waitperson to skip the wraps, and you are so low-carb.

Weighing the Dessert Decision

Don't let your dinner friends urge you into eating a big dessert because "you deserve it." What you really deserve is to continue the healthy low-carb lifestyle that's working so well for you.

In my dining out experiences, I've been guilty of indulging in sumptuously sweet endings on occasions. And there have been times I've paid for it by feeling fuzzy, sluggish, and downright awful for three or four days afterwards. After those indulgences, I've always been furious with myself, because one serving of dessert can make the scales go up as much as 3 pounds overnight. By making the decision to partake, I betray myself, and I set my healthy low-carb lifestyle back. Is a piece of chocolate cake really worth it?

Only you can be the judge on this one. It's your body and your health. Just be careful with desserts. Order some juicy strawberries topped with real whipped cream and a cup of hot, spiced tea or a frothy cappuccino (ask them to hold the sugar in the cappuccino). If you really must splurge, order a dessert for everyone at the table to share, and have just one or two bites. You'll be glad you didn't eat the whole thing.

Chapter 19

Brown-Bagging It, Low-Carb Style

In This Chapter

▶ Packing your lunch and lovin' it

▶ Creating a tasty low-carb lunch

▶ Looking at the prepackaged frozen possibilities

Recipes in This Chapter

▶ Waldorf Salad to Go

*A*fter a tasty, nutritious low-carb breakfast (see Chapter 6 for recipes that fit the bill) and a mid-morning low-carb snack (see Chapter 14), lunchtime comes rolling around. At this point in the day, most folks choose one of three options: They skip the midday meal, head to a restaurant, or turn to their lunch bag or refrigerator.

Right out of the gate, I'm here to rule out the first option. Any healthy eating lifestyle encourages you not to skip meals, and your low-carb lifestyle is no different. Skipping meals tends to make you ravenous and brings the possibility of overeating at your next real meal. In addition, food provides your body with fuel, and skipping meals can leave you feeling sluggish. Eating lunch can determine how you feel by mid-afternoon, as well as maintain afternoon alertness and boost your energy levels.

As for the remaining lunch options — eating out and eating in — either can be enjoyable as well as low-carb healthy. From my experience, the trusty brown bag (or some snazzier version of a lunch carrier) is an easy option, and it's the most conducive to maintaining your low-carb lifestyle. In this chapter, I tell you why packing your lunch is a stellar option, and I provide you with all sorts of tips, tricks, and suggestions (including a recipe) for controlling carbs when the clock strikes noon.

Bagging the Benefits of Taking Your Lunch

In my years in the corporate world, I ate out all the time. But then I finally got smart and started taking my lunch to work with me. It took a little getting used to, but once I did it, I almost dreaded going out. I'd prepare as much as I could the night before in plastic sandwich bags and small plastic containers to cut down on time in the mornings, and like everything else in life, after I got the program down, it was just part of my routine.

With healthier eating being a priority, more and more people are packing their lunches. If you want to eat exactly what you like and what gives you energy, and you want to know for sure what's in your lunch, then brown-bagging is a great option. Planning your lunch puts you in total control of your midday carb counts. And, controlling what you put in your mouth is what your healthy low-carb lifestyle is all about at the end of the day, the beginning of the day, and the middle of the day!

Don't get me wrong. You may like to go out with co-workers or friends occasionally for lunch. That's great so long as you watch for hidden carbs in seemingly carb-friendly lunch entrees (see Chapter 18 for some dining out hints).

The benefits of packing your lunch far outweigh the downside of taking the time to do it. With a low-carb lifestyle, packing your lunch at least a few days a week falls into that "try it, I think you'll like it" category. Anything new sometimes seems intimidating, and the thought of adding one more thing to your already overloaded schedule may make you tremble. But look at some benefits of toting your lunch and see what you think after your read them.

- **Introducing flexibility:** One of the great benefits I enjoyed about brown-bagging was the flexibility it allowed me. If I was buried in work at my desk, I could eat right there and then take a walk afterward. Brown-bagging also allows you to run errands at lunch. You can eat your lunch at work and still have time to run an important errand in the middle of the day. I always felt like I was getting ahead in the busy game of life rather than wasting an hour standing in line or waiting for my food and then rushing through my meal to get back to work on time.

- **Enjoying variety:** Variety is the spice — ah, yes! And who better knows the spice of your low-carb life better than you. Breaking up your work week and taking your lunch even a few days a week will add variety to your days. And if you can work in even a 10-minute walk, you'll enjoy variety and possibly relieve some stress at the same.

✔ **Escaping:** On the days I didn't have errands to run during my lunch hour, I'd go to a nearby park, take my shoes off, and enjoy lunch in my own little world. Often I'd take a book and do a little reading, and other times I'd make grocery lists or to-do lists. (I even turned off my cell phone sometimes.) I'd always be refreshed after lunch in the park.

✔ **Saving time:** At first you may think, "I don't have time to pack a lunch." I'm here to encourage you to just try it for a couple weeks and see how much time you'll actually save. You rush around all day at work because you never have enough hours in the day. But if your lunch is packed and waiting for you when lunchtime rolls around, I'll bet that after it takes you 10 minutes to eat, you'll be sitting there for the first few days thinking, what do I do now? I got so that I dreaded the days that I had to go to a restaurant and fight the crowds at lunch. I got back to my desk more stressed than when I left for an hour that was supposed to be a break. Well, give yourself a break —pack your lunch!

✔ **Saving money:** By packing a lunch each day, you probably save at least $4 per day, which is more than $1,000 a year. Bet you can think of something to do with that extra grand.

When toting my lunch, I prefer to do it in style. If you don't already own one of those cute little insulated bags, then it's time for a treat. I have one that's black with a leopard insert, and it's cuter than a button. I think I paid $5 for it at a discount store. You just pop the gel packs that come with the bag in the freezer, and they keep your food very cold until lunchtime.

If you take hot soups in your lunch, then a thermos with a wide-mouth top is another must-have. Pouring soups in and out is much easier if you have the wide mouth as opposed to that skinny little opening in some insulated vacuum containers. If you have a microwave available at work, you don't need a thermos. Just pack frozen soup in your little lunch bag without any frozen bags, and by lunchtime, the soup has started to thaw and just needs a few minutes in the microwave.

Be sure to keep cold foods cold (below 40 degrees) and hot foods hot (above 140 degrees). Bacteria thrive best in the range of 40 to 140 degrees. Don't take a chance on eating food that could be hazardous to your health.

If you have a low-carb friend at work, eating lunch with her once a week may be fun. Take turns — one week you bring the low-carb lunch, and the next week your friend brings it. You can either go to the park or eat together in the office lunchroom. You'll add a little variety to your lunch routine, and you and your friend can share your low-carb lifestyle tricks and tips.

Packing Delightful Low-Carb Lunches

Think about your lunch entree as much as you do your dinner entree. All of your meals as part of your low-carb lifestyle are important, but lunch is supposed to give you a boost and a jump-start for the rest of the day. You can pack so much low-carb delicious variety into your lunch bag. And there's a huge element of satisfaction when you know what you're having when lunchtime rolls around. And if you pack some of your favorite low-carb foods in your lunch bag, you'll probably find yourself really looking forward to lunch instead of dreading going out and fighting the crowds in a restaurant. I always throw in a small resealable bag of crunchy veggies that can pinch-hit as snacks if I get hungry mid-morning or in the middle of the afternoon.

When shopping for lunch ingredients, steer clear of processed meats and lunch meats, because they're full of preservatives, hidden carbs, hidden sugars, and sodium. Go straight to the deli counter instead.

Sensational salads

If you've been with me for most of this book, you've long forgotten that boring iceberg lettuce. Instead, you're keeping your favorite prewashed leafy greens and crunchy salad veggies on hand. Make plenty of your favorite homemade vinaigrette dressing (see Chapter 8 for recipes) to keep around also.

Find a plastic container that fits your tummy. In other words, take enough to fill you up at lunch. Fill it with leafy greens. If you had chicken for dinner the night before, add some chunks of chicken. Tuna is good on top of a salad too. Don't forget about fresh fruits, cheeses, and nuts for crunch. If you don't want to combine all the ingredients in the morning, just pack your leafy greens in the plastic container and put the other ingredients in individual self-sealing plastic bags. Keep a supply of paper plates at work, combine all the ingredients at lunchtime, and top with your favorite dressing.

Put your salad dressing in a small, self-sealing bag, and place it in the container with your salad mixings. If the bag should leak, the dressing doesn't end up all over the inside of your lunch tote.

Waldorf Salad to Go

This salad makes the best lunch ever, and it's light but filling enough to keep you going all afternoon. Because it contains mayonnaise, keep it cold on the way to work in your insulated lunch bag with two of the little "ice" packets that come with the bag — frozen of course. One freezer bag on the top and one on the bottom of the plastic container are quite adequate. Refrigerate it until lunchtime. Enjoy this great lunch treat to go.

Preparation time: *15 minutes*

Refrigeration time: *3 hours or overnight*

Yield: *6 servings*

2 tablespoons freshly squeezed lemon juice	*1 cup whole white or red seedless grapes, halved*
2 tablespoons plus ½ cup mayonnaise	*½ cup chopped walnuts*
2 cups diced apples (preferably Jonathan)	*½ pint heavy whipping cream*
2 to 3 cups cubed white meat chicken	*2 packets Splenda sugar substitute*
1 cup finely chopped celery	

1 Combine the lemon juice and 2 tablespoons mayonnaise, mixing well. Place the diced apples in a medium mixing bowl. Pour the mayonnaise mixture over the diced apples and toss until the apples are well coated.

2 Combine the chicken, celery, grapes, and walnuts with the apple mixture.

3 Whip the heavy cream until soft peaks form. Stir the Splenda into the remaining ½ cup mayonnaise and fold the mayonnaise mixture into the whipped cream.

4 Fold the whipped cream and mayonnaise mixture into the chicken mixture.

5 Refrigerate until chilled, about 3 hours, or overnight if you're planning it for lunch the next day.

Per serving: Calories 494 (From Fat 373); Fat 42g (Saturated 13g); Cholesterol 108mg; Sodium 199mg; Carbohydrate 16g; Dietary Fiber 2g (Net Carbohydrate 14g); Protein 18g.

Wonderful wraps

Wraps make a great low-carb lunch and are quick to prepare. The combinations of wraps are endless (see Chapter 15 for lots of wrap recipes and ideas). You can, for instance, wrap up the Waldorf Salad I discuss in the preceding section. There are very few of your favorite ingredients you can't wrap up!

You can prepare your wraps in advance and place them in tightly sealed plastic wrap or take the ingredients in your lunch tote and roll them at work.

Consider these wrap ideas for your lunch:

- ✔ Hummus is low in carbs and is delicious in a low-carb tortilla with fresh bell peppers, cucumbers, and tomatoes.

- ✔ Drizzle some Italian dressing on a low-carb tortilla, add a slice of deli turkey, and pile on fresh salad greens. Drizzle a little more dressing on top of the greens, roll it, and you're set.

- ✔ Wrap black soybeans, red onions, a bit of cilantro, a touch of olive oil, and shredded cheddar cheese in a low-carb tortilla or even a lettuce leaf.

- ✔ Combine a dab of your favorite mustard (Dijon or some other delicacy) with a dab of mayo and mix well. Spread the mustard-mayo combo on a whole-wheat, low-carb tortilla. Top with a slice of deli turkey (or chicken). Chop half a piece of provolone cheese, and sprinkle it in the middle of the tortilla on top of the meat. Add some chopped tomatoes and finely chopped Italian parsley and roll it up.

- ✔ Try your favorite marinated vegetable salad in a low-carb tortilla (turn to Chapter 12 for a recipe idea).

Instead of a tortilla as a base for your wrap, use 2 or 3 pieces of deli ham, turkey, or chicken for a change in venue. Something as simple as deli ham with a slice of cheese rolled up can be very satisfying. I also like a slice of deli turkey spread with cream cheese and rolled tightly.

Luscious leftovers

You're cooking up a storm these days, and some awesome quick and nutritious low-carb meals are coming out of your kitchen: homemade soups (see Chapter 7), meats (see Chapter 11), fish entrees (see Chapter 9), and some great veggie dishes (see Chapter 12). Obviously, all this cooking means more and more leftovers frequenting your fridge — which is when low-carb cooking really gets fun. You cook once and eat the meal twice, saving time and money in the process. What a great combination!

Maybe you had a great plate of steamed veggies for dinner. Those veggies are perfect for lunch the next day served cold with your favorite low-carb dip or some ranch salad dressing. You can use hummus for a veggie dip too.

Another great leftover for lunch is quiche. I happen to like cold quiche, but if you prefer it warm, just pop it in the microwave at work (see Chapter 6 for great quiche recipes). Coming in a close second to quiche in the race for the lunchbox are frittatas. So if you're making frittatas for Sunday morning breakfast, think about making a couple extra for Monday's lunch. You'll get to the point that you look forward to having leftovers from a great-tasting low-carb meal at home so that you can take them for lunch the next day.

Because soup is hot, you eat it more slowly, and it gives your brain time to talk to your stomach and say, "Hey, I'm full now." Soup is great at lunchtime (see Chapter 7 for some recipes). Here are a few souper tips (sorry, I couldn't resist):

- Liven up your soups with shredded cheese. Just pack a small amount of shredded cheese in a self-sealing plastic bag and sprinkle the cheese on top of your heated-up soup.

- If you use a vacuum bottle to tote your soup, preheat the bottle with boiling water for about 5 minutes before placing the hot soup in the thermos, and your soup will stay hotter longer.

Little lunch packables

Don't forget to include some delightful side items in your lunchbox, like low-carb yogurt, unsweetened applesauce, string cheese, or nuts. If you like fruit in your yogurt, pack frozen blueberries in a self-sealing plastic bag. By lunchtime, they're thawed and ready to stir into your yogurt. Add a packet of Splenda sugar substitute and sprinkle in some crunchy pecans, and you have a real treat for lunch.

Vacuum-sealed packets of salmon and tuna in water are great lunch packables that can be rolled in a low-carb tortilla, stirred with a little mayo and hard-boiled egg, or eaten plain with tomato slices.

Fresh fruit kabobs

Prepare seasonal fresh fruit, such as strawberries, melon, and kiwi, with cubes of various cheeses like Swiss, medium cheddar, or mozzarella. Alternate the fruit and cheese on wooden skewers. You can tightly wrap these prepared kabobs in plastic wrap and include them in your lunchbox. These kabobs are especially good in the summer because they're so refreshing. You can also make a very quick dip for these kabobs with cream cheese, a packet of Splenda, and enough light cream to blend with the mixer to make the mixture dippable.

Delicious desserts

No, I haven't forgotten dessert in your lunchbox. I'm a dessert lover after all. Here are few ways to end your lunch on a sweet yet light note:

✔ **Fruit:** You can cut melon into chunks and tote them in plastic containers or self-sealing plastic bags. Other fruit options are tangerines, nectarines, dark plums, grapes, kiwi, apples, strawberries, blueberries, blackberries, or pears or peaches every now and then (pears aren't the lowest-carb fruit around). There are also new low-carb canned fruits packed in their own juices that are great. You can find them at most grocery stores. Just watch the sugar content and the calorie counts.

✔ **Sugar-free gelatins and puddings:** You can make sugar-free gelatin or pudding at home, put it in a small plastic container with a lid, and pop it in your lunch bag. I suggest you make the gelatin and pudding, even though you can find them in the grocery store already made and packaged. They're rather pricey, and you can make a whole batch for what you'd pay for one small prepackaged container.

✔ **Meringue cookies:** Throw a few in a little container and indulge with a hot cup of tea. Speaking of meringues, you can pack a meringue shell in a plastic container and some fresh fruit in another plastic container and then dump the fruit in the meringue shell after you have your lunch. Your co-workers will be jealous of your dessert. Try doing some low-carb baking on the weekends, and you'll have sweet treats to tote with you all week. (Chapter 13 has several meringue recipes that you're gonna love.) Ah — the decadence of packing a low-carb lunch.

Peeking in the Frozen Food Case

I encourage you to make your own lunches at home, but realistically, I also know that doing so isn't always possible. And some new dinners popping up in your grocer's frozen food case boast low-carb counts and taste just dandy.

Shop the frozen food section at the grocery store with care. I offer you a word of caution not to read only the front of the food package that offers you the net carb count. Instead, read the entire Nutrition Facts label on the back of the package (flip to Chapter 3 to become a label-reading expert). Check for hidden sugars, sodium, as well as the calorie counts. Sometimes the calorie counts are off the charts, and what good does that do you?

If you take a frozen dinner to work with you, make sure that a freezer is available for storage of your entree until you pop it in the microwave at lunch. Letting the frozen dinner thaw before you cook it isn't a good idea.

Chapter 20

Cooking Dinner in a Low-Carb Heartbeat

*Y*ikes! You just came flying through the door from a long day, it's 6:30 p.m., and you don't have a clue what's for dinner. Sound a bit familiar? How would you like to change this picture? There seems to be a strange myth associated with low-carb healthy living and cooking. The myth is that you have to spend hours in the kitchen to serve up nutritious meals. Take it from an old-fashioned, Midwestern cook — nothing is farther from the truth. By shifting a couple gears, your low-carb kitchen can turn out all kinds of delicious meals quickly. You can also become more creative in your cooking, which is great news for your low-carb lifestyle because it brings variety to your table.

Recognizing the Power of a Plan

If you're flying through the door at 6:30 p.m. without a clue of what you're going to prepare for dinner, that can spell trouble. But take it one step further: If the refrigerator is running on empty, you're really up a creek. I know that planning sounds like something you just don't have time to do, but it can really pay off by actually saving you time in the end. Imagine walking in the door at 6:30 p.m. with the fridge and cupboards full of low-carb staples, and you have already planned a menu for the evening. What a concept, huh? The time that you'll save simply by not stopping at the grocery store on your way home is huge — and you don't have to stand in those aggravating after-work checkout lines. When you have a plan, you're not roaming the kitchen waiting for an idea for dinner to jump out of the cupboard at you. You're armed and ready, reducing stress and complementing your low-carb lifestyle with a great preplanned healthy meal. Feel the power of preplanning! In Chapter 3, I help you stock your kitchen with all the low-carb staples you need to make it through the day. Check it out. Go ahead. I'll wait right here.

Having no dinner plan and no healthy, wholesome foods to work with is one of the easiest ways to get into trouble with your low-carb lifestyle. Think about it. What do you do? You either rummage through the cupboards and come up with some old snack foods that make you feel miserable after you eat them, or you jump in your car and are so tired and hungry that you turn into the first drive-thru fast food restaurant you see.

I graciously give you the key to creating quick, healthy, low-carb meals in one word — *planning*. Planning ahead makes creating menu options that fit your low-carb lifestyle a pleasure rather than a chore.

Planning ahead isn't that difficult — trust me. You do it all the time or at least most of the time: If you have to be at work at 8 a.m., you plan ahead to give yourself time to shower and dress, grab some coffee and breakfast, and drive to work so you arrive on time. Lunchtime rolls around, and you may plan to dine out with a friend or co-worker, or you may have thought ahead and brought your lunch to work (see Chapter 19 for ideas for brown-bagging it). Heck, you may have even planned to run some errands or work out right after work before you head home.

But this is where the picture gets murky for many folks. What do you do about dinner? Surprisingly, research shows that more than 70 percent of Americans don't decide what they're going to eat for their evening meal until well after 4 p.m. But doesn't it make sense that you'd plan what you're going to have for your evening meal? After all, you owe it to yourself as a reward for surviving the long day.

Plan ahead and keep some smart snacks on hand so you can nibble on something healthy and low-carb while you're cooking a quick dinner. Nuts are always good, and I like to crunch on celery with a little dilled cream cheese while I cook. If you love dill pickles, roll up a crunchy pickle spear in a slice of deli turkey. Sometimes foods with crunchy textures ward off hunger pangs better than other choices.

The freezer is your friend

Keeping your freezer stocked with frozen veggies, meats, and even frozen herbs really helps you in your quest for healthy, low-carb meals in minutes. If you run out of the fresh stuff in the fridge, you need back-ups in the freezer. Be sure to add items to your grocery list as you take them from your freezer.

Keep in mind that homemade soups and stews freeze well, so make a big batch on the weekend and stick it in your freezer. Then simply pop the frozen item in the fridge to thaw as you're running out the door to work. When you get home that night, you have homemade soup in minutes.

You can also opt for freezing individual servings in those semi-disposable freezer containers. Use containers of the same size so you can stack them nicely in the freezer, thus maximizing space. These containers are inexpensive, and I find them at the dollar store in packages of four for a dollar. They come in all shapes and sizes, and I use them over and over. Freezing individual servings adds another option for grabbing something from the freezer to take to work for lunch.

A list is your lifesaver

Buy one of those to-do or list-type notepads with a magnet on the back and stick it in the middle of your fridge. Tie a pen or pencil to another magnet. (This method should be incorporated after you stock your low-carb kitchen with basics; see Chapter 3 for details.)

When you find a recipe that's appealing to you and you don't have the ingredient, write it on the list. When you're close to running out of something in the pantry, the fridge, or the freezer, write it on the list. Some people even go so far as categorizing their lists according to produce, frozen foods, fresh vegetables, meats — you get the picture. That method may sound like overkill, but it can actually save you time in the grocery store, and you like to save time, don't ya?

Scheduling a Week of Low-Carb Meals

The country club even has chili night on Wednesday, so why not adopt a similar schedule for your house? Look at your week and your household's favorite meals. I suggest you create a two-week schedule with ten different meal varieties, and then you can begin to mix and match as the weeks progress.

Your new meal schedule for a week may look something like the following. You can accomplish this full week of meals by going to the grocery store no more than twice a week. Do your main shopping over the weekend and then stop by the store once during the week for some fresh produce. That's it! And because you're becoming a master planner and list maker, these trips to the grocery store should be no sweat.

- **Monday: Slow Cooker Night.** Mondays are hectic, but you may have time on Sunday nights to prepare something to pop in the slow cooker as you dash out the door on Monday morning. Your slow cooker offers variety in very low-carb meals. See Chapter 16 for slow cooker recipes.

- **Tuesday: Stir-Fry Night.** Stir-frying is without a doubt one of the quickest ways to a complete nutritious meal. If you had chicken in the slow cooker on Monday night, you may have leftovers to toss in your stir-fry. Look for varieties of frozen veggies, especially the packaged kinds, for stir-frying. Grocery stores are beginning to package fresh produce the same way. See Chapters 11 and 12 for some stir-fry recipes.

- **Wednesday: Packet Cooking Night.** Packet cooking is a quick and easy way to prepare nutritious meals, and there's very little clean-up. You can cook anything from fish to chicken to a combination of meats and veggies. (See the "Packet Cooking" section later in the chapter.)

- **Thursday: Grilling Night.** You can grill steak, pork chops, lamb, chicken — the choice is yours. And to jazz up your grilling night, just plan ahead and place the meat in a marinade on Wednesday night before you go to bed. Also, do yourself a favor and invest in a grilling basket for veggies, so you can prepare your whole meal on the grill.

- **Friday: Soup and Salad Night.** Have a variety of greens on hand, some fresh veggies, and even some deli meats and cheeses for your big salad night. Buy prewashed, ready-to-eat greens, and just dump them in a big salad bowl with your other low-carb ingredients of choice and some homemade vinaigrette (see Chapter 8 for recipes). For soup, have homemade soup in the freezer that you made in advance (see the section "The freezer is your friend," earlier in the chapter), or whip up a quick batch (check out Chapter 7).

Variety is the spice of life, and this menu plan is just the beginning. When you get into the swing of scheduling your meals, all kinds of other quick ideas will come to you. Here are two more to consider working in:

- **Breakfast Night:** Breakfast isn't just a morning meal anymore. Check out some quick breakfast recipes in Chapter 6 and have breakfast for dinner once in a while.

- **Skillet Supper Night:** Be sure to include skillet suppers in your schedules (see the "Skillet Suppers" section later in the chapter). Skillet suppers are hearty meals, and you cook the whole meal in one skillet. If you want to add a salad, you're good to go quickly with little cleanup.

Rosemary Steak

The rub for this recipe is an incredible combination of flavors and spices that results in one of the best steaks ever if you're looking for a little variety rather than just another steak. If you haven't cooked with fresh rosemary, do yourself a culinary favor — I guarantee you're in for a treat!

Preparation time: *5 minutes*

Refrigeration time: *25 minutes*

Cooking time: *8 to 10 minutes*

Yield: *4 servings*

4 boneless New York strip steaks, 6 ounces each

2 cloves garlic, minced fine

1 tablespoon olive oil

2 tablespoons finely minced fresh rosemary

1 teaspoon lemon zest

½ teaspoon sea salt

1 teaspoon pepper

4 fresh sprigs of rosemary for garnish (optional)

1 With a sharp knife, score both sides of the steaks very shallowly in a diamond pattern.

2 In a small bowl, combine the garlic, olive oil, rosemary, lemon zest, sea salt, and pepper, mixing well. Rub the mixture on the steaks. Refrigerate for at least 25 minutes.

3 Grill the steaks on a gas grill on medium-high heat for about 4 minutes on each side, or until desired doneness (4 minutes per side will give you medium-rare steaks).

4 Slice the steaks diagonally in ½-inch slices. Garnish with fresh rosemary sprigs, if desired.

Per serving: Calories 278 (From Fat 124); Fat 14g (Saturated 4g); Cholesterol 93mg; Sodium 372mg; Carbohydrate 1g; Dietary Fiber 0g (Net Carbohydrate 1g); Protein 35g.

Chicken and Veggie Stir-Fry

This recipe is quick, quick, quick — with a hearty flavor and fresh taste. It'll work great on one of your stir-fry nights. The great thing is that you dump it all in one skillet and have a meal in literally minutes. Stir-fry and skillet meals are great for your low-carb lifestyle because they get you in and out of the kitchen quickly and provide a wonderful home-cooked healthy meal. Depending on how many you're serving, you might even be lucky enough to have some leftovers for lunch the next day. To make this dish even easier to prepare, pick up fresh mushrooms that are already sliced and peppers that are already cut up (in the frozen section). To thaw your frozen stir-fry veggies in this recipe, just put them in the fridge in the morning. They'll be good to go by dinnertime.

Preparation time: *10 minutes*

Cooking time: *About 20 minutes*

Yield: *8 servings*

1 pound skinless boneless chicken breast

2 cloves garlic, minced

1 medium yellow onion, sliced

1 can (14 ounces) bean sprouts, drained

1 can (8 ounces) sliced water chestnuts, drained

4 ounces sliced fresh mushrooms

1 cup mixed frozen bell peppers (not necessary to thaw)

1 package (16 ounces) frozen stir-fry veggies, thawed

1 cup chicken broth

1 teaspoon freshly grated gingerroot

¼ cup soy sauce

1 Cut the chicken into thin strips. Using a large skillet or wok, cook the chicken over medium heat, stirring often until juices run clear in chicken, about 7 minutes.

2 Add the garlic and onion to the chicken in the skillet and cook for 3 minutes.

3 Add the bean sprouts, water chestnuts, mushrooms, peppers, and stir-fry veggies. Cook the mixture for 3 to 4 minutes or just until crisp-tender.

4 Combine the broth, gingerroot, and soy sauce. Stir the broth mixture into the skillet mixture. Bring to a boil and continue cooking for 1 minute.

5 Serve immediately.

Per serving: Calories 107 (From Fat 18); Fat 2g (Saturated 1g); Cholesterol 32mg; Sodium 648mg; Carbohydrate 8g; Dietary Fiber 3g (Net Carbohydrate 5g); Protein 15g.

Salmon Fillets with Tarragon Cream Sauce

This recipe is a culinary delight, and it's a great way to take in some of those important omega-3s (discover the importance of omega-3s in Chapter 9). Serve this with some steamed veggies on the side, and you have a meal that guests will think you spent hours in the kitchen preparing. Ah, the secrets of quick cooking pay such great dividends.

Preparation time: *10 minutes*

Cooking time: *12 to 15 minutes*

Yield: *4 servings*

2 scallions (white part only)	*1 teaspoon cornstarch*
1 Roma tomato	*⅔ cup light cream*
2 tablespoons butter	*¼ cup dry sherry*
4 fresh salmon fillets (about 4 ounces each)	*2 tablespoons finely chopped fresh tarragon*
Salt and pepper	

1 Finely chop the scallions. Remove the seeds from the tomato and finely chop. Set both aside.

2 Melt the butter in a large, heavy skillet over medium heat. Season the fillets with salt and pepper to taste.

3 Place the fillets in the skillet and cook for 6 to 8 minutes, turning only once. Transfer the fish to a platter and cover with aluminum foil to keep warm.

4 Add the scallions to the skillet and cook over low heat for 3 minutes. Stir occasionally and don't allow them to brown.

5 Remove the skillet from the heat and stir in the cornstarch. Return to low heat and slowly stir in the cream and sherry. Stirring constantly, let the mixture simmer until it thickens — about 3 or 4 minutes.

6 Add the tarragon and the chopped tomatoes to the cream sauce in the skillet, stirring to combine well. Season with salt and pepper to taste. Spoon the sauce over the fillets. Serve immediately.

Per serving: Calories 281 (From Fat 160); Fat 18g (Saturated 9g); Cholesterol 106mg; Sodium 247mg; Carbohydrate 3g; Dietary Fiber 0g (Net Carbohydrate 3g); Protein 26g.

Packet Cooking

You're going to love this style of low-carb cooking! Wrapped in parchment paper or foil, the contents steam while the juices of the meat, fish, or poultry mingle with the herbs you've chosen. And the vegetables present a flavorful and nutritious burst when you serve the packet. Packet cooking is kind of like a mini pressure cooker minus the pressure, and it's *fast*. Foods are cooked at high temperatures, usually 425 to 450 degrees. Less fat is needed because you're using high temperatures, and food cooks in its own juices, keeping it moist and upping the concentration of the natural flavors of the food.

You can cook *anything* in a packet — well not a cake — but fish, poultry, meats of all kinds, veggies, and even fruits for desserts. This packet cooking is good stuff, I tell you!

If that isn't enough to get you into low-carb packet cooking made easy, here are a few more reasons for you to jump in:

- ✔ **You can cook an entire meal in handy individual servings.** You can cook your veggies and meat together in individual packets. Cut those veggies a bit smaller than usual so they'll be done at the same time the meat is.

- ✔ **Packet cooking makes make-ahead meals a snap.** Just prepare the packets the night before, and when you walk through the door, simply preheat the oven while you're changing into something more comfortable. Pop the packets in the oven, and dinner is served!

- ✔ **You can cook the packets in the oven or on the grill.** If it's a hot summer night, you can stay inside in the air conditioning while your packet meal cooks on the grill and doesn't heat up the entire house.

- ✔ **The individual servings are great if your family can't all sit down to dinner at the same time.** When a hungry member of the family comes through the door, just pop a packet in the oven, and he'll have a hearty and healthy fresh meal in minutes.

Parchment paper and aluminum foil both work, and I love the presentation of parchment paper for those times when a dramatic touch is nice, when time is of the essence and convenience is a must. My vote, however, is solidly behind heavy-duty aluminum foil. Foil packets offer the following advantages:

- ✔ They easily withstand the high temperatures of packet cooking whether it's in the oven or on the grill.

- ✔ They produce more liquid, because they're more airtight than the parchment packets.

✔ They make crimping and sealing the packet a breeze.

✔ They allow you to prepare food in advance, which you can't do with parchment.

If you're wondering how to fold these little packets, see Figure 20-1. These particular instructions are geared for foil, and they're just one of many different ways to fold your packet (see Chapter 9 for some instructions on using parchment paper for cooking fish in a packet).

The key to successful packet cooking is making sure the seal is very tight throughout the cooking.

Drugstore Wrap

Figure 20-1:
Wrap it
up, and I'll
take it.

Place the food in the center of a rectangle of foil. Leave enough foil to fold the sides and ends.

Bring the sides together at the top and fold down + over, several times.

Fold the short ends up + over several times and crimp to seal the package.

ready to grill!

With packet cooking, you can cook many foods in individual servings in 10 to 20 minutes, and the cleanup consists of tossing the foil or the parchment. Cooking individual servings also reduces the cooking time, which means you get out of the kitchen faster. Isn't this time-saving stuff fun?

Quick cooking hints

Here are some tips to help speed up your cooking and reduce your overall time in the kitchen:

✔ Use your microwave for melting butter and thawing foods quickly.

✔ Keep two sets of measuring cups on hand so you don't have to wipe one out or wash it when measuring consecutive ingredients.

✔ Clean up as you go along so you get out of the kitchen faster. Doing so also makes the cooking time seem shorter.

✔ Use your freezer to cut down on prep time. Freeze shredded cheeses, and they will keep for a long time and are easily accessible. Chop fresh red, green, and yellow bell peppers in ½ cup quantities and freeze them in self-sealing plastic bags and freeze. Do the same with onions in ¼ cup quantities and fresh basil and Italian parsley in smaller quantities. These are great time-savers for stir-fries, soups, casseroles, and skillet suppers.

Steamed Fish and Veggies

Fish and veggies are a great combination in packet cooking because they both cook so quickly. You're going to be amazed at the flavors that packet cooking captures and the way the process accentuates the herbs and spices. This one is sure to spoil you and spur you on to more packet cooking that's so low-carb user friendly.

Preparation time: *10 minutes*

Cooking time: *15 to 18 minutes*

Yield: *1 serving (can easily be doubled)*

Nonstick cooking spray

1 whitefish fillet, 4 ounces

½ cup thinly sliced zucchini

½ cup thinly sliced yellow squash

2 teaspoons fresh lemon juice

½ teaspoon finely chopped fresh Italian parsley

½ teaspoon salt-free lemon pepper seasoning

¼ teaspoon finely chopped fresh dill

1 Preheat the oven to 450 degrees. Spray a 12-x-15-inch piece of heavy-duty aluminum foil with the cooking spray. Place the fish in the middle of the foil.

2 Place the zucchini and squash on top of the fish fillet. Sprinkle with the lemon juice, parsley, lemon pepper, and dill.

3 Fold the foil over and fold the edges in twice, making a pouch for the fish fillet. Place on a baking sheet.

4 Bake for 15 to 18 minutes, until the veggies are crisp-tender and the fish easily flakes with a fork.

Per serving: Calories 174 (From Fat 62); Fat 7g (Saturated 1g); Cholesterol 70mg; Sodium 62mg; Carbohydrate 5g; Dietary Fiber 1g (Net Carbohydrate 4g); Protein 23g.

Skillet Suppers

I've been cooking for a long time, and I still rely on my cast-iron skillets and Dutch oven. In fact, I can't cook without them! My Grandad McCracken bought them for me a hundred years ago for a wedding gift. I'm still using the same ones! (See Figure 20-2 for a picture of a cast-iron skillet.) I'll admit that new, heavy-bottomed skillets are available that do *almost* as good a job holding heat as the cast iron. (But cast iron definitely has its merits, and it's like anything else you're accustomed to — cast iron is just comfortable for me.) So don't shy away from these great recipes just because you may not cook in cast iron. Use whatever cookware puts you in your own cooking comfort zone. Just get cookin'!

Cooking with cast iron has a bit of a reputation of being difficult to deal with — especially getting it ready to use for the first time. But I just found out that there's a company out there that now makes preseasoned, ready-to-use cast iron cookware. (If you're interested in finding out more about cast iron, you can check out *Cast-Iron Cooking For Dummies,* written by Tracy Barr and published by Wiley.)

Skillet suppers may seem kind of old-fashioned, but they fit very well into your low-carb healthy lifestyle and your desire for quick meals. Skillet suppers also conjure up a feeling that you're eating comfort food, which is always welcome to low-carbers. If you have a pretty skillet, you can take it directly to the table and serve from it. Dinner is ready in a matter of minutes with very little cleanup.

Figure 20-2:
Skillet
supper,
anyone?

cast-iron
skillet

Zucchini Skillet Supper

10
LESS THAN

It's all in the skillet! Fresh ingredients cook up quickly, and the skillet doubles as a serving platter — it goes straight from stovetop to the table, so it's no-muss, no-fuss cooking. Your rewards are a great meal and low-maintenance cleanup. This is low-carb comfort food at its freshest and finest. And the end result is pretty too.

Preparation time: *12 minutes*

Cooking time: *15 to 18 minutes*

Yield: *8 servings*

2 tablespoons olive oil	2 teaspoons dried oregano
4 cups diced zucchini	¼ teaspoon salt
1 cup chopped carrots	Pepper
1 cup finely chopped yellow onion	⅓ cup picante sauce (find the type with lower sugar and carb counts)
¾ cup finely chopped celery	2 teaspoons Dijon mustard
½ red bell pepper, sliced thin	1 medium tomato, diced
½ teaspoon garlic powder	2 cups shredded Monterey Jack cheese
2 teaspoons dried basil	

1 Heat the olive oil over medium heat in a large 12-inch, heavy skillet or a small Dutch oven. Add the zucchini, carrots, onion, celery, red pepper, and garlic powder to the oil, and cook until the veggies are crisp-tender.

2 In a small bowl, combine the basil, oregano, salt, pepper to taste, picante sauce, and Dijon mustard. Pour the mixture into the skillet with the veggies and cook, stirring for 3 minutes until well mixed.

3 Stir in the tomatoes just to heat them through.

4 Dish immediately onto individual serving plates and top with the cheese so that it melts over the veggies.

Per serving: *Calories 171 (From Fat 110); Fat 12g (Saturated 6g); Cholesterol 25mg; Sodium 361mg; Carbohydrate 8g; Dietary Fiber 2g (Net Carbohydrate 6g); Protein 8g.*

Tarragon Chicken with Apples

This is a very special meal on the low-carb side because it lends a bit of sweetness. It's a tad bit higher in carb counts, but it isn't off the charts by any means. So languish in this very special and quick entree.

Preparation time: *5 to 8 minutes*

Cooking time: *30 to 35 minutes*

Yield: *4 servings*

2 tablespoons butter, divided

4 boneless, skinless chicken breasts, 4 ounces each

¼ teaspoon salt

⅛ teaspoon pepper

2 medium tart apples, peeled and sliced

½ cup apple juice

¼ cup light cream

¼ cup plus 1 tablespoon cool water

1 teaspoon cornstarch

1 tablespoon finely minced fresh tarragon

1 Using a large, nonstick, heavy skillet, melt 1 tablespoon of the butter. Brown the chicken on both sides, about 8 minutes per side over medium heat. Sprinkle with the salt and pepper and remove from the skillet. Cover to keep warm.

2 In the same skillet, cook the apples in the remaining 1 tablespoon butter just until tender, 6 to 7 minutes. Remove from the skillet and cover to keep warm.

3 Add the apple juice to the skillet, stirring constantly for about 4 minutes, until the juice is reduced by half. Combine the cream and ¼ cup water to make a milk mixture, and add it to the apple juice in the skillet.

4 Return the chicken breasts to the skillet and cook for 10 minutes, or until the juices from the chicken run clear.

5 In a small bowl, combine the 1 tablespoon water and the cornstarch so there are no lumps and stir the mixture into the juices in the skillet. Bring to a boil, cooking and stirring for about 2 minutes, or until the mixture begins to thicken.

6 Add the apples and tarragon and heat through.

Per serving: Calories 259 (From Fat 104); Fat 12g (Saturated 6g); Cholesterol 88mg; Sodium 208mg; Carbohydrate 15g; Dietary Fiber 2g (Net Carbohydrate 13g); Protein 24g.

Turkey Brats and Cabbage

This great skillet supper provides a bit of a crunch at the end of the day. You're going to need a nice large skillet for cooking this one, and I recommend using a Dutch oven if you have one. Be sure to start your onions cooking first so you can keep the crunch in your cabbage.

Preparation time: *10 minutes*

Cooking time: *30 minutes*

Yield: *4 servings*

Small head green cabbage (about 1½ pounds)	*1 tablespoon olive oil*
1 medium yellow onion	*¾ teaspoon garlic powder*
1 package (20 ounces) turkey bratwurst	*½ teaspoon pepper*
Nonstick cooking spray	*2 tablespoons soy sauce*

1 Cut the cabbage in quarters through the core and remove the core. Cut the cabbage in ¼-inch slices. Set aside.

2 Cut the onion in half and then in ½-inch slices. Set aside.

3 Cut the bratwursts into 1-inch pieces

4 Coat a large, heavy skillet (or Dutch oven) with the cooking spray. Cook the bratwurst pieces over medium-high heat for about 8 minutes, or until they're browned on all sides. Drain (depending on how lean your brats are) and remove the bratwurst pieces from the skillet. Set aside and keep warm.

5 Using the same skillet, add the olive oil and the onion slices. Stirring often, cook for about 5 minutes. Then add the cabbage and continue cooking the onions and cabbage for another 6 minutes. Sprinkle with the garlic powder, pepper, and soy sauce, cooking and stirring for an additional 4 minutes.

6 Return the bratwurst pieces to the skillet and cook an additional 2 minutes. Cover and reduce the heat to low. Simmer for about 5 minutes, or until the vegetables are tender and the bratwurst pieces are cooked through.

Variation: *Feel free to substitute the brats with a specialty sausage. I buy a chicken sausage with spinach, fontina, and roasted garlic that's nothing short of divine. And the great news is that these sausages have 1 gram of carbs each. Be adventuresome and shop around a bit — you may be delightfully surprised at what you find.*

Per serving: *Calories 353 (From Fat 169); Fat 19g (Saturated 5g); Cholesterol 124mg; Sodium 1,630mg; Carbohydrate 14g; Dietary Fiber 5g (Net Carbohydrate 9g); Protein 34g.*

30-Minute Chicken

Here you have "quickie chicky." By cooking the chicken on high heat and sealing it in aluminum foil, the chicken cooks quickly, and the juices are sealed in, making the end result tantalizingly moist. With the veggies, this entree needs no other sides, making it a very quick low-carb meal.

Preparation time: *10 minutes*

Cooking time: *30 minutes*

Yield: *4 servings*

Nonstick cooking spray

4 boneless skinless chicken breasts

1 medium yellow onion, sliced thin

¼ teaspoon pepper

½ teaspoon salt-free seasoning blend

½ pound fresh mushrooms, sliced

2 medium zucchinis, sliced

1 can (14½ ounces) diced tomatoes, undrained

¾ teaspoon dried basil

½ teaspoon dried oregano

2 cloves garlic, minced fine

4 tablespoons freshly grated Parmesan cheese

1 Preheat the oven to 450 degrees. Coat a 9-x-13-x-2-inch baking dish with the cooking spray.

2 Place the chicken in the baking dish and top with the onion slices. Sprinkle with the pepper and seasoning blend.

3 Layer the mushrooms over the chicken and layer the zucchini on top of the mushrooms.

4 In a medium bowl, combine the tomatoes with the basil, oregano, and garlic. Pour the tomato mixture over the chicken and vegetables. Cover tightly with aluminum foil.

5 Bake for 30 minutes, making sure the chicken juices run clear at the end of the baking time. Remove from the oven and sprinkle with Parmesan cheese.

Per serving: *Calories 202 (From Fat 41); Fat 5g (Saturated 2g); Cholesterol 67mg; Sodium 284mg; Carbohydrate 12g; Dietary Fiber 4g (Net Carbohydrate 8g); Protein 29g.*

Quick low-carb quesadillas

I suggest you always have whole-wheat, low-carb tortillas on hand (they keep for quite a while in the refrigerator), as well as shredded cheeses in the freezer. With those two ingredients available, you can whip up some low-carb quesadillas in a hurry. Just preheat the broiler and place the low-carb tortillas on a baking sheet. Top with shredded cheddar cheese and, if you like, a little chopped onion, diced tomato, drained green chiles, or whatever carb-conscious ingredients you have on hand. Place the tortillas under the broiler. Watch them carefully and, when the cheese begins to melt, fold the tortillas in half and broil them until crisp (this happens very quickly). Cut into wedges and serve with a nice salsa.

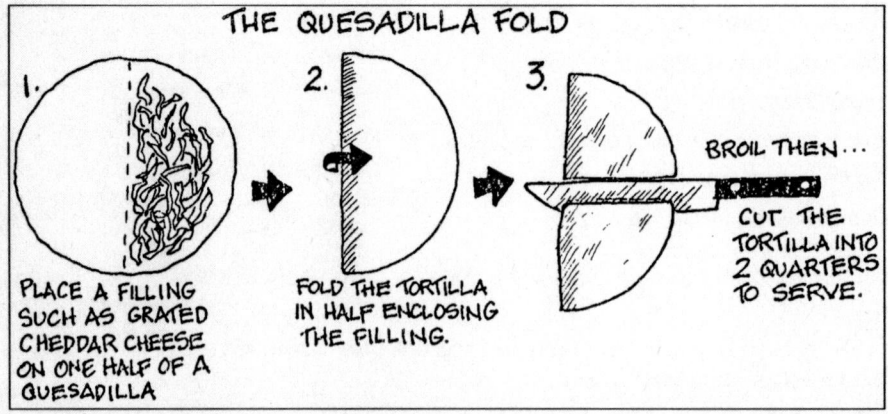

THE QUESADILLA FOLD

1. PLACE A FILLING SUCH AS GRATED CHEDDAR CHEESE ON ONE HALF OF A QUESADILLA

2. FOLD THE TORTILLA IN HALF ENCLOSING THE FILLING.

3. BROIL THEN... CUT THE TORTILLA INTO 2 QUARTERS TO SERVE.

Always practice safe leftover-handling procedures by transferring cooked food to shallow containers, covering tightly, and refrigerating promptly. The bacterial content of unrefrigerated food can double in 20 minutes. Be sure to eat leftovers within a couple days.

Part V
The Part of Tens

The 5th Wave   By Rich Tennant

"Oh, I have a very healthy relationship with food. It's the relationship I have with my scale that's not so *good*."

In this part . . .

First, I show you ways to simplify your low-carb cooking. My suggestions include things like buying certain prepared foods and using your grill and slow cooker. You find a chapter with a list of foods that are packed full of so much of the right stuff — including cruciferous veggies, nuts, blackberries, and black soybeans — that you'll be able to eat more of them and still lose weight. I know you're thirsty for even more information than I've packed between the front and the back covers of this book, so I include a list of Web sites offering lots of free stuff — free low-carb information and free online low-carb magazines and low-carb e-zines — and other helpful material, such as online pedometer support and information and nutritional Web sites that you can spend hours navigating. They all offer support on your yellow brick road to a healthy low-carb lifestyle.

Chapter 21

Ten Easy Ways to Simplify Your Low-Carb Cooking

In This Chapter

▶ Planning ahead and staying prepared

▶ Letting someone else do the work

▶ Using quick and easy cooking techniques

*T*ricks to simplify your low-carb cooking include everything from stocking up on low-carb staples to investing in handy kitchen gadgets. This chapter includes several ideas to make your time in the kitchen a little easier and get you out of there a little faster, without sacrificing great low-carb meals.

Keep an Ongoing Shopping List

Buy one of those list pads with a magnet on the back, stick it on your fridge, and keep a running list of low-carb staples and ingredients you run out of. Keeping a list on the fridge saves you a ton of time when you go grocery shopping. You don't have to rack your brains in the produce section trying to remember what you used up three days ago. Nothing is worse than having your heart set on trying a new recipe and finding out midway through making it that you're short some ingredients because you didn't make a list.

Plan Meals in Advance

Do yourself a big favor, and don't wait until 4:30 p.m. to figure out what you're going to make for dinner tonight. Planning your meals in advance is a biggie if you want to be successful in your low-carb healthy lifestyle. After you get accustomed to planning your meals, you'll find that doing so not only simplifies your low-carb cooking life but keeps your weight in check. Planning ahead helps keep you from eating whatever is available, which could easily be foods loaded with carbs. (See Chapter 20 for more on planning meals.)

Stock Your Kitchen with Low-Carb Basics

Make sure you have a well-stocked low-carb pantry. I don't expect you to initially spend a couple hundred dollars stocking your pantry. As you continue on your low-carb path, I think you'll find it natural to pick up an extra package of frozen veggies just in case you don't have fresh ones on hand the next time you stir up a meal. (See Chapter 3 for stocking your low-carb pantry.)

Buy Food Already Prepared for You

The grocery store offers a ton of real timesavers these days. No longer do you have to spend time chopping veggies, because they come pre-chopped in the frozen food section *and* in the fresh produce section. Tasty lettuce and greens combinations are already washed and pre-packaged — just add dressing. The deli is another good stop for things including freshly sliced cheeses and fresh-cut deli meats like turkey, chicken, and ham, which aren't usually full of preservatives. The deli folks have all the nutrition available, but you usually have to ask for it.

When you're working late, you may want to pick up one of those broasted whole lemon chickens, which are tasty and quite acceptable in your low-carb lifestyle. Just watch out for all of those prepared salads in that ready-to-eat case — stay away from them, please. Also be wary of precut fruits, because they're often overpriced.

Prepare Your Veggies in Steamer Baskets

If you don't have a stainless steel steamer basket, I strongly suggest you buy this kitchen gadget. Steamer baskets are cheap, and you can adapt them to various-sized pots that are already in your cupboard. Steamed veggies maintain almost all of their nutritional value. (Slide over to Chapter 12 for some great veggie recipes.) After you eat crisp-tender veggies from a steamer basket, you'll never want to see boiled and waterlogged veggies again — much less eat them. You can also use your steamer for fish and shellfish.

Have Parchment Paper on Hand

Parchment paper is wonderful stuff. If you're not familiar with its many advantages, give it a whirl. You can use it to line cookie sheets and baking dishes or to wrap food in (see Chapter 9 for a great halibut recipe cooked in a parchment packet). Parchment paper is coated on both sides, usually with silicon, and comes on a roll like wax paper. You just tear off what you need. You'll find it at the grocery store with the aluminum foil and wax paper. Parchment paper may look delicate to you, but don't let looks fool you: It withstands high heat, and whatever you cook on it won't stick to the paper! (And check out Chapter 20 for some great packet recipes that use foil.)

Consider a Slow Cooker

If you don't own a slow cooker, I encourage you to make this low-carb invest-ment. Preparing healthy, delicious meals is a major goal of your low-carb healthy lifestyle, and a slow cooker helps you accomplish just that. If you don't have experience with one of these little timesaving gadgets, you don't need long to get the hang of it. It'll be one of your many new low-carb best friends (besides me, of course). See Chapter 16 for some great low-carb slow cookin' recipes.

Get Out the Grill

I can't cook without my outdoor gas grill, and I love my tabletop inside grill. Both grills make low-carb cooking so easy and quick, and they cut fat because it just drips away. Outdoor grilling makes everything taste better, and there isn't much that you can't throw on the grill — steaks, chops, chicken, fish, shellfish, veggies, and even some fruits for desserts. (For some pretty awesome grilling suggestions, scoot on over to Chapters 11, 17, and 20.) I bet you already have an outdoor grill, but you may want to consider investing in an inside tabletop grill too. These grills are fairly inexpensive, and you don't have to buy one of the fancy schmancy brand-name ones. Grillin' is great and very compatible with your low-carb lifestyle.

Organize Your Low-Carb Recipes

In addition to keeping *Healthy Carb Cookbook For Dummies* handy in your kitchen, I know you have other sources for low-carb recipes. Because variety is one of the major keys to success in your low-carb healthy lifestyle, consider organizing not only your lifestyle but your recipes too. If you can, designate a shelf just for low-carb books. If you have loose recipes printed on 8½-x-11-inch paper, three-hole punch them and put them in a binder. This organization doesn't have to be fancy. Grab some binder dividers and organize your recipes by category. If you cut recipes out of a magazine, tape them on a piece of 8½-x-11-inch paper so your recipe pages are uniform. If you want to be fancy, color-code your sections with different colored paper. You may want to start two notebooks — one for recipes you've tried and are definitely keepers and another one for new recipes you want to try. You'll no longer look all over the place for that recipe when it's time to get cookin'!

Eyeball Portion Control

Measuring food amounts has never been something that I've been interested in doing — in the literal sense of getting out a measuring cup. But you and I both know that if you don't measure somehow, it's easy to super-size your portions, which isn't going to get you where you want to be with your low-carb lifestyle. With just a little practice, you can eyeball portion sizes in comparison to things such as the palm of your hand, baseballs, tennis balls, and other familiar items. Here's a list to get you well on your way to making portion decisions:

- 2 ounces cheese = a pair of dominoes
- 1 teaspoon butter = tip of your thumb, or 1 dice
- 3 ounces fish, meat, or poultry = the size of a computer mouse
- 1 tablespoon oil = tip of your thumb to the first joint
- ½ cup veggies or fruit = half of a tennis ball
- 1 cup of veggies or greens = your fist
- 1 medium piece of fruit = a baseball
- 1 tablespoon salad dressing = half of a golf ball

Chapter 22

Ten Foods to Eat More Of

*E*at more and weigh less. No, I'm not kidding. You really can eat more and lose weight, but not without making trade-offs and choices. When you're walking the line of a low-carb life, you know that controlling your carbs is just part of the equation. Watching those calories is important, too, and don't forget being on the lookout for bad fats. So, with a little tweak here and there, you can eat more food and take in fewer carbs and calories, lowering your bad fat intake. And with a smidgen of movement every day — *voilà!* You're a happier (and slimmer) camper!

In this chapter, I look at some foods that are squarely on the low-carb champions list — *plus* they can help you burn calories. How, you ask? Well, they have low carb counts and high fiber counts — a one-two punch that puts them low on the glycemic index. And, as you know if you've read Chapter 2, foods low on the glycemic index satisfy your hunger longer, control cravings a little better, and keep you out of the peaks and valleys of blood sugar spikes. Eating good carbs more often and not letting yourself get really hungry are secrets to this amazing healthy lifestyle (see Chapter 2 on good grazing habits). Many of the foods listed in this chapter can be between-real-meal snacks as well as part of great low-carb meals. Happy grazing!

Broccoli

I hope you like broccoli because it sure likes you and your low-carb, healthy lifestyle. Broccoli is considered a "super food" because it's full of nutrients and packed with fiber. Just ½ cup broccoli contains almost a whole day's worth of vitamin C. The green veggie also fires your metabolic furnace, helping your body burn calories (fat).

Eat raw broccoli for snacks — either on its own or with a bit of dip to spice things up. (Just don't go too heavy on the dip, or you'll cancel out all the good stuff you're getting.) And steamed broccoli isn't the only way to prepare this great veggie. Flip through your favorite cookbooks or jump online to explore your options with new broccoli recipes.

Bell Peppers

You can dress bell peppers up and take them anywhere! They can be a snack, an appetizer, an entree (Chapter 12 has a great recipe for stuffed peppers), an ingredient in a wrap, or a side dish, and they're packed with vitamin C and a high concentration of key antioxidants. You can't lose with the bright rainbow of red, yellow, orange, and green bell peppers. (The red and yellow varieties are especially sweet.) Cut peppers into crispy strips and carry them with you for quick and refreshing snacks with some of your favorite low-carb dip (dip away in Chapter 14). Just seeing this rainbow of colors will brighten up your mood!

Dark, Leafy Greens

Thinking green gets you far on the yellow brick road of a low-carb, healthy lifestyle. You'll be knocking on the door of wellness before Dorothy can even click her ruby red slippers together. The antioxidants in the dark, leafy greens are off the charts and help prevent chronic disease.

When it comes to leafy greens, your choices are vast and varied, from spinach to lettuces and salad greens with a bunch more green bunches in between. There's more to your leafy green low-carb life than just another boring salad or side dish. You can spice things up with sauces, herbs, and spices and take the green stuff from ho-hum to yum-yum! For example, head to Chapter 8 for a Stir-Fried Lettuce recipe. (For more on the benefits of green leafy stuff, flip to Chapter 8).

Cabbage, Cauliflower, and Other Cruciferous Veggies

In addition to broccoli, cruciferous vegetables include cabbages, cauliflower, turnips, and radishes. Whether you eat a variety of these veggies raw, cooked with an entree, or as a main meal, you've got a win/win situation. Their protective health benefits are impressive, and they have the low-carb counts and high fiber counts that are so important to your low-carb lifestyle. So graze as often as you wish with these guys. (Veg out on veggies in Chapter 12 for lots of great info plus recipes to tease your palate!)

Nuts and Seeds

Almonds, walnuts, pumpkin seeds, sunflower seeds . . . the list goes on and on. You've probably heard that eating a few nuts a day will help you lose more weight. The keyword here is *few* — that means not a whole bag. Nuts and seeds are good sources of vitamin E and essential fatty acids. Their protein and fat contents make them satisfying craving controllers and between-meal snacks. Get in the habit of carrying a little snack-sized bag around with you for the times when you get that pesky growl in your tummy. For more nutty info, see Chapter 14.

Sliced Turkey Breast

Keep slices of turkey breast in your fridge for snacks. You'll find it very satisfying for grazing and very kind to your carb counts. If you're in a hurry for some sustenance, plain slices are great on their own. If you have a bit more time, you can roll it around a cold piece of asparagus to get protein and a vegetable in one handy nibble. Or spread a little cream cheese on a slice of turkey, sprinkle some fresh chives across the top, and then roll it up for another tasty snack.

Fish

Fish, for the most part, is perfect for your low-carb lifestyle. Make the choice to broil, grill, poach, or bake your fish, and you're home free. Some oily fishes, such as salmon, herring, and sardines, provide healthy omega-3 fatty acids. Omega-3s aid in cholesterol reduction and the prevention of cardiovascular disease and high blood pressure. Visit your fresh fish counter often. Remember: Eat more fish — lose more weight.

When it comes to fish, the only thing you really have to watch out for is the preparation. Obviously, battered and deep-fried are no-nos.

Blackberries

Blackberries are highly recommended for almost any low-carb lifestyle. Why are such little fruits so important? Well, they're low on the glycemic index and don't make your insulin spike. Add to that the fact that ½ cup of blackberries contains lots of vitamin C and a little over 3 grams of fiber that knocks the net carb count down to about 6 grams. So go ahead and stir a few fresh blackberries into some Greek yogurt (which has low carb counts) for a real low-carb treat.

Tea

If you're feeling hungry or raving for a craving of some sort, try a cup of hot tea. It should take away your craving. And even better than the quick craving fix, that little cup of tea is loaded with antioxidant properties (even more if it's green tea). Tea also speaks a discouraging word to blood clots and helps reduce fat levels in the blood. Relax for a few minutes and make any time teatime.

Black Soybeans

Black soybeans are one of the best-kept secrets in the universe. These little rascals not only taste great and work wonderfully in recipes that call for some kind of beans, but they're also good for you and your healthy low-carb lifestyle. I use them in chili, soups, stews, and some bean salads, and they make great black bean dip. One cup of these little jewels contains 16 grams of carbs and 14 grams of fiber for a net carb count of only 2 grams! (See Chapter 15 for a great recipe using black soybeans.)

Chapter 23

Ten Carb-Counting Web Sites

*I*n this chapter, I list ten of my favorite informational Web sites that I know to be reliable. In living a low-carb, healthy, and active lifestyle, knowledge is golden. Learning as much as you can about nutrition, carb control, and caloric intake and output will make you not only a *happier* person but a *healthier* person, too. These Web sites give you the opportunity to build your bank of good carb knowledge. I bet you'll discover some things you didn't know about nutrition and the low-carb world. Most importantly, have fun with this!

In navigating the Internet for information, please keep in mind that just as you're in charge of your low-carb lifestyle and what goes in your body, you're also in charge of what goes in your head. It's okay to be skeptical, because some folks posting information online are less than ethical and less than knowledgeable. At the other end of the spectrum, absolutely incredible and credible information is literally at your fingertips to help you and support you with your low-carb healthy lifestyle. So get online and be smart!

CarbSmart

CarbSmart (www.carbsmart.com) is a retailer of over 1,300 products for people living the low-carb lifestyle. CarbSmart serves both the United States and Canada and is dedicated to helping everyone currently following or considering a low-carb lifestyle. Not only is CarbSmart *the* shopping source for products supporting low-carb lifestyles, but it also offers a free online magazine. *CarbSmart Magazine* contains over 400 articles of interest to the new or experienced low-carber. I've known the owner of CarbSmart, Andrew DiMino, personally every since I started writing low-carb cookbooks. Andrew is a jewel, and you're sure to be treated well at CarbSmart. No matter which low-carb lifestyle you follow, check out this site for great information and products and be sure to sign up for the free online magazine.

Fabulous Foods

Fabulous Foods (www.fabulousfoods.com) is an enormous general food and cooking Web site that offers a large array of low-carb articles and recipes (many with full color photos), as well as a free biweekly low-carb e-zine. If you're looking for an active message board community, you'll find that at Fabulous Foods, too; trading tips and recipes with other low-carbers is fun, as is offering each other support in your low-carb lifestyle. Editor Cheri Sicard, who coincidentally co-wrote *U.S. Citizenship For Dummies* (published by Wiley), told me that low-carbers make up the site's largest niche audience. She started the low-carb e-zine about six years ago when she began a low-carb diet and couldn't find enough interesting recipes. "In those days, low-carb products and information were scarce, outside of the Atkins books," Cheri said. "I started to post the recipes on the site that I was using to lose weight. We never expected it to take off the way it did."

The enthusiastic low-carb audience inspires the folks at Fabulous Foods to continually add new low-carb recipes and content to the site, so check back often or sign up for the free low-carb e-zine and get great low-carb content delivered to your e-mail inbox. I've been getting Cheri's newsletter for several years now, and I'm always excited to see what's new!

Low Carb Luxury

Low Carb Luxury (www.lowcarbluxury.com) doesn't manufacture or sell low-carb products; rather, it's the consumer voice of the low-carb, sugar-free, and specialty food industry. The company emphasizes the science, health, well-being, longevity, and strength of those living the low-carb, healthy lifestyle. This Web site has tons of useful free information, with a great guide for low-carb beginners. Even if you've been low-carbing for a while, you'll probably find some new nugget of information here. Be sure to sign up for the free online magazine while you're browsing the site. Low Carb Luxury is exceptionally well designed and easy to navigate.

Sassy Stepper

Sassy Stepper (www.sassystepper.com) is quite a character and was created to be your "Move More Motivator," encouraging you to move more every day. Besides Sassy Stepper revealing the Secret Motivation of the Pedometer to you, I'll reveal that Sassy Stepper is my creation, and this is my Web site. In my ten-plus years as a low-carber, I've learned the hard way that what you eat isn't the whole picture to a successful low-carb lifestyle. You gotta move more, and pedometer stepping works for me. I think most of us take life way too seriously, especially when it comes to weight. So I created Sassy to try to lighten things up a bit and, with grins and giggles, get low-carbers all over the world to become Sassy Steppers and have fun losing weight, moving more, and being healthier than ever. So come join Sassy Stepper and me online and let's have some fun and share some grins as well as some serious business about moving more with a pedometer in our healthy and active low-carb lifestyle. (For more about pedometer walking, see Chapter 5.)

Mendosa.com's Glycemic Index and Glycemic Load Values

At www.mendosa.com, you find a directory of articles, columns, and informative links compiled by Rick Mendosa, a freelance journalist specializing in diabetes. There's great free information on this site with tons of links to other informational sites — it's a wealth of good information relating to your low-carb lifestyle as well as encouragement for you to keep up the good work! The big low-carb payoff on Rick's page is the information available at www.mendosa.com/gilists.htm. This portion of the Web site has what I think to be the most comprehensive and most complete glycemic index and glycemic load lists currently on the Web. Don't miss it. This list will help you make good food choices for your low-carb, healthy lifestyle. For more information on the glycemic index and glycemic load, see Chapter 2.

USDA National Nutrient Database

The Nutrient Data Laboratory (NDL) (www.nal.usda.gov/fnic/foodcomp) and its predecessor organizations in the U.S. Department of Agriculture (USDA) have been compiling and developing food composition databases for over a century. The major focus of NDL is to maintain the USDA National Nutrient Database, a repository of information for 100 nutrients and over 7,300 foods.

NutritionData

The NutritionData (ND) Web site (www.nutritiondata.com) provides valuable nutrition facts and calorie counts for all foods and recipes. Created and maintained by fitness and health folks Ron and Lori Johnson, ND tells you, in simple terms, what's good and bad about the foods you eat and helps you select foods that best meet your dietary needs. ND's database contains over 7,000 foods in over 21,000 serving sizes.

Medline Plus

Medline Plus (www.nlm.nih.gov/medlineplus) is a service of the U.S. National Library of Medicine and the National Institutes of Health. On this Web site, you can find a plethora of information about health, wellness, and disease along with over 165 interactive tutorials. The Health Topics link provides you with a long list of places to start your search for information. Watch out: You can easily spend hours on this site. But maybe that's not such a bad thing. . . .

Food and Nutrition Information Center

The Food and Nutrition Information Center (FNIC) (www.nal.usda.gov/fnic) is a leader in online global nutrition information. This site gives you calorie counts and levels of calcium, folate, saturated fats, and other nutrients for some 10,000 brand-name foods. One of my favorite parts of the FNIC site is the Consumer's Corner that offers recipes and information about food and nutrition topics in the news.

Carbs Information

This Web site (www.carbs-information.com) is a gem, and I discovered it quite by accident and am delighted to be able to share it with you. You can find answers to hundreds of questions about carbs and diet nutrition and all kinds of useful links. For starters, the site answers questions and provides information about carbohydrates, dietary fiber, glycemic issues, low-carb diets and how they stack up, low-carb products, and net carbs. The site is easy to navigate, and I think it'll be helpful in answering some question that may pop up for you on the low-carb lifestyle road. Enjoy poking around and seeing what you come up with — I did!

Common Abbreviations and Metric Conversion Guide

Note: The recipes in this cookbook were not developed or tested using metric measures. There may be some variation in quality when converting to metric units.

Common Abbreviations

Abbreviation(s)	What It Stands For
C, c	cup
g	gram
kg	kilogram
L, l	liter
lb	pound
mL, ml	milliliter
oz	ounce
pt	pint
t, tsp	teaspoon
T, TB, Tbl, Tbsp	tablespoon

Volume

U.S Units	Canadian Metric	Australian Metric
¼ teaspoon	1 mL	1 ml
½ teaspoon	2 mL	2 ml
1 teaspoon	5 mL	5 ml
1 tablespoon	15 mL	20 ml
¼ cup	50 mL	60 ml
⅓ cup	75 mL	80 ml
½ cup	125 mL	125 ml
⅔ cup	150 mL	170 ml
¾ cup	175 mL	190 ml
1 cup	250 mL	250 ml
1 quart	1 liter	1 liter
1½ quarts	1.5 liters	1.5 liters
2 quarts	2 liters	2 liters
2½ quarts	2.5 liters	2.5 liters
3 quarts	3 liters	3 liters
4 quarts	4 liters	4 liters

Weight

U.S. Units	Canadian Metric	Australian Metric
1 ounce	30 grams	30 grams
2 ounces	55 grams	60 grams
3 ounces	85 grams	90 grams
4 ounces (¼ pound)	115 grams	125 grams
8 ounces (½ pound)	225 grams	225 grams
16 ounces (1 pound)	455 grams	500 grams
1 pound	455 grams	½ kilogram

Measurements

Inches	Centimeters
½	1.5
1	2.5
2	5.0
3	7.5
4	10.0
5	12.5
6	15.0
7	17.5
8	20.5
9	23.0
10	25.5
11	28.0
12	30.5
13	33.0

Temperature (Degrees)

Fahrenheit	Celsius
32	0
212	100
250	120
275	140
300	150
325	160
350	180
375	190

(continued)

_____

Temperature (Degrees) *(continued)*

Fahrenheit	Celsius
400	200
425	220
450	230
475	240
500	260

Index

• *C* •

cabbage
  benefits of eating, 330–331
  Chinese, 114
  German Cabbage Soup, 104
  savoy, 115
  shopping for, 191
  Turkey Brats and Cabbage, 320
  for wraps, 248
cake
  cheesecake, quick, 243
  Dirt Cake, 227
Calico Tomato Salad, 125
California Fishermen's Soup, 108
calories
  artificial sweeteners and, 24
  average consumed, 66
  counting, 13
  defined, 31
  in eggs, 84
  food labels and, 53
  low GL carbs and, 37
  metabolism and, 31–32
  in sugar, 23, 25, 207
  in sugar alcohols (polyols), 25
canned and jarred goods
  fruit, 208
  shopping for, 45–46
  tomatoes, 124
carbohydrates. *See also* counting
    carbohydrates
  in black soybeans, 28, 100
  blood-sugar level and, 34
  in chicken, 152
  complex, 22, 26–27
  daily recommended intake, 12
  described, 11–12, 22
  in eggs, 84
  fiber and, 26–27
  in fish, 132–133
  food labels and, 53–54
  in fruit, 208
  gram counters, 42
  healthy choices, 13–14, 29–30
  hidden, 278, 302
  not so healthy choices, 13, 30
  simple, 22
  stored as fat, 12

Carbs Information (Web site), 336
CarbSmart Magazine, 334
CarbSmart (Web site), 333–334
Caribbean Style Black Soybean Soup, 107
carrots, 44, 191, 198
cashews, 235
casseroles
  Artichoke Heart Casserole, 202
  Casserole of Chicken, Artichokes, and
    Mushrooms, 273
Cast-Iron Cooking For Dummies
    (Barr, Tracy), 317
cast-iron skillet, 317
catfish, blackened, 147
cauliflower
  benefits of eating, 330–331
  Cauliflower and Broccoli with Cheese and
    Bacon, 282
  Creamy Whole Cauliflower, 201
  puree, 204
  seasonings and sauce for, 198
  shopping for, 191
Celery Stick Tuna Delight, 240
cheese
  about, 14
  Apricot-Cheddar Brunch Toast, 98
  Arugula, Radicchio, and Goat Cheese
    Salad, 117
  Cauliflower and Broccoli with Cheese and
    Bacon, 282
  Cheese and Spinach Dumplings, 165
  Cheese and Spinach-Stuffed Chicken, 161
  cheeseburger, 294
  cheesecake, quick, 243
  Cheese-Stuffed Ground Round Patties,
    185–186
  Cheesy Hot Steak Wraps, 255
  Cherry Tomato and Mozzarella Salad,
    124–125
  cottage cheese dips, 242, 244
  cream cheese dips, 242
  Ham and Cheese Frittata, 93
  Mexican Cheese Omelet, 88
  Mozzarella Cheese Soup with Fresh
    Mushrooms, 102
  Peanut Butter and Cream Cheese
    Wraps, 252
  Ricotta Dip for Fruits, 246
  for salads, 119

• U •

• V •

• W •

BUSINESS, CAREERS & PERSONAL FINANCE

0-7645-5307-0   0-7645-5331-3 *†

Also available:
- Accounting For Dummies †
  0-7645-5314-3
- Business Plans Kit For Dummies †
  0-7645-5365-8
- Cover Letters For Dummies
  0-7645-5224-4
- Frugal Living For Dummies
  0-7645-5403-4
- Leadership For Dummies
  0-7645-5176-0
- Managing For Dummies
  0-7645-1771-6

- Marketing For Dummies
  0-7645-5600-2
- Personal Finance For Dummies *
  0-7645-2590-5
- Project Management For Dummies
  0-7645-5283-X
- Resumes For Dummies †
  0-7645-5471-9
- Selling For Dummies
  0-7645-5363-1
- Small Business Kit For Dummies *†
  0-7645-5093-4

HOME & BUSINESS COMPUTER BASICS

0-7645-4074-2   0-7645-3758-X

Also available:
- ACT! 6 For Dummies
  0-7645-2645-6
- iLife '04 All-in-One Desk Reference
  For Dummies
  0-7645-7347-0
- iPAQ For Dummies
  0-7645-6769-1
- Mac OS X Panther Timesaving
  Techniques For Dummies
  0-7645-5812-9
- Macs For Dummies
  0-7645-5656-8

- Microsoft Money 2004 For Dummies
  0-7645-4195-1
- Office 2003 All-in-One Desk Reference
  For Dummies
  0-7645-3883-7
- Outlook 2003 For Dummies
  0-7645-3759-8
- PCs For Dummies
  0-7645-4074-2
- TiVo For Dummies
  0-7645-6923-6
- Upgrading and Fixing PCs For Dummies
  0-7645-1665-5
- Windows XP Timesaving Techniques
  For Dummies
  0-7645-3748-2

FOOD, HOME, GARDEN, HOBBIES, MUSIC & PETS

0-7645-5295-3   0-7645-5232-5

Also available:
- Bass Guitar For Dummies
  0-7645-2487-9
- Diabetes Cookbook For Dummies
  0-7645-5230-9
- Gardening For Dummies *
  0-7645-5130-2
- Guitar For Dummies
  0-7645-5106-X
- Holiday Decorating For Dummies
  0-7645-2570-0
- Home Improvement All-in-One
  For Dummies
  0-7645-5680-0

- Knitting For Dummies
  0-7645-5395-X
- Piano For Dummies
  0-7645-5105-1
- Puppies For Dummies
  0-7645-5255-4
- Scrapbooking For Dummies
  0-7645-7208-3
- Senior Dogs For Dummies
  0-7645-5818-8
- Singing For Dummies
  0-7645-2475-5
- 30-Minute Meals For Dummies
  0-7645-2589-1

INTERNET & DIGITAL MEDIA

0-7645-1664-7   0-7645-6924-4

Also available:
- 2005 Online Shopping Directory
  For Dummies
  0-7645-7495-7
- CD & DVD Recording For Dummies
  0-7645-5956-7
- eBay For Dummies
  0-7645-5654-1
- Fighting Spam For Dummies
  0-7645-5965-6
- Genealogy Online For Dummies
  0-7645-5964-8
- Google For Dummies
  0-7645-4420-9

- Home Recording For Musicians
  For Dummies
  0-7645-1634-5
- The Internet For Dummies
  0-7645-4173-0
- iPod & iTunes For Dummies
  0-7645-7772-7
- Preventing Identity Theft For Dummies
  0-7645-7336-5
- Pro Tools All-in-One Desk Reference
  For Dummies
  0-7645-5714-9
- Roxio Easy Media Creator For Dummies
  0-7645-7131-1

* Separate Canadian edition also available
† Separate U.K. edition also available

Available wherever books are sold. For more information or to order direct: U.S. customers visit www.dummies.com or call 1-877-762-2974.
U.K. customers visit www.wileyeurope.com or call 0800 243407. Canadian customers visit www.wiley.ca or call 1-800-567-4797.

 WILEY

SPORTS, FITNESS, PARENTING, RELIGION & SPIRITUALITY

0-7645-5146-9

0-7645-5418-2

Also available:
- Adoption For Dummies
  0-7645-5488-3
- Basketball For Dummies
  0-7645-5248-1
- The Bible For Dummies
  0-7645-5296-1
- Buddhism For Dummies
  0-7645-5359-3
- Catholicism For Dummies
  0-7645-5391-7
- Hockey For Dummies
  0-7645-5228-7

- Judaism For Dummies
  0-7645-5299-6
- Martial Arts For Dummies
  0-7645-5358-5
- Pilates For Dummies
  0-7645-5397-6
- Religion For Dummies
  0-7645-5264-3
- Teaching Kids to Read For Dummies
  0-7645-4043-2
- Weight Training For Dummies
  0-7645-5168-X
- Yoga For Dummies
  0-7645-5117-5

TRAVEL

0-7645-5438-7

0-7645-5453-0

Also available:
- Alaska For Dummies
  0-7645-1761-9
- Arizona For Dummies
  0-7645-6938-4
- Cancún and the Yucatán For Dummies
  0-7645-2437-2
- Cruise Vacations For Dummies
  0-7645-6941-4
- Europe For Dummies
  0-7645-5456-5
- Ireland For Dummies
  0-7645-5455-7

- Las Vegas For Dummies
  0-7645-5448-4
- London For Dummies
  0-7645-4277-X
- New York City For Dummies
  0-7645-6945-7
- Paris For Dummies
  0-7645-5494-8
- RV Vacations For Dummies
  0-7645-5443-3
- Walt Disney World & Orlando For Dummies
  0-7645-6943-0

GRAPHICS, DESIGN & WEB DEVELOPMENT

0-7645-4345-8

0-7645-5589-8

Also available:
- Adobe Acrobat 6 PDF For Dummies
  0-7645-3760-1
- Building a Web Site For Dummies
  0-7645-7144-3
- Dreamweaver MX 2004 For Dummies
  0-7645-4342-3
- FrontPage 2003 For Dummies
  0-7645-3882-9
- HTML 4 For Dummies
  0-7645-1995-6
- Illustrator CS For Dummies
  0-7645-4084-X

- Macromedia Flash MX 2004 For Dummies
  0-7645-4358-X
- Photoshop 7 All-in-One Desk
  Reference For Dummies
  0-7645-1667-1
- Photoshop CS Timesaving Techniques
  For Dummies
  0-7645-6782-9
- PHP 5 For Dummies
  0-7645-4166-8
- PowerPoint 2003 For Dummies
  0-7645-3908-6
- QuarkXPress 6 For Dummies
  0-7645-2593-X

NETWORKING, SECURITY, PROGRAMMING & DATABASES

0-7645-6852-3

0-7645-5784-X

Also available:
- A+ Certification For Dummies
  0-7645-4187-0
- Access 2003 All-in-One Desk
  Reference For Dummies
  0-7645-3988-4
- Beginning Programming For Dummies
  0-7645-4997-9
- C For Dummies
  0-7645-7068-4
- Firewalls For Dummies
  0-7645-4048-3
- Home Networking For Dummies
  0-7645-42796

- Network Security For Dummies
  0-7645-1679-5
- Networking For Dummies
  0-7645-1677-9
- TCP/IP For Dummies
  0-7645-1760-0
- VBA For Dummies
  0-7645-3989-2
- Wireless All In-One Desk Reference
  For Dummies
  0-7645-7496-5
- Wireless Home Networking For Dummies
  0-7645-3910-8

HEALTH & SELF-HELP

0-7645-6820-5 *†   0-7645-2566-2

Also available:
- Alzheimer's For Dummies
  0-7645-3899-3
- Asthma For Dummies
  0-7645-4233-8
- Controlling Cholesterol For Dummies
  0-7645-5440-9
- Depression For Dummies
  0-7645-3900-0
- Dieting For Dummies
  0-7645-4149-8
- Fertility For Dummies
  0-7645-2549-2

- Fibromyalgia For Dummies
  0-7645-5441-7
- Improving Your Memory For Dummies
  0-7645-5435-2
- Pregnancy For Dummies †
  0-7645-4483-7
- Quitting Smoking For Dummies
  0-7645-2629-4
- Relationships For Dummies
  0-7645-5384-4
- Thyroid For Dummies
  0-7645-5385-2

EDUCATION, HISTORY, REFERENCE & TEST PREPARATION

0-7645-5194-9   0-7645-4186-2

Also available:
- Algebra For Dummies
  0-7645-5325-9
- British History For Dummies
  0-7645-7021-8
- Calculus For Dummies
  0-7645-2498-4
- English Grammar For Dummies
  0-7645-5322-4
- Forensics For Dummies
  0-7645-5580-4
- The GMAT For Dummies
  0-7645-5251-1
- Inglés Para Dummies
  0-7645-5427-1

- Italian For Dummies
  0-7645-5196-5
- Latin For Dummies
  0-7645-5431-X
- Lewis & Clark For Dummies
  0-7645-2545-X
- Research Papers For Dummies
  0-7645-5426-3
- The SAT I For Dummies
  0-7645-7193-1
- Science Fair Projects For Dummies
  0-7645-5460-3
- U.S. History For Dummies
  0-7645-5249-X

Get smart @ dummies.com®

- **Find a full list of Dummies titles**
- **Look into loads of FREE on-site articles**
- **Sign up for FREE eTips e-mailed to you weekly**
- **See what other products carry the Dummies name**
- **Shop directly from the Dummies bookstore**
- **Enter to win new prizes every month!**

* Separate Canadian edition also available
† Separate U.K. edition also available

Available wherever books are sold. For more information or to order direct: U.S. customers visit www.dummies.com or call 1-877-762-2974.
U.K. customers visit www.wileyeurope.com or call 0800 243407. Canadian customers visit www.wiley.ca or call 1-800-567-4797.

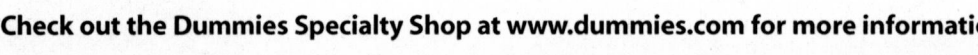